A Complete Guide to the Science Section of the National Board Exam for Funeral Services

First Edition (Revised)

David R. Penepent, PhD

Program Director of Funeral Services Administration
State University of New York at Canton
Canton, New York

President of Anubis Publications Inc.
3 Harrison Street
Norwood, New York

A N U B I S

PUBLICATIONS, INC.

ESTD 2020

Copyright © 2023 Anubis Publication Inc.

No part of this publication may be reproduced, duplicated or transmitted in any form, means, including photographing, recording, or other electronic or mechanical methods, including but not limited to emailing, without the prior written permission of the publisher, except in reviews and certain other non-commercial use permitted by copyright laws.

ISBN: 979-8-9891595-4-3 **(Paperback - Revised Edition)**
ISBN: 979-8-9891595-1-2 **(Hardcover)**
ISBN: 979-8-9891595-2-9 **(Digital)**
ISBN: 979-8-9891595-3-6 **(Audiobook)**

The glossary of terms and content outlines used in this publication are the intellectual property of the American Board of Funeral Service Education and are being used with expressed permission. No part of the outlines or glossary of terms may be reproduced, duplicated or transmitted in any form, means, including photographing, recording, or other electronic or mechanical methods, including but not limited to emailing, without the prior written permission from the American Board of Funeral Service Education, 992 Mantua Pike, Suite 108, Woodbury Heights, NJ 08097.

Published and Distributed by:

Anubis Publication Inc.
3 Harrison Street
Norwood, New York 13668
585-356-4929
dpenepent@deatheducationassessmentdrills.com

Printed by: Lightning Press
Totowa, New Jersey 07512
www.Lightning-Press.com

Contributing Authors

David R. Penepent, PhD is the President and Owner of Anubis Publications Inc. Dr. Penepent has been a funeral director and embalming practitioner for over 30 years. A graduate of the Simmons Institute of Funeral Services in Syracuse, New York, he earned a Bachelor's of Arts degree in Psychology from the University of Wisconsin Oshkosh; A Master's of Arts degree in Organizational Management from the University of Phoenix; and a Doctorate of Philosophy degree in Leadership and Organizational Change from Walden University. Currently, he is the Funeral Services Administration Program Director at the State University of New York at Canton. Dr. Penepent wrote the Restorative Art, OSHA, and Preparation for Final Disposition sections of this book. He lives in Norwood, New York with his wife and has three children and one grandson.

Darien B. Cain, M.S. is a New York State Licensed Funeral Director/Embalmer for Cleveland Funeral Home Inc., in Watertown, NY. After growing up in Clayton, NY, Darien obtained a Bachelor's of Science in Biology from the State University of New York (SUNY) at Potsdam. She then completed a Bachelor's of Technology in Funeral Services Administration at SUNY Canton. In 2020 Darien became a full-time Lecturer for SUNY Canton's Funeral Services Administration program. She recently completed a Master's of Science in Management from SUNY Potsdam and earned the Chancellor's Award for Student Excellence. Darien is currently pursuing her doctoral degree in Education at Liberty University. Darien contributed to multiple sections of this book, including Embalming, Preparation for Final Disposition, Microbiology, Pathology, and Anatomy. She lives in Watertown, NY, with her husband Ian, a Captain in the U.S. Army, whose lips are featured in this book.

Barry Walch, M.Ed. has been a funeral service professional since 1975. After practicing for 10 years in New Hampshire, he was selected as an instructor, and later became Program director, in the Mortuary Science Program at the State University of New York at Canton. His degrees are: Associate of Funeral Service from New England Institute, a Bachelor's in Chemistry from Colby College, and a Master's of Education, with a concentration in Counseling from University of New Hampshire. While at SUNY Canton, he taught Chemistry, Embalming, Pathology, Microbiology, Counseling, and the History of Funerals. He has received several university awards including "Golden Apples," Greek Advisor of the Year, Stellar Advisor, and Distinguished Faculty 2018. He is still a funeral practitioner. As a Professor Emeritus at the college, he continues to write, teach, lecture and tutor current students, with the stated goal of increasing the number of qualified funeral directors in our nation. Professor Walch wrote the Embalming, Thanatochemistry and Preparation for Final Disposition sections of this book. He lives in Canton, New York with his wife and enjoys spending time with his grandchildren.

Dedication

When I began my career in funeral services, one of the many people who believed in me was my mother, Concetta (Connie, to all) Florence Penepent. She was my financial, spiritual and emotional support throughout this journey. Even though she died in 2002, she remains a part of everything I do and accomplish. The Mother's Day before she died, I wrote this poem for her, expressing my love and appreciation for all that I have become as a man. I dedicate this book to you, Mom, with love.

Concetta F. Penepent 1923-2002

A Tribute to My Mom

Your gentle guidance has immeasurably influenced all that I have done,
all that I do, and all that I will ever do.
Your sweet spirit has been indelibly imprinted on all that I have been,
all that I am, and all that I will ever be.
Thus, you are part of all that I accomplish and all that I become.

When I help my neighbor, your helping hand is there as well.
When I comfort the bereaved, your compassionate love is my tool for healing.
When I ease the pain of friends, they owe a debt of gratitude to you.
When I show a child a better way, either by word or by example,
you are the teacher once removed.

Likewise, when I succeed with any educational achievement,
you are the professor emeritus who embedded in me the importance of knowledge.

Hence, everything I do reflects the values you taught me;
any wrong that I right, any heart I brighten,
any gift that I share or burden I may lighten,
is in its own small way a tribute to you.

I love you Mom and
Thank you for giving me the Gift of Life.

Acknowledgements

A review manual of this magnitude takes a considerable amount of time and effort to complete. Dr. Thomas Taggart was my professor when I attended the Simmons Institute of Funeral Services in Syracuse 35 years ago. He developed the concept of taking the American Board of Funeral Service outline and using it as part of the review process. There is a plethora of information to be covered that could potentially be on the National Board Exam. Dr. Taggart's outline became crucial to creating a summary of the information in consistent form. Over the years, he updated the information as the outlines changed and information was added, deleted and revised. When he retired in 2016, the review manual went unedited, and over the past seven years, the ABFSE outlines for the science section has been revised twice with no edits to Dr. Taggart's NBE Review Manual. This manuscript used Dr. Taggart's review manual as a starting point and incorporated all the changes in the curriculum outlines made by ABFSE. We have added graphics and diagrams to better serve the students in preparing for the NBEs. Finally, we created an audio version for students who learn best by listening to the material. This book was greatly influenced by Dr. Taggart's initial notes.

Words cannot express my sincere gratitude to my colleague Darien Cain for the hours of work she put into writing the various sections in this book, in addition to editing the many drafts. While funeral directing was not her original career path, her choice to become a funeral director has blossomed into a vocation in which she has applied her knowledge in the profession to become an outstanding professor of funeral services at the State University of New York at Canton. Her teaching style and ability to connect with the students has earned her the Stellar Advisor Award in 2023. In addition, while pursuing her Master's degree at SUNY Potsdam, Darien earned the Chancellor's Award for Distinguished Student, an honor very few students achieve. These are two honors that distinguish her as an asset to the profession. The contributions she has made to funeral service education and the profession has undoubtedly been advanced because of her career choice five years ago.

Barry Walch is a wealth of information and knowledge. As a funeral service educator for 35 years, he has prepared hundreds of students for this profession. His unique teaching style makes learning this information memorable and applicable to real life experiences. In 2022 he decided to retire from education but still had a desire to teach in some capacity. He continues to lecture with Advanced Funeral Service Education Programs and conducts weekly tutoring sessions, via ZOOM, with students preparing for the NBEs. Barry's contributions to this book, as well as his advice as to how it should be organized has certainly improved this edition.

Many of the photographs in this book were taken by Gregory E. Kie, Senior Media Relations Manager and College Photographer, whose prowess as a photographer has enhanced this book immensely. I owe a great deal of gratitude to Zachery Micheal Smith for designing the cover of this book and for creating some of the graphics. A special thanks to Jade Kenyon for giving me permission to use her perfectly symmetrical face for teaching facial proportions. And finally, a special thank you to Captain Ian Cain for his service to this great nation in the US Army, 10th Mountain Division. I appreciate the countless hours that Darien spent working on this book, which meant family sacrifices. With a humble heart, words do not express my appreciation for your understanding. Oh yes, thanks for letting us use your mouth to explain the arcs of the lips in this book.

David R. Penepent, PhD

TIPS on How to
Pass the National Board Exam

The National Board Exam (NBE) should never be taken for granted. Even if you received good grades in mortuary school, a considerable amount of preparation is necessary to pass the Science section of the NBE successfully. The following are some tips on how to prepare for the exam.

Tip 1: Know the Exam

According to the Conference National Board Exam Science Study Guide (2022), the exam is divided into four specific areas, with a specific number of questions per section:

> - Embalming Section comprises 41% of the questions – 62 items
> - Restorative Art comprises 23% of the questions – 34 items
> - Preparation for Final Disposition comprises 19% of the questions – 28 items
> - Hard Sciences, a/k/a Funeral Service Sciences comprises 17% of the questions – 26 items
> - Conference Beta Test for future exams comprises 15 questions, but these questions don't count towards your final score.

Total 165 Questions

Tip 2: Preparing to Study

Identify what you do not know as a starting point. Using the Death Education Assessment Drill (DEAD) simulator, take a 150-question science test. The first test will become an indicator and provide a roadmap of what needs to be studied. Identify what types (subject matter) of questions you got wrong. Use this textbook to look up the right answers. The key here is to develop an understanding of why you got the questions wrong and why your answer is not the right one.

Use the DEAD simulator to focus in on specific areas. For example, if you got 10 pathology questions wrong, use the simulator to create mini quizzes to further narrow the scope of material that needs to be studied. DO NOT memorize the questions and answers; that is not studying. Memorizing questions and answers is low level learning, and retention of the material will be minimal.

Tip 3: Test Smart, Not Hard

Questions on the NBE have four answers. Try to make it a 50/50 question by reducing the answers down to 2 possible answers. For example:

> Deoxygenated blood from the upper extremities enters the heart through which vessel?
> A. Iliac Vein
> B. Inferior Vena Cava
> C. Superior Vena Cava
> D. Femoral Vein

Excluding the pulmonary vein, deoxygenated blood returns to the heart in the vascular system. Analyze the question and identify key terms. The question is asking for *deoxygenated blood* from the *upper extremities,* which means from the head and arms. The iliac and femoral veins are both from the lower extremities, so these two answers can be eliminated. That leaves answer B and C. Superior means above; thus, the answer must be C.

Tip 4: Scenario Questions

Scenario questions are comprehension of the material type questions. If you understand the material, you will understand the scenario question: For example:

> What vein in the human body carries deoxygenated blood towards the heart?
>   A. Iliac Vein
>   B. Inferior Vena Cava
>   C. Superior Vena Cava
>   D. Pulmonary Vein

All veins carry deoxygenated blood to the heart except for the pulmonary vein. Arteries carry oxygen rich blood away from the heart, except for the pulmonary artery, which is the only artery in the human body that carries deoxygenated blood to the lungs to be oxygenated.

> Where does blood from the hand enter the heart?
>   A. Pulmonary Vein
>   B. Inferior Vena Cava
>   C. Superior Vena Cava
>   D. Pulmonary Artery

Immediately, A & D can be eliminated because those are internal vessels within the heart, which leaves answers B and C. The hand is part of the upper extremities, which would eliminate the inferior vena cava, which returns deoxygenated blood from lower extremities. Superior means above; thus, the answer must be C (Superior Vena Cava).

Tip 5: DO NOT Change Your Answer

Once you select an answer, move on! Don't second guess your answer. The majority of the time students change their answers, they usually select and change the answer to the wrong one. Your first answer is usually the correct answer.

Tip 6: Use DEAD to your Advantage

Use the DEAD simulator nightly and do between 150 and 300 questions as part of your study ritual. The key is to consistently score 85% and above on each quiz and full-length test. Research has shown that students who have scored consistently above 85% on five or more full length practice exams usually pass the NBEs. Several factors influence the outcome of the exam, but like any exam, the more you study and prepare for the exam, the more likely the chance of receiving a favorable outcome.

Tip 7: Know Vocabulary Terms

Science is straightforward and most of the questions revolve around a comprehensive understanding of the vocabulary terms. There are flash cards that can be purchased; however, creating your own flashcards is more effective. Each chapter has the current American Board of Funeral Service Education glossary. One of the problems with definitions on Quizlet or purchased flashcards is that some of the definitions have changed and are outdated.

Creating flashcards involves a thorough process that aids in remembering the terms. Only create cards on terms you need to review.

Tip 8: Do Not Get Nervous

Test anxiety does play an important role in the outcome of the exam. Being a little nervous prior to the NBE is normal and is part of a heightened awareness of the importance of the exam. Worrying and self-doubt are negative feelings that could shift positive energy to negative energy, causing the mind to lose its focus on the goal of passing the exam. Having a positive attitude and doing the necessary studying prior to the exam will reduce some of this anxiety. Effective study habits that limit distractions (cell phones, social media and procrastination) will help to create a feeling of accomplishment, which could reduce stress.

Tip 9: Take a Review Session & Private Tutoring

Most mortuary science programs have a capstone course that reviews all the material learned throughout the curriculum. Anubis Publications offer five 2-day review courses for the Science section. See www.deatheducationessdrills.com website (under *Resources*) for more information.

Some students need to have concepts re-explained. Some tutoring experiences are very expensive and require students to make long term commitments. Anubis Publications offers semi-private tutoring sections at $30/per hour. The sessions are led by experienced mortuary science professors who tailor the sessions to their needs. See www.deatheducationessdrills.com website (under *Resources*) for more information. Students who benefit the most from these sessions come prepared with questions about specific topics.

Tip 10: What if I Fail?

Failure is good as long as you learn from your mistakes, correct your behavior, and move forward towards success. Failure is bad when you keep making the same mistakes repeatedly and expect a different outcome.

If you fail the NBE, keep your results and bring them to a tutoring session. In January 2023, the Conference began providing information on the concepts missed on the exam. Even though the actual questions are not known, these concepts can be remediated in a private review session with our professors. During the tutoring session, these concepts can be the focus for remediation.

Table of Contents for Science Section

Domain I

Domain II

Domain III

Domain IV

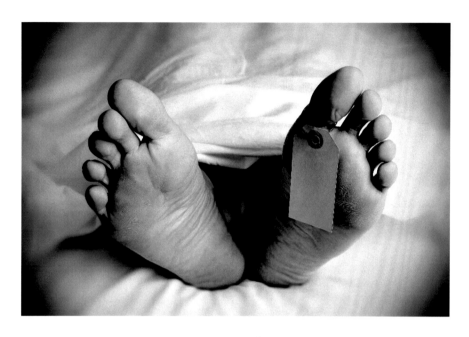

Domain I

Embalming
Thanatochemistry
Occupational Health and Safety

Embalming

Embalming can be traced back through history to the Ancient Egyptians and their mummification practices. The word "embalm" comes from the prefix "em-," meaning in or about, and the suffix "-balm," meaning **resinous** (*an amorphous, nonvolatile solid or soft side substance, natural exudation from plants: tars, saps)* substance. In the present day, we think of embalming for the purposes of open casket services, allowing families to have that last memory image and assisting them in those tasks of mourning (see counseling section in Arts book).

Embalming is regulated by various governing bodies such as **OSHA** (*Occupational Safety and Health Administration: A governmental agency with the responsibility for regulatory and enforcement of safety and health matters for most United States employees; an individual State OSHA agency may supersede the U.S. Department of Labor OSHA regulations*), the **FTC** (*Federal Trade Commission*), **EPA** (*Environmental Protection Agency*), **State Health Departments**, etc. Embalming licensure and regulations vary from state-to-state. For example, in New York, you must complete your degree in mortuary science from an accredited program, complete and pass both NBEs, complete a year residency in a funeral home, and pass the state funeral law exam. Note: In New York State, it is a combined funeral director/embalmer license. Some states have a separate embalmer's license. The following websites have state licensure requirements for funeral directing and embalmers:

https://nfda.org/education/resources
https://theconferenceonline.org/wp-content/uploads/2022/07/Regulations-in-Licensing-2021-updated-June-2022.pdf

Legally, according to the Federal Trade Commission (FTC), embalming is not required by law unless there is a public health hazard. However, embalming may be a funeral home policy for public viewing and does require permission from the family. At the point of removal or first call, you may obtain verbal permission to embalm. Some states also require written permission, which is a good funeral home practice even if not required by law. Written permission also needs to be obtained for procedures other than embalming. These include autopsies, which may be requested by the coroner or medical examiner or requested by the family. Organ and tissue donation must have written authorization (usually obtained by the Organ Procurement Organization). Removal of medical devices such as pacemakers for cremation must have written permission. Major restorations such as tissue excision or reduction of tissue must also have written permission.

Along with legal considerations, there are moral and ethical considerations when it comes to embalming and the prep (preparation/embalming) room. Embalmers need to ensure and maintain the respect, dignity, and confidentiality of all decedents. A high level of professional standards in the prep rooms must be maintained by keeping the room a private and sacred place for embalming and preparation. The prep room should be limited to only licensed funeral professionals, registered residents and students in mortuary science programs, those authorized by family members, and law enforcement (governmental – i.e., M.E./Coroner) personnel. Decedents should always be covered to maintain dignity and respect.

Human remains are a deceased person's body, which also includes **cremated remains** (the carbon *elements remaining after the cremation process of a dead human body has concluded*), and a **cadaver** *(a dead human body used for medical purposes, including transplantation, anatomical dissection, and study).*

Embalming is *a process of chemically treating the dead human body to reduce the presence and growth of microorganisms, slow or retard organic decomposition, and restore an acceptable physical appearance.* The purpose of embalming can be broken down into 4 main reasons: sanitation, disinfection, **temporary** preservation, and restoration. **Sanitation** is *a process to promote and establish conditions that minimize or eliminate biohazards.* The embalming room and environment need to be kept clean and sanitized at all times to protect the human remains from complications, such as tissue gas, and the embalmer and other personnel from harm or possible infections. This is different from **disinfection** which is *the destruction and/or inhibition of most pathogenic organisms and their products in or on the body* (see Microbiology for control of microorganisms pp. 268 - 271). Disinfection is aimed at the deceased human body. Human remains need to be safe to protect public health, such as service attendees. Many people falsely assume embalming lasts forever. This is untrue; embalming only temporarily preserves the body for the purpose of providing time for funeral services. Eventually, **decomposition** *(the separation of compounds into simpler substances by the action of microbial and/or autolytic enzymes)* will continue to break down the human remains.

A variety of factors will affect how long preservation lasts, including but not limited to chemical choices, body conditions, temperature, length of time between death and embalming, and the amount of water that is present. Note: Embalming can be reversed in the presence of an abundance of water. Restoration is to recreate a natural form and state, allowing viewability and a positive memory picture for the service. This would include cosmetic work.

There are four types of embalming: vascular, cavity, surface, and hypodermic. **Vascular** (arterial, capillary) embalming utilizes the circulatory system, specifically the arteries for injection and veins for drainage. **Cavity** embalming is used to treat the body cavities (thoracic, abdominal, pelvic, cranial) and the lumina of the hollow viscera. This is done with a trocar (See instruments p. 48) to aspirate *(remove)* bodily fluids and inject cavity chemicals. **Hypodermic** embalming is done by injecting embalming chemicals into tissues directly using a trocar or syringe. Surface embalming is when chemicals are applied to external or internal surfaces directly. An example of this would be applying gels to areas of **desquamation** *(skin slip).*

Before any type of disposition is made, **identification of the decedent needs to occur**. This is arguably one of the most important steps that needs to be taken. There are many ways that identification can occur. The best possible source is matching DNA. However, identification by next-of-kin, photos, fingerprints, dental records, blood samples, and personal effects (worst form) can be made. **NOTE:** If, during the initial observations and identification process, anything suspicious is present, the police should be notified. Law enforcement may then contact a **coroner** (*an official of a local community who holds inquests concerning sudden, violent, and unexplained deaths)* or a **medical examiner** (*an official elected or appointed to investigate suspicious or unnatural deaths, a medical doctor)* for further investigation and a possible autopsy.

Once identification occurs and is concluded, the embalming process may begin (with the appropriate permission, verbal and/or written). The first step in this process is sanitation and protection practices. Both to disinfect the body, sanitize the environment, and protect ourselves as embalmers. Embalmers need to use **universal precautions** *(acting as if every human remains infectious)* and utilize personal protective equipment (PPE) (see OSHA section for proper PPE). PPE includes but is not limited to gloves, gowns, shoe covers, face masks, impermeable aprons, goggles, face shields, and/or coveralls. Note: respirators may be included in PPE but must pass OSHA regulations and fit test requirements (see OSHA section). PPE should be disposable for easy cleanup, especially with highly infectious cases. During the embalming process, all embalmers should follow maximum hygiene practices and standards, including but not limited to handwashing, cleaning fingernails, rinsing oral and nasal cavities, and showering. Once the protective precautions have been taken by the embalmer, the human remains can be sanitized and disinfected. This initial disinfection creates a safe working environment for the embalmer by eliminating any pathogens or surfaces infectious materials present on the remains.

There are three stages of disinfection during the embalming process:

1. **Primary disinfection** is done before injection (spraying with disinfectant chemicals and washing the human remains);
2. **Concurrent disinfection** occurs during the embalming process (placing instruments in a sterilizing tray and washing throughout the embalming process);
3. **Terminal disinfection** occurs at the end (sterilizing equipment, washing the body, washing the table).

Primary disinfection includes practices like bathing the body with soap and water and disinfecting the orifices with a chemical and cotton in the eyes, nose, and mouth. Extra precautions may include packing the orifices (nose, throat, anus, and vagina) to prevent purge and expulsion of gasses and fluids. Some embalmers choose to do this procedure post-embalming. Sheets and clothing need to be washed and properly folded before returning them to the family. Permission needs to be obtained before discarding, burying, or cremating any belongings. Any articles of clothing, sheets, or pouches that are contaminated with blood or bodily fluids need to be disposed of in a biohazard container. Regular trash cans should be used for normal everyday waste that is not contaminated with bodily fluids. A sharps container should be used to dispose of sharp objects (scalpels, razor blades, pins). Plastic bottles can be recycled if they are rinsed and placed in a recycling bin with the cap off. If the bottle is contaminated with bodily fluids, it should be disposed of in the biohazard container.

As death professionals, there are some basic terms and their meanings that need to be understood:
1. **Thanatology,** or *the study of death.*

2. **Death** is the *irreversible cessation of all vital functions or irreversible total cessation of metabolic activity.* There are different classifications of death.
   ➢ **Clinical death** is when the *heart and lungs stop* but can be restored.
   ➢ **Brain death** is when the *brain stops functioning and is irreversible.*
   ➢ Somatic or **biological death** is the *death of the whole body.*

➢ Finally, **cellular death** is the *death of individual body cells*. Cellular death can occur antemortem (before death) or postmortem (after death). **Antemortem cellular Death** may be necrosis, *the pathological death of cells due to lack of oxygen* (decubitus ulcers, gangrene), or **necrobiosis**, *the physiological death of the cells of the body followed by their replacement with living tissue* (cellular life cycle).

Body Changes During and After Death

There are many signs that someone is "dead." These include decomposition, presence of macroorganisms such as maggots, cessation of circulation and respirations, complete muscular relaxation, **rigor mortis** (*postmortem stiffening of the body muscles, begins 4-6 hours after death, lasts 4-6 hours, results from ATP depletion*), **algor mortis** (*postmortem cooling of the body*), **livor mortis** (*postmortem lividity/cadaveric lividity, postmortem intravascular red-blue discoloration-can be removed through embalming*), and changes of the eye including cloudiness, loss of luster, flattening, and pupil dilation. Although a person may appear dead, there are various tests that can be done both by the funeral director or by medical professionals to see determine death.

1. Expert tests can only be done by medical professionals. These include: using a stethoscope to detect heart sounds, an ophthalmoscope to look for eye response, encephalograms to detect brainwaves, and electrocardiograms to detect heart waves.
2. Inexpert tests for death may be done by a funeral director, which include: a ligature test by tying a ligature around a finger to see if swelling occurs, an ammonia injection test to see if a skin reaction occurs, feeling for a pulse, listening for respirations, and placing a mirror in front of the mouth to see if it becomes foggy.

AGONAL/ANTEMORTEM CHANGES

There are visible and physical changes that occur when a person is dying. This is known as the **moribund or agonal period** (*the dying state, the time period immediately before somatic death*). During this time period, the biological systems are shutting down and may experience a variety of reactions. The **death rattle** may be observed: *a noise that is caused by air passing through a residue of mucus in the trachea and pharynx*. There may be a **death struggle** in which the body has *semi-convulsive twitches* or **cadaveric spasms** in which there is a *prolongation of muscle contraction*. There may also be temperature changes that occur within the body. The body may decrease in temperature (**agonal algor**), which is typical, or in some cases, the body may increase in temperature (**agonal fever**). As the body is dying, the blood begins to **coagulate** (become more viscous) and starts to settle. *The settling of blood and/or fluids to dependent portions of the body is known as* **hypostasis**. This hypostasis will result in livor mortis discoloration, and eventually, as the blood cells break down (**hemolysis**), it will turn into a postmortem stain. The body may also experience **agonal edema** (*abnormal accumulation of fluids*) or **agonal dehydration** (*loss of moisture*). However, as the body begins to die, bacteria will continue to thrive. These bacteria will eventually move primarily from the gastrointestinal tract throughout the body as cellular permeability changes. This is known as bacterial translocation - often noticed as a green discoloration in the abdomen. These changes may be affected by a variety of factors, such as gas and therapeutic agents (chemotherapy, blood thinners, antibiotics). Gas may be present in the body because of a pleural cavity tear (**subcutaneous emphysema**) or **gangrene**. **Gangrene can be classified in three ways**: **dry** (body part that has died and has little blood and remains

6

aseptic, arterial obstruction), **wet** (is moist as a result of venous obstruction, may have a bacterial infection), and **gas** (as a result of an infected wound and the presence of anaerobic gas forming bacillus pathogens *(such as Clostridium perfringens-* See Microbiology p. 273 and Pathology p. 233).

POST MORTEM CHANGES

Like the agonal period, there are many physical and chemical changes that occur postmortem. Note these may all be affected by the cause and manner of death. Manner of death is classified as suicide, homicide, natural, accidental, or unknown. Cause of death is what actually killed the person, for example, myocardial infarction, uncontrolled diabetes, etc.

POST MORTEM PHYSICAL CHANGES

The first physical change is algor mortis. **Algor mortis** is the *postmortem cooling of the body to the surrounding temperature.* This may be **intrinsically** *(from within the body)* affected by **corpulence** *(obesity)* which could slow cooling. It may be affected **extrinsically** *(from the environment/outside the body)* by the amount of clothing the decedent has on, the temperature of the environment, and the humidity of the environment.

The second physical change is related to moisture. Dehydration is the loss of moisture from the body. This may be due to evaporation if the environment is extremely dry and hot. **Desiccation** is the *extreme point of dehydration and moisture loss.* **Imbibition** is postmortem edema, *which is the absorption of the fluid portion of the blood by tissues.* **Gravitation**, or the flow of fluids to dependent portions of the body, may also occur.

Finally, the third physical change is the increased viscosity of the blood. **Agglutination** is the *intravascular (within the vessels) increase in blood viscosity due to the clumping of particulate-formed elements in the blood vessels.*

POST MORTEM CHEMICAL CHANGES

1. Decomposition

The first major chemical change is decomposition. Decomposition can be affected by many intrinsic factors such as age, sex, corpulence, cause and manner of death, bacterial/parasitic activity, pharmaceutical agents, or extrinsic factors such as air temperature, moisture levels of the environment, bacterial/parasitic activity, pressure on the body, and presence of animals or vermin (maggots, lice, rats, etc.).

There are various types of decomposition:

a. The first type is **autolysis**, *the self- destruction of cells by their own enzymes without microbial assistance.* This can be done by lysosomes of the cell.

b. The second type is **fermentation**, *the bacterial decomposition of carbohydrates into simple sugars* (polysaccharides that break down through saccharolysis to

7

monosaccharides). **Proteolysis** is the *decomposition of proteins*. Proteolysis has two forms:

1) **Putrefaction**, *the decomposition of proteins by the action of enzymes from anaerobic bacteria* (no air to skin, more odor),
2) **Decay**, the *decomposition of proteins by enzymes of aerobic bacteria*.

Proteolysis results in proteins breaking down into their amino acid building blocks. There are 20-22 essential amino acids that have a basic formula of NH_2-CHR-COOH - an amino group, an alpha carbon, any aliphatic or aromatic radical, and a carboxyl group. These amino acid bonds are what become affected by the presence of formaldehyde to fix tissues. Putrefaction can result in the presence of Ptomaines (skatole, indole, cadaverine, and putrescine), which are nitrogenous and can cause microorganisms like *E. coli* to fester and increase the formaldehyde demand of the remains.

Lipolysis is the *decomposition of fats into fatty acids* (16/18 carbons long, broken apart by hydrolysis). **Hydrolysis** is the *breakdown with the assistance of water*. Decomposition can create many end products, such as ammonia, ammonium compounds, hydrogen, hydrogen sulfide, mercaptan, nitrogen, carbon dioxide, water, methane, phosphoric acid, and sulfuric acid, resulting in five cardinal signs:

a. Color changes (marbling, green, black),
b. Odor,
c. **Purge** (*postmortem evacuation of any substance from an external orifice of the body because of gas and/or internal pressure*),
d. **Desquamation** (*skin-slip, the separation of the epidermis from the underlaying dermis because of putrefaction*), and
e. Gas accumulation.

Carbohydrates are the first body compound to break down, followed by proteins, fats, and lastly, bones. When it comes to viscera (organs), the order of putrefaction begins with the lining of the membrane of the trachea and larynx (*Note* - the pregnant uterus decomposes first in pregnant individuals, and the brain decomposes first in babies and infants, due to water composition). The last organ to decompose in the adult female is the non-pregnant uterus and the prostate in the adult male.

The stages of decomposition are:

a. freshly deceased,
b. bloating,
c. active decay,
d. advanced decay,
e. skeletal remains.

2. pH

The second chemical change in the body after death is pH change. pH relates to the degree of acidity or alkalinity of the body on a scale from 0-14. 0 is completely acidic, and 14 is completely basic. However, the body hovers around 7, which is neutral. Blood during life has a pH of 7.35-7.45. When the body is in rigor mortis, the pH may drop down to 5-6 (very acidic).

During advanced decomposition, the pH will increase to a more alkaline state around 11, due to the ammonium-based byproducts.

3. Rigor Mortis

Another chemical change is rigor mortis. **Rigor mortis** is *the postmortem stiffening of the body's muscles by natural body processes.* At the time of death, the body is in a state known as **primary flaccidity.** As the body depletes its ATP (energy) stores, the muscles will continue to contract (for 4-6 hours) until all the ATP is depleted, which leaves those muscles contracted. At the point of full contracture, **full rigor** is taking place. Full rigor may stay for another 4-6 hours until the muscle cells begin to decompose (proteolysis), thus relaxing the contracture. Once the body has come out of rigor, the body reaches **secondary flaccidity.** After rigor has ended, it cannot go back to a normal state (rigor mortis is a one-way process). Note: The best time for embalming is during primary flaccidity, before rigor, and before proteolysis occurs. Rigor begins with the eyes and continues throughout the body and relaxes in the same way.

Progression of Rigor Mortis

Time After Death	Event	Appearance	Circumstances
2 – 6 hours	Rigor begins	Body becomes stiff and stiffness moves down body	Stiffness begins with the eyelids and jaw muscles after about 2 hours, then center of the body stiffens, then arms and legs
12 hours	Rigor complete	Peak rigor is exhibited	Entire body is rigid
15 – 36 hours	Slow loss of rigor	Loss of rigor in small muscles first, followed by larger muscles	Rigor lost first in head and neck, and last in bigger leg muscles
36 – 48 hours	Rigor totally disappears	Muscles become relaxed	Many variables can extend rigor beyond the normal 36 hours

Rigor mortis may be affected by temperature, age, muscle mass, sex, pregnancy, cause of death, and condition of the muscles (less muscle mass = less extreme rigor). If embalming takes place after the onset of rigor, manual manipulation of the body (flexing, moving limbs, massaging, rotating) may loosen up the body and relax the rigor for better distribution and absorption.

4. Discolorations

Discolorations may also be a chemical change that could occur after death. During the agonal period, hypostasis occurs as fluids and blood begin to settle. This settling causes livor mortis (postmortem lividity, cadaveric lividity), an intravascular discoloration that may be removed through embalming. If the body is untouched for a prolonged period of time, hemolysis occurs, which is the breakdown of red blood cells, causing the blood pigments to seep into the surrounding tissues, thus becoming extravascular (outside the vessels). *This extravascular discoloration is called* **postmortem stain**. Postmortem stains cannot be removed through arterial embalming. To remove this discoloration, bleaching techniques are used before or during embalming or cosmetic application will be needed post-embalming.

9

5. Postmortem caloricity

The last chemical change is **postmortem caloricity**. *This is when the body has an increase in temperature after death* as a result of continued cellular metabolism. This may be due to various factors such as poisoning of the body or digestion of food.

PREPARATION OF THE BODY

Once there is an understanding of the changes that occur before and after death, the embalming process can begin. The embalming process begins with a pre-embalming analysis or case analysis. This analysis should be documented in an embalming report. This analysis identifies intrinsic and extrinsic factors related to the body in order to plan the best embalming techniques.

Some *intrinsic factors* we may take into consideration are:
  a. Cause and manner of death,
  b. Pathological conditions of the body,
  c. Moisture levels of the body,
  d. The temperature of the body,
  e. Discolorations of the body,
  f. Presence of gas,
  g. Weight (Corpulence- *obesity*, or emaciation - severely underweight),
  h. Exsanguination (*total loss of blood*),
  i. Medication use, or the presence of illicit drugs.

Some *extrinsic factors* we may encounter are:
  a. Atmospheric conditions (moisture, precipitation, pressure),
  b. Temperature,
  c. Presence of microbes,
  d. Vermin or macroorganisms (lice, maggots),
  e. Postmortem **interval** (PMI: *length of time between death and embalming*),
  f. Skills of the embalmer.

These conditions will affect various aspects of the embalming process.

Once the pre-embalming analysis has been completed, the remains are prepared for the embalming process:

Step 1 - Preliminary Procedures: The first thing is to place the decedent on the embalming table and remove all clothing, medical tubing, adhesives, bandages, etc. Documentation and creating an inventory of all items that are with the body is an important part of the intake process. Permission from the next-of-kin as to the proper disposal or return of the items should be given and signed.

Step 2 - Primary Disinfection: Begin the primary disinfection by using a disinfectant spray and swab the orifices (mouth, ears, nose, eyes). It is a good practice to spray the entire human remains with a disinfectant prior to embalming to kill any microbes that are on the remains when received. Let the disinfectant set for a period of time before the next step.

Step 3 - Washing of Body: After topical (surface) disinfection, wash the entire body, including the hair, with antibacterial soap, water, and a sponge.

POSITIONING

Step 4 - Head: Once the remains are washed and disinfected, the body needs to be positioned on the table, similar to the approximate position the remains will look in the casket. The head should be elevated on a head block (similar to the way the head will be placed on the pillow during casketing) with the head tilted at a *15-degree angle to the right* (to give the appearance that the decedent is looking towards the funeral attendants). The head should never be back and looking towards the ceiling. Exceptions are when the decedent is severely overweight, in which the head should be positioned forward for the most natural appearance, or if positioning is restricted due to pathological/physical abnormalities of the body (wheelchair bound, arthritis, etc.).

Step 5 - Arms and Hands: Hands typically are folded across the abdomen and placed on top of each other (usually, the left hand is on top if there is a wedding ring or band). Positioning blocks and devices may be needed to keep the limbs in place during the embalming process.

Step 6 - Shaving: The objective is to make the person look as natural and reposed as possible. This may require shaving the face (**ALWAYS** ask permission before shaving or removing facial hair). Use shaving cream or soap to shave the face. Never dry shave the face of the deceased. This will cause a razor burn. Finally, use massage cream (or a lanolin/oil-based product) to re-hydrate the tissues and create a base for cosmetics. For decedents with a darker complexion, some funeral directors use cocoa butter or silicone spray to prevent the skin from turning ashy.

SETTING FEATURES
After the body is positioned, the features may be set. NOTE: Some funeral directors do the positioning and setting of the features later in the embalming process.

Step 7 - Eyes: The first feature to be set are the eyes. After the eyes have been disinfected, eye caps should be placed underneath the eyelids. Kalip, Vaseline, or massage cream may be applied to the eye caps to re-hydrate tissues and help keep the eyelids closed. Eye caps may be cut if necessary. *The eyelids should abut each other in the lower one-third of the eye orbit* to give the most natural appearance. The eyelashes should not get trapped under the eyelid and should be clean from creams used to set the eye caps.

If the eye is sunken, cotton or mortuary putty (mastic paste) may be placed behind the eye cap to give the eye a more normal shape. Tissue builder may also be utilized after embalming to assist in appearance and shape.

If eye enucleation (removal of the eye) or corneal sclera button removal has occurred, the entire eye socket should be cleaned and disinfected. A cauterant should be applied and remain during the embalming process. This will prevent leaking and cauterize the blood vessels ruptured during the eye enucleation process. The eye socket should be filled with either cotton or mortuary putty (mastic paste) with an eye cap to create a normal almond shape and appearance.

Ecchymosis (*bruising*) of the eye may also be present and should be taken into consideration. Bruising can be treated pre-embalming by injecting a bleaching chemical into the bruised area subcutaneously. Over-manipulation of the eyelids will cause ecchymosis. See restorative art section.

Step 8 - Mouth: The second feature to be set is the mouth. Special attention needs to be given to how the mouth is set because *the mouth gives the body its expression in death* (the eyes give expression in life). When observing a deceased in a casket, people usually are drawn to look at the mouth. Care should be given when manipulating the mouth and lips; the lips may be brittle or dehydrated, and the teeth may be sharp. The decedent may have natural teeth, dentures (should be removed and disinfected), implanted teeth, or no teeth at all. In the absence of teeth, a mouth former, cotton, mortuary putty or cardboard may be utilized to create the natural shape of the mouth.

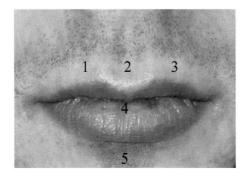

The five arcs in the line of the upper lip

There are five arcs in the line of the upper lip; it should not be straight across; observe the hunting bow shape. The corners of the mouth should align with the center of the eyes to maintain appropriate facial proportions. Cotton may be needed in the corner of the lips to maintain mouth form and prevent concavity.

There are three main ways that the mouth could be closed: via the needle injector, musculature (mentalis) suture, or mandibular suture.

Needle Injector	A mechanical device that injects injector needles/pins into the jaw bones. The wires are then twisted and pulled together to hold the jaw in place.
Musculature suture a/k/a Frenulum suture	Method of mouth closure in which a suture is passed under the top lip into the nostril, through the septum of the nose, back through the second nostril under the top lip, and then through the mentalis muscle of the chin. The ligature is then tied to keep the jaw in place. Also known as the mentalis suture or frenulum (*a fleshy strip of tissue that attaches two body parts together*) suture.

Mandibular suture	Method of mouth closure in which a suture is passed under the top lip into the nostril, through the septum of the nose, back through the second nostril under the top lip, and then around the mandible bone of the jaw. To prevent a divot underneath the chin, move the ligature back and forth, and pull the center of the divot down, separating the connecting tissue. The ligature is then tied to keep the jaw in place.

If the lips do not stay closed and together, the embalmer may use massage cream, Kalip, petroleum jelly, or wet cotton strips. If these methods do not work, the embalmer may utilize an adhesive, such as Aron Alpha (a common super glue type for the dead).
NOTE: Adhesives should not be applied until after the embalming process is completed. In extreme situations, a subcutaneous (beneath the skin) or intradermal (hidden) suture may be used.

In cases where prognathism (buck tooth or jaw protrusion) is present, obtaining prior permission is essential to either: realign teeth, extract teeth, make an incision posterior and transverse through the frenulum of the lower lip to stretch the skin or show the teeth (the least invasive method).

VESSEL SELECTION

STEP 9 - Raising Vessels: Once the features have been set, the embalmer is able to select the appropriate vessels for use in the embalming process. Remember, arteries carry blood away from the heart and are the site of injection during embalming. Arteries are creamy white in appearance and have thick walls and a lumen that remains open when incised. Veins carry blood back to the heart and are the site of drainage during embalming. Veins generally have a blue appearance and collapse when incised.

There are six major injection sites: (See Anatomical and Linear Guides pp. 39-44)

Artery	Accompanying Vein	General Location	Notes
Right Common Carotid (most commonly used)	Right Internal Jugular	The right side of the neck	Great for distribution to the head and hands. Able to insert a drainage device into the vein close to the right atrium for drainage. Note: Watch for over-injection of the face. It may be difficult if the decedent has clothing with low necklines.
Left Common Carotid	Left Internal Jugular	The left side of the neck	Great for distribution to the head and hands. Note: Watch for over-injection of the face. It may be difficult if the decedent has clothing with low necklines.

Right Axillary	Right Axillary	Right armpit	Great for clearing the hands and fingers. Watch for buildup of fluids if I.V.s had been used in a medical setting.
Left Axillary	Left Axillary	Left armpit	Great for clearing the hands and fingers. Watch for buildup of fluids if I.V.s had been used in a medical setting.
Right Femoral	Right Femoral	Right hip crease/ inner thigh	The furthest vein from the right atrium could be difficult if the decedent has corpulence and may have plaque present causing intravascular resistance.
Left Femoral	Left Femoral	Left hip crease/ inner thigh	The furthest vein from the right atrium could be difficult if the decedent has corpulence and may have plaque present causing intravascular resistance.

Although these are the major injection sites, there are many supporting vessels that may be utilized in autopsy, donor, and special cases. These vessels include the brachial arteries, radial arteries, ulnar arteries, popliteal arteries, anterior tibial arteries, posterior tibial arteries, subclavian arteries, arch of the aorta, and iliac arteries.

There are many factors that will influence vessel selection, such as accessibility, proximity to the aorta and right atrium (for distribution and drainage), size of the vessel, and intrinsic/extrinsic factors governing the body. These body factors include but are not limited to age, biological sex, weight/adipose tissue composition, body disfigurements (such as arthritis), pathological disruptions (tumors, necrosis), moisture levels (edema, dehydration), trauma (accidents, surgeries, suicides, etc.), if an autopsy has taken place, if tissue/organ donation has taken place, and cause/manner of death.

Some other factors that may affect the vascular system and selection include:
(See Pathology, pp. 240-241)

Atheroma	Fatty deposits
Arteriosclerosis	Thickening of arteries
Varices	Varicose veins
Clots	Thick clumps of blood and tissues
Embolus	Free-floating particles in the bloodstream. It may be a clot or air bubble, or thrombi that has broken free.
Thrombus	A stationary clot or particle that restricts blood flow.

Phlebitis	Inflammation of the vein
Hemorrhage	Rupture of the vein
Endocarditis	Inflammation of the lining of the heart
Tuberculosis	Disease causing fluid in the lungs
Febrile diseases	May cause dehydration
Trauma	It may be affecting a particular location.

Once the appropriate vessel has been determined, the location of the selected vessel is found using anatomical limits and guides. *See **Anatomical and Linear guides** to review how to locate the vessels* (pp. 39-44). Using a sharp scalpel, a 2" to 3" incision is made in the general location of the vessels. Using an aneurysm hook(s), blunt dissection is necessary to expose the vessels. This blunt dissection will help clear away connective tissue (fascia), muscle, and adipose tissue. Once the arteries and veins have been located, the fascia and nerve tissue need to be detached for the vessel to become exposed and prepared for the embalming process.

Note: Blunt dissection needs to be completed with precision and care to avoid rupturing the vessels (especially the vein, once it is nicked, the blood may obscure the view into the incision). Once the connected tissue is cleared away, ligatures are placed around the vessels. Two ligatures are used around the artery and two around the vein to appropriately tie them off during and after the embalming process. After applying the ligatures, the vessels can be opened for injection and drainage.

To open the artery, a few different incisions may be made. A **transverse incision**, in which there is a right angle to the long axis of the incision, may be used, a **longitudinal incision** down the long axis of the vessel, a **T-incision** which combines transverse and longitudinal, or the **triangular/wedge** incisions, which is made up of two opposite diagonal cuts to create an inverted "V."

Once the vessels are opened, a cannula (a/k/a arterial tube) can be inserted into the artery and held in place with arterial fixation hemostats, and a drainage device (such as the angular spring forceps or a drain tube connected to a discharge hose) may be inserted into the vein to start drainage. After the insertion of these devices, vascular injection may take place.

EMBALMING SOLUTION CREATION

STEP 10 - Chemicals: Selecting the appropriate embalming chemicals will vary with each embalming depending on the pre-embalming analysis. The cause of death and the intrinsic and extrinsic factors play very important roles when selecting the proper embalming chemicals that will result in optimal preservation, disinfection, and restoration of the human remains. Once the proper chemicals have been selected, mixing them into the embalming machine, establishing and setting the appropriate pressure, and monitoring distribution are all key components to ensure proper distribution.

CHEMICAL COMPOSITION

Arterial fluid refers to the concentrated fluid that comes from a manufacturer in a bottle. An arterial solution is when that arterial fluid is mixed with water in the embalming machine.

As previously mentioned, selecting appropriate embalming chemicals is dependent on many different factors that are noted in the pre-embalming analysis. During the embalming process, arterial and accessory chemicals are selected to create a solution that will be injected into the human remains. Post embalming and after cavity aspiration, cavity fluid is injected, typically using a gravity method with a cavity fluid applicator connected to a trocar. Finally, paraformaldehyde, such as gels and powders, is used in certain embalming situations that require topical/surface treatment. These paraformaldehyde chemicals are usually made from 37% formaldehyde or what is also known as formalin.

Formaldehyde (also known as methanal - HCHO) is a one-carbon aldehyde that is a common preservative and arterial chemical because of its ability to denature and fix proteins (See Thanatochemistry, pp. 81-83). The index of the fluid is the strength or the percentage of formaldehyde that is contained in the bottle. This is measured in grams of formaldehyde gas dissolved in 100 ml of water.

Index: (Grams of formaldehyde gas/ 100 mL water)

A strong or high index fluid is 26% - 36% of formaldehyde.
A medium-index fluid is 16% - 25% formaldehyde.
A weak or low-index fluid is 5% - 15% formaldehyde.

Formaldehyde is not the only arterial chemical that can be used for embalming. Glutaraldehyde (a 5-carbon dialdehyde – $C_5H_8O_2$) is also a preservative and great disinfectant. This chemical can also be used for jaundice cases to remove yellow discoloration and can work with various pH levels. Glutaraldehyde is also beneficial against tissue gas because it has the ability to kill spores, unlike many other chemicals. Some disinfectants used to clean instruments and equipment have glutaraldehyde as their main chemical.

Methanol is also becoming increasingly popular as a preservative arterial fluid and is a component in many arterial chemicals.

Phenol (carbolic acid) can be used in arterial solutions as a preservative but is more commonly used as a bleaching agent or surface embalming agent. Extreme caution should be exercised when using phenol-based products because they tend to be a contributing factor to some kidney cancers.

Cavity fluids are injected into the body cavities using an applicator and a trocar. Cavity treatment is done after the aspiration process is completed. Cavity fluid injection is used to treat the hollow viscera and tissues that may not have been reached during arterial embalming.
Remember, decomposition occurs from the inside-out. The viscera contain many anaerobic bacteria that will continue to thrive in the body after death, causing decomposition, bloating, and gases. Cavity treatment will slow this occurrence.

Supplemental fluids are used for purposes other than preservation and disinfection.

Jaundice fluids work to remove yellowing discolorations and restore the natural coloring of the decedent. **Note**: *High levels of formaldehyde in jaundice cases may cause the conversion of bilirubin (the pigment causing the yellow coloring) to biliverdin, which will result in a green discoloration of the remains. Jaundice fluids are low index or contain glutaraldehyde or methanol.*

Accessory chemicals are used in addition to arterial and cavity chemicals. These are chemicals such as powders, gels, bleaching agents, and sealing agents.

ARTERIAL CHEMICALS:

Preservatives work to inactivate saprophytic bacteria and alter enzymes to slow decomposition.

Modifying agents:

There are many modifying agents that are added to fluids and solutions to create the desired effects and overcome issues that occur due to the factors presented by the body.

Modifying Agent Type	Description	Examples
Dyes	**Inactive dyes** (non-cosmetic): Coloring added to fluid bottles to differentiate fluids does not give coloring to the decedent. **Active dyes** (cosmetic): Coloring added to fluids and solutions to restore a natural coloring and appearance to the decedent. Typically, a pink/red coloring.	Natural coloring agents (not stable): vegetable-based ex. Cudbear, carmine, cochineal. Synthetic coloring agents (most common): coal-tar based ex. Eosin, erythrosine, ponceau, and amaranth. Sustainable/Green fluids use F.D. Red 3 (food coloring).

Anticoagulants (water-conditioners, water softeners)	Help against the coagulation of blood. Reduce blood viscosity (thickness). Sequestering/chelating agents to combat calcium and other ions found in hard water.	Borates, EDTA, Salts, Citrates, Epsom salt.
Buffers	Affect the pH (acid-base) balance within the solution and tissues. Important for rigor mortis cases, as the pH can drop into the acidic range. Want to maintain a normal neutral body pH (around 7).	Borates, Carbonates, phosphates, salts of EDTA, citrate.

Humectants	Help to retain moisture in the tissue. Beneficial for cases of dehydration.	Glycerine, sorbitol, glycols, polyhydroxy alcohols, lanolin (emulsified oils).
Surfactant (wetting agents, surface tension reducers, penetrating agents, surface-active agents)	Reduce surface tension. Reduce molecular cohesion of liquid. Allows for penetration across permeable membranes.	Anionic (dissolved in H_2O to create negatively charged anions): soap, alkyl sulfonates Cationic (dissolved in H2O to create positively charged cations): quaternary ammonia compounds. Nonionic (no charge): hydroxyls, ethers (Amphoteric (either – or +).
Vehicles	Serve as a solvent. Solvents are agents that dissolve a solute. Ex. In a saltwater solution, salt is the solute, and water is the solvent.	Water, alcohol, sorbitol, glycerin.
Perfuming agents/Masking agents/ Deodorizing Agents	Work to combat smell and odors.	Sassafras, oil of wintergreen, benzaldehyde, esters. Many people will also use "cherry charm," a common custodial chemical often used for cleaning vomit.

Supplemental fluids:

Pre-injection	Injected before arterial chemicals open up the vascular system. Helps relieve rigor, control pH, and remove clots.
Co-injection	Injected in conjunction with arterial chemicals to enhance the vascular chemical effects.

Accessory Chemicals:

Hardening compounds	Powdered chemicals that can absorb excess liquid	Plaster of Paris, clay, wood powder, kitty litter
Mold prevention agents	Prohibit the growth of mold.	Paradichlorobenzene, cresol
Preservative powders	Powdered chemicals that can disinfect the area and absorb excess liquid	Paraformaldehyde, alum
Sealing agents	Used in incisions to absorb moisture and liquid.	Powders, creams, spray, gels
Bleaching agents	Used to lighten up areas of the skin and treat surface problems	Phenol, cavity fluid, specialty chemicals with proprietary ingredients.

EMBALMING SOLUTION

Once the fluids have been selected, the embalming fluids must be mixed in the embalming machine tank, creating a solution. This includes two vital topics: dilution and diffusion.

Dilution of arterial chemicals is the process of attaining proper fluid concentration by adding water. The first level of dilution is **primary dilution.** *This is created by adding water to our embalming fluid in the machine (embalmers do primary dilution).* **Secondary dilution** *is the weakening of the embalming fluid by the fluids within the body, both vascular and interstitial.*
For example, 16 ounces of formaldehyde-based fluid is added to the embalming machine with 1 gallon of water (primary dilution). When injecting this fluid into the vessels, the remains already contain water, and this combines with the fluids being injected, further watering down the formaldehyde solution causing secondary dilution. Embalming solutions should be created using the Standard Dilution Formula. See Thanatochemistry on how to calculate dilution formula (pp. 84-85).

Diffusion is the net movement of anything. Many times, in embalming, this is achieved through osmosis. **Osmosis** is *the passage of a solvent from an area of low solute to an area of high solute across a permeable membrane to achieve an equal concentration of solvent/solute.* This is when embalming fluids seep out of the capillaries into the interstitial fluids across the permeable membranes and penetrate the surrounding tissues (creating that delayed firming effect).

There are three types of solutions that are involved with osmotic pressure and movement:

Hypotonic	A solution having a lower concentration of solute. Ex. Solution A: has 80% water and 20% solute versus Solution B: has 20% water and 80% solute. Solution A: is hypotonic (less solute, will lose water)	Ideally, an embalmer wants a slightly hypotonic solution for embalming to prevent over-dehydration.
Isotonic	The solution has an equal concentration of solute compared to water. Ex. Solution A: has 80% water and 20% solute versus Solution B: has 80% water and 20% solute. They are isotonic because they are equal.	
Hypertonic	A solution having a higher concentration of solute. Ex. Solution A: has 80% water and 20% solute versus Solution B: has 20% water and 80% solute. Solution B is hypertonic (more solute, will draw in water)	Hypertonic solutions should be used for cases with edema. The higher concentration of the fluids will help to draw out water. This will dehydrate normal cases and cause the graying effect.

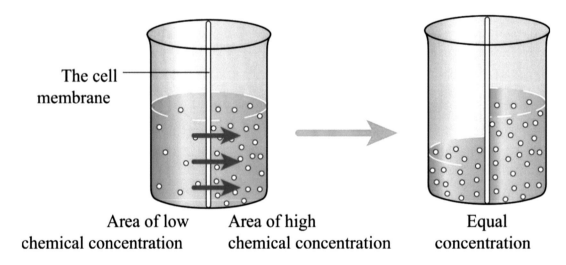

The cell membrane

Area of low chemical concentration   Area of high chemical concentration   Equal concentration

Pressure filtration is positive intravascular pressure that causes fluid to go through the capillary wall into the interstitial fluids (moving intravascularly to extravascularly).

Dialysis is the separation of substances due to the diffusion rates through a semipermeable membrane. Separation of crystalloid from a colloid.

Gravity filtration is when gravitational forces pull fluids downwards to dependent portions of the body.

PRESSURE AND FLOW

Step 11 - Setting the Machine Pressure and Flow: After the solution is created, the embalming machine is to be turned on, and the pressure must be set. To set the appropriate pressure, the embalmer must first review that **pressure** *is the action of a force against an opposing force.* When the solution enters the body, many people think of pressure in terms of blood pressure. Blood pressure is the pressure exerted by the blood on the walls of the vessels. This is measured in millimeters of mercury (for example, 120/80, the two numbers reflect systolic and diastolic pressure). The embalmer wants to simulate blood pressure during injection to properly achieve total body distribution. When turning on the embalming machine (leaving the stopcock off so no fluid enters the body), the pressure that is read on the machine is potential pressure. **Potential pressure** *is the total pressure that the machine is currently able to produce due to the motor.* Once that stopcock is turned on and the solution enters the body, the pressure may change. This new reading is the **actual pressure,** *the pressure that is actually flowing into the body.* By taking the initial potential pressure (reading #1) and subtracting the actual pressure (reading #2), you will find the differential pressure.

Potential Pressure - Actual Pressure = Differential Pressure

What causes this difference? The answer is intravascular and extravascular resistance. **Intravascular resistance** *results when there are items in the blood vessels that block the flow of blood and fluid.* Examples may be emboli, thrombi, plaque, or clots. **Extravascular resistance** *is a blockage or force outside of the vessels that may be affecting flow and distribution.* Examples may be tumors or bones that are pressing on the vessels. Other factors such as the postmortem interval **PMI** (time between death and embalming), presence of rigor mortis, and stage of decomposition may affect the pressure needed to embalm. Typical injection pressure is 10-20 lbs. for the body and drops to 2-3 lbs. for the head. Ideally, the embalmer will use the lowest pressure possible to achieve distribution into the head and prevent over-injection to the head and face. The face should be injected last to prevent over injection.

The **rate of flow** *is the speed that the injection is occurring. The rate of flow is the amount of fluid being injected per minute (ounces per minute).*

INJECTION AND DRAINAGE

Step 12 – Injection and Drainage: After the pressure is set, the solution can be injected into the artery, and drainage will begin from the vein. There are various injection and drainage methods that may be utilized during embalming.

Injection Method	Description
One point injection	Injection occurs from one artery with its accompanying vein.
Multi-point injection	More than one injection site is used.
Six-point injection	All 6 major injection sites (R. common carotid, L. common carotid, R. axillary, L. axillary, R. femoral, L. femoral) are used.
Restricted Cervical Injection	Utilizing a "Y" shaped cannula to inject into both the right and left common carotid simultaneously to obtain even facial distribution.
Split Injection/Drainage	Injection takes place at an artery in one location, while drainage is at a different location. Example: injection into the right common carotid with drainage from the right femoral vein.

Drainage Method	Description
Continuous drainage	Injection and drainage occur simultaneously.
Alternate drainage	Drainage occurs when the injection is paused. Drainage and injection occur opposite from each other.
Intermittent drainage	The injection is continuous, and drainage is switched on and off.
Heart Tap	Drainage is primarily from aspiration of the right atrium with the trocar.
Closed drainage	No drainage is taking place. (Great for dehydrated and emaciated cases to maintain water/moisture).

NOTE: Injection at any point may be distal or proximal. **Distal** embalming is when the cannula (or arterial tube) is placed so that *injection occurs away from the trunk of the body* (i.e., into the head, down the arm, down the leg). **Proximal** embalming is when the cannula is positioned so that *the injection goes toward the trunk of the body*. Some embalmers who use restricted cervical injection method, embalm the head first, ligate the distal common carotids and then inject proximal. Those embalmers who inject from the right common carotid artery first, inject distal at the end of the embalming process, depending on the collateral distribution of the solution in the final stages of the embalming process. Distal injection should always be at a low rate of flow and pressure to prevent distention in the right eye and face.

22

Once the solution is moving into the body, there are various signs that distribution is occurring. Superficial vessels can become distended (hint: look in the temporal region of the head and the vessels on the back of the hands and tops of the feet). Adequate drainage is another sign. Color changes of the decedent, such as the clearing of livor mortis in the fingertips and ears, and a natural color due to the movement of dyes can also indicate distribution.

Signs of diffusion of the embalming fluids include the firming of tissues, drying of tissues, tissue distention, and bleaching. In individuals with darker complexions, a pinkish hue (under the hands, feet, and lower and upper extremities) can be observed for adequate distribution when using chemicals with active dyes.

Drainage refers to the drainage of blood, interstitial fluid (fluid surrounding body cells), lymphatic fluid, or embalming fluid from the body. Typically done through a vein, drainage removes intravascular discoloration from flushing out the capillaries close to the skin. Drainage also works to prevent swelling and removes microorganisms to slow decomposition. Drainage can be improved or stimulated through increasing pressure, manually massaging the body parts towards the heart, raising the limbs, using instruments (or chemicals) to remove clots, and using pre-injections with anticoagulant agents. If needed, drainage can occur from a different drainage site or through a heart tap (see chart above on drainage methods).

SUTURING

Step 13 – Closing Incision Points: Upon completion of the embalming process, the point of injection incision needs to be sutured to adequately prevent leakage. There are multiple different sutures that may be utilized:

Suture	Description
Baseball	Starting underneath and coming up through the skin. Then crossing over to the other side. Creates a criss-cross pattern similar to the stitching on a baseball.
Inverted baseball	This uses the technique of the baseball suture. However, it starts from the top of the skin and goes inward. Creates a flatter suture.
Intradermal (Hidden)	Single: The needle begins underneath the incision and is brought up through the subcutaneous tissue, NOT through the skin. This follows a back-and-forth motion across each side of the incision. Double: utilizes two needles on either side of the incision; think of tying your shoes with two laces.
Worm (draw)	Similar to the single intradermal, except it fully penetrates the skin.

Whip (roll)	The needle passes through both sides of the incision simultaneously. The needle is then brought back over to go back through both sides again. Hint: push the needle through and "whip" it back over.
Locking	Follows the same pattern as the whip, except after going through both sides of the incision, "lock" it by going through the loop created by excess ligature before pulling it tight. Creates the shape of an "H."
Purse String	A series of small stitches through the dermis is made around the circumference of the opening. The ends of the ligature are knotted within the opening, drawing the suture together.

Staples and adhesives could also be used to close incisions. See Restorative Art, pp. 160-161.

CAVITY EMBALMING

Step 14 – Cavity Embalming: Once arterial embalming is complete; the next step is cavity embalming. Cavity embalming can occur immediately after arterial embalming but sometimes is performed after a few hours delay ensuring diffusion has happened.

Cavity embalming is the direct treatment of body cavities. The process consists of aspiration to remove fluid trapped in the hollow organs and injection to introduce fluid to these spaces. This works to treat the areas that do not receive adequate fluid and disinfection through arterial embalming. This is a key factor that will slow (or retard) decomposition as carbohydrates will breakdown in the gastrointestinal tract causing gases and purges.

To adequately perform cavity embalming, an adequate review of the abdominal regions is essential. The four-abdominal quadrants consist of four regions drawn using one horizontal and one vertical plane. The nine-abdominopelvic regions are created by transverse (horizontal) lines drawn across the body at the 10th rib and at the superior iliac spines, and two sagittal lines drawn from the nipples down to the inguinal ligaments. The chart below shows them in the correct anatomical orientation.

Four Abdominal Quadrants (remember Anatomical Position-See Restorative Art, pp. 116 & 117 and Anatomy p. 286 & 287):

Upper Right Quadrant	Upper Left Quadrant
Lower Right Quadrant	Lower Left Quadrant

Nine Abdominopelvic Regions:

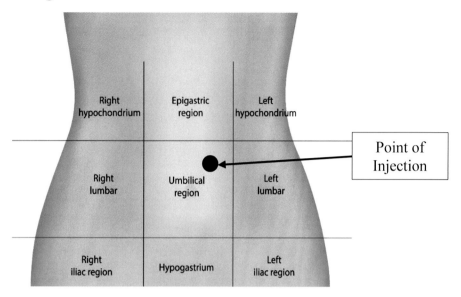

To start aspiration, the trocar should be inserted **2" to the left and 2" above** the umbilicus (belly button). The trocar should then be aimed at specific viscera using the trocar guides listed below:

Viscera	Location
Stomach	Towards the left mid-axillary line and left fifth intercostal space.
Cecum	1/4th of the distance from the right anterior-superior iliac spine to the pubic symphysis.
Urinary bladder	Towards the median line of the pubic bone (pubic symphysis)
Right atrium of the heart	Towards the lobe of the right ear.
Brain	Through the cribriform plate through the nose. Note: This is mainly for baby/infant cases, cases with cerebral hemorrhage, gas within the cranial cavity.

Once the aspiration has been completed, injection of cavity fluid may occur. With injection, the trocar is hooked up either to an injection machine or to a gravity injector. The trocar is inserted back into the same spot (2" to the left and 2" above the belly button), and undiluted cavity fluids are injected. Cavity fluids are meant to be undiluted and contain no modifying agents. Ideally, a minimum of two bottles of cavity fluid (32 oz.) should be used on a standard case. One bottle for the thoracic region and one for the pelvic region. After injection, a trocar button should be placed in the puncture hole, or a purse string-suture should be used. Re-aspiration and re-injection may be needed if there is advanced decomposition, ascites (fluid buildup in the abdomen), or continuous gas/purge issues. After re-aspiration and re-injection, a purse-string suture may be used to completely close the puncture wound, followed by applying a liquid adhesive and Webril.

POST EMBALMING TREATMENT

Step 15 - Additional Embalming Treatment: After cavity embalming, there may be factors within the body that need additional treatment. If an area is lacking distribution, hypodermic and surface embalming may be needed.

Hypodermic embalming utilizes a needle and syringe or a trocar to introduce an embalming solution directly into muscle tissue. This is utilized frequently with autopsy and donation cases.

Surface embalming is used to treat problems affecting the skin and surface tissues. For example, if there is a blister on the skin, the blister should be drained and dried. A surface pack may be utilized with cotton and cavity fluid to treat and dry the area before cosmetic and restoration work. Also, hypodermically injecting a 50/50 mixture of a phenol base and cavity fluid solution directly into the petrified area will eradicate and cauterize the decomposition. Gels may also be used for surface embalming. When using gels, plastic should cover the area to ensure that the formaldehyde gases do not escape.

Once the embalming is complete, a post-embalming analysis should be done to examine and review the remains and results. The person may need to be placed in plastic garments. The garments could be stockings that cover the feet and calves, pants or capris to cover the genital and leg area, coveralls to cover the torso, or Unionalls that cover the entire body except for the hands and head. Gels and powders may be placed inside the garments to help absorb moisture or fluids. These garments may go under the clothing to help against leakage.

This concludes the embalming process.

Factors Affecting Embalming and Special Cases

There are many factors and cases that affect embalming. This next section will describe the embalming procedures and processes that should be used when a decedent presents these complications.

INFANT EMBALMING

Infants less than one year of age have specific considerations. These infants generally have a higher water composition (75% compared to the normal 60% after a year old). Their skin is also very delicate and thin. The probability of skin-slip or desquamation is greater in newborns and infants than in adults immediately following death. When positioning and embalming the child remains, remember that family members may wish to hold and cradle the baby before or during the services.

A baby's mouth will not close normally. They may have a slight pucker. The lips should be brought together with petroleum jelly to retain moisture and keep them together. Eye caps will need to be cut to fit.

Embalming may occur from the normal six vessels. However, these vessels will be very small and could be difficult to get to depending on the size and development stage of the fetus/baby.

The abdominal aorta may be used as a point of injection. To reach this, make a 2-3" incision in the middle of the abdomen to the left of the midline. Note: The intestines may have to move. A "U" shaped incision may also be used from the clavicle to the bottom of the rib cage and across the inferior margin of the sternum.

Some embalmers use the umbilicus on newborns. To locate the artery above the umbilical clamp, make the umbilicus flat. The most medial vessel is the artery, and with a very small arterial tube, this vessel can be injected. Because of the size and weight of the infant, 4 to 6 lbs. of pressure with a low rate of flow is recommended. Also, if possible, the pulse setting should be used because the underdeveloped vascular system is accustomed to this type of flow and pressure.

Another technique used is embalming by immersion. This is when a tub is filled with the embalming solution, and the baby is wrapped in a blanket or sheet and immersed in the solution. Immersion may take up to 8 hours and requires the container holding the baby to be covered in plastic so that the formaldehyde gas is allowed to penetrate the tissue. Within those 8 hours, the baby should be rotated and resubmerged in more fluid for even distribution.

If the baby has been autopsied (which is very common), placing weight into the cranial cavity will create a normal feeling if the baby is held. Incisions should be leakproof and covered (Recommend using suture adhesive, Webril, and a plastic burrier underneath a baby cap).

PURGE

Purge is the postmortem evacuation of any substance from an external orifice (eyes, ears, nose, mouth, vagina, anus) due to pressure. Purge can be a result of gas buildup, decomposition, pressure from injection, and pathological conditions.

The appearance of a purge varies depending on where the purge is originating:

Stomach purge	Sour smell, brown coffee-ground-like appearance
Lung purge	Generally frothy and white or pink in color
Brain purge	A creamy white appearance, usually coming from the nose or ears
Rectal purge	Feces
Embalming fluid	Pinkish liquid, the appearance of the chemical you are injecting

Purge from the nose and mouth can be treated using the nasal tube aspirator to remove the fluid. Purge can also be removed through aspiration using the trocar. The trachea can also be tied off to prevent purge from escaping. Orifices can also be packed with cotton and gels to cauterize and plug the areas.

When purge occurs, in addition to the aspiration of the oral and nasal cavities, re-disinfection and resetting of the mouth features are important. Cotton soaked with purge fluids could cause bacterial growth, and there is a potential for decomposition, odors, and insect infestation.

OBESITY

Obese bodies may affect the selection of arteries. Excess skin and adipose tissue may cause difficulty locating the vessel. Obesity can also cause excess pressure on the body, causing a purge. To treat obese bodies, the head should be positioned straight (to maintain normal appearance and diminish rolls when placed in the casket), and the head and shoulders should be raised to allow gravity to assist with drainage. Stronger/higher index chemicals should be used at a larger volume to ensure proper distribution across the entire body. The "50-pound rule" is an old rule that is sometimes used when embalming obese human remains. The rule states that for every 50 lbs. of body weight, 1 gallon of embalming solution should be injected. This rule is sometimes used to combat secondary dilution on edematous or obese human remains. Due to body factors that may be present with obesity, multi-point injection may also be needed.

AUTOPSY EMBALMING

An **autopsy** (necropsy, postmortem exam) is *a postmortem examination of the organs and tissues of a body to determine the cause of death or pathological condition*, done after death and usually before embalming. An autopsy is used to determine the cause and manner of death.

Autopsies may be clinical, in which they are ordered by a doctor or medical facility. Or they may be medico-legal, in which they are ordered by the **Medical Examiner,** *a medical doctor who has been hired to determine suspicious and unnatural deaths (they perform the autopsy),* or a **coroner**, *which is an elected community official to investigate suspicious or unnatural deaths (does not have to be a medical doctor).*

Autopsies may be full or partial. Full autopsies examine the entire body by creating a "Y" shaped incision from both shoulders to a point in the center of the chest and then down to the genital area, and an incision around the back of the head. With full autopsies, all of the internal organs (or viscera) will be removed for study and dissection and may be placed back into the abdominal cavity (sometimes in a viscera bag) and loose sutured before being released to a funeral home. A partial autopsy will only look at part of the body. In some cases, depending on the perceived cause of death, a more in-depth autopsy may be required in which other parts of the body such as the back, face, or arms may be dissected.

These cases pose extra problems for the embalming process. When embalming a body that has been autopsied, the embalmer should first place the body on the table and do the pre-embalming analysis. Along with the autopsy, the body may have other factors, such as trauma or decomposition present.

Once the remains are on the table and washed, all incisions should be opened. The viscera should be removed and placed into a separate container lined with a viscera bag and treated with accessory chemicals or cavity fluids. Note: this container should be covered to mitigate fumes from escaping while the organs are being soaked. The breastplate, and the **calvarium**. (*the dome-like superior portion of the cranium that is removed during a cranial autopsy)* should also be treated separately. Once the cranial cavity is open, the vertebral arteries left from the autopsy need to be clamped off to close the arterial system and allow the distribution of fluid in the face and neck region. This will also prevent the spraying of fluid during the injection.

Next, the six vessels should be found that are going to be utilized for injection: both common carotids, both subclavian or axillaries, and right and left iliac. However, due to the nature of some autopsies, these vessels may be damaged or severed, in which case additional vessels may be used. In addition to the arteries, the veins should also be located and clamped off (using hemostats) to create residual pressure in the arterial system. This will force fluids into the capillary beds and further aid in the distribution of fluids.

When injecting up the right and left common carotids, each injection should be done separately using a low rate of flow and 2 to 5 pounds of pressure. At the beginning of the injection process, as the fluid is being injected distal, the embalmer pulls back the scalp to the exposed base of the occipital bone. The vertebral arteries will squirt small amounts of fluid. The vertebral arteries need to be clamped individually to create back pressure that will allow fluid to penetrate into the facial tissues.

Ligatures should be placed around each of these vessels. This ligature is used to secure the arterial tube during embalming and to tie off the artery after injection. Inject each arterial point separately, with an injection to the head and face last. If the distribution is not occurring, a hypodermic injection may be needed and used as a supplemental procedure. Once injection takes place, aspirate any fluid that has settled in the abdominal and thoracic cavities immediately to limit occupational exposure to the chemicals and bodily fluids. An autopsy aspirator (or bell aspirator) should be used; however, a normal trocar or nasal tube aspirator could be used. Once the bodily fluids have been removed, the cavities should be fully dried. Accessory chemicals (such as paraformaldehyde powders or hardening compounds) may be added to further treat and absorb fluids that are present. The viscera may then be placed back into the cavity in a viscera bag that has been closed with ligature or a zip-tie. Placing the viscera in a box and putting it at the foot of the casket is unethical and an improper procedure. Also, cremating viscera in a cremation unit that is the unit of another person is considered commingling of human remains and is illegal.

Paraformaldehyde powder should be placed on the bottom of the abdominal/thoracic cavity and the top of the viscera bag to absorb post-embalming fluids. Placing viscera in the body cavity without being contained in a viscera bag is not recommended. This could lead to rapid decomposition.

Note: The small intestines may need to be cut to release gases that have built up. Once the bagged viscera are then placed back in the body cavity, the breastplate should be placed on top and secured with a ligature. The chest flaps (or side walls) should be hypodermically treated, covered in a paraformaldehyde gel, and then brought together for suturing. Tissue drawing hemostats are used to hold the sidewalls of the torso together during the suturing process. Typically, a double ligature baseball suture is used to suture long incisions, such as those presented in an autopsy case. The cranial cavity should also be dried, and coated with a paraformaldehyde gel and hardening compound, followed by a large amount of absorbent cotton, to fill the void space.

The cranial cavity should have some weight added, such as a small sandbag or cotton, to resemble the normal head weight (remember, people may touch the body). The calvarium must be secured back to the rest of the skull. This can be done through sutures, adhesives, or calvarium clamps. The suturing method uses the temporalis muscle to secure the calvarium in place. Once the temporalis is secure on the right side, the ligature goes over the top of the calvarium and secures the temporalis on the other side. The problem with this method is that older people will have muscle loss, and the anchoring points may loosen.

Using a calvarium clamp is a widely used method for securing the calvarium. The process begins with filing a notch at the 90° angle on the temporal bone using a rat-tail file. While filing the notch, the rat-tail file needs to be rotated while making the in-and-out movements on the skull bone. The file will become clogged with bone fragments. To remove the bone fragments from the file, a small wire brush or a file board should be used during and after the process. Once the notch has been carved on both sides, cotton is placed in the skull, and a calvarium clamp is placed in both notches. With a flathead screwdriver, the clamps are tightened until both halves are firmly secure.

The third method is to use liquid adhesive, such as Aron Alpha, to secure the calvarium to the skull. For this method to be effective, both parts of the skull must be dried and free of moisture. Start at the top and dispense the entire tube using a 360° motion while holding the calvarium in place. The calvarium must be held in place for about 2 minutes for the adhesive to dry. Some embalmers use suturing powder to rub over the incision to rebuild the bone.

Regardless of which of the above methods are used to secure the calvarium in place, mortuary putty should be used to cover-up the incision made by the bone saw during the autopsy. This will prevent a suture line from showing through on the forehead post-embalming.

The scalp should be returned to its natural position and sutured in place. Watch for hair, as the hair can get stuck in the incision, causing the suture to be loose and a source for leaking. Cutting back the hair around the incision about 1/8 inch and using hair combs are recommended to create a strong suture.

Once the embalming process is completed, the human remains should be washed, dried, and placed in industry-specific plastic garments. Depending on the extent of the autopsy, coveralls or Unionalls are recommended. Normal cavity embalming does not occur because the viscera have been treated during the embalming process. Using Webril and liquid adhesive, the autopsy abdominal and thoracic sutures should be sealed and covered. For the cranium, a plastic barrier should be placed under the head and then tucked underneath prior to family viewing. Some embalmers cut a small slit in the casket pillow, or remove stuffing, to recess the head back.

ORGAN AND TISSUE DONATION

All 50 states in the United States uphold the Uniform Anatomical Gift Act, in which any person 18 or older can pledge to be an organ or tissue donor after death for research, transplantation, and educational reasons. Organ donation can include hearts, lungs, liver, kidneys, pancreas, and intestines. Tissue donation can also include eye tissue, valves, skin, and bone.

The embalming process itself is very similar to the process for autopsy cases. NOTE: human remains that have been autopsied can potentially be donor cases. Due to the nature of the donation process, supporting vessels need to be located to aid in the injection and distribution of fluid. Hypodermic embalming will be key for donor cases such as skin and bone donors to treat the exposed tissue areas.

For long bone (arm and leg bones) donors, the void caused by the removal process may be replaced with PVC rods, which simulate the appearance and structure of the removed bones. These rods should not be removed during the embalming process. The embalmer should work around the prosthetic devices. Once the embalming is completed, the exposed area should be dried with absorbent cotton and paraformaldehyde powder should be applied prior to suturing. Using a double strand baseball suture, the area should be closed, followed by using liquid adhesive and Webril placed over the incisions.

Skin donation may occur in full thickness, where the skin is removed down to the muscle or adipose tissue, or partial thickness, where only a few layers are taken. Some tissue recovery institutions use a device known as *dermatome* (memorize this term) to remove the outer most layer of the skin (epidermis). It is becoming more common for procurement specialists to remove skin and connecting tissue to increase the shelf life of the donation. In either recovery procedure, the human remains should be embalmed as if the skin was not removed. Some fluids will leak through during the embalming process. A large, clear plastic sheet should be applied to the exposed area(s) to prevent chemical and pathological exposure. These areas should be treated, post-embalming, with paraformaldehyde gels and powders. Post-embalming, the human remains of skin recovery cases should be placed in Unionall plastic garments. An absorbing pad should be placed on the posterior part, followed by paraformaldehyde powder. Paraformaldehyde powder should be placed on the exposed anterior areas void of skin tissue and covered with an absorbing pad. Additional paraformaldehyde powder should be applied on top of the pad and along the sides.

Eye enucleation is a very common tissue donation case. Some procurement specialists remove the entire eye, while others remove only the corneas, leaving the vitreous (a gel-like fluid that fills the eye) and the shell of the eye in place. Pre-embalming, in either case, the eye should be treated with either a small cavity pack inserted in the eye socket or in the eye shell. This will cauterize any blood vessels that may have ruptured during the enucleation process. Be careful not to over-manipulate the area. Over-manipulation could cause ecchymosis (bruising). Too much cavity fluid or phenol-based products in the eye could cause bleaching. Post-embalming, the cavity pack should be removed, and the eyelids should be disinfected using an orifice cleaning agent and cotton. To set the eye features, either a mortuary putty or suture seal may be used to fill the eye orbit. Some embalmers use cotton behind the eye caps; however, this practice may cause wicking, resulting in moisture around the eyes. Eye caps should be placed with stay cream on the exterior of the cap and mortuary putty on the underside (See the Restorative Art section for more care for Organ and Tissue Recovery cases (p. 161).

DISCOLORATIONS

Discolorations *are an abnormal color change in or on the body.* Discolorations may occur before death (antemortem) or after death (postmortem) and may cause problems with restoration and cosmetizing. Some of these discolorations can be treated through the embalming process to minimize their effects. Discolorations may be generalized across the entire body or localized to one location on the body. There are six classifications of discolorations.

The first classification is **blood discolorations**. These are discolorations resulting from changes in blood composition, content, or location. They may be intravascular (within the vessel) or extravascular (outside of the vessel). Intravascular discolorations may be removed through embalming and drainage. Once the discolorations have diffused out of the vessels (extravascular), they cannot be removed through embalming. They may be treated through lightening with bleaching agents or cosmetic work. See the Restorative Art section for bleaching (pp. 154).

Type of discoloration	Name of discoloration	Treatment
Antemortem-Intravascular	Hypostasis	Settling of blood and fluids to dependent portions of the body. Blue/black discoloration. Removed through embalming.
Antemortem-Intravascular	Carbon Monoxide Poisoning	Cherry red discoloration. Removed through embalming.
Postmortem-Intravascular	Livor mortis, cadaveric lividity, postmortem lividity	The discoloration results from the settling of blood and fluid. Removed through embalming.
Antemortem-Extravascular	Ecchymosis (bruising)	May inject a bleaching agent into the area. It may accompany swelling. Cosmetic work.
Antemortem-Extravascular	Petechia	Pinpoint bleeding. Cosmetic work.
Antemortem-Extravascular	Hematoma	Bruise and blood-filled swelling. May inject a bleaching agent. Cosmetic work.
Postmortem-Extravascular	Post mortem stain	Caused by hemolysis (breakdown of red blood cells) after prolonged settling of blood and fluids. Bleaching agents can be used along with cosmetic work.

The second classification is **pathological discolorations**. These are antemortem discolorations that are the result of diseases.

Discoloration	Cause/information	Treatment
Gangrene	Wet Gangrene: Venous obstruction, red to black color Dry Gangrene: Arterial issues, dark red-brown to black color	Hypodermic and surface embalming.

Jaundice (Icterus)	Liver disease, bile problems, and blood disease. Poor liver function.	Jaundice fluids, low-index fluids, counterstains, cosmetics. Note: Methanol-based cavity fluid on cotton used as a surface compress can help draw out discolorations from jaundice on the face and hands. Be sure to use massage cream to prevent dehydration.
Addison's disease	Bronze discoloration	Cosmetic work.
Leukemia	Petechia	See blood discolorations.
Meningitis	Blotchy red skin, petechia, purpura	See blood discolorations.
Lupus Erythematosus	Scaling, red muscular rash	Surface embalming for scaling and cosmetic work.

The third discoloration type is **surface discoloration**. These may occur antemortem or postmortem. These include adhesives, blood, grease, ink, iodine, oil, paint, and tobacco stains. Mechanical aids such as soap and sponges or cloths may be used. Chemical aids like solvents can also be used. Note: lemon juice will remove tobacco stains. Surface discolorations should be removed prior to embalming to verify they are removable and to not block signs of distribution during the injection.

The fourth type of **discoloration is due to embalming**. These are postmortem discolorations that result from the embalming process. They may include razor burns, which could be darkened due to dehydration. These should be covered with massage cream and cosmetics. Another example is formaldehyde gray, which results from the reaction of formaldehyde with hemoglobin (creating methyl-hemoglobin). Chemical burns around the mouth and nose may also result from chemical purge. These areas should be covered with massage cream so that the acids in the purge don't damage the skin tissue.

The Fifth Classification is due to **Skin Issues**.

Skin Issue	Treatment
Skin lesions: change in structure produced during the course of a disease or injury	1. Disinfect lesion. 2. If the skin is broken (skin slip/desquamation, abrasions), the skin may be removed. 3. If the lesion is a blister or vesicle, the blister should be punctured and drained, and the skin should be left intact. 4. Hypodermic and surface embalming may be used. 5. Once the tissues are firm and dry, cosmetics can be applied.
Pustular and ulcerative lesions: Boils, carbuncles, furuncles, ulcers, pustules, fever-blisters (herpes)	1. Aspirate or drain pus. 2. Disinfect the area. 3. Hypodermic or surface embalm area. 4. Once tissues are firm and dry, cosmetics can be applied

The last classification is **discolorations due to decomposition**. Decomposition may result in a marbling appearance and green, yellow, and black discolorations. Decomposition cases should be embalmed with very high-index fluids. Depending on the level of decomposition, waterless embalming may be used. **Waterless embalming** *is when there is no water added to the embalming machine. The concentrated arterial fluid is diluted with supplementary chemicals and modifying agents.* Hypodermic embalming and surface embalming should be utilized to fully treat the body. The body should be placed in plastic garments and may need to be placed in a disaster pouch or a Zeigler case in advanced stages of decomposition.

There are other cases in which discolorations may be present:

Refrigeration	Refrigeration may cause dehydration, which may cause discolorations. Should add a humectant to your embalming solution and use lanolin-based massage cream.
Hanging	Death by hanging may cause petechia and ligature marks. Protrusion of the tongue and ecchymosis of the eye may also be present.
Burns	See the restorative art section for the treatment of burns. (p. 155-156)
Gunshot wounds	Gunshot powder may cause burns.
Exsanguination	Total blood removed from the body causes a white/pale color.

VASCULAR CONDITIONS

When vascular difficulties such as arteriosclerosis are present, various procedures may be used to mitigate the effects. Pre-injections may be used to release clots and open the vascular system for primary injection. Co-injections may also be used to supplement primary injection chemicals. Pressure and rate of flow can be adjusted to account for intravascular and extravascular resistances. Drainage aids such as spring angular forceps can be utilized to remove clots. Various drainage methods, such as alternate or intermittent drainage, can be used to help build pressure within the system to remove clots and particles. See Pathology for diseases affecting the cardiovascular system (pp. 240-241).

DECOMPOSITION

Decomposition cases should be treated with large volumes of concentrated fluid to ensure the entire body is disinfected and treated. Waterless embalming, in which supplemental fluids are used for dilution instead of water, may be used for extreme cases. The use of specialty fluids is recommended as either a co-injection or a pre-injection. Ideally, six-point embalming should occur to treat all portions of the body. Hypodermic and surface embalming should also be used to treat any areas not getting distribution. Cavity embalming should be done immediately after embalming to prevent further decomposition and gases from occurring. Re-aspiration and re-injection may be necessary.

Decomposition cases should be placed in Unionall garments with accessory chemicals and perfuming agents to absorb moisture and mask odor. For advanced embalming cases, they should be placed in a disaster pouch in the casket or alternative container. A Zeigler case may also be necessary for extreme cases.

TISSUE GAS

Tissue gas can have many different causes. Subcutaneous Emphysema is when a tear is present in the pleural cavity, which can result in **crepitation**, *a crackling sound* when the chest is pressed. *C. perfringens* can cause tissue gas, or gas gangrene. Decomposition can also cause gas. During the embalming process, 16 oz of Dispray (disinfectant spray) or 8 to 10 oz of San Venio as a co-injection is recommended. Gas can be treated through aspiration, lancing, and channeling. Depending on the type of gas, multi-point injections may be necessary to fully treat the body and the cause.

MYCOTIC INFECTION

Mycotic infections are fungal infections. Fungal infections are common among those with immune deficiencies, such as AIDS. Many of these infections, such as Candida, have spores. See Microbiology section (pp. 278-279). These spores can be released into the air if gases are released from the body. The use of proper disinfection techniques and personal protective equipment (PPE) is essential to prevent occupational exposure. Universal precautions should be used in all embalming cases as a barrier to bloodborne pathogens, chemical exposures, and potential infectious viruses and bacterial infections.

MOISTURE CONSIDERATIONS

DEHYDRATION:

Dehydration occurs when water and moisture are lost or removed from the body. This may result due to hemorrhaging, exsanguination, febrile diseases (such as AIDS, Tuberculosis), burns, refrigeration, or a dry, warm environment.

To combat dehydration, large volumes of diluted fluid should be used. The embalmer will want to add humectants to the solution as well to help retain moisture. Pre-injection may be avoided to prevent further loss of moisture. Closed drainage may be needed to retain moisture as well. Cool water should be used in the solution to prevent the searing effect of formaldehyde on the tissues and promote distribution. Lanolin can be added to the embalming solution in the last gallon of injection. Using lanolin in the first gallon of injection could potentially clog the capillary bed and cause an uneven distribution of fluid.

Lanolin or oil-based massage cream should also be applied to the hands and face to help retain and absorb moisture into the tissues. In the restoration and cosmetic phase, tissue fillers may be added to plump up tissues.

EDEMA

Edema is classified when there is a 10% increase in water/fluid. Edema may be generalized across the entire body or localized in a specific area. Edema may also be intercellular (between cells), intracellular (within cells), or in the cavities. Edema can be the result of various things, including phlebitis, congestive heart failure, renal failure, lymph obstruction, alcoholism, trauma, steroids, and allergic reactions.

Type of edema	Where it is located
Dependent edema	Result of gravity, the lowest portion of the body
Anasarca	Generalized across the entire body
Ascites	Abdominal cavity
Pitting edema	Intercellular edema results in imprint when pressed. Common in diabetes patients.
Hydrothorax	In the Thoracic and pleural cavities
Hydropericardium	Within the pericardial sac
Hydrocele	Within the scrotum
Hydrocephalus	Within the cranial cavity

Edema can cause many problems for embalming, such as excess distention of tissues, swollen features, desquamation, leakage, and distortion of the body.

Edema can be treated with manual aids such as elevation of the body for gravity and the application of compress bandages that will apply pressure to force out liquids. Edema can also be treated through the embalming process by utilizing a large volume of medium to strong fluid solution. Slow injection should take place to allow for full distribution and drainage. The incision may be left open for a period of time for drainage purposes. Waterless embalming may be necessary for extreme cases. Epsom salts may also be added to the solution to create a hypertonic solution to draw moisture out.

The Epsom salt technique needs to be used with extreme caution because, if done incorrectly, this process will cause extreme damage to the embalming machine. Most embalmers use specialty chemicals that are designed for edematous cases. The results are just as effective as the Epsom salt technique without damaging the embalming machine. Channeling and wicking may also be utilized to remove excess fluids from the neck region.

Edema cases should be aspirated immediately after injection and treated with a high index cavity fluid. The next day, the human remains should be re-aspirated and re-injected with cavity fluid.

FROZEN HUMAN REMAINS

Frozen human remains should be left to thaw out completely before embalming. The freezing of cells can cause them to burst due to the water content (think of a water bottle freezing in your car over the winter and causing it to crack).

A strong (high index) solution should be created with warm water and injected slowly into the body. Allow time for distribution and diffusion as the body continues to thaw. The use of hot water should be avoided because it will create false rigidity.

EFFECTS OF DRUGS AND RADIATION

Chemotherapy drugs used to treat cancer may cause filtration issues within the body. This may result in excess nitrogen waste, leading to an increased formaldehyde demand within the body to overcome the excess nitrogen. Chemotherapy may also affect the permeability of cells.

Radiation is also a common treatment for diseases such as cancer. Some examples of radioactive isotopes are: Cobalt 60, Iodine 131, Phosphorus 32, Radium 226, Gold 198, and S.R. 89. People who receive large doses of radioactive isotopes must be hospitalized less than 30 mCi. mCi = Millicurie: The amount of radioactive material in which 37 million atoms disintegrate each second:

mCi= 37 million Atoms disintegrate/ per Second

Radiation must be below 30 mCi for unautopsied bodies and below 5 mCi for autopsied bodies to be safe for embalming. If above these levels, the embalming should be in a hospital morgue under the direction of a radiation protection or safety officer.

To embalm a radiation case:

1. Use rubber gloves and a heavy rubber apron.
2. Use large volumes of running water consistently throughout the embalming process.
3. Minimize contact with the body.
4. Prevent contamination of the floor.
5. Wash all instruments.
6. Use non-porous clothing.
7. Waste material should be incinerated (utilize hospital).
8. Gloves should be able to soak in water and soap.
9. If you are contaminated, seek medical attention and talk with a radiation safety officer.

Behind antibiotics, corticosteroids and anti-inflammatory drugs are the second most common type of drug used. They are used to decrease inflammation and immune responses in the body. They may be used for many conditions, such as asthma, allergies, and inflammatory bowel disease. Use of them can cause fluid retention, high blood pressure, decreased cell membrane permeability, waterlogging of tissues, perforations of the gut, weight gain, fungal infections, and bruising. Embalming techniques will vary depending on the factors presented by the body.

SHIPPING DECEDENTS

There are many factors to consider when shipping human remains. Timelines are important. How long is the postmortem interval between death and embalming? How long is the body being held before shipping? How long will the shipment take? Where is the body going? What are the temperature changes that the body will be experiencing?

Overall, all human remains that are being shipped should have a six-point injection to ensure distribution across the entire body. The features should not be glued to allow for possible disruption during transportation. All orifices should be treated and packed. The body should be in Unionall garments with powders and masking agents to absorb leakage and mask odors that may occur.

Copies of the embalming report should always be sent with the human remains and retained in the funeral home file for legal coverage.

Note: When shipping decedents, if the remains are casketed, the bed should be at the lowest position, and if the casket is metal, the locking mechanism plug should be placed in the shipping envelope attached to the outside of the shipping container. If metal caskets are sealed tight, the altitude will cause the metal casket to cave in, resulting in damage to the casket and possibly the human remains. See Preparation for Disposition section (pp. 199 - 201).

ANATOMICAL LIMITS AND GUIDES

Part 1: **Definitions**

- Anatomical Guide
    - ➢ Locating a structure by reference to an adjacent structure
    - ➢ Understanding within the scope of where things are
    - ➢ Ex. On a guided campus tour, the guide may say the library is next to the campus center building
    - ➢ Ex. The heart is medial to the lungs
- Linear Guide
    - ➢ A line drawn or visualized on the surface of the skin to represent a deeper structure
    - ➢ Being able to point out where things are on the body
    - ➢ Ex. A plastic surgeon draws dotted lines around the nose of a patient before surgery to detail where they will make their incisions
    - ➢ Ex. A line drawn from the shoulder to the elbow will show where the humerus bone is located.
- Anatomical Limits
    - ➢ The point of origin and termination of a structure
    - ➢ Where something starts and ends
    - ➢ Ex. Your house may be located on Middle Road that starts at a turn off of Cross Road, and ends at a turn into Main Street
    - ➢ Ex. The sternocleidomastoid muscle in the neck originates at the sternum and terminates at the mastoid process, thus the name

Example Questions: (Answers on p. 49)

1. A line drawn or visualized on the surface of the skin to represent the approximate location of some deeper-lying structure describes the:

    A. Linear guide
    B. Anatomical guide
    C. Place of incision
    D. Linear line

2. A point of both origin and termination in relation to adjacent structures also used to designate the boundaries of arteries describes the:

    A. Linear guides
    B. Anatomical guides
    C. Anatomical limits
    D. Topographical human anatomy

Part 2: **Guides and Limits for Particular Vessels**

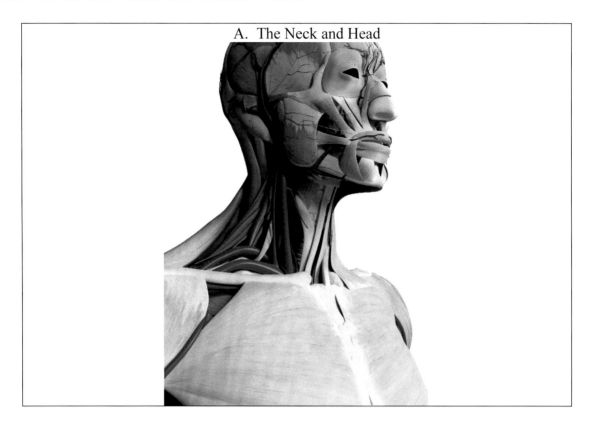

A. The Neck and Head

Vessel	Anatomical Guide	Linear Guide	Anatomical Limit	Accompanying Vein
Common Carotid Arteries	The right and left common carotids are posterior to the medial border of the sternocleidomastoid muscle	Draw a line from the sternoclavicular articulation (where the clavicle meets the sternum) to the bottom of the earlobe	The right common carotid: begins at the right sternoclavicular articulation and extends to the superior border of the thyroid cartilage. The left common carotid: begins at the level of second costal cartilage and extends to the superior border of the thyroid cartilage	Internal Jugular Veins: Superficial and lateral to the carotids (Vein-Nerve-Artery)

Facial Arteries	Along inferior border of mandible just anterior to the angle of the mandible			Facial Veins
Subclavian Arteries	The clavicle		Right: begins at the sternoclavicular articulation and terminates at the lateral border of the first rib Left: begins at the level of the second costal cartilage and terminates at the lateral border of the first rib	Brachiocephalic Veins
Axillary Arteries	Posterior to the medial border of the coracobrachialis muscle	Through center of the base of axillary space (middle of the armpit) and parallel to long axis of the upper extremity when abducted	Begins at the lateral border of the first rib and terminates at the inferior border of the tendon of the teres major muscle	Axillary Veins: Medial and superficial to the axillary arteries
Brachial Arteries	Lies posterior to the medial border of the belly of the biceps brachii muscle	From center of base of the axillary space to center of forearm just below the bend of the elbow	Begins at the inferior border of the tendon of the teres major muscle and terminates at a point just inferior to the antecubital fossa (middle of elbow)	Basilic Veins: Medial and superficial to the brachial arteries
Radial Arteries	Just lateral to the tendon of flexor carp radialis muscle	On surface of forearm from center of the antecubital fossa to the center of the base of the index finger	Extends from a point approximately 1 inch below the bend of the elbow to a point over the base of the thumb	Radial veins

41

Ulnar Arteries	Just lateral to the tendon of flexor carp ulnaris muscle	On surface of forearm from center of the antecubital fossa to a point between the ring and pinky fingers	Extends from a point approximately 1 inch below the bend of the elbow to a point over the pisiform bone (in the wrist above the pinky finger)	Ulnar veins

Example Questions: (Answers on p. 49)

1. The anatomical guide for the ulnar artery states that it lies:

    A. Lateral to the tendon of the flexor carpi ulnaris muscle and medial to the tendon of the flexor digitorum superficialis muscle.
    B. Medial to the tendon of the flexor carpi ulnaris muscle and lateral to the tendon of the flexor digitorum superficialis muscle.
    C. Lateral to the tendon of the flexor carpi radialis muscle.
    D. Directly medial and deep to the tendon of the flexor carpi radialis muscle.

2. The artery which terminates at the inferior border of the teres major muscle is the:

    A. Subclavian
    B. Vertebral
    C. Axillary
    D. Brachial

3. The linear guide for the common carotid artery may be described as a point from the _____ to the anterior surface of the lobe of the ear.

    A. Mastoid process of the temporal bone
    B. Sternocleidomastoid muscle
    C. Sternocleidomastoid articulation
    D. Sternocleidomastoid artifact

A. The Leg

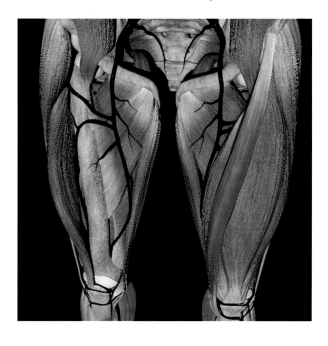

Vessel	Anatomical Guide	Linear Guide	Anatomical Limit	Accompanying Vein
External Iliac Arteries	The medial border of the psoas major muscle			External iliac vein
Femoral Arteries	Through the center of the femoral triangle bounded laterally by the sartorius and medially by the adductor longus muscle	On surface of thigh from center of inguinal ligament to center point on the medial condyle of the femur	Begins at the point posterior to the center of the inguinal ligament and terminates at the opening in the adductor magnus muscle	Femoral veins: Medial at the inguinal ligament, progressing to immediately posterior at the apex of the femoral triangle
Popliteal Arteries	Begins at the opening of	Through the center of		Popliteal veins

	adductor magnus muscle (hunter's canal) and terminates at the interior border of popliteus muscle	popliteal space parallel to the long axis of lower extremity		
Anterior Tibial Arteries		From the lateral border of the patella to the anterior surface of the ankle joint		Anterior tibial veins
Posterior Tibial Arteries		From center of popliteal space to point midway between medial malleolus and calcaneus		Posterior tibial veins
Dorsalis Pedis Arteries		From the center of the anterior surface of the ankle joint to a point between the first and second digits		Dorsalis pedis veins

Example Questions: (Answers on p. 49)

1. A parallel or transverse incision made midway between the medial malleolus and calcaneal tendon can be used to access the
   A. AnteriorTibial Artery
   B. PosteriorTibial Artery
   C. Popliteal Artery
   D. Facial Artery

2. The femoral artery is found _____ to the Sartorius muscle
   A. Medial
   B. Superficial
   C. Lateral
   D. Deep

3. The femoral vein progresses to immediately posterior to what part of the femoral triangle?
   A. Apex
   B. Top
   C. Medial Border
   D. Lateral Border

Anatomical Directions

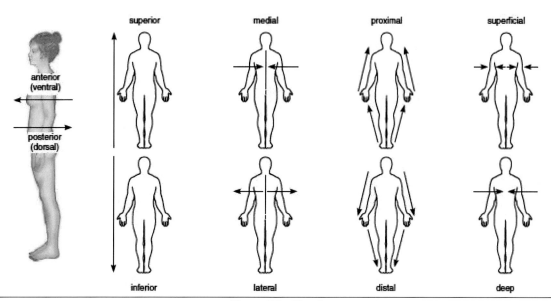

Front Vs. Back	
Anterior/Ventral	Posterior/Dorsal
The front side of a structure	The backside of a structure
	Hint: Think a dorsal fin on a dolphin
Ex. The navel is on the anterior side of the body	Ex. The occipital bone is posterior to the parietal bones

Up Vs. Down	
Superior/Cranial	Inferior Vs. Caudal
Towards the head of a structure, top side	Towards the feet of a structure, bottom side
Ex. The head is superior to the torso	Ex. The feet are inferior to the torso

Center Vs. Outside	
Medial	**Lateral**
Towards the center of a structure, towards the middle	Towards the outside of a structure, to the side
Ex. The heart is medial to the lungs	Ex. The eyes are lateral to the nose

Near Vs. Far	
Proximal	**Distal**
Towards a structure, near	Away from a structure, far
Ex. The sternum is proximal to the clavicles	Ex. The fingers are distal to the shoulder

EMBALMING ROOM INSTRUMENTS AND EQUIPMENT

There are various pieces of equipment that embalmers utilize during the embalming process.

A major piece of equipment that is vital to the embalming process is the embalming machine. The embalming machine may be a pressure machine that uses an electrical pump to create pulsating or non-pulsating pressure, such as Porti-boy, Sawyer, Duotronic, and Dodge Embalming Machine. Pulsating pressure simulates the heartbeat and can help with clot removal. Although these machines have many benefits, such as a wide pressure range, constant pressure, and large volume tanks, they can break down. A backup embalming machine readily available is essential. They may also need frequent servicing and require constant monitoring during injection and use.

The embalming machine could also be gravity driven, in which a vat hangs from the ceiling to create pressure (0.43 lbs. of pressure per one foot of elevation, or ½ lbs. every 14", 1 lb. for every 28") for injection. The key here is pressure. Pressure needs to be applied to overcome intravascular and extravascular resistance that may be present. Hand pumps are not common anymore, but they resemble large hypodermic syringes attached to a bottle apparatus. Through this, the embalmer is able to create pressure for injection or a vacuum for aspiration. Bulb syringes are self-contained rubber manual pumps that can create pressure for injection (they cannot be used for aspiration due to one-way valves). Air pressure machines using mechanical or hydraulic pressure are also options.

Another important type of equipment is for aspiration and injection (for cavity embalming). Although the trocar is the main instrument for aspiration, there are various types of apparatuses that this instrument needs to attach to in order to aspirate the hollow organs in the human body. The trocar may hook up to a hydro aspirator, which is an apparatus that is connected to the water supply. When the water turns on, it creates a suction to aspirate (withdraw) fluids and waste. Electric aspirators use motors to create suction. Note: there is a water line to keep the motor lubricated. Finally, the newest aspirator being used is a waterless aspirator which uses centrifugal force to create suction. Both the electric and waterless aspirators work best in prep rooms with low water pressure. Hand pulps and bulb syringes are historical instruments that use manually created pressure to inject and aspirate. Note: bulb syringes have one-way valves and cannot be used for aspiration.

Embalming rooms need appropriate embalming tables. These tables should be made of impermeable, non-porous material (porcelain, fiberglass, stainless steel) and should have a hole for drainage. Many tables also have the ability to tilt to utilize gravity. These are different from dressing tables, as dressing tables do not tilt and do not have drainage holes. However, many firms use combo prep/dressing tables. Along with these tables, there should be impermeable positioning devices to position the body correctly. These devices could be used to lift the head, fold the arms, lift the shoulders, etc.

Hair dryers and curling irons are key in the prep room to dry clothing and style the hair of the decedent.

Electric spatulas are electrically heated blades used to move excess fluid in swollen tissues. They help to remove edema. However, when using them, you want to have a layer of massage cream between the tissues and the spatula to ensure that the tissues do not become burned or seared.

Body lifts are designed to move decedents easily without adding physical stress to the lifter.

Sterilizers are for safety to ensure that instruments are sterilized. If an autoclave is utilized, the steam under pressure should be above 100°C.

Some firms have refrigeration units or coolers. These coolers should be kept between 38 and 40°F for the best results. Too cold, and the body will freeze; too warm, and the rate of decomposition will increase.

There are also many instruments and supplies that should be utilized during the embalming process. These include but are not limited to:

Instrument/Supplies	Purpose
Arterial Tube/Cannula	Used to inject embalming fluid into the arteries. Various shapes and sizes.
Needle Injector	A mechanical device used to inject injector needles/pins into the jawbone to close the mouth.

Scalpel	A handle and blade used for incisions.
Aneurysm hook/needle	An embalming instrument that is used for blunt dissection and in raising vessels.
Scissors	May be sharp-sharp, sharp-blunt, blunt-blunt (referring to each blade), or bandage scissors, used for cutting.
Groove director	Used to guide tubes into vessels.
Bone Separator	Used to maintain elevation of vessels, usually plastic or wood. (Also great for cleaning under fingernails)
Hemostats (forceps)	Used to clamp vessels. It may be straight or curved and can lock in place.
Spring Forceps	Used for holding tissues, cotton, etc. Also used for restoration and holding open veins for drainage to remove clots.
Whitney Spreaders, incision spreaders	Used to hold incisions open.
Razor	Used to shave the decedent.
Drain tubes	Used to insert into a vein to aid drainage.
Suture needles	S, C, or Loopuyt shaped, used to close incisions by suturing with a ligature (string).
Nasal tube aspirator	Used to aspirate the nose and throat area.

Autopsy aspirator	Used to aspirate the body cavities after an autopsy. The head is flush with the tissues.
Trocars	The sharp, hollow tube is used to aspirate body cavities and inject cavity fluid. Various sizes depend on the body. It may also be used for hypodermic embalming.
Hypodermic syringes and needles	Used to inject embalming chemicals hypodermically and to inject restorative chemicals such as tissue builder.
Trocar button	Used to plug the hole made by the trocar. Looks like a screw and is placed with a trocar button applicator.
Arterial fixation forceps	Used to hold arterial tubes in place in the arteries and prevent leakage.

Eye caps	Thin plastic dome-shaped disks are used to close the eyes and maintain the normal shape of the eye.
Mouth formers	A piece of plastic used to maintain the shape of the mouth during closure.
Kalip or Lip cement	Used to close the lips.
Adhesive glue	Aron alpha, rubber cement, super glue. Used to close eyelids and lips when needed.
Plastic garments	Unionalls, coveralls, capris, shorts, pants. Plastic garments are used to cover the decedent body or extremities, prior to clothing, and to prevent bodily fluids from leaking on the clothing.
Cotton and Webril	Used to wipe tissues, swab orifices, and pack incisions.
Solvent chemicals	Used to remove stains and cleanse makeup brushes. An example is acetone or Dry wash by Dodge.
Preservative chemicals	Embalming chemicals are used to inactivate bacteria and slow decomposition.
Bleaching agents (phenol)	Used to lighten areas of the skin.
Disinfectant chemicals	Chemicals are used for cleaning and to destroy or inhibit pathogenic organisms. Used on the body, instruments, table, walls, floors, etc.
Sealers	Sealing agents are used to prevent leakage. It may be in powder or liquid form.

Answer Key:

p. 39   1. A   2. C

p. 42   1. C   2. C   3. B

p. 44 & 45   1. B   2. A   3. C

49

Glossary for Embalming

Abdominal anatomical regions - Two systems of nomenclature employed for designating portions of the abdomen, which include a 9-region plan and a 4-quadrant plan.

Abrasion - Antemortem injuries resulting from friction of the skin against a firm object resulting in the removal of the epidermis.

Abut - To bluntly adjoin another structure; for example, the line of eye closure.

Accessory chemical - A group of chemicals used in addition to vascular (arterial) and cavity embalming fluids; most are applied to the body surface.

Action level/AL (exposure limits) - A concentration of 0.5 ppm of formaldehyde calculated as an 8-hour TWA concentration as defined by OSHA.

Active dye - An agent that will impart permanent color to tissues.

Actual pressure - Pressure indicated by the injector gauge needle when the arterial tube is open, and the arterial solution is flowing into the body.

Adipocere (grave wax) - Wax-like material produced by saponification of body fat in a body buried in alkaline soil.

Aerobic - Characterized by the presence of free oxygen.

Aerosolization - Dispersed minute particles of blood and water that become atomized and suspended in the air.

Agglutination - Increased viscosity of blood brought about by the clumping of particulate-formed elements in the blood vessels.

Agonal algor - Decrease in body temperature immediately before death.

Agonal coagulation - A change from a fluid into a thickened mass of blood immediately before death.

Agonal dehydration - Loss of moisture immediately before death.

Agonal edema - Escape of blood serum from an intravascular to an extravascular location immediately before death.

Agonal fever - Increase in body temperature immediately before death.

Agonal - A period of time immediately before death.

Agonal translocation - Redistribution of endemic microflora on a host-wide basis immediately before death.

Algor mortis - Postmortem cooling of the body to the ambient temperature.

Alternate drainage - Method of injection and drainage in which embalming solution is injected, and then the injection is stopped while drainage is opened.

Amino acid - The building block of protein.

Anaerobic - Characterized by the absence of free oxygen.

Anasarca - Generalized edema in subcutaneous tissue.

Anatomical guide - Descriptive reference for locating arteries and veins by means of identifiable anatomical structures.

Anatomical limits - Points of origin and termination in relation to adjacent structures used to designate the boundaries of arteries.

Anatomical position - Used as a reference in describing body parts to one another in which the body is erect, feet together, palms forward, and thumbs are pointed away.

Aneurysm - Localized abnormal dilation of a blood vessel resulting in a weakness of the vessel.

Aneurysm - Embalming instrument that is used for blunt dissection and raising vessels.

Aneurysm needle - Embalming instrument that is used for blunt dissection with an eye in the hook portion of the instrument for placing ligatures around raised vessels.

Angular spring forceps - Drainage instrument designed for the removal of venous blood clots.

Anomaly - Deviation from normal.

Antecubital fossa - Triangular depression in front of the bend of the elbow.

Antemortem - Before death.

Anterior - Anatomical term of position and direction denoting the front or forward part.

Anterior superior iliac spine - A palpable bony protuberance located on the ilium.

Anticoagulant - Ingredient of embalming fluids that retards the natural postmortem tendency of blood to become viscous and prevents adverse reactions between blood and other embalming chemicals.

Apparent death - Condition in which the manifestations of life are feebly maintained.

Arterial fluid - Concentrated preservative embalming chemical for injection into the arterial system during vascular embalming.

Arterial solution - Mixture of arterial fluid and water used for arterial injection and may include supplemental fluids.

Arterial tube - Instrument used to inject embalming fluid into the vascular system.

Arteriosclerosis - Disease of the arteries resulting in thickening, hardening, and loss of elasticity of the arterial walls.

Articulation - Juncture between two or more bones or cartilage.

Ascites - Accumulation of serous fluids in the peritoneal (abdominal) cavity.

Asepsis - Freedom from infection and from any form of life; sterility.

Asphyxia - Death beginning in the lungs due to an insufficient intake of oxygen.

Aspiration - Removal of gas, fluids, and semi-solids from body cavities and hollow viscera by means of suction with an aspirator and a trocar.

Atheroma - Fatty degeneration or thickening of the walls of the larger arteries occurring in atherosclerosis.

Autoclave - Apparatus used for sterilization by steam pressure.

Autolysis - Self-destruction of cells; decomposition of all tissues by enzymes of their own formation without microbial assistance.

Autopsy - A postmortem examination of the organs and tissues of a body to determine the cause of death or pathological condition.

Bactericide - Substance used to destroy bacteria.

Biohazard - Biological agent or situation that constitutes a hazard to humans.

Biohazardous waste - Any potentially infective, contaminated waste that constitutes a hazard to humans in the workplace.

Biological death - Irreversible somatic death.

Bischloromethyl ether/BCME - A carcinogen potentially produced when formaldehyde and sodium hypochlorite come into contact with each other.

Bleach (sodium hypochlorite) - Chlorine-containing compound used for disinfection of inorganic/inanimate surfaces.

Bleaching agent - Chemical used to lighten skin discoloration.

Blood - Tissue that circulates through the vascular system and is composed of approximately 22% solids and 78% water.

Bloodborne pathogens - Microorganisms present in human blood that can cause disease in humans.

Bloodborne Pathogen Standard - OSHA mandate (29 CFR 1910.1030) regulating the employee's exposure to blood and other body fluids.

Blood discoloration - Condition resulting from changes in blood composition, content, or location, either intravascularly or extravascularly.

Blood vascular system - Circulatory network composed of the heart, arteries, arterioles, capillaries, venules, and veins.

Blunt dissection - Utilizing manual techniques or round-ended instruments that separate rather than cut the superficial fascia surrounding blood vessels.

Boil (furuncle) - Deep-seated inflammation in the skin, which usually begins as a subcutaneous swelling in a hair follicle.

Bridge suture (interrupted suture) - Temporary suture consisting of individual stitches employed to sustain the proper position of tissues.

Buffer - Substance capable of neutralizing acids and bases to maintain a constant pH.

Bulb syringe - Self-contained manual pump made from soft rubber designed to create pressure to deliver arterial fluid as it passes through one-way valves located within the bulb.

Cadaver - Dead human body used for medical purposes.

Cadaveric lividity (livor mortis) - Intravascular red-blue discoloration resulting from postmortem hypostasis of blood.

Cadaveric spasm (instantaneous rigor) - Immediate stiffening of the muscles of a dead human body.

Calvarium - Superior portion of the cranium removed during cranial autopsy.

Calvarium clamp - Device used to reattach the calvarium to the cranium after a cranial autopsy.

Canalization - Formation of new channels in tissue.

Capillary - Semi-permeable minute blood vessels allowing for the diffusion of arterial embalming fluid.

Capillary permeability - Ability of substances to diffuse through capillary walls into the tissue spaces.

Carbohydrate - Compound of hydrogen, carbon, and oxygen that is an aldehyde or ketone derivative of polyhydroxy alcohol.

Carbuncle - Circumscribed inflammation of the skin and deeper tissues that ends in suppuration and is accompanied by systemic symptoms.

Carcinogen - A cancer-causing chemical or material.

Case analysis (embalming analysis) - Evaluation of the dead body prior to, during, and after the embalming procedure is completed.

Cavitation - The formation of cavities in an organ or tissue, frequently seen in some forms of tuberculosis.

Cavity embalming - Direct treatment of the contents of the body cavities and the lumina of the hollow viscera, usually accomplished by aspiration and injection of chemicals using a trocar.

Cavity fluid - Concentrated embalming chemical injected into the cavities of the body following the aspiration of the body; it can also be used in hypodermic and surface embalming.

Cellular death - Death of the individual cells of the body.

Center of arterial solution distribution - Ascending aorta and/or arch of the aorta.

Center of venous drainage - Right atrium of the heart.

Centrifugal force machine - Embalming machine that uses an electrical pump to create pulsating and non-pulsating pressure.

Chelate - Substance used as an anticoagulant in embalming solutions that binds metallic ions.

Chemotherapy - Application of chemical agents in the treatment of disease in humans, primarily cancer, causing an elevated preservative demand.

Clinical death - Phase of somatic death lasting from 5-6 minutes during which life may be restored.

Coagulating agent - Chemical or physical agents that bring about coagulation.

Co-injection fluid - Primarily used to supplement and enhance the action of vascular (arterial) solutions.

Coma - Death beginning in the brain due to irreversible cessation of brain activity and loss of consciousness.

Communicable disease - Disease that may be transmitted either directly or indirectly between individuals by an infectious agent.

Concurrent disinfection – Disinfection carried out during the embalming process.

Concurrent drainage - Occurs continuously during the vascular injection.

Condyle - Rounded articular process on a bone.

Contaminated laundry - Laundry that has been soiled with blood or other potentially infectious materials.

Contaminated sharps - Any contaminated object that can penetrate the skin including needles, scalpels, broken glass, and exposed ends of wires.

Cornea - Transparent part of the tunic of the eyeball that covers the iris and pupil and admits light into the interior.

Corneal sclera button - Portion of the cornea recovered for transplantation in situ.

Coroner - Elected or appointed official of a local community who may or may not have medical training and holds inquests concerning sudden, violent, and unexplained deaths.

Cosmetic fluid - Arterial fluid that contains active dyes intended to restore a more natural skin tone.

Counterstaining - Technique using active dye in an attempt to cover internal discolorations such as jaundice.

Crepitation - Crackling sensation produced when gases trapped in tissues are palpated, as in subcutaneous emphysema or tissue gas.

Creutzfeldt-Jacob Disease/CJD - Rare degenerative disease of the brain with unknown etiology caused by a prion.

Cribiform plate - Thin, medial portion of the ethmoid bone of the skull used as a point of entry for cranial aspiration.

Death - Irreversible cessation of all vital functions.

Death rattle - Noise made by a moribund person caused by air passing through a residue of mucous in the trachea and posterior oral cavity.

Death struggle - Semi-convulsive twitches that often occur before death.

Decay - Decomposition of proteins by enzymes of aerobic bacteria.

Decedent care report - Documentation of body conditions and subsequent treatments when sheltering or preparing a body for visual identification prior to cremation; or for a body received from another facility.

Decomposition - Separation of compounds into simpler substances by the action of microbial and/or autolytic enzymes.

Dehydration - Loss of moisture from body tissue, which may occur antemortem or postmortem; the removal of water from a substance.

Desiccation - Extreme dehydration often resulting in post-embalming discolorations.

Desquamation (skin slip) - Separation of the epidermis from the underlying dermis as a result of putrefaction.

Dialysis - Separation of substances in solution on the basis of differences in their ability to pass through a semipermeable membrane.

Differential pressure - Difference between potential and actual pressure.

Diffusion - See **Solution diffusion**

Discoloration - Any abnormal color in or upon the human body.

Disease - Any deviation from or interruption of the normal structure or function of a body part, organ, or system.

Disinfectant - An agent, usually chemical, applied to inanimate objects/surfaces to destroy most disease-causing microbial agents, excluding bacterial spores.

Disinfection - Destruction and/or inhibition of most pathogenic organisms and their products in or on the body.

Distribution - See **Solution distribution**

Drain tube - Drainage instrument used to aid the removal of venous blood.

Drainage - Removal of blood, blood clots, interstitial and lymphatic fluid, and arterial solution during vascular embalming, usually through a vein.

Drench shower - OSHA-required safety device for a release of a copious amount of water in a short time.

Dry gangrene (ischemic necrosis) – Necrosis resulting from localized deprivation of arterial blood supply.

Ecchymosis - Bruising discoloration of the skin caused by the escape of blood into the extravascular tissues.

Edema - Abnormal accumulation of fluids in tissues or body cavities.

Electric aspirator - A device that uses a motor to create suction for the purpose of aspiration.

Electric spatula (tissue reducer) - Electrically heated blade which may be used to dry moist tissue, reduce swollen tissue, and restore contour to natural form.

Embalming - Process of chemically treating the dead human body to reduce the presence and growth of microorganisms, to temporarily inhibit organic decomposition, and to restore an acceptable physical appearance.

Embalming report - Detailed listing of body conditions and treatments performed by funeral personnel for all bodies received into a facility for preparation.

Engineering controls - Mechanical systems and devices of a facility designed to minimize exposure to occupational hazards.

Enzyme - Organic catalyst produced by living cells and capable of autolytic decomposition.

Excision - To remove by cutting out; the area from which tissue has been removed.

Exposure incident - Specific eye, mouth, other mucous membrane, non-intact skin, or parenteral contact with blood or other potentially infectious materials that results from the performance of an employee's duties.

Exsanguination - Loss of blood to the point where life can no longer be sustained.

Extravascular - Outside the blood vascular system.

Extrinsic - From outside the body.

Eye enucleation - Removal of the eye for tissue transplantation, research, and education.

Eye caps - A thin, dome-like plastic shell placed beneath eyelids to restore natural curvature and maintain the position of posed eyelids.

Eyewash station - OSHA-required emergency safety device providing a steady stream of water for flushing the eye.

Fatty acid - Product of decomposition of fats.

Febrile - Characterized by a high fever, causing dehydration of the body.

Fermentation - The microbial (enzymatic) decomposition of carbohydrates under anaerobic conditions.

Fever blister - Lesion of the mucous membrane of the lip or mouth.

Firming - Rigidity of tissue due to the chemical reaction.

Fixation - Act of making tissue rigid as a result of protein solidification.

Fixative - Agent employed in the preparation of tissues for the purpose of maintaining the existing form of the structure.

Formaldehyde/HCHO- Colorless, strong-smelling gas that, when used in solution, is a powerful preservative and disinfectant; a known carcinogen.

Formaldehyde demand (preservative demand) - Amount of formaldehyde required to effectively preserve remains.

Formaldehyde gray - Gray discoloration of the body caused by the reaction of formaldehyde with hemoglobin to form methyl hemoglobin.

Formaldehyde Rule - OSHA (29 CFR 1910.1048) regulation limiting the amount of occupational exposure to formaldehyde.

Gangrene - Death of body tissues due to deficient or absent blood supply.

Gas gangrene - Antemortem form of gangrene, associated with anaerobic gas forming bacilli, most commonly, *Clostridium perfringens*.

Gravity filtration - Extra vascular settling of preservative fluids by gravitational force to the dependent areas of the body.

Gravity injector - Apparatus used to inject arterial fluid; relies on gravity to create the pressure required to deliver the fluid.

Gray (Gy) - The derived unit that measures a dose of absorbed radiation.

Groove director - Instrument used to guide drainage devices into veins.

Hand pump - Historical instrument resembling a large hypodermic syringe attached to a bottle apparatus; used to create either pressure for injection or vacuum for aspiration.

Hardening compound - Chemical in powder form that has the ability to absorb moisture and/or preserve tissue; used in cavity treatment of autopsied cases.

Hazard Communication Standard - (29 CFR 1910.1200) OSHA regulation that deals with identifying and limiting exposure to hazardous chemicals within the workplace.

Hazardous material - Agent exposing one to risk.

Hematoma - Tumor-like swelling of blood.

Heme - The red pigment of the hemoglobin.

Hemoglobin - Iron-containing pigment of red blood cells functioning to carry oxygen to the cells.

Hemolysis - Destruction of red blood cells that releases heme.

Hepatitis - Inflammation of the liver.

Hepatitis B Virus/HBV - Infectious bloodborne virus.

High-index fluid - Special arterial fluid with a high HCHO content.

Human remains - The body of a deceased person, including cremated remains.

Humectant (restorative fluid) - Chemical that increases the capability of embalmed tissue to retain moisture.

Hydroaspirator - Apparatus that utilizes a water supply to create suction and is used to aspirate the contents of the body's cavities.

Hydrocele - Abnormal accumulation of fluids in the scrotal sac.

Hydrocephalus - Abnormal accumulation of cerebrospinal fluid in the ventricles of the brain.

Hydrolysis - Decomposition with water as one of the reactants.

Hydropericardium - Abnormal accumulation of fluid within the pericardial sac.

Hydrothorax - Abnormal accumulation of fluid in the thoracic cavity.

Hygroscopic - Readily absorbing moisture.

Hypertonic - Solution having a greater concentration of dissolved solute than the solution to which it is compared.

Hypodermic injection - Injection of embalming chemicals directly into the tissues through the use of a syringe and needle or a trocar.

Hypostasis - Process of blood and/or other fluids settling to the dependent portions of the body that can occur in the antemortem, agonal, or postmortem period.

Hypotonic - Solution having a lesser concentration of dissolved solute than the solution to which it is compared.

Imbibition - Swelling and softening of tissues and organs as a result of absorbing moisture from adjacent sources.

Inactive dye - Agent that will not impart permanent color to tissues; generally used to impart color to a chemical.

Incision - A clean cut into tissue or skin made with a scalpel to access arteries and veins.

Index - Strength of embalming fluids indicated by the number of grams of pure formaldehyde gas dissolved in 100 ml of solution; usually refers to a percentage.

Infant - A child less than one year of age.

Infectious disease - Condition caused by the growth of a pathogenic microorganism in the body.

Inferior - Anatomical term of position and direction denoting towards the feet or underlying structure.

Inguinal ligament - Anatomical structure forming the base of the femoral triangle; extends from the anterior superior iliac spine to the pubic tubercle.

Injection - Act or instance of forcing fluid into the vascular system or directly into tissues.

Injection pressure - Amount of pressure produced by an injection device to overcome initial intravascular and/or extravascular resistance on or within the vascular system.

Intercellular - Between the cells of a structure.

Intercostal space - Space between the ribs.

Intermittent drainage (restricted drainage) - Method of drainage in which the drainage is stopped at intervals while the injection continues.

Interstitial fluid - Substance in the supporting connective tissues surrounding body cells.

Intracellular fluid - Protoplasmic substance inside body cells.

Intravascular - Within the blood-vascular system.

Intravascular pressure - Force created as the flow of embalming solution is established, and the arterial walls expand and contract, resulting in the filling of the capillary beds and the development of pressure filtration.

Intrinsic - From within the body.

Isotonic - Solution having an equal concentration of dissolved solute as the solution to which it is compared.

Jaundice - Condition characterized by excessive concentrations of bilirubin in the skin and tissues, cornea, body fluids, and mucous membranes with a resulting yellow appearance.

Jaundice fluid - Low-formaldehyde arterial fluid with bleaching and coloring qualities for use on bodies with jaundice.

Laceration - Wound characterized by irregular tearing of tissue.

Larvicide - Substance used to kill insect larvae.

Lateral - Anatomical term of position and direction denoting away from the mid-line.

Lesion - Abnormal change involving any tissue or organ due to disease or injury.

Ligate - To tie off any vessel or structure upon completion of embalming.

Linear guide - Line drawn or visualized on the surface of the skin to represent the approximate location of some deeper-lying structure.

Lipolysis - Decomposition of fats.

Lumen - Cavity or opening of a hollow structure.

Lysin - Hydrolytic enzyme that acts destructively upon cells and tissues.

Lysosome - Organelle within but separate from a cell containing hydrolytic enzymes that break down proteins and certain carbohydrates.

Maggot - Insect larvae, especially flies.

Masking agent (perfuming agent) - Chemical found in an arterial fluid having the capability of displacing an unpleasant odor or of altering an unpleasant odor so that it is converted to a more pleasant one.

Massage - Manipulation of tissue in the course of preparation of the body.

Medial - Anatomical term of position and direction denoting toward the mid-line.

Medical examiner - Elected or appointed official of a local community with a medical degree who holds inquests concerning sudden, violent, and unexplained deaths.

Microorganism - A microscopic organism, especially a bacterium, virus, or fungus.

Microbial enzyme - The enzymes of microorganisms; a source of the enzymes that contribute to decomposition.

Modifying agents - Chemicals within the arterial fluid to deal with varying demands predicated upon the condition of the deceased, the environment, and the preservative to be used.

Moist gangrene – necrotic tissue that resulting from inadequate venous drainage accompanied by the invasion of saprophytic bacteria.

Mold preventative - Agent, which will prohibit the growth of mold.

Moribund - In a dying state; in the agonal period.

Mortuary putty – a pliable compound used to fix or fill.

Mouth former - A feature–setting device that is placed in the mouth to provide shape the contour of the lips.

Multiple-site injection - Vascular injection from two or more arteries.

Nasal tube aspirator - An instrument used to aspirate the throat by means of the nostrils.

Necrobiosis Antemortem, physiological death of the cells of the body followed by their replacement.

Necrosis - Pathological death of tissue still a part of the living organism.

Needle injector – a feature-setting device used for mouth closure designed to implant metal pins into bone.

Nephritis - Inflammation of the kidneys can cause an increase in nitrogenous waste.

Nitrogenous waste - Metabolic by-products such as urea and uric acid that contain nitrogen and tend to neutralize formaldehyde.

Non-cosmetic fluid - An arterial fluid that does not contain active dyes and will not impart a color change upon the body tissues.

Occupational exposure - Reasonably anticipated skin, eye, mucous membrane, or parenteral contact with blood or other potentially infectious materials that may result from the performance of a worker's duties.

One point injection - Injection and drainage from one location.

Osmosis – Passage of pure solution from a solution of lesser concentration to one of greater solute concentration when the two solutions are separated by a semipermeable membrane; the primary mechanism by which preservation occurs.

Packing forceps - Embalming instrument used to fill the external orifices of the body with absorbent material.

Palpate - To examine by touch.

Parenteral – introduced into the body by piercing mucous membranes or the skin barrier through such events as needle sticks, human bites, cuts, and abrasions.

Petechia - Antemortem, pinpoint, extravascular blood discoloration visible as purplish hemorrhages of the skin.

Pharmaceutical agents - Drugs or medicines that change the biochemistry of the blood.

Pitting edema - Condition in which interstitial spaces contain such excessive amounts of fluid that the skin remains depressed after palpation.

Positioning devices - Preparation room equipment for properly positioning bodies prior to, during, and after vascular embalming.

Plastic garments – Used to contain leaking and manage odors; different types include pants, coveralls, stockings, sleeves, capri pants, and Unionalls.

Positioning device - Equipment used to position the body before, during, and after the decedent care.

Posterior – An anatomical term of position and direction that denotes towards the back.

Postmortem - Period that begins after somatic death.

Postmortem caloricity - The rise in temperature after death due to continued cellular metabolism.

Postmortem chemical change - Change in the body's chemical composition that occurs after death.

Postmortem physical changes - A change in the form or state of matter without any change in chemical composition.

Postmortem stain - Extravascular color change that occurs when heme seeps through the vessel walls and into the body tissues.

Potential pressure - The pressure indicated by the injector gauge needle when the embalming machine is running, and the rate of flow is closed.

Preparation room – Facility wherein embalming, dressing, cosmetizing, or general decedent care is performed.

Preservative - A chemical that inactivates saprophytic bacteria and attempts to arrest decomposition by converting body tissue to a form less susceptible to decomposition.

Preservative powder - Chemical in powder form, typically used for surface embalming of the remains.

Pressure filtration – Passive transport system enabling the passage of arterial solution from the capillary to the tissue fluid.

Primary dilution - Strength of embalming solution mixed in the embalming machine.

Primary disinfection - Disinfection carried out prior to the embalming process.

Procurement - The recovery of organs or tissues from a cadaver for transplantation.

Protein - Biochemical compound that is a polymer of many amino acids.

Proteolysis - Decomposition of proteins.

Ptomaine -Any one of a group of nitrogenous organic compounds formed by the action of putrefactive bacteria on proteins; indole, skatole, cadaverine, and putrescine.

Pubic symphysis - The fibrocartilage that joins the two pubic bones in the median plane.

Purge - Postmortem evacuation of any substance from an external orifice of the body because of internal pressure.

Pus - Liquid product of inflammation.

Putrefaction - Decomposition of proteins by the action of enzymes from anaerobic bacteria.

Rate of flow - Speed at which fluid is injected; measured in ounces per minute.

Razor burn (razor abrasion) - A darkened, air-dried area on the skin resulting from the removal of the epidermis while shaving

Re-aspiration - Repeated aspiration of a cavity.

Restoration - Treatment of the deceased in an attempt to recreate natural form and color.

Restricted cervical injection - Method of injection wherein both common carotid arteries are initially raised to control the entry of arterial solution into the head.

Rigor mortis - Postmortem stiffening of the body muscles by natural body processes.

Saccharolysis - Decomposition of sugars.

Sanitation - A process to promote and establish conditions that minimize or eliminate biohazards.

Saponification - Process of soap formation; as related to decomposition, the conversion of fatty tissues of the body into a soapy, waxy substance called adipocere, or grave wax.

Saprophytic bacteria - Bacteria that derive their nutrition from dead organic matter.

Scalpel - A two-piece-embalming instrument consisting of a handle and a blade used to make incisions and excisions.

Sealing agents - Material used to provide a barrier or seal against any type of leakage of fluid or blood.

Secondary dilution - Weakening of the embalming fluid by the fluids in the body, both vascular and interstitial.

Septicemia – A condition characterized by the presence of bacteria in the blood

Sequestering agent - A chemical agent that isolates metal ions so they cannot react with blood or water.

Sharps container - OSHA required, puncture-resistance, a leak-proof receptacle for proper disposal of sharp objects.

Shell embalming – Vascular embalming in which only the skin or superficial portion of the body receives arterial solution.

Solute - A substance dissolved in a solvent to form a solution; the component of a solution present in a lesser amount.

Solution - A homogeneous mixture of one or more substances (solutes) dissolved in a sufficient quantity of solvent.

Solution diffusion (arterial solution diffusion) - Passage of some components of the injected arterial solution from an intravascular to an extravascular location; movement of the arterial solution from the capillaries into the interstitial fluids and subsequently the cells.

Solution distribution (arterial distribution) - The movement of solution from one point of injection throughout the arterial system and into the capillaries.

Solvent - A substance that does the dissolving in a solution; the component of a solution present in a greater amount.

Somatic death - Death of the organism as a whole.

Split injection - Injection from one site and drainage from a separate site.

Sterilization - Process of completely removing or destroying all life forms and their products on or in a substance.

Stillborn - Dead at birth.

Subcutaneous - Situated or occurring beneath the skin.

Superficial - Toward the surface.

Superior - Anatomical term of position and direction denoting *towards the head* or elevation in place or position.

Supplemental fluid - Fluid injected for purposes other than preservation and disinfection. Supplemental fluids generally fall into one of three categories: pre-injection, co-injection, and humectants or restorative fluids.

Surface compress - A wet or dry cloth applied firmly to a body part.

Surface embalming - The direct contact of body tissues with embalming chemicals.

Surface discoloration - A discoloration due to the deposit of matter on the skin surface. These discolorations may occur antemortem, during, or after embalming of the body; adhesive tape, ink, iodine, paint, and tobacco stains.

Surface pack - An absorbent material, compressed, saturated with an embalming chemical, and placed in direct contact with the tissue.

Surfactant (surface tension reducer, wetting, penetrating, or surface-active agent) - Chemical that reduces the molecular cohesion of a liquid so it can flow through smaller apertures.

Tardieu spots - Post-mortem extravascular blood discoloration caused by the rupture of minute vessels as blood settles into the dependent areas of the body.

Terminal disinfection - Institution of disinfection and decontamination measures after the preparation of the remains.

Test of death - Any procedure used to prove a sign of death.

Terminal disinfection - Disinfection carried out after the embalming process.

Tissue gas - Postmortem accumulation of gas in tissues or cavities brought about by an anaerobic gas-forming bacillus, *Clostridium perfringens*.

Transverse - Anatomical term of position and direction denoting lying at right angles to the long axis of the body.

Trauma - A physical injury or wound caused by external force or violence.

Trocar - Sharply pointed surgical instrument used in cavity embalming to aspirate the cavities and inject cavity fluid. The trocar may also be used for supplemental hypodermic embalming.

Trocar button - A plastic threaded screw-like device for sealing punctures and small round trocar openings.

Trocar guide - A line drawn or visualized on the surface of the body or a prominent anatomic structure used to locate internal structures during cavity embalming, from the point of reference 2 inches to the left of and 2 inches superior to the umbilicus.

Unionall - Plastic garment designed to cover the entire body from the chest down to and including the feet.

Universal precautions - An approach to infection control in which all human blood and certain human body fluids are treated as if known to be infectious.

Vacuum breaker - Apparatus that prevents the back-siphoning of contaminated liquids into potable water supply lines or plumbing cross-connections within the preparation room.

Vehicle - Liquids that serve as a solvent for embalming fluids.

Viscera - Internal organs enclosed in the body cavity.

Viscosity - The thickness of a liquid.

Water conditioner - An agent used to remove elements from a water supply.

Work practice controls - A procedure that reduces the likelihood of exposure to a hazard by altering the manner in which a task is performed, prohibiting the recapping of needles, and not allowing blood splatter or aerosolization of blood while draining during the embalming process.

Thanatochemistry

Chemistry for Embalmers is a survey of the wide variety of concepts and principles which relate to funeral service. In particular, the preservation and disinfection of human remains, and the safety concepts and practices for the embalmer are covered. Chemistry is the study of the properties of materials based on the fundamental understanding of scientific principles.

Objectives of a Funeral Service Chemistry course include the ability to identify and properly protect against dangerous chemicals and to understand the signs of chemical exposure. The student will know the components of the different types of fluids and other preparations used and will be able to make selections of the proper chemicals for specific embalming problems. The science of decomposition and preservation of proteins through embalming is of fundamental importance as a means of fully serving bereaved families.

There are different fields of Chemistry, including Inorganic (*the study of metals and nonmetals which may be trace components of life processes, including salts and oxides)*, Organic (*the study of carbon-based molecules which are found in living things and their byproducts)*, Biochemistry (*a branch of science concerned with the chemical and physicochemical process and substances that occur within living organism,)* and **Embalming Chemistry** (*the special reactions and molecules that convert protein to a material that resists decomposition)*. **Thanatochemistry** is another term for the study of the chemical processes related to human remains and their postmortem treatment.

BEGINNING CHEMISTRY

The universe is made up of matter (*anything that has mass and takes up space*) and energy. Matter is composed of atoms. Some atoms can react with other atoms to form molecules which are how the roughly 30,000,000 known different molecules are formed. Matter can be described in two general ways: physical properties and chemical properties. Physical properties are characteristics that can be observed about the material. These observations cannot change the composition of the material (or what it is made of). Examples of physical properties include the state (*solid, liquid, or gas at room temperature*), solubility (*how much will dissolve in a particular solvent*), color, density (*mass per unit volume, such as the density of water is 1 gram per cubic centimeter- g/cm^3*), odor, taste, and conductivity (*ability to carry an electric current in a wire*).

states of matter

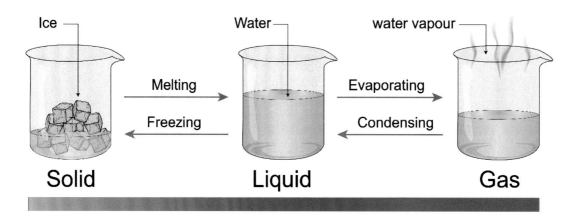

Ice — Melting → Water — Evaporating → water vapour

Freezing ← Condensing ←

Solid   **Liquid**   **Gas**

The **states of matter** (*solid, liquid, and gas*) are due to the **cohesion** (*attraction among the atoms or molecules of that material*) between the molecules of the material and the energy it takes to cause them to pull away from each other. All atoms and molecules are constantly in motion. The total amount of movement of the particles is known as heat. The measurement of this movement, on average, is the temperature. The atoms of solids are attracted to each other by a force called cohesion. The atoms of solids do not change places in relation to each other. However, they vibrate while remaining in place. The higher the temperature, the faster the atoms vibrate. The concept of vibrational energy in solids can be understood when it is observed that metal expands when heated and shrinks when cooled. The increased heat causes the vibrations to be more forceful, so the distance between the atoms increases; thus, the metal expands.

In the case of liquids, the movement of the atoms is such that they collide with each other in perfectly elastic collisions. These collisions are forceful enough to keep the atoms bouncing around and exceed much of the cohesive force that would exist if it were solid. Liquids occur because they fit in the narrow range of overcoming enough of the cohesion to move freely but not enough energy to exceed all that attraction. The idea of removing heat to slow down the atoms is easily demonstrated by cooling a liquid until it becomes a solid. At the **freezing point** (*the temperature at which a liquid becomes solid*), the low energy of the atoms is insufficient to overcome cohesion.

A gas is composed of atoms that have very little cohesion, so little energy is needed for them to overcome the cohesion and fly away from their open container. Gases fill an enclosed container.

The states of water are a good way to solidify these concepts. Ice has the least molecular energy. Warming the ice until it melts has added heat; thus, the molecules move faster until they break the cohesion and can move about in the container as a liquid. Keep heating, and the water will boil, producing steam which is the gas phase of water. The molecules in steam contain so much energy they separate from each other readily.

66

Water has other factors related to the state that are important to embalmers. The first is evaporation which is the loss of water to the air at temperatures below boiling. Bodies dry out due to surface evaporation, and solution mixes in the embalming machine change due to evaporation. Evaporation occurs because the heat energy in the water breaks some of the cohesive attractions, and some of the molecules break free and go into the air. The other related concept is sublimation which is when water molecules evaporate from ice and do not go through a liquid phase.

Test your understanding of the kinetic energy (energy in motion) of molecules by explaining how the solubility of formaldehyde gas in water changes as the temperature of that solution goes up.

Other terms related to physical properties are **liquefaction** (*melting a solid to become liquid)*, **vaporization** (*heating a liquid to become a gas*), **condensation** (*cooling gas to become liquid)*, **viscosity** (*resistance to the flow, the thickness of a liquid, i.e., a gel is more viscous than water)*, and **surface tension** (the *tendency of a liquid to form a skin-like surface due to strong cohesion among the molecules)*. Water beading up on a waxy surface shows surface tension.

Physical changes are events such as crumbling a piece of chalk, melting a solid, evaporating a liquid to a gas, or dissolving a salt in water. The substance still has the same chemical makeup before and after the physical change.

Chemical properties are the other way to describe matter. Chemical properties are the ability of one material to react with other atoms or molecules to produce new material. Examples of chemical properties include **flammability** (*ability to burn)*, **coagulation** (*clumping, thickening)*, **decomposition** (*breaking apart of protein molecules)*, reactivity with **formaldehyde** (*embalming or preservation)*, and **neutralization** (*reacting an acid with a base)*. If a reaction **does not** occur, that is a chemical property too. For example, being nonflammable is a chemical property which means the substance in question does not burn.

Chemical changes always have products that are different from the reactants at the completion of the reaction. Chemical changes always require or result in two different substances being involved in the reaction.

SUBATOMIC PARTICLES, ATOMS, PERIODIC TABLE

Atom structure

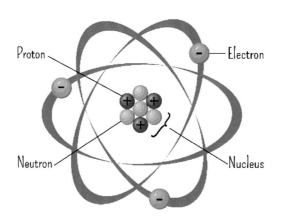

Protons are the most important subatomic particle for establishing the identity of the element. Found in the nucleus, the number of protons is specific for each element and is used to determine the **Atomic Number** (*the element number shown on the Periodic Table*). The element is determined by the atomic number. Elements are listed on the Periodic Table in order of increasing atomic number. Protons have a mass of 1 Atomic Mass Unit (amu) and a charge of +1. For example, all carbon atoms have an atomic number of 6, meaning every carbon atom has 6 protons (+6).

Neutrons are also found in the nucleus; they have a mass of 1 amu and a charge of zero (0). Neutrons contribute to the mass of the atom. Since protons and neutrons both have a mass of 1 amu: they can be added together to find the **Atomic Mass** of the atom. For example, carbon has 6 protons and 6 neutrons. (6 protons x 1amu) + (6 neutrons x 1 amu) gives carbon an atomic mass of 12.

Atomic mass = number of protons + number of neutrons.

The number of neutrons often varies among different atoms of the same element but exists in known ratios of different **isotopes** (*same number of protons and atomic number but a different number of neutrons*) in nature. A common example is Carbon. Carbon-12 has the standard 6 neutrons, but Carbon-14, an isotope, has 8 neutrons (but still has 6 protons).

The third subatomic particle is the electron which has almost no mass and a -1 charge. The electrons are found in orbitals around the nucleus. In atoms, the number of electrons must equal the number of protons to have an overall net charge of 0. Carbon has 6 protons (+6) and, therefore must have 6 electrons (-6) to have an overall charge of 0 [(-6) + (+6) = 0].

Number of Electrons (-) = Number of Protons (+)

Substances that are composed of one type of atom are called elements. These pure substances cannot be broken down by any chemical means. The elements on the left side of the periodic table are metals, and those on the right are nonmetals. The dividing line is a stairstep line starting with Boron, separating Al from Si, Ge from As, etc.

A few particular elements (H, N, O, F, Cl, Br, I) are diatomic, meaning they naturally occur in pairs due to their bonding tendencies. For example, Oxygen is a naturally occurring gas with the formula O_2.

Groups are the vehicles displayed in columns; periods or rows are horizontal. Group 1 are alkali metals (Li, Na, K, Rb, Cs, Fr), Group 2 are alkaline earth metals (Be, Mg, Ca, Sr, Ba, Ra), Group 7 are halogens (Cl, F, Br, I, At), Group 8 are noble gases (He, Ne, Ar, Kr, Kr, Xe, Rn).

MIXTURES

A mixture, in the simplest terms, is a combination of **two or more** substances not chemically united and in no definite proportion by mass. Any time two or more materials are found together in close contact, it is a mixture. Mixtures can vary in specificity from the simplicity of this definition to a true solution which has specific physical properties that are measurable and repeatable.

A **suspension** (*mixture of two or more materials that remain mixed with mechanical stirring but will separate when the agitation stops*) is a nonspecific mixture with the property that one phase can hold up or suspend the other. Using milk and a chocolate powder drink mix as an example, the chocolate particles are so small that when the mix is shaken or stirred, they remain distributed, fairly evenly throughout the container. After a few minutes, however, the chocolate powder begins settling to the bottom, and the milk appears white again. Products that are labeled as "Shake Well Before Using" are suspensions. ***Any fluid in the embalming room which has noticeable layers in the bottle is a suspension.*** The "solutes" in a suspension can be removed using a filter. The **cellular** portion of the blood is a suspension. When blood is collected in a tube, the cells will sink to the bottom, and the liquid phase will remain above it.

A solution is a much more specific type of mixture. There is a physical attraction between the **solvent** (*the material doing the dissolving of the solution, usually a liquid or gas)* and the **solutes** (*the smaller portion of the mixture)* that causes the solution to form.

An example:

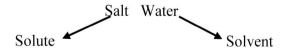

Periodic Table of the Elements

	1	2	3	4	5	6	7	8	9	10	11	12	13	14	15	16	17	18
1	1 1.008 H HYDROGEN																	2 4.003 He HELIUM
2	3 6.941 Li LITHIUM	4 9.012 Be BERYLLIUM											5 10.811 B BORON	6 12.011 C CARBON	7 14.007 N NITROGEN	8 15.999 O OXYGEN	9 18.998 F FLUORINE	10 20.180 Ne NEON
3	11 22.990 Na SODIUM	12 24.305 Mg MAGNESIUM											13 26.982 Al ALUMINIUM	14 28.086 Si SILICON	15 30.974 P PHOSPHORUS	16 32.066 S SULPHUR	17 35.453 Cl CHLORINE	18 39.948 Ar ARGON
4	19 39.098 K POTASSIUM	20 40.078 Ca CALCIUM	21 44.956 Sc SCANDIUM	22 47.867 Ti TITANIUM	23 50.942 V VANADIUM	24 51.996 Cr CHROMIUM	25 54.938 Mn MANGANESE	26 55.845 Fe IRON	27 58.933 Co COBALT	28 58.693 Ni NICKEL	29 63.546 Cu COPPER	30 65.38 Zn ZINC	31 69.723 Ga GALLIUM	32 72.64 Ge GERMANIUM	33 74.922 As ARSENIC	34 78.971 Se SELENIUM	35 79.904 Br BROMINE	36 83.798 Kr KRYPTON
5	37 85.468 Rb RUBIDIUM	38 87.62 Sr STRONTIUM	39 88.906 Y YTTRIUM	40 91.224 Zr ZIRCONIUM	41 92.906 Nb NIOBIUM	42 95.95 Mo MOLYBDENUM	43 98.907 Tc TECHNETIUM	44 101.07 Ru RUTHENIUM	45 102.91 Rh RHODIUM	46 106.42 Pd PALLADIUM	47 107.87 Ag SILVER	48 112.41 Cd CADMIUM	49 114.82 In INDIUM	50 118.71 Sn TIN	51 121.76 Sb ANTIMONY	52 127.60 Te TELLURIUM	53 126.90 I IODINE	54 131.29 Xe XENON
6	55 132.91 Cs CAESIUM	56 137.33 Ba BARIUM	57-71 La-Lu Lanthanide	72 178.49 Hf HAFNIUM	73 180.95 Ta TANTALUM	74 183.84 W TUNGSTEN	75 186.21 Re RHENIUM	76 190.23 Os OSMIUM	77 192.22 Ir IRIDIUM	78 195.08 Pt PLATINUM	79 196.97 Au GOLD	80 200.59 Hg MERCURY	81 204.38 Tl THALLIUM	82 207.2 Pb LEAD	83 208.98 Bi BISMUTH	84 (209) Po POLONIUM	85 (210) At ASTATINE	86 (222) Rn RADON
7	87 (223) Fr FRANCIUM	88 (226) Ra RADIUM	89-103 Ac-Lr Actinide	104 (261) Rf RUTHERFORDIUM	105 (262) Db DUBNIUM	106 (266) Sg SEABORGIUM	107 (264) Bh BOHRIUM	108 (269) Hs HASSIUM	109 (268) Mt MEITNERIUM	110 (281) Ds DARMSTADTIUM	111 (280) Rg ROENTGENIUM	112 (285) Cn COPERNICIUM	113 (286) Nh NIHONIUM	114 (289) Fl FLEROVIUM	115 (288) Mc MOSCOVIUM	116 (292) Lv LIVERMORIUM	117 (294) Ts TENNESSINE	118 (294) Og OGANESSON

GROUP →
PERIOD

Atomic Number — 8
Atomic Mass — 15.999
Symbol — O
Name — OXYGEN

Lanthanide Series

57 138.91 La LANTHANUM	58 140.12 Ce CERIUM	59 140.91 Pr PRASEODYMIUM	60 144.24 Nd NEODYMIUM	61 (145) Pm PROMETHIUM	62 150.36 Sm SAMARIUM	63 151.96 Eu EUROPIUM	64 157.25 Gd GADOLINIUM	65 158.93 Tb TERBIUM	66 162.50 Dy DYSPROSIUM	67 164.93 Ho HOLMIUM	68 167.26 Er ERBIUM	69 168.93 Tm THULIUM	70 173.05 Yb YTTERBIUM	71 174.97 Lu LUTETIUM

Actinide Series

89 (227) Ac ACTINIUM	90 232.04 Th THORIUM	91 231.04 Pa PROTACTINIUM	92 238.03 U URANIUM	93 (237) Np NEPTUNIUM	94 (244) Pu PLUTONIUM	95 (243) Am AMERICIUM	96 (247) Cm CURIUM	97 (247) Bk BERKELIUM	98 (251) Cf CALIFORNIUM	99 (252) Es EINSTEINIUM	100 (257) Fm FERMIUM	101 (258) Md MENDELEVIUM	102 (259) No NOBELIUM	103 (262) Lr LAWRENCIUM

Legend: ALKALI METAL · ALKALINE EARTH · TRANSITION METAL · BASIC METAL · SEMIMETAL · NONMETAL · HALOGEN · NOBLE GAS · LANTHANIDE · ACTINIDE

This physical attraction is the most important part of the concept of solubility and explains the specific properties of this type of mixture. The reason why a suspension does not stay mixed is that the particles are too large. No matter how science has tried, there is no way to mechanically grind the material into individual atoms or molecules. Unless the solute particles are at the individual atom or molecule size, they will not remain suspended. Only a solvent with the correct properties is able to pull a solute material apart on the molecular level. This is where the phrase "like dissolves like" comes into play. A solute that is polar (an unequal sharing of electrons – partially charged), water, for example, can separate the ions of salt from each other and hold them in a permanent state of being separated from each other. The salt ions are effectively insulated from each other, and they will not recombine to remake the salt as long as there is enough water to maintain adequate separation.

The interaction between solute and adequate solvent to maintain **solvation** (*dissolving a solute in a solvent*) explains several of the properties of solutions. Solutions are **homogeneous** (*having the same composition throughout*) because the randomness of molecular movement in a liquid keeps it mixed thoroughly. Solutions have a **specific solubility** (*maximum amount of solute per amount of solvent at a known temperature*) because it requires a certain amount of solvent to keep the ions separate. The ions are attracted to the water molecules, so they remain dissolved permanently; solutions never separate. Solute particles are impossible to see because they are too small; solutions are clear, although not necessarily colorless. Another term for a true solution is a crystalloid. The term means crystal-like because the hydrated ions are distributed in a pattern. The crystalloid concept is important for understanding osmosis during arterial injection. The serum portion of the blood is partly a solution because of glucose and salt being dissolved within the solution.

Physical properties can be used to describe true solutions. A **saturated** solution has dissolved its maximum amount of solute at a specific temperature. An **unsaturated** solution still has room for more solute. More specific expressions of concentrations include percent by weight or volume, by ratio like **1:100 or parts per million** (*ppm*), or the specific measure for formaldehyde solutions called **index** (*grams of HCHO per 100 ml of solution, it has no units*)

A supersaturated solution, for some reason, exceeds the known solubility, but it is a temporary condition. An example of a supersaturated solution is fog, which is an excess of water dissolved in the air. When warm moist air cools, the water usually precipitates as rain, especially if there is enough air movement to cause the water droplets to collide, thus making drops big enough to fall as rain. The fog usually persists until the wind picks up to cause collisions or the temperature goes down enough to precipitate out as dew. If the temperature goes up, the warmer air will dissolve more moisture, and the fog will dissipate.

A colloidal suspension, more commonly called a colloid, is a special type of suspension. The suspended particles are between 1 and 100 nanometers (10^{-9}m) in diameter, which is very small but still not as small as individual atoms or ions. These particles are small enough to be stirred up by collisions with the liquid or gas which is suspending them. The particles are too small to be seen under normal illumination but are large enough to be seen as sparkles when a beam of light shines through the mixture. This is called the Tyndall Effect. Colloidal solutes can pass through man-made filters but not through membranes like capillaries. This is a second factor in the explanation of osmosis for embalming purposes.

Examples of colloids are dust in the air, coffee, virions suspended in water, edema-removing supplemental fluids, and proteins suspended in water. Blood is partially a colloid because plasma proteins, especially albumin, are suspended in the plasma.

OSMOSIS

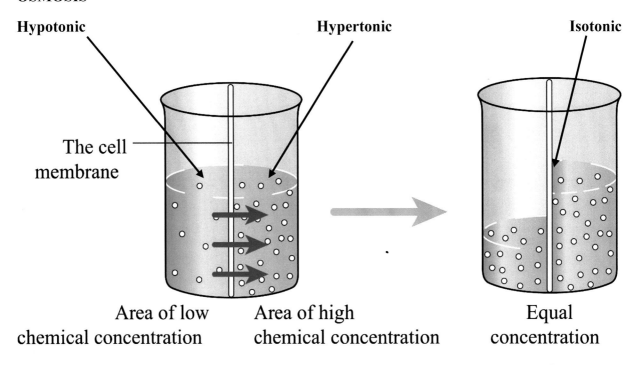

Osmosis (*the passage of solvent through a semi-permeable membrane from the side which has the higher water content to the side which has lower water content; from hypotonic to hypertonic solution*) is explained in terms of the attraction that water and solutes have for each other.

The dissolving of polar molecules occurs because the solute particles are pulled apart, according to the concept of like dissolves like, into individual ions by the force of the solvent. This is like the attractive force between magnets in that they do not have to touch to exert force on each other. The attraction can occur over a short distance. Consider a special container whose walls will allow water molecules to pass through but keep the solute inside. The walls would be similar to a window screen; the spaces allow the small water molecules to pass through (as air does) but keep the large solutes confined inside. This special container does exist; for embalmers, it is the capillary. Capillaries have very small pores, which allow water and dissolved solutes to pass through. Those pores are too small to allow the osmotically active colloidally suspended molecules to escape from the capillary. The result is that water is drawn out of the tissues into the capillaries.

Embalmers use osmosis to adjust the amount of water in the tissues. An **edematous body** (*containing an excess of fluid in interstitial and intracellular space*) must have the water content removed to regain a natural appearance. An edema-reducing chemical is added to the injection solution. This supplemental fluid is the colloid portion of the mixture. The colloidal particles of this special fluid cannot pass through the capillary wall. Instead, they attract water out of the tissues back through the capillary wall into the vascular system. The excess water is then removed as venous drainage. The crystalloid portion of the mixture is HCHO and water. The HCHO passes through the capillary wall into the tissues for preservation. The edema-removing chemical is the **hypertonic** (*high concentration of osmotically active solutes*) side of the membrane; the moisture-laden tissues are the hypotonic side. Water flows from the side where it is in excess (the wet tissues) to the side where the attracting solutes are (inside the capillary). The flow of water will cease when the two sides are **isotonic** (the *concentration of solutes is equal on both sides of the capillary wall*).

ACID & BASE CHEMISTRY

The concept of acidity is rooted in the behavior of water. Water exhibits a small degree of **self-dissociation** (*the separation of water molecules into hydrogen H^+ and hydroxide OH^-*). The H^+ ion is a single proton; this is the ion that is responsible for acidity. The ratio of dissociated atoms to undissociated atoms in pure water is 1:10,000,000. Expressed in exponential form, this ratio is 10^{-7}. The algebraic manipulation signified by the letter p means to multiply the exponent by -1 and remove the 10 from the expression completely. Thus p (10^{-7}) is 7. When the concentration of hydrogen ions, H^+, in a sample of water, is 10^{-7}, the pH is 7. This is the neutral point of the acid/base scale. The concentration of H^+ can be increased by adding a compound known to release H^+, such as HCl, which is hydrochloric acid. In this case, the ratio of H^+ to undissociated water is larger, for example, 1:10,000. This is the same as 10^{-4}. Using the p function to express pH, it is 4, which is much more acidic than pure water. The full pH range is 1 to 14. Any value above 7 is labeled as alkaline or basic; any value below 7 is acidic, and 7 is neutral. The pH of healthy human remains has a pH range from 7.35 to 7.45.

Inorganic acids contain at least one hydrogen, which is written at the beginning of the formula. The haloacids are HF, HCl (the acid of the stomach), HBr, and HI. Other inorganic acids include H_2SO_4 and H_3PO_4. There are many others. Organic acids include lactic acid, citric acid, acetic acid, and formic acid. Inorganic acids are much stronger than organic acids.

Inorganic bases contain OH^-, the hydroxide polyatomic ion, as part of their molecular formula. A metal is bonded to the OH to form molecules such as NaOH, LiOH, and Ca $(OH)_2$. The organic base of interest to embalmers is ammonia, NH_3. This does not appear to have any OH polyatomic ion as part of the formula. However, when dissolved in water, the unbonded pair of electrons on the nitrogen center attracts the H^+ from water molecules, thus leaving an increase of the OH^- in the solution. When the hydrogen is attached to the previously unbonded electrons on the nitrogen center, this new polyatomic ion, NH_4^+, is called ammonium.

This reaction is NH_3 +   HOH $\rightarrow$ $NH_4^+OH^-$

ammonia +   water $\rightarrow$ ammonium hydroxide

The neutralization reaction is the reaction of an acid with a base to yield salt and water. If the exact equal amount of acid and base react, the final pH will be 7.

$$HCl \; + \; NaOH \quad \rightarrow \quad NaCl \; + \; HOH$$

$$acid \; + \; base \qquad \rightarrow \quad salt \qquad + \quad water$$

In the case of short-chain organic acids, the resulting product is known as the salt designated by adding -ate to the name of the molecule:

$$CH_3COOH \; + \; NaOH \qquad \rightarrow \quad CH_3COO^- Na^+ \; + \; HOH$$

$$acetic \; acid \quad + \; sodium \; hydroxide \; \rightarrow \; sodium \; acetate \; + \; water$$

In the case of long-chain organic acids, which are known as lipids but are often called fatty acids, the product is labeled as a soap instead of a salt. This is called the saponification reaction. When human fats react with a base, which could happen if an unembalmed body is buried in alkaline soil, the product is called adipocere or grave wax.

ORGANIC CHEMISTRY

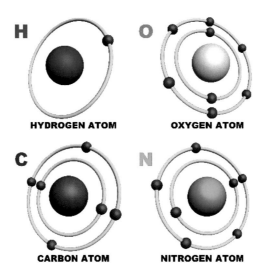

The carbon-containing molecules which are found in living things are called organic compounds. They are comprised mostly of C, H, O, and N. The main structure is the carbon chain or ring to which functional groups are attached. All organic molecules are covalent or coordinate covalent bonded molecules. When the molecule contains only carbon and hydrogen, it is called a hydrocarbon. When a hydrocarbon has only a single bond between the carbons of the chain, it is called an alkane. If there is a double bond, it is called an alkene, and if there is a triple bond, it is an alkyne. The name of the molecule is based on the number of carbons in the chain and the type of bonds present.

When an alkane is oxidized (loses electrons), an atom of oxygen will attach between carbon and one of the hydrogens. This first step in the oxidation series of an alkane is called alcohol. Alcohol is used primarily for disinfection and preservation, although some specific alcohols have special properties that benefit embalming practice. Alcohol preserves and disinfects on contact by dehydrating the tissues. The functional group is written as R-OH.

When alcohol, whose functional group is on a terminal carbon, is oxidized, it will form an aldehyde. This step of the oxidation series occurs by removing one hydrogen from the carbon center plus the hydrogen from the OH functional group. This leaves oxygen attached to the carbon by a double bond. The term aldehyde is the contraction of "**alcohol dihydride**." Aldehydes are used mostly as preservatives and disinfectants. Formaldehyde and glutaraldehyde are two aldehydes used in embalming. The functional group is written as R-CHO.

If the alcohol functional group is on a carbon that is NOT terminal when the hydrogen is removed from the alcohol functional group, the oxygen with a double bond remains on that same inner carbon. This type of molecule is a ketone. Its functional group is written R-CO – R' where the R's must represent at least one carbon. Ketones are excellent solvents to remove grease, oil, paint, and cosmetic stains.

The next step in the oxidation series is an organic acid. In this reaction, an oxygen atom attaches between the carbon and hydrogen of the aldehyde functional group, leaving the double-bonded oxygen on its original carbon. The functional group is written as R-COOH. Organic acids are also called carboxylic acids because the -COOH functional group is called the carboxyl group.

The final step of the oxidation series of an alkane ends in $CO_2 + H_2O$. In fact, all hydrocarbons and nearly all organic molecules oxidize fully to just these same two products.

An organic molecule that does not contain carbon is ammonia, NH_3. Ammonia qualifies as organic because it is part of amino acids. As such, it is a product of protein degradation and is removed by the kidneys in the form of urea. Ammonia, one of the products of decomposition, is of special concern to embalmers because it neutralizes HCHO instead of allowing it to denature the protein.

The reaction of ammonia with HCHO yields the waxy solid called urotropin. This is both good and bad for embalmers. The good aspect is the neutralization of HCHO in a spill emergency, plus the knowledge that disposing of HCHO into the sewer system is harmless because HCHO is neutralized so promptly. The bad part is the neutralization of HCHO in cases of massive decomposition. An increased level of ammonia in the body due to decomposition or disease, such as kidney failure, will cause the body to have an increased formaldehyde demand.

BIOCHEMISTRY

Digestion of protein

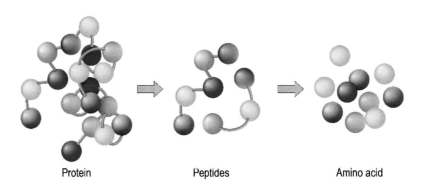

Protein   Peptides   Amino acid

Amino acids are known as the building blocks of life. Amino acid molecules, as their name shows, have a base end (amino the same root as ammonia) and an acid end. This property of having both base and acid properties is called amphoterism. The structure of an amino acid is such that they allow nearly limitless molecules to be made by reacting the acid end of one with the base end of another. This forms a peptide bond. Molecules composed of less than 50 peptide bonds are called polypeptides. A protein is a polypeptide at any length. Each time a peptide bond is formed, a molecule of water is produced. Proteins are susceptible to degradation by water because an excess of water can reverse the peptide reaction. This process of being broken down by the water is called hydrolysis.

Proteins are extremely complex molecules. They are very large and have a specific composition that is determined by the DNA of the cell which synthesized the protein. They also have a specific three-dimensional shape which is necessary for them to function properly. Some proteins use their structure to hold two molecules in the proper location and orientation so they can react. Proteins are biological catalysts or enzymes when they work in this manner. The molecules which enzymes specifically act upon are called the substrate. The name of an enzyme is usually derived from the material that it acts upon with the suffix "*ase*" added to the end of the word. For example, ***lipase*** is an enzyme that acts on lipids, and protease acts upon protein.

Both Amino Acids Create a Peptide Bond

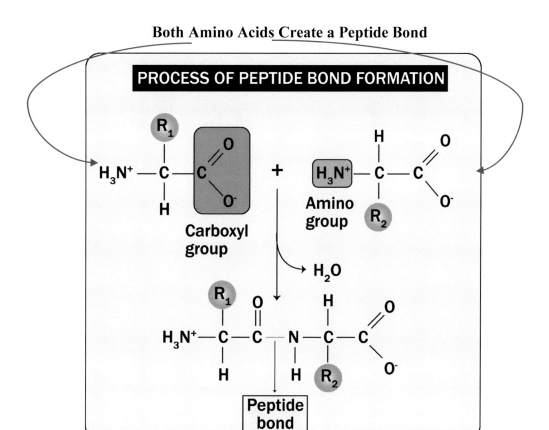

Proteins are responsible for the structure, regulation, and function of the body. Tissues which are proteins, include skin, muscle, hair, glands, and internal organs. Albumin is a plasma protein that has osmotic activity, hemoglobin is a protein that transports oxygen, and enzymes catalyze reactions in the body. The capsid of a virion is protein, while cellular microbes use proteins for structure, enzymes and toxins.

The highly specific nature of protein shape is their weakness. If the three-dimensional form is changed, it will not function properly. Altering the structure is called denaturing the protein because it does not work in its natural way. The coagulation proteins are denatured, they become more compressed and firmer. Heat is one way to coagulate protein, just as the white of an egg, which is the protein albumin, becomes firm when cooked. Preservatives like HCHO and glutaraldehyde coagulate protein by cross-linking between adjacent peptide bonds. For each cross-link formed, a molecule of water is produced. Drainage is recommended to prevent hydrolysis from reversing the cross-linking reaction that just occurred. Water can reverse embalming by hydrolysis; it is important to keep embalmed bodies dry.

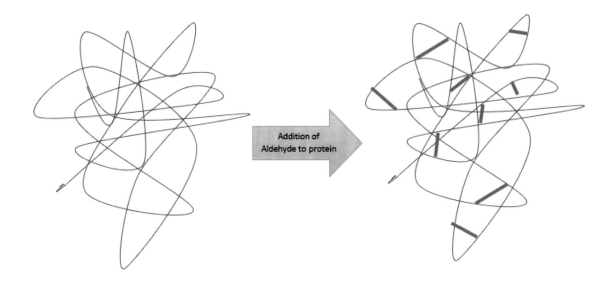

The above figure is a cross-link reaction.

Autolytic enzymes are a special type of protein. These enzymes are contained in most cells and have the purpose of degrading the cell when it dies. After death, these enzymes contribute to decomposition. Denaturing these enzymes with embalming fluid slows down decomposition.

DECOMPOSITION

The breakdown of body proteins is caused by several forces and reactions. One of the purposes of embalming is to slow or delay the progress of this eventuality until final disposition. Autolysis and hydrolysis are noted above. Putrefaction is decomposition caused by saprophytic anaerobes (without oxygen). Decay is decomposition caused by aerobic (with oxygen) saprophytes. These microbes secrete enzymes that break down peptide bonds. The is so prevalent in all living things that proteolytic enzymes have evolved to be very effective at this site. Degradation of the peptide bond is the source of ammonia in decomposing bodies. Another reaction that occurs is fermentation which is the conversion of carbohydrates to carbon dioxide, water and sometimes alcohol.

Chemical changes post-mortem involves many things. The pH of human remains changes after death. As cells that are oxygen starved still engage in some metabolism after death, they release lactic acid. This increases the acid content of the body, causing pH to decrease. Once all the cells are dead, decomposition continues, which releases ammonia, thus causing the pH to increase well into the alkaline range. Embalming occurs best at pH = 7.4. However, human remains will typically be more acidic, even dropping as low as pH=5, post-mortem. Rigor mortis occurs when the body is depleted of ATP and is not able to relax muscle constriction, thus causing the muscle fibers to shorten in a physical change. Rigor mortis releases when the muscle fibers decompose, which is a chemical change. Hydrolysis breaks down protein, especially erythrocyte

78

cell membranes, which causes the release of pigments into the tissues. This is the cause of post-mortem stains. Stomach acid and the normal digestive flora treat the human remains as any other protein-based material that they readily dissolve, so decomposition is rapid in the abdominal region.

HOW EMBALMING CHEMICALS WORK

Preservatives react with proteins to temporarily halt decomposition. They do this by denaturing proteins. As noted above, HCHO cross-links adjacent peptide bonds to coagulate the molecule. Once denatured, a protein cannot function as it did in life. This allows many interconnected ways that the body is protected from decomposition. Besides coagulation which causes firmness of the tissues, reacting with the peptide bond alters the target (more appropriately, the substrate) from the action of proteolytic enzymes of saprophytes. Since these enzymes are proteins, they also are denatured and could not act on the peptide even if it were still in its normal form. The cell walls of bacteria, the capsids of virions, and the cell membranes of other microbes contain proteins that are also denatured, resulting in the death or inactivation of the microbe. Many of the odors of decomposition are inactivated by preservative chemicals as well.

The chemical mechanisms of preservation are also responsible for disinfection. The alteration of protein structure kills or inactivates microbes. The protein of their cell walls or cell membranes is fatally denatured. The enzymes microbes secrete to break down host tissues and are denatured, thus they cannot provide the nutrients for life. Drawing a distinction between disinfection and preservation is difficult because their functions overlap.

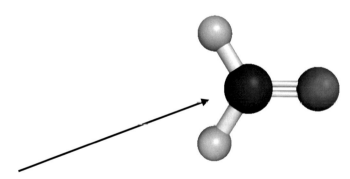

FORMALDEHYDE (HCHO)

As the most common chemical used in embalming, the properties of HCHO must be well understood. This is a single-carbon aldehyde commercially produced by the oxidation of methanol, the single-carbon alcohol. The proper scientific name is **methanal** which denotes that it is a one-carbon aldehyde. HCHO is a gas at room temperature. The saturated solution of HCHO in water is specifically called formalin. Formalin is an industrial material that is one of the most widely used chemicals in manufacturing. The index (*grams of HCHO per 100 ml of solution*) is 37. An index is similar to percent because its ratio is based on 100 ml of the total solution, but the industry standard is to use an index. An index is determined by weight; when formalin is described in terms of volume, HCHO is 40% of the volume of the solution. Formalin must be stabilized with 7% to 12% methanol to prevent the formation of the solid called paraformaldehyde. Paraformaldehyde is used in autopsy powders, and HCHO is off-gassed when paraformaldehyde encounters moisture, which then preserves proteins.

HCHO is classified as an irritant; efforts to classify it as a carcinogen have been unsuccessful partly because HCHO is found in trace amounts in healthy normal human cells as part of metabolic reactions. Every effort must be made to decrease HCHO exposure in the workplace. This includes proper ventilation, covering the injection machine tank, removing background sources like autopsy powder from the workspace, rinsing any spilled HCHO down the drain with cold water, and removing contaminated waste from the embalming room promptly.

Since HCHO is a gas, it must be dissolved in water to be injected. Being aware that warm gases have higher kinetic energy than cold gases and that gas will expand to fill its container, there are two important rules about working with HCHO. The first is to use cool to cold water to dilute the injection solution. Use cold water to mop up spills and rinse any HCHO residue down the drain. Remember, ammonia neutralizes HCHO into harmless urotropin; it is environmentally safe to use the sewer for disposal. The second rule is to always keep the cover on the machine and the caps on the bottles to reduce HCHO vapor in the air.

Embalming with HCHO can cause the tissues to take on a "formaldehyde gray" color, so dyes are added to prevent this condition. The amount of HCHO needed to accomplish embalming is called formaldehyde demand. This is an estimate of the amount of protein in human remains with extra consideration given to decomposition and/or massive bacterial infection. Lipid tissue is not fixed with HCHO, so the formaldehyde demand is not dictated by corpulence (obesity). Demand is based on the quantity of protein and ammonia present.

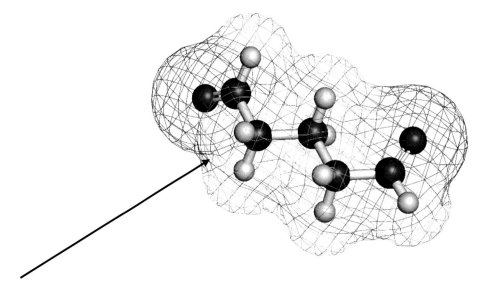

GLUTARALDEHYDE (OHC (CH₂)₃CHO)

Glutaraldehyde is a five-carbon dialdehyde which means it has a -CHO functional group on each terminal carbon. It is a liquid at room temperature and, as such, has very little effect on air quality. This chemical can be used to embalm any type of case but is usually reserved for jaundice cases as a means of preventing the formation of biliverdin (*green discoloration resulting from the reduction of bilirubin by HCHO or other chemicals*). Glutaraldehyde has the special value of destroying bacterial spores. This makes it a valuable disinfectant for soaking instruments that come in contact with intestinal contents where spores may reside. Sporulating bacteria that are important to embalmers include *Bacillus anthracis, Clostridium tetani, Clostridium perfringens, and Clostridium difficile.*

PHENOL

Phenol is the simplest alcohol of the aromatic (ring structure) molecule called benzene (a 6-carbon ring structure with alternating double bonds). This molecule has been known since coal was mined from the ground; it is a product of coal formation. At that time, it was called carbolic acid because, even though it is an alcohol, it exhibits an acid pH. The hydrogen of the alcohol functional group is hydrolyzed away from the molecule, which means it is a proton in a water solution. This is the definition of an acid. This is a weak acid; this property gives it a disinfectant value. Phenol is an excellent disinfectant for surfaces and tissues. It cannot be injected through most embalming machines because it can damage rubber seals in the pump. Phenol has the benefit of bleaching (lightening) the discoloration of blood pigments in the tissue. Phenol is also good for topical (surface) compresses and hypodermic injection.

ARTERIAL FLUIDS

There is a distinction between **arterial fluid** and **arterial solution**. Fluids are products purchased from an embalming chemical supplier. When the fluid is diluted in the embalming machine, this becomes the arterial solution. This dilution in the tank is known as the primary dilution. The secondary dilution occurs when the arterial solution mixes with the moisture in the human remains during the embalming process.

The most complex of the injected solutions is the arterial injection. It contains the widest range of components of any of the types of fluids. The wide variety of arterial fluids available gives the modern embalmer a nearly limitless range of choices. Uses for different types of arterial fluids are discussed in the Embalming section (pp. 16-19).

Special Arterial Fluids are a distinct group that has enhanced preservative and disinfectant capabilities. They are used in difficult situations like decomposition, tissue gas, contagious disease, and long-term storage. They might sacrifice cosmetic value and economy, but they are important for those needing special treatment.

Jaundice fluids are known to have a low HCHO index. The purpose of this is to prevent the oxidation of bilirubin to biliverdin which has been known to happen. This is an oxidation-reduction reaction, while HCHO is an oxidizer, so it is likely there is another mechanism at work causing this color change. Although glutaraldehyde has been used for jaundice cases, many commercial embalming fluids utilize a low-index formaldehyde solution or methanol.

81

SUPPLEMENTAL CHEMICALS

Fluids that have special properties to assist or improve the embalming process are known as supplemental. Supplemental fluids are added to the arterial injection solution of the machine to accomplish special effects depending on the postmortem condition of the human remains.

Pre-injection fluids are injected through the machine prior to the injection of arterial fluid. Pre-injection fluids are like arterial fluids, with the distinction that there are no preservatives in the fluids. This allows the embalmer to rinse out thick blood, adjust pH, add moisture to the tissues, identify areas of poor distribution, open circulation, and flush out the vascular system, making the cells receptive to formaldehyde. Pre-injection fluids are used as co-injection fluids when they are combined with arterial fluid in the embalming solution (also known as supplemental fluids).

Co-Injection Supplemental Fluid

Edema-reducing fluids are added to the arterial injection to use osmosis to remove tissue fluids. These osmotically active molecules are too large to fit through the pores of the capillaries, so they are trapped inside. Water, which does fit through those pores, is attracted by the large molecules into the capillaries. This water is removed by the venous drainage. The injected fluid is on the hypertonic side (the *hypertonic solution has a higher concentration of solutes compared to the hypotonic solution*), and the body, which had an abundance of water, is on the hypotonic side. Injecting with low pressure is necessary to avoid counteracting water diffusion with intravascular pressure.

Modifying Agents

Modifying agents are chemicals that are added to the arterial fluid or solution to mitigate issues that are present in the human remains or may become present during the embalming process. These include issues such as pH levels and discolorations of the body.

Humectant fluids are used to retain moisture in the body. Hydrated remains look more natural than dehydrated human remains. Alcohols that have two -OH functional groups are called glycols. Ethylene glycol is a 2-carbon glycol. This is used as a humectant. Glycerol is a 3-carbon trihydroxy (*containing 3 -OH functional groups)* alcohol. Also called glycerin, it is a viscous liquid that is sometimes used in hand creams and lotions. Glycerin is water soluble, so it works well as a humectant in arterial injections. Another humectant is Sorbitol, which works by absorbing water into its molecular structure and holding it there to become larger. Lanolin, the oil that comes from sheep, is another humectant that is also used as a surface moisturizer or massage cream to prevent dehydration of the skin. Lanolin is also in some arterial fluids.

Dyes are supplemental chemicals. Eosine, erythrosine, Ponceau Red, and amaranth are all synthetic dyes used in cosmetic arterial fluids. Active or staining dyes remain in the tissues once they are injected. Inactive or non-staining dyes are used as markers in pre-injection chemicals (or are simply colors added to the fluid for identification purposes, such as blue, green, or purple) but can be rinsed out if they are too intense.

BUFFERS

EDTA is chelating agent. Chelate is derived from the word "claw." This chemical holds ions in its claws. Removing certain ions from the blood can help the embalming process greatly. Those ions include H^+, OH^-, and Ca^{2+}. Control of hydrogen and hydroxide ions adjusts the pH. So EDTA functions as a buffer. Another type of buffer is to use a weak acid and its sodium salt. The salt and the acid reach an equilibrium. If there is an excess of H^+, the Na is replaced in the salt with H^+. If there is a lack of H^+, the acid releases enough to reestablish the equilibrium. Examples of these buffer systems include citric acid/ sodium citrate and boric acid/sodium borate.

Additionally, EDTA can remove metallic ions (such as calcium ions) that make water 'hard,' which makes it a water softener.

ANTI-COAGULANTS (Hard Water Conditioning Agents)

The presence of calcium ions in the blood may contribute to post-mortem clotting. Thick blood causes problems with embalming, so the removal of Ca^{2+} is necessary. EDTA and sodium citrate remove these ions.

SURFACTANTS

Human bodies are oily, and embalming solutions are water-based. There is a problem here because oil and water don't mix. Water will bead up on an oily surface. The surface tension of water is significant due to its property of strong cohesion. Water molecules are attracted to themselves and have no attraction to an oily surface. The HCHO and other molecules remain trapped in the water droplets. The answer is to use a 'surface active agent, but its name is a contraction of **surfactant.** The surfactant most commonly used in embalming is sodium lauryl sulfate, but sometimes sulfonate molecules are used instead. They all contain sulfur which is unusual for embalming chemicals. They work by "diluting" the water slightly, so the water molecules are farther from each other and exert a less attractive force on each other (a/k/a surface tension reducers or penetrating agents).

ACCESSORY CHEMICALS

Accessory Chemicals are not injected through the machine; they are used in other ways. Examples of accessories are adhesives, pore closers, cosmetics, absorbent powders, preservative powders, bleaches, cauterants, and surface disinfectants.

A significant accessory chemical is a phenol base product which is used because of its bleaching and cauterizing properties.

Another significant class of accessory chemicals is cavity fluid. Used as supplied by the manufacturer, this is injected directly into the body cavities where hollow organs do not receive an arterial injection. Cavity fluids contain the classes of chemicals that preserve and disinfect, plus surfactants and vehicles, but not those which add cosmetic value. Some cavity fluids have an index higher than 37, which is the saturation point of HCHO in water. The reason for the higher index of formaldehyde is because methanol is the vehicle instead of water. The solubility of this chemical is greater due to the methanol as a vehicle for the chemical.

THE DILUTION FORMULA

The concentration of HCHO in an injection solution is one of the most important concepts in embalming. The solution strength (%) should range between 0 and 8. A solution strength below 2% does not guarantee disinfection, and the above 8% (water-less embalming) leads to cauterizing the capillaries leading to walling off. Normal dilution of a solution is between 2 and 3.5% of HCHO per gallon. Different arterial fluids have different indexes; there is no standard mix to use for every case. To calculate the concentration of the arterial solution, the Standard Dilution Formula is used to determine the percentage of formaldehyde in the tank. The concept behind this formula is that there is the same number of molecules of HCHO in the fluid bottle as there is in the embalming reservoir if only water is added.

Change the formula to the familiar version: $C_1 \times V_1 = C_2 \times V_2$, where subscript 1 is in the bottle, and subscript two is diluted in the tank. Other ways to denote the concentration and volume may be used, but the concept is the same. A small amount of fluid with a high concentration is equal to a lot of fluid containing a low concentration.

Tricky parts of the dilution formula get in the way of easily solving this formula. The concentration should be given in the index, although percent may be substituted. Be sure to keep the same units of volume; ounces are usually best because the fluids come in 16-ounce bottles. The other thing to remember is that the index of formalin is 37, but for calculations, substitute 36.

Preparing for the NBE

Dilution Formula Question:

Facts you need to know:
   a. 1 gallon = 128 oz.
   b. 1 bottle = 16 oz. of fluid
   c. C = Concentration of fluid or solution
   d. V = Volume of fluid or solution
   e. On the left side of the equation is the fluid in the bottle (C_1 and V_1)
   f. On the right side of the equation is the solution in the embalming machine (C_2 and V_2)

On the NBEs, they give all the values and the correct answer. X represents what needs to be solved. Here is the secret to getting this question right every time:

The embalmer adds 2 gallons of water to the embalming machine and desires a 2% dilution of formaldehyde solution. The fluid was a 32 index. How much fluid did the embalmer add to the tank?

What is known?
1. 2 gallons of water = 128 oz x 2 gallons = 256 oz.
2. The concentration of the fluid is 32 index
3. The concentration of the solution in the tank is 2%

The answer is given on the exam:
a. 12 oz
b. 14 oz
c. 16 oz
d. 18 oz

There are two ways to calculate the dilution formula.
1. You may solve the equation normally by plugging in the known values.

$$32 \times V_1 = 2 \times 256$$
$$32 \times V_1 = 512$$
$$V_1 = \frac{(2 \times 256)}{32}$$
$$V_1 = 16 \text{ oz.}$$

2. You may use the checks and balances method by plugging in the four multiple-choice answers for the unknown to see if the math is the same on each side of the equation.

Using answer B: $C_1 \times V_1 = C_2 \times V_2$

$$(32 \times 14) = (2 \times 256)$$
$$448 = 512$$

Are these two values equal? No. Go to the next value.

Adjust up or down depending on the value received.

$$(32 \times 16) = (2 \times 256)$$
$$512 = 512$$

Are these two values equal? YES! Answer is C.

Glossary for Thanatochemistry

Accessory chemicals - Any chemical used in the preparation of human remains that is not 4 injected into the arterial system or cavities.

Acids - Substances that yield hydrogen ions in an aqueous solution.

Adipocere (grave wax) - A wax-like material produced by saponification of body fat.

Alcohols - An organic compound containing one or more hydroxyl (-OH) groups.

Aldehyde - An organic compound containing one or more -CHO groups.

Amides - Derivatives of carboxylic acids in which a hydroxyl group is substituted with an amine or ammonia having the general formula of R-CONH-R'.

Amines - An organic compound containing nitrogen with the general formula of R-NH2.

Amino acid - The building blocks of proteins that contain an amino group (-NH2) and a carboxyl (-COOH) group.

Amphoterism - Any compound that can act as both an acid and a base in an aqueous solution.

Anticoagulants - Chemical agents that retard the tendency of the blood to become more viscous.

Arterial fluid - Concentrated preservative chemicals used primarily for arterial embalming.

Arterial solution - A mixture of arterial fluid and water used for arterial injection with the possible inclusion of supplemental fluids.

Atom - The smallest particle of an element that has all the properties of the element.

Autolysis - Self-digestion or self-destruction of the body by enzymes.

Bases - Substances that yield hydroxide ions in an aqueous solution.

Biochemistry - That branch of chemistry dealing with compounds produced by living organisms.

Boiling - Conversion of a liquid into a vapor state through the action of heat.

Bond - An attractive force that holds together the atoms, ions, or groups of atoms in a molecule or crystal.

Buffers - Substances capable of maintaining a constant pH by neutralizing both acids and bases.

Carbohydrates - A compound of hydrogen, carbon, and oxygen that is an aldehyde or ketone derivative of polyhydroxyl alcohol.

Carboxylic acid (aka Phenol) - An organic compound that contains a carboxyl group (C(=O)OH)

Cavity fluid - Concentrated preservative chemicals used in cavity embalming.

Chemical change - A change that results in the formation of a new chemical substance(s).

Chemical properties - Characteristics of a substance observed during or after a chemical reaction.

Chemistry - The study of matter and the changes it undergoes.

Coagulation - The process of converting soluble protein to insoluble protein by physical or chemical means.

Colloid - A solute that can pass through filters but not membranes.

Combustion - Rapid oxidation that produces heat and light.

Compound - A substance consisting of two or more elements combined chemically in definite proportions by mass.

Concentrated solution - A solution containing a relatively large amount of solute.

Concentration - The ratio of a solute to the solution or solvent.

Condensation - A change of state of matter from a gas to a liquid.

Covalent - A chemical bond formed between two atoms by the sharing of electrons.

Crystalloid - A solute that can pass through a membrane.

Decay - The gradual decomposition of dead organic matter by the enzymes of aerobic bacteria.

Dehydration - The removal of water from a substance.

Denaturation - The disruption and breakdown of a protein by heat or chemicals.

Desiccation - A complete or nearly complete deprivation of moisture.

Dialdehyde - An organic compound containing two aldehydes (-CHO) groups.

Diffusion - The movement of molecules or other particles in solution from an area of greater concentration to an area of lesser concentration until the uniform concentration is reached.

Dilute solution - A solution containing a relatively small amount of solute.

Disinfectant - An agent, usually chemical, applied to inanimate/surfaces objects to kill most disease-causing microbial agents, excluding bacterial spores.

Dye - Natural or synthetic compounds that are used to impart color to another material.

Elements - Simple substances which cannot be decomposed by ordinary chemical means.

Embalming chemistry - The study of those types of matter and changes in matter related to the disinfection, preservation, and restoration of human remains.

Enzyme - A protein that acts as a biological catalyst.

Ester - An organic compound with the general formula RCOOR.'

Fats - A combination of saturated fatty acids and glycerol that is semisolid at room temperature.

Fermentation - The microbial decomposition of carbohydrates under anaerobic conditions.

Formalin - Formaldehyde gas dissolved in water at 37% by weight and 40% by volume.

Formula - A symbolic expression of the chemical composition or constitution of a substance.

Freezing - A change of state of matter from a liquid to a solid by the loss of heat.

Gases - A state of matter that has no definite shape or volume

The hardness of water - The condition of water that results from dissolved minerals and metallic ions.

Humectants - Chemicals that increase the capability of tissues to retain moisture.

Hydrate - A compound in which there is a union between water and certain substances when they crystallize.

Hydrolysis - A chemical reaction in which a substance is broken down or dissociated by water.

Hydrogen bond - A non-chemical bond that creates surface tension.

Hypertonic solution - A solution having a greater concentration of dissolved solute than the solution to which it is compared.

Hypotonic solution - A solution having a lesser concentration of dissolved solute than the solution to which it is compared.

Imbibition - The swelling and softening of tissues and organs as a result of absorbing moisture 44 from adjacent sources.

Index - The strength of embalming fluids indicated by the number of grams of pure formaldehyde gas dissolved in 100 ml of solution.

Inorganic chemistry - That branch of chemistry that studies the properties and reactions of elements, excluding organic or certain carbon-containing compounds.

Ion - An atom or group of atoms with a positive or negative electrical charge.

Ionic - A chemical bond formed between oppositely charged atoms

Isotonic solution - A solution having an equal concentration of dissolved solute as the solution to which it is compared.

Ketone - A class of organic compounds with the general formula R(CO)R' formed by the oxidation of a secondary alcohol.

Liquid - A state of matter having a definite volume but no definite shape.

Matter - Anything that has mass and occupies space.

Melting - A change of state of matter from a solid to a liquid by the addition of heat.

Metal - An element marked by luster, malleability, ductility, and conductivity of electricity and heat.

Mixture - A combination of two or more substances not chemically united and that exist in no 24 fixed proportion to each other.

Minimum lethal dose (MLD) - The smallest dose of a poison that produces death.

Modifying agent - Chemicals incorporated into commercial preservative fluids to meet the varying demands of embalming procedures.

Molecule - A group of two or more atoms joined by chemical bonds.

Neutralization - The reaction of an acid and a base to produce salt and water.

Nonmetal - Any element that is generally dull in appearance, has a low density, has a low 36 melting point, and is not a good conductor of heat or electricity.

Oils - A combination of unsaturated fatty acids and glycerol that is a liquid at room temperature.

Organic chemistry - That branch of chemistry that deals with certain carbon-containing compounds.

Osmosis - The passage of a solvent from an area of lesser concentration to an area of greater concentration through a semi-permeable membrane.

Oxide - A compound consisting of oxygen combined with only one other element. Parts per million (ppm) – a method of expressing low concentrations; 1 ppm is equivalent to milligrams per liter.

Peptide bond – A bond formed from a dehydration reaction between the amino group on one amino acid with the carboxyl group on another amino acid.

Periodic table – A tabular arrangement of the elements, ordered by their atomic number, electron configurations, and recurring chemical properties.

pH - The measure of hydrogen ion concentration of a solution.

Physical change - A change in the form or state of matter without any change in chemical composition.

Physical properties - Characteristics of a substance that are observed or measured without a change in chemical composition.

Poison - A substance capable of causing illness or death to an organism.

Polymerization - A chemical reaction in which two or more molecules combine to form larger molecules that contain repeating structural units.

Pre-injection/capillary wash - The introduction of a non-preservative solution to prepare the vascular system before the injection of the preservative solution.

Pre-injection fluid - Fluids designed to clear the vascular system of blood and enable the arterial solution to distribute more effectively.

Preservative - Substances used to inhibit protein decomposition and inactivate enzymes.

Preservative demand - The amount of preservative necessary to properly embalm human remains.

Protein - A biological component that is a polymer of many amino acids.

Perfuming agent (masking agent) - Chemicals having the capability of altering an unpleasant odor.

Putrefaction - The decomposition of proteins by the enzymatic activity of anaerobic bacteria.

Quaternary ammonium compound - Surface disinfectants that are generally used for disinfection of skin, oral and nasal cavities, as well as instruments.

Salt - Any group of substances that result from the reaction between acids and bases other than water.

Saponification - The hydrolysis of a fat and a strong base to produce glycerol and the salt of a fatty acid.

Saturated solution - A solution containing the maximum amount of solute a solvent is able to hold at a certain temperature and pressure.

Solid - A state of matter having a definite shape and volume.

Solubility - The measure of how well a solute mixes with a solvent.

Solute - A substance dissolved in a solvent to form a solution.

Solution - A homogeneous mixture of one or more solutes dissolved in a sufficient quantity of solvent.

Solvent - A substance that dissolves a solute in a solution.

States of matter - A physical property of matter (solid, liquid, or gas)

Sublimation - A physical change of state during which a substance changes directly from a solid to a gas.

Supplemental fluid - Fluids injected for purposes other than preservation and disinfection that will enhance the actions of the arterial solution.

Substrate - The material upon which an enzyme acts.

Surface tension - The molecular cohesion at the surface of a liquid forming a membrane-like layer.

Surfactant (surface tension reducers/wetting agents/penetrating agents) - Chemicals that will reduce the molecular cohesion of a liquid and thereby enable it to flow through smaller openings.

Suspension - A solute that will not pass through filters or membranes.

Thanatochemistry - The study of those physical and chemical changes in the human body that are caused by the process of death.

Thiol (mercaptan) - An organic compound containing the group -SH

Toxin - A poisonous substance that is organic in nature.

Unsaturated solution - A solution containing less than the maximum amount of solute a solvent is able to hold at a certain temperature and pressure.

Urotropin - The neutralization product of formaldehyde and ammonia.

Vehicle - Liquids that serve as solvents for the components of embalming fluids and solutions.

Viscosity - The measure of the resistance to the flow of a liquid.

Wax - A type of lipid formed from the combination of unsaturated and/or saturated fatty acids 2 and high molecular weight alcohols.

The Occupational Safety and Health Act of 1970 - OSHA

1. The Background and Function of OSHA

a. **Application** - In 1970, Congress enacted the Occupational Safety and Health Act. That Act created the Occupational Safety and Health Administration ("OSHA") within the Department of Labor. OSHA has been charged with the responsibility to protect the nation's employees by implementing new safety and health programs, providing research into occupational safety, instituting a recordkeeping system and reporting to track job related injuries and illness, establish training programs, and develop and enforce mandatory job safety and health standards.

In general, OSHA extends to all employers in the 50 states, the District of Columbia and all other territories under federal government jurisdiction. Coverage is provided directly by federal OSHA or through an OSHA-approved state program. Approximately half of the states conduct OSHA-approved state programs - these are typically referred to as "state-plan-states." New York, for example, is a state-plan-state.

Any person or business that is engaged in business and has employees are subject to the OSHA standards. However, OSHA does not cover self-employed persons. Therefore, if a funeral home is a sole proprietorship with the owner serving as the only employee, the funeral home would not be subject to OSHA requirements. However, if the funeral home has one employee, then they would be subject to the standards.

b. **Enforcement** - To enforce the standards, OSHA is authorized under the Act to conduct workplace inspections. OSHA compliance officers will conduct the inspection. Typically, such inspections can be triggered by fatal accidents on the job site, employee complaints, or random inspections of any industry that OSHA is targeting. Following the inspection, the OSHA officer will conduct a closing conference with the employer to discuss all unsafe or unhealthful conditions observed on the inspection. At this time, all apparent violations for which a citation may be issued are discussed. The compliance officer will submit a report to the OSHA state director with a recommendation as to proposed penalties.

The state director may issue citations and propose penalties for those citations. When issued a citation or notice of a proposed penalty an employer may request an informal meeting with the OSHA state director to discuss the case. If the employer does not contest the citation, the employer must correct the cited hazard by the prescribed date.

c. General Duty Clause - The OSHA law states that each employer has a "general duty" to furnish each of its employees with a place of employment free from recognized hazards that are causing or likely to cause death or serious physical harm to employees as well as comply with specific occupational safety and health standards promulgated under the Occupational Safety and Health Act. The General Duty Clause, however, will not apply if there is specific safety and health standard or regulation dealing with the hazard.

This "General Duty" covers "recognized hazards" which are dangers recognized by the employer's industry or industry in general, by the employer, or by common sense, regardless of whether the condition is covered by a specific safety or health standard or regulation. The compliance issue then becomes whether the employer knew of or could have known of the hazardous condition with reasonable diligence.

Specific standards include the safety and health standards contained under the OSHA General Industry Standard for all industries, found at 29 C.F.R. 1910 in the Code of Federal Regulations, and, for construction, under the Construction Standard, found at 29 C.F.R. 1926 in the Code of Federal Regulations.

d. Inspections

An inspection begins with the arrival of a compliance officer and an opening conference at which time the inspector will present identification, advise the employer of the reason for the visit, and outline the scope of the inspection. Subsequent to this conference, all required safety and health records will be reviewed, including: OSHA forms 300 (LOG of Work-Related Injuries and Illnesses for the worksite), 300A (Yearly Summary of Work-Related Injuries and Illnesses), and 301 (Report of Occupational Injuries and Illnesses that are Recordable). These records may be kept on a computer if a computer can produce equivalent forms when needed.

Types of OSHA Inspections:

- **Routine/Program** - General Compliance Inspection - Sometimes, based on data obtained from a state's Workers' Compensation Commission, through an Employer's First Report of Injury, the entire worksite could be inspected from basement to ceiling.

- **Target Inspection** - This is an inspection directed to employers who are deemed or perceived to have a potential exposure for their employees to a specific occupational safety and health hazard. This can take the form of a Local Emphasis Program or a National Emphasis Program. Working with Formaldehyde could be a target.

- **Complaint Inspection** - This is an inspection based on a complaint filed, usually by an employee, with OSHA alleging a specific safety or health hazard or hazards or violations of enacted rules, regulations or standards. The employee has the right to remain anonymous.

- Employees are **protected from retaliation** for raising workplace health and safety concerns and for reporting work-related injuries and illnesses. Section 11(c) of the Occupational Safety and Health Act of 1970 (OSH Act) prohibits employers from retaliating against employees for exercising a variety of rights guaranteed under the OSH Act, such as filing a safety or health complaint with OSHA, raising a health and safety concern with their employers, participating in an OSHA inspection, or reporting a work-related injury or illness.

- **Accident Inspection** - This is an inspection done usually because of a serious accident. The scope of the inspection will be narrow and be generally limited to the accident site. The focus of the inspection will be whether or not a law, standard or regulation was violated during the accident occurrence, but additional violations found, that may not relate to the accident itself, can and will be cited.

- **Follow-Up Inspection** - This occurs at the site of a prior violation and is conducted to verify that the required hazard abatement has been made within the prescribed time given in the prior issued citation.

   e. A recordable occupational injury or illness is an occupational injury or illness that results in a fatality, a lost workday, restricted work, or a non-fatal case without a lost workday that requires:
   1) transferring the employee to another job;
   2) termination of employment;
   3) medical treatment other than first aid; or
   4) involving loss of consciousness or restriction of work or motion.

Contagious diseases are considered work-related and recordable if the employee is infected at work. A pre-existing injury or illness that is significantly aggravated by the work environment is also recordable, and injuries and illnesses that occur when an employee is on work-related travel status, and engaged in work activities, are recordable.

A *few low-hazard industries, such as funeral service,* designated by standard industrial classification (SIC) number (SIC Code 726), are NOT required to maintain OSHA forms 300, 300A and 301, **unless** the specific employer has been ordered to do so. ***Small employers with ten or fewer employees at any time during the calendar year are also exempt from these recordkeeping requirements, unless otherwise required to maintain them.***

During an inspection, the inspector has a right to interview employees privately and without the presence of management or the employer. The inspector also has the right to interview management privately and without the presence of an employee representative.

During an inspection, the inspector will take photographs, make any necessary measurements, and, in a case involving a health issue, may do environmental testing. An OSHA inspector does not, however, have the right to take identifiable photographs of remains.

At the close of the inspection, the inspector will hold a separate closing conference for the employer and its representative, and with the employees and their representatives. The purpose of this conference is to advise of potential violations found, which will then be submitted to the inspector's supervisor for a final determination as to whether or not a citation penalty will be issued.

   f. Penalties and Fines - If a penalty is issued, a serious violation can carry a civil penalty of not more than $14,502.00 for each violation in which there is a substantial probability that death or serious physical harm could occur. An other-than-serious violation also carries a maximum civil penalty of up to $14,402.00 for each violation. No penalties are issued for other-than-serious violations unless there are ten or more citations.

Other penalties than can be assessed include a civil penalty of not more than $145,027.00 for each violation deemed to be a willful or repeated violation, with a minimum required penalty of not less than $14,402.00 for each willful violation.

If the willful violation causes death to an employee, there is a provision for a criminal fine of not more than $10,000.00 or imprisonment of not more than six (6) months. If the conviction is for a second offense, the criminal penalty is punishment of a fine of not more than $20,000.00 or by imprisonment of not more than one (1) year, or both. Failure to correct a violation carries a civil penalty of not more than $14,502.00 per day for each day during which the violation continues. Making a false statement carries a maximum criminal fine of not more than $20,000.00 or imprisonment of not more than one year, or both, for falsifying representations or certifications on any application, record, report, plan or other document filed or required to be maintained. Violations of any posting requirements carry a civil penalty of up to $7,000.00 for each separate violation.

2. THE HAZARD COMMUNICATION STANDARD (29 C.F.R. 1910.1200)

a. Purpose - The purpose of the Hazard Communication Standard is to assure that hazards of all chemicals are evaluated, whether produced or imported, and that the information concerning their hazard is transmitted to employers and employees through a comprehensive written **Hazard Communication Program** and through the development and update of **Safety Data Sheets (SDS)** by chemical manufacturers and importers of each hazardous chemical they produce or import, at no cost to the purchasing employer. *The employer is required to maintain an up to date 16-section Safety Data Sheet (SDS)* for each hazardous chemical in the workplace. Note that Material Safety Data Sheets (MSDS) are outdated and not aligned with current Globally Harmonized System (GHS) standards.

b. The Hazard Communication Program - The Hazard Communication Program must be written, maintained at each workplace, and contain information indicating how the criteria that are part of the Hazard Communication Standard will be met for labels and other forms of warnings, the Safety Data Sheets, and for employee information and training.

The written Program must also include a list of the hazardous chemicals known to be present, using an identity that is referenced on the appropriate Safety Data Sheet, and describe the methods used to inform employees of the hazards of non-routine tasks and the hazards associated with chemicals contained in unlabeled or improperly labeled containers in their work area. Additional requirements may be needed for state specific regulations, including the Chemical Information List.

A **Safety Data Sheet** is not required for consumer products used in the work area, if the use results in a duration and frequency of exposure which is not greater than what could reasonable be experienced by consumers when the product is used by the purpose intended.

The best funeral home practice is to keep two sets of Safety Data Sheets, one set in the prep-room with the chemicals and the other in an office. In the event of a chemical spill or emergency exposure incident, safety information about the chemical needs to be readily available. Digital copies of the SDS can also be retained on a funeral home computer. Employees need to be aware how to access this digital information in an emergency situation.

      c. Labeling - The employer must ensure that each container of hazardous chemicals is marked with the product identifier, supplier identification, signal words (DANGER or WARNING), hazard statement, precautionary statements, and appropriate hazard pictograms. Portable containers of hazardous chemicals, that are transferred from labeled containers, do not have to be labeled <u>if</u> they are intended *only* for the immediate use of the employee who performs the transfer.

      d. Training - Employers must provide employees with training on the hazardous chemicals in the workplace at the time of initial assignment and whenever a new physical or health hazard is introduced. The employees must be informed of the requirements of the Hazard Communication Standard, any operations in their work areas where hazardous chemicals are present, and the location and availability of the written Hazard Communication Program, the prepared list of hazardous chemicals, and the applicable Safety Data Sheets.

      The training must also include methods and observations that may be used to detect the presence or release of hazardous chemicals in the work area, the physical and health hazards of the chemicals in the work area, the measures that can be taken by employees to protect themselves from these hazards, and the details of the Hazard Communication Program.

      The employer should maintain training records to verify that the required training has been completed. These records should include the date of the training, the trainer's name and credentials, the name of the employee involved in the training, and, most importantly, a clear statement of the subject of the training given.

3. THE FORMALDEHYDE STANDARD (29 C.F.R. 1910.1048)

This section is very important for the National Board Exam.

a. **Purpose and Scope** - This Standard requires an employer to identify <u>all</u> employees who may be exposed at or above the **Action Level (AL)** or the **Short-Term Exposure Limit (STEL)** and accurately determine the exposure of each employee so identified.

Important Formaldehyde Exposure Limits:

Permissible Exposure Limit	**PEL**	0.75 ppm
Action Level	**AL**	0.50 ppm
Short-term exposure limit	**STEL**	2.00ppm (for 15 minutes, not be exceeded more than 4x per day)
Time weighted average	**TWA**	8-hour workday
Immediate danger to life and health	**IDLH**	20.00ppm

The Formaldehyde Standard applies to all occupational exposure to formaldehyde. It requires each employer to sample and verify that no employee is exposed to an **air borne concentration of formaldehyde which exceeds the permissible exposure limit (PEL) of 0.75 parts formaldehyde per million parts (0.75 ppm) of air, as an eight-hour time weighted average (TWA), or an airborne concentration exceeding 2 parts formaldehyde per million parts (2.0 ppm) of air, as a fifteen-minute short-term exposure limit (STEL).**

Documentation of this sampling must be maintained with the employer's records and must be made available, upon request, to the employee, to an employee representative, and to an OSHA inspector.

Sampling must be performed during preparation and must be repeated every time there is a change in production, equipment, processes, personnel, or control measures that may result in a new or additional exposure.

Employees shown to be at or above the **Action Level (AL) of 0.5 ppm, as an eight-hour time weighted average**, by the initial monitoring must be re-monitored at least every six months, or, **if above the STEL of 2.0 ppm as a 15-minute short-term exposure limit, at least once per year** *until* **the results from two (2) consecutive sampling periods, taken at least seven days apart, show that the employee exposure is below the Action Level and the STEL.**

If employee exposure is over the TWA or the STEL, the employer must develop and implement a **written plan** to reduce employee exposure to or below the TWA or the STEL and give written notice to the employee. The written notice must contain a description of the corrective action being taken to decrease exposure.

b. **Regulated Areas** - Regulated areas are those areas where the concentration of airborne formaldehyde exceeds the TWA or the STEL. The Formaldehyde Standard requires that all entrances and access ways to the regulated areas must be posted with signs stating:

"Danger: Formaldehyde. Irritant and Potential Cancer Hazard. Authorized Personnel Only."

    c. Methods of Compliance - Engineering controls and work practice controls must be implemented if necessary to reduce or maintain exposure at or below the AL and the STEL limits. If not adequate, they must be supplemented by the use of Personal Protective Equipment.

Engineering controls: those items designed for safety, such as a sharps container or fume hood.

Work practice controls: tasks we complete to keep us safe, such as placing sharps into the sharp's container, or washing hands.

    Respirators must be used in an emergency, which is defined as an occurrence that results in an uncontrolled release of a significant amount of formaldehyde. The term significant is NOT defined in the Standard. An example of a significant release:

    In a plastics factory where formaldehyde is available at full strength (37 % by weight as formalin) in 55-gallon drums and often moved around on a forklift 4 or 5 drums at one time. If the drums should fall and split open causing a spill in an area where unprotected workers are, this would be significant. In the funeral home setting, it would be nearly impossible to have a release that would be considered significant. One 16 oz. bottle of 32 index fluid becoming broken or spilling its contents would not be significant.

    Respirator usage, if required, mandates an employer to implement a **respirator protection program,** including respirator fit tests consistent with the Respiratory Protection Standard which is described in OSHA Respiratory Protection Standard, 29 C.F.R. 1910.134.

    d. Personal Protective Equipment - The employer must provide Personal Protective Equipment and clothing to employees at no cost and enforce their usage.
    Potential eye and skin contact with liquids containing ***one percent (1%)*** or more formaldehyde requires the use of personal protective clothing, goggles and face shield.
    Containers for contaminated clothing or equipment must have signs stating:

    "Danger: Formaldehyde-Contaminated Clothing or Equipment.
    Avoid Inhalation and Skin Contact."

    e. Housekeeping and Emergencies - Quick drench showers must be provided when there is a possibility of a splash of the solution containing *one percent* or greater formaldehyde.
    Eyewash facilities must be provided if there is any possibility that an employee's eyes may be splashed with solutions containing 0.1 percent or greater formaldehyde.
    Leaks and spills must be cleaned promptly by trained employees wearing Personal Protective Equipment.

    f. Medical Surveillance - *A medical surveillance program is required for all employees exposed to concentrations of formaldehyde at or exceeding the Action Level of 0.5 ppm, as an eight-hour time weighted average, or the short-term exposure limit (STEL) of two parts formaldehyde per million (2.0 ppm) of air as a 15-minute short-term exposure limit.*

Medical surveillance must be made available for any employee who develops signs and symptoms of overexposure to formaldehyde and for all employees exposed to formaldehyde in emergencies consistent with the requirements of the Formaldehyde Standard.

Results of medical examinations and tests are to be retained consistent with the provisions of the Access to Employee Exposure and Medical Record Standard, 29 C.F.R. 1910.1020. **That OSHA Standard requires retention for the duration of employment plus thirty (30) years.** *This is very important and could be on the NBEs.*

g. Medical Removal - An employee, based on a physician's examination and recommendation regarding employment restrictions or removal from current formaldehyde exposure, must be transferred to a position having no or significantly less exposure to formaldehyde.

The transfer must be to comparable work for which the employee is qualified or can be trained in a short period (up to six months), or where formaldehyde exposure is at least below the Action Level of 0.5 ppm.

The employee's pre-removal current earnings, seniority and benefits are to be maintained during the transfer to other employment. If no other employment is available, earnings, seniority and other benefits are to be maintained until a determination is made that the employee can return to the original job, or until a determination is made that the employee can NOT return to the workplace with formaldehyde exposure, or for six (6) months, whichever comes first.

h. Hazard Communication - All mixtures or solutions of formaldehyde greater than 0.1% formaldehyde and materials capable of releasing formaldehyde into the air under reasonable foreseeable conditions of use, at concentrations reaching or exceeding 0.1 ppm, are subject to the Formaldehyde Standard Hazard Communication Requirements that include, at a minimum, specific health hazards of cancer, irritation and sensitization of the skin and respiratory system, eye and throat irritation, and acute toxicity.

An employer in compliance with the Formaldehyde Standard does not need a separate written hazard communication program for formaldehyde as long as formaldehyde is included in the hazard communication program. If the employer is not in compliance with the Formaldehyde Standard, as would be the case where there is an overexposure, the employer is required to develop, implement and maintain a separate written hazard communication program for formaldehyde exposure that, at a minimum, describes the requirements for labeling, Safety Data Sheets, other forms of warning, and the requirements for employee information and training to be met.

Formaldehyde labelling must comply with the requirements of the Hazard Communication Standard, 29 C.F.R. 1910.1200.

i. Training - Where objective data demonstrates that employees are not exposed to formaldehyde at 0.1 ppm, training is NOT required, other than that required by the Hazard Communication Standard, 29 C.F.R. 1910.1200. All employees who are assigned to workplaces where there is an exposure to formaldehyde at or above 0.1 ppm must be trained at the time of initial assignment and whenever a new exposure to formaldehyde is introduced into the work area. Training must be repeated at least annually.

Required training must include, among other things, the use and understanding of the contents of Safety Data Sheets, medical surveillance, health hazards, safe work practices, Personal Protective Equipment, spills, and emergencies.

A record of employee training should be maintained to verify that the training has been completed as required and include the date the training was given, the employees trained, the identity of the trainer, and the contents of the training.

j. Recordkeeping - If the employer determines that NO monitoring is required under this Standard, the employer must maintain a record of the objective data relied upon to make this determination.

If an employer determines that monitoring is required under this Standard, the employer must establish and maintain an accurate record of all measurements taken to monitor employee exposure to formaldehyde. This record must include the date of measurement, the operation being monitored, methods of sampling and analysis, and evidence of their accuracy and precision, the number, duration time, and results of samples taken, and the types of protective devices worn. The report must also include the names, job classifications, social security numbers, and exposure estimates of employees whose exposure is represented by the actual monitoring results.

Records must be maintained of all sampling and monitoring of employee exposure to formaldehyde, medical surveillance, and respiratory fit testing.

Exposure records must be kept for thirty (30) years, and medical records for employment plus thirty (30) years consistent with OSHA Standard 1910.1020, Access to Employee Exposure and Medical Records.

Respiratory fit testing records must be maintained, *if respirators are required*, until they are replaced by a more recent record.

4. THE BLOODBORNE PATHOGEN STANDARD 29 C.F.R. 1910.1030

a. Purpose and Scope - The Bloodborne Pathogen Standard applies to all occupational exposure to blood or other potentially infectious material (OPIM) and mandates the use of Universal Precautions, the treatment of all human remains as being infectious. Each employer with one or more employees with occupational exposure must have a written Exposure Control Plan (ECP) to eliminate or minimize employee exposure and survey the job site, by job classification, to determine the actual exposure to employees, as well as evaluate all tasks and procedures where exposure can occur.

A **bloodborne pathogen** is defined as a pathogenic micro-organism present in human blood that can cause disease in humans. These pathogens include, but are not limited to, Hepatitis B Virus (HBV) and Human Immunodeficiency Virus (HIV).

Occupational exposure under the Bloodborne Pathogen Standard is defined as reasonable anticipated skin, eye, mucous membrane, or parenteral contact with blood or other potentially infectious materials that results from performance of an employee's duties.

As defined by the Standard, *other potentially infectious materials* include semen, vaginal secretions, cerebrospinal fluid, synovial fluid, pleural fluid, pericardial fluid, peritoneal fluid, amniotic fluid, saliva and dental prostheses, any bodily fluid that is physically contaminated with blood, bodily fluids in situations where it is difficult or impossible to differentiate between body fluids and any unfixed tissue or organ (other than intact skin) from a human (living or dead).

b. Exposure Control Plan - The required written **Exposure Control Plan (ECP)** must include, as part of its elements, an exposure determination of the worksite, a schedule and method of implementation for engineering and work practice controls, the required Hepatitis B vaccination and post-exposure evaluation and follow-up, communication of hazards to employees, recordkeeping, and the procedures for evaluating circumstances of exposure incidents.

The written Exposure Control Plan (ECP) must be accessible to employees and reviewed and updated at *least annually* and wherever necessary to reflect new or modified tasks or procedures that effect occupational exposure, and new and revised employee positions with occupational exposure.

An employer, at least *annually*, must also consider the selection and implementation of appropriate effective, commercially available, safer control devices for *sharps injury protection*. The employer must solicit non-managerial employees, who are potentially exposed to injuries from contaminated sharps, for their input to identify, evaluate, and select effective sharps injury protection devices. This consideration should be documented and include the date of consideration, the device or control being considered, the name of the employer providing input, the decision reached, and the basis of the decision.

1) **Universal Precautions** - When, under circumstances in which differentiation between body fluid types is difficult or impossible, *all* human blood, certain human body fluids, and any unfixed tissue or organ (other than intact skin) must be considered potentially infectious.

2) **Engineering and Workplace Controls** - Engineering and workplace controls must first be used to eliminate or minimize employee exposure. If occupational exposure remains after the implementation of these controls, personal protective equipment must be used. Readily accessible hand washing facilities must be provided. When this is not feasible, either an appropriate antiseptic hand cleaner in conjunction with clean cloth/paper towels or antiseptic towelette to be followed as soon as feasible by washing with soap and running water. Employees must wash their hands immediately, after removal of gloves or other personal protective equipment. Mucous membranes must be flushed with water immediately following contact of such body areas with blood or other potentially infectious materials. See Microbiology section for Microorganism Control Practices (pp. 266-268).

3) **Contaminated Needles and Sharps** - Contaminated needles and sharps must not be bent, recapped or removed unless the employer can demonstrate that no alternative was feasible or that such action is required by a specific medical or dental procedure. Shearing or breaking of contaminated needles is prohibited. Contaminated reusable sharps must be placed in appropriate containers until properly re-processed. These containers must be puncture-resistant, labeled or color coded as to content and hazard, leak-proof on the sides and bottom and stored and processed in such a way that employees are not required to reach into the container where the sharps have been placed.

4) **Prohibitions** - Eating, drinking, smoking, applying cosmetics or lip balm, and handling contact lenses in work areas are prohibited where there is a reasonable likelihood of occupational exposure. Food and drink must not be placed or stored near blood or other potentially infectious materials. All procedures must be performed in such a manner as to minimize splashing, spraying, spattering, and generation of droplets.

5) **Personal Protective Equipment** - *Personal protective equipment must be used and must be provided to employees at NO cost to the employee.* This includes gloves, gowns, laboratory coats, face shields or masks, and eye protection that does not permit blood or other potentially infectious material to be passed through or reach an employee's work clothes, street clothes, undergarments, skin, eyes, mouth or other mucous membranes under normal conditions of use and duration of time that the personal protective equipment will be used.

   The personal protective equipment must be cleaned, laundered, disposed of, repaired or replaced at no cost to the employee. The employer must also ensure the workplace is maintained in a clean and sanitary condition and implement appropriate written schedules for cleaning and decontamination.

6) **Housekeeping** - Contaminated sharps must be immediately discarded in containers that are closable, puncture-resistant, leak-proof on sides and bottom, and labeled or color-coded in accordance with the Bloodborne Pathogen Standard. All contaminated work surfaces must be decontaminated after completion of procedures, immediately when surfaces are overly contaminated, after any spill, and after or at the end of the work shift if the surface becomes contaminated since the last cleaning. Disposal of all regulated waste must comply with all applicable state and federal regulations.

7) **Warning Labels** - The Bloodborne Pathogen Standard requires that warning labels be placed on containers of regulated waste, refrigerators and freezers containing blood or other potentially infectious materials and other containers used to store, transport, or ship blood or other potentially infectious materials. The labels must include this Legend: **"BIOHAZARD"** and the Biohazard symbol. Red bags or red containers may be substituted for labels.

8) **Vaccination** - The Bloodborne Pathogen Standard requires that the **Hepatitis B vaccine** and vaccination series be made available to all employees who have occupational exposure. It also requires that all medical evaluations and procedures, including the Hepatitis B vaccine, booster doses, vaccination series and post-exposure evaluation and follow-up, must be made available at *no cost to the employee*, at a reasonable time and place and be performed by or be under the supervision of a licensed physician or other licensed health care professional, as well as be provided according to current U.S. Public Health Service recommendations.

The Hepatitis B vaccination itself must be made available to employees after they have received the appropriate training and within ten (10) days of their initial assignment to a position with occupational exposure unless the employee has previously received the complete Hepatitis B vaccination series, antibody testing has revealed that the employee is immune, or the vaccination is contraindicated for medical reasons. An employee who declines to accept the vaccination must sign and date a **mandatory Hepatitis B Vaccination Declination** which must be presented to the employee exactly as written in the regulation.

9) **Post-Exposure Follow Up** - In a case of a exposure incident, the Standard requires post-evaluation follow-up to include documentation of the route of exposure and circumstances under which the exposure occurred, identification and documentation of the source individual, unless this is unfeasible or prohibited by state or local law, the testing of the source individual's blood as soon as possible after the incident, after any required consent is obtained, to determine HBV and HIV infection, unless the source individual is already known to be infected, post-exposure counseling and prophylaxis follow-up at no cost to the employee in accordance with current Centers for Disease Control and Prevention (CDC) Guidelines for Hepatitis B, Hepatitis C, and HIV.

10) **Training** - The Bloodborne Pathogen Standard has specific training requirements that include giving a copy of the Standard itself and an explanation of its contents to the employee. The employee must also be given an explanation of the epidemiology and symptoms of bloodborne diseases, the modes of transmission of bloodborne pathogens, explanation of the employer's required written **Exposure Control Plan**, and the means by which the employee may obtain a copy of the Plan.

The employee must be given, under the training program, an explanation of the appropriate methods for recognizing tasks and other activities that may involve exposure to blood or other potentially infectious materials, and explanation of the use, limitations and methods that would prevent or reduce exposure, including appropriate engineering controls, work practices and personal protective equipment and information on the proper use, location, removal, handling, decontamination, disposal of appropriate personal protective equipment.

The employee must be given information on the Hepatitis B vaccine, information on the appropriate action to take and the person to contact in an emergency involving blood or other potentially infectious materials and an explanation of procedures to follow if an exposure incident does occur, including the method of reporting the incident and the medical follow-up that will be made available.

The employee must also be given information on post-exposure evaluation and follow-up that the employer is required to provide to the employee following an exposure incident, must be trained in the use and recognition of the signs and labels and/or color-coding required by the Bloodborne Pathogen Standard and be given an opportunity for questions and answers with the person conducting the training who must be knowledgeable in the subject matter.

11) **Recordkeeping** - Training records, under the Bloodborne Pathogen Standard, must be kept for ***three (3) years*** from the date in which the training occurred and include the dates of the training sessions, the contents or summary of the training sessions, names and qualifications of the person conducting the training and names and job titles of all persons attending the sessions. These records will be reviewed by OSHA inspectors and must be available for examination and copying by the employee.

There is also a requirement, *unless* the employer is specifically *exempt* from maintaining the otherwise required OSHA log of injuries and illnesses, due to the employer's standard industrial code (SIC) classification as a low-hazard industry, to establish a ***Sharps Injury Log*** that describes the type and brand of device involved in an exposure incident, the department or work area in which the exposure incident occurred and an explanation of how the incident occurred. No special form is required, but the Sharps Injury Log must be recorded and maintained to protect the confidentiality of an injured employee and be maintained for the same period of time as the OSHA log of injuries and illnesses.

5. PERSONAL PROTECTIVE EQUIPMENT STANDARDS 29 C.F.R. 1910.132, 133, 135, 136, 137 AND 138

a. General - Personal protective equipment must be provided, used and maintained in a sanitary and reliable condition whenever it is necessary by reason of hazards of processes or environment, chemical hazards, radiological hazards, or mechanical irritants encountered in a manner that may cause impairment or injury in the function of any part of the body through absorption, inhalation, or physical contact.

Personal protective equipment may include personal protective equipment for the eyes, face, head and extremities, protective clothing, respiratory devices and protective shields and barriers. Employers are responsible to ensure the use, adequacy, proper maintenance and sanitation of personal protective equipment, even if the employees provide their own personal protective equipment.

b. Workplace Assessment - The employer is required to assess the workplace to determine if hazards are present or likely to be present that require the use of personal protective equipment. If they are present, the employer must explain to the employees when personal protective equipment is to be used and ensure that each affected employee uses properly fitted personal protective equipment that will protect the employee form the identified hazard. Any equipment that is defective or damaged shall not be used, and all equipment must be specifically designed to be used with the specific hazard encountered. Respiratory protection is covered under a separate Standard, which is 1910.134.

The Standard requires an employee to verify that the required workplace hazard assessment has been performed through a *written certification* that documents the assessment and identifies the workplace evaluated, the person certifying that the evaluation has been performed and the dates of the assessment.

c. Training - The Standard requires an employer to provide training sufficient to inform employees of when personal protective equipment is necessary, what type of personal protective equipment is necessary, how to properly wear personal protective equipment, the limitations of personal protective equipment and the proper care, maintenance, useful life and disposal of personal protective equipment *before* employees can be allowed to perform work requiring the use of personal protective equipment.

Re-training is necessary when changes in the workplace or in the type of personal protective equipment to be used makes the previous training obsolete or when an employer demonstrates that the employee does not have the required understanding or skill to properly use the required personal protective equipment. The employer must keep a *written certification* that contains the name of each employee trained, dates of the training and the subject matter of the training.

29 C.F.R. 1910.133 contains the specific requirements for eye protection, 29 C.F.R. 1910.135 contains the specific requirements for head protection, 29 C.F.R. 1910.136 contains the specific requirements for foot protection, 29 C.F.R. 1910.137 contains the requirements for electrical protective equipment, and 29 C.F.R. 1910.138 contains the specific requirements for hand protection.

6. THE RESPIRATORY PROTECTION STANDARD 29 C.F.R. 1910.134

a. General - The Respiratory Protection Standard requires that when effective engineering controls are not feasible to control occupational injury or disease caused by breathing contaminated air, an employer *must* provide respirators suitable for the intended purpose. Contaminated air may include potentially harmful levels of hazardous gases or vapors and/or potential respiratory hazards such as dust, mist, fumes, sprays, or airborne particles, as well as airborne biologic hazards.

As of July 1, 2004, OSHA will apply the general Respiratory Protection Standard, 29 C.F.R. 1910.134, to respiratory protection against *Tuberculosis.*

b. Respiratory Protection Program (a/k/a The Program) - The Standard requires that when respirators are necessary to protect the health of employees or whenever respirators are required by an employer, the employer must establish and maintain a written Respiratory Protection Program with required worksite procedures for required respiratory use in routine and foreseeable emergency situations.

The Program must be *worksite specific* and be updated as necessary to reflect changes in workplace conditions that affect respiratory use. The written Respiratory Protection Program must include procedures for selecting respirators, *medical evaluation of employees required to us respirators,* fit test procedures for tight fitting respirators, procedures for proper use of respirators in routine and foreseeable emergency situations and procedures and schedules for cleaning, disinfecting, storing, inspecting, repairing, discarding or otherwise marinating respirators. The Program must also contain procedures to ensure adequate air quality, quantity and flow of breathing air into atmosphere supplying respirators, if this type of respirator is in use.

Employees must be trained in the respiratory hazards to which they are potentially exposed, during routine and emergency situations and in the proper use of respirators, including putting them on or removing them, and limitations in their use and their maintenance. The Program must also contain procedures for regularly evaluating the effectiveness of the Program.

When a written Respiratory Protection Program is required, the employer must designate a Program Administrator, qualified by appropriate training or experience commensurate with the complexity of the written Respiratory Protection Program to administer or oversee the Program and to conduct required evaluations of Program effectiveness. All respirators under the Program shall be provided, along with required training and medical evaluations, at no cost to the employee.

    c. **Voluntary Respirator Usage** - If respiratory protection is not required, but employees voluntarily choose to use their own or employer-provided respiratory protection, even when such protection is not mandated, the employer is NOT required to have a full Respiratory Protection Program as indicated, but must still ensure that the employees are medically able to use the respirators, ensure that respirators are properly cleaned, stored and maintained and provide voluntary respirator usage with the information contained in 29 C.F.R. 1910.134, Appendix D, which provides information for employees using respirators when such respirators are not required under the Respiratory Protection Standard.

    d. **Respiratory Selection** - Respirator selection, when a respirator is required, must be based on the employer's evaluation of the respiratory hazards to which the employee is exposed and workplace and user factors that affect respiratory performance and reliability. The respirators that are selected must be NIOSH (National Institute for Occupational Safety and Health) certified and used in compliance with the conditions of their certifications. The employer's evaluation of the respiratory hazard must include a reasonable estimate of the employee exposure to respiratory hazards and an identification of a contaminant, chemical state and physical form. If employee exposure cannot be identified or reasonably estimated, the employer must consider the atmosphere to be immediately dangerous to life or health. The employer shall select a respiratory appropriate for the level of hazard identified. The respiratory hazards to be considered include *biological,* as well as *chemical hazards.*

    e. **Medical Evaluation** - The requirement for a medical evaluation is to determine the employee's physical ability to use a respirator *before* the employee is fit tested or required to use or allowed to voluntarily use a respirator in the workplace. This evaluation, which must be performed by a physician or other licensed health care professional, is necessary since a respirator does present a restriction on an individual's respiratory system and may be medically contraindicated for the particular individual.

    The evaluation includes a medical questionnaire to be administered confidentially and the employee must be provided the opportunity to discuss the questionnaire and the examination results with the physician or other licensed health care professional. The employer must provide the physician or other licensed health care professional information about the actual type and weight of the respirator to be used, the duration and the frequency of the respiratory use, the expected physical work effort, and additional information as to any additional personal protective clothing or equipment to be worn and the temperature and humidity extremes that may be accounted *before* the physician makes a recommendation as to the employee's ability to use the respirator.

    The medical recommendation regarding the employee's ability to use the respirator must be written and must contain any limitations in respirator usage related to the medical condition of the employee or the workplace conditions and contain a specific, clear determination as to whether the employee is medically able to use a respirator, the need for any follow-up medical evaluations and a statement that physician or licensed health care professional has provided the employee with a copy of the written recommendations.

f. Fit Testing - The requirements for fit testing are specific and contained in Appendix A to the Respiratory Protection Standard, 29 C.F.R. 1910.134. Before any required use, the employee must be fit tested on the same make, model, style and size of the respirator that will be used. Fit testing can be performed, for the employer, by an outside industrial hygienist or qualified health care professional and must include a qualitative or quantitative fit test as described by the Respiratory Protection Standard in Appendix A. Fit testing must be done prior to initial use, whenever a different face piece is used, at least annually thereafter and whenever there is a change in the employee's facial appearance/physical condition that warrants additional testing.

g. Training - Employees who are required to use respirators must receive comprehensive and understandable training in their usage at least annually and more often if necessary. This training must include why a respirator is necessary and how improper fit, usage, or maintenance can compromise the protective effect of the respirator. The employee must also be trained in the limitations and capacities of the respirator being used, how to use the respirator effectively in emergency situations, including situations in which the respirator malfunctions and how to inspect, put on, remove, use, and check the seals of the respirator.

The training must also include procedures for maintenance and storage and the recognition of the medical science and symptoms that may limit or prevent effective use of the respirator, along with the general requirements of the Respiratory Protection Standard. Training must be given prior to requiring the employee to use the respirator in the workplace with retraining administered annually and when there are changes in the workplace or type of respirator that render previous training obsolete. Retraining must also be done when there are changes in the workplace or the type of respirator that render previous training obsolete, or whenever the employee's usage of the respirator indicates that retraining is required.

While the Respiratory Protection Standard does not require employers to keep training records, this should be done as a matter of practice to verify that training has been completed as required, the date of the training, the scope of the training, the employee being trained, and the identity of the trainer.

7. AIR CONTAMINANTS 29 C.F.R. 1910.1000

This Standard contains tables that list chemicals and the exposure limits for each substance stated as a ceiling value or as an 8-hour time-weighted average. To achieve compliance, administrative or engineering controls must first be determined and implemented wherever feasible. When administrative or engineering controls are not feasible to achieve full compliance, personal protective equipment must be used to keep employee exposure to the listed air contaminants within the limits prescribed by 29 C.F.R. 1910.1000.

Whenever respirators are to be used, their usage shall comply with the Respiratory Protection Standard 29 C.F.R. 1910.134.

8. QUICK DRENCH SHOWERS AND EYE WASHES 29 C.F.R. 1910.1048(i)(2)(3) and 1910.151

OSHA Standard 1910.1519(c) specifically requires that where the eyes or body of any person may be exposed to injurious corrosive materials, suitable facilities for quick drenching or flushing of the eyes and body shall be provided within the work area and available for <u>immediate</u> use should an employee get splashed with an injurious corrosive/destructive material. A shower or eye wash station that is located in another room, that would require an employee to pass through a door or to move more than a few steps, would not be in compliance with the requirements of this Standard.

To ensure that the equipment is operating properly and available for immediate emergency use, and employer must also, on a regular basis, test the unit's operation and should document this test to prove it was done.

In addition, under the specific OSHA Formaldehyde Standard, 29 C.F.R. 1910.1048(i)(2)(3), there is a requirement that states: "If employees' skin may become splashed with solutions containing 0.1% or greater Formaldehyde, the employer shall provide conveniently located quick drench showers and ensure that affected employees use these facilities immediately. If there is any possibility that an employee's eyes may be splashed with solutions containing 0.1% or greater Formaldehyde, the employer shall provide acceptable eye wash facilities within the immediate work area for emergency use."

Hands-free eye wash stations are the best option.

9. NEW FOR OSHA AS OF JANUARY 1, 2015

a. As of January 1, 2015, all employers must report to OSHA:

> ➤ All work-related fatalities with 8 hours.
> ➤ All work-related inpatient hospitalizations, all amputations and all losses of an eye with 24 hours.

b. The OSHA revised recordkeeping rule includes two key changes:
> ➤ First, the rule updates the list of industries that are exempt from the requirement to routinely keep OSHA injury and illness records, due to relatively low occupational injury and illness rates.
> ➤ Second, the rule expands the list of severe work-related injuries that all covered employers must report to OSHA.

c. State-Plan State Regulations:

There are 27 states and U.S. territories that have their own OSHA-approved occupational safety and health programs called State Plans. State Plans are required to have standards that are at least as effective as OSHA's.

All State Plans have recordkeeping and reporting requirements in place. These requirements are at least equivalent to OSHA's previous reporting requirements for fatalities and catastrophes. In addition, several states have different or additional requirements that may already be in line with OSHA's revision.

All State Plans have begun reviewing their current reporting and recordkeeping requirements to determine how they compare to OSHA's new reporting requirements.

d. Hazard Communication:

The Hazard Communication Standard (HCS) is now aligned with the Globally Harmonized System (GHS) of Classification and Labeling of Chemicals. This update to the Hazard Communication Standard (HCS) will provide a common and coherent approach to classifying chemicals and communicating hazard information on labels and safety data sheets (SDS). The revised standard will improve the quality and consistency of hazard information in the workplace, making it safer for workers by providing easily understandable information on appropriate handling and safe use of hazardous chemicals. This update will also help reduce trade barriers and result in productivity improvements for American businesses that regularly handle, store, and use hazardous chemicals while providing cost savings for American businesses that periodically update safety data sheets and labels for chemicals covered under the hazard communication standard.

List of OSHA Acronyms

ACGIH – American Conference of Governmental Industrial Hygienists

AL – Action Level

E.P.A. – Environmental Protection Agency

F.T.C. – Federal Trade Commission

G.H.S. – Globally Harmonized System

HBV – Hepatitis B Virus

HCHO – Formaldehyde

H.C.S. – Hazardous Communication Standard

NIOSH – National Institute for Occupational Safety and Health

OPIM – Other Potentially Infectious Material

OSHA – Occupational Safety and Health Act OR Administration

P.E.L. – Permissible/Prolonged exposure limit

pH Potential of Hydrogen

P.P.E. – Personal Protective Equipment

ppm – Parts Per Million

S.D.S. – Safety Data Sheet

STEL – Short-term exposure limit

T.W.A. – Time-weighted average

Glossary for OSHA

Action level/A.L. (exposure limits) - Concentration of 0.5 ppm of formaldehyde calculated as an 8-hour T.W.A. concentration as defined by OSHA.

Biohazard - biological agent or situation that constitutes a hazard to humans.

Biohazardous waste - any potentially infective, contaminated waste that constitutes a hazard to humans in the workplace.

Bloodborne pathogen - microorganism present in human blood that can cause disease in humans.

Bloodborne Pathogen Standard - OSHA mandate (29 CFR 1910.1030) regulating the employee's exposure to blood and other body fluids.

Drench shower - OSHA-required safety device for a release of a copious amount of water in a short time.

Eyewash station - OSHA-required emergency safety device providing a steady stream of water for flushing the eye.

Formaldehyde/HCHO - colorless, strong-smelling gas that when used in solution is a powerful preservative and disinfectant; a known carcinogen.

Formaldehyde Standard - OSHA (29 CFR 1910.1048) regulation limiting the amount of occupational exposure to formaldehyde.

Hazard Communication Standard - (29 CFR 1910.1200) OSHA regulation that deals with identifying and limiting exposure to hazardous chemicals within the workplace.

Hazardous material - agent exposing one to risk.

Hepatitis B virus/HBV - infectious bloodborne virus.

Occupational exposure - reasonably anticipated skin, eye, mucous membrane, or parenteral, contact with blood or other potentially infectious materials that may result from the performance of a worker's duties.

Permissible exposure limit (PEL) - 0.75 ppm of formaldehyde present over an 8-hour time weighted average.

Short term exposure limit (STEL) - 2 ppm of formaldehyde present over a 15-minute time weighted average.

Domain II

Restorative Art

Restorative Art

Chapter Overview

This section of the review manual will discuss the basic principles of Restorative Art as it relates to the practice of funeral services. On the National Board Exam, there are 34 questions, or about 23% of the exam which is related to Restorative Art. In addition to discussing the terminology associated with Restorative Art, this section will describe techniques for restoration and recreation in preparation of deceased human remains for public visitation. The goal of Restorative Art is to create a peaceful repose of the human remains so the bereaved can have a positive memory picture of their loved one.

Introduction to Restorative Art

Restorative Art *is the care of the deceased to recreate a natural form and color.* When death occurs, the human body changes metabolically and physically results in the ceasing of biological functions. The deceased human remains, left unattended over a period of time, will eventually begin to decompose and experience putrefaction. Embalming retards the natural decomposition of human remains and facilitates the foundation for restorative art. The main objective of restorative art is to create a positive memory picture so the bereaved can memorialize their loved ones and begin the grieving process.

Restorative art takes different forms for the embalmer and restorative artist. There is **minor restorative art**, which is a *restoration that requires minimal effort, takes little time to complete, and involves little skill.* An example of this is cosmetizing the human remains prior to visitation or services. **Major restorative** *art requires a longer period of time, involves extensive reconstruction, and requires technical skills* that are usually acquired over a practitioner's career. An example of this type of restorative art would be reconstructing a face after the deceased experienced trauma from a car accident.

In cases of sudden death, the importance of restorative art becomes even more important to the family. A funeral director's main job is to take the death event and help people connect to their own grieving experience. Death, whether it is of natural causes, a result of a long illness, or a traumatic event, requires people to bring closure to the relationship so they can reinvest in new relationships. The psychological effect on the immediate family and close friends requires the bereaved to view their loved-one in a state of repose, at peace from the manner that caused the death event. This positive memory picture that is created with restorative art, if done properly, brings respect and dignity to the deceased and jump-starts the grieving process for the bereaved.

The funeral practitioner holds a professional responsibility to create this positive memory picture as part of their obligation to the community to do the best for the dead while caring for the emotional needs of the bereaved. If done correctly, the embalmer/restorative artist will receive not only accolades for their investment of time, talent, and technique but also their reputation for caring for the dead in a proper manner that could result in future business from others. Improperly done, the embalmer/restorative artist and the funeral home run the risk of a lawsuit.

As learned in the chapter on Mortuary Law, embalming is a form of **mutilation** because it *alters the natural state of human remains from their original condition.* This is why it is important to obtain oral or written permission prior to the embalming process. Hence, when doing major restoration of human remains, the prudent funeral director should obtain written permission for the restoration prior to engaging in any invasive procedures.

In my career, I had two events that could have resulted in litigation. The first event was when I removed a single hair from an elderly woman's mole on her chin. This single hair was an identifying mark for the grandchildren. The situation was rectified by excusing the family from the room and reattaching the hair. Procedures such as this should never be performed in front of family members.

The second situation was irreparable. The family gave permission to embalm the human remains with the understanding that no cosmetics be applied to her remains. After the embalming process, the remains did not need cosmetics because the active dyes in the chemicals gave her a natural appearance. Upon viewing the remains, the family was aghast and requested that the cosmetics be removed. I took a tissue and rubbed the deceased face and hands, revealing that no cosmetics were applied. The potential negligence, in this case, hinged upon failure to disclose the fact that the embalming chemicals had active dyes that could not be removed from the fluids. This fact needed to be disclosed to the family prior to embalming, and written permission needed to be obtained, explaining how active dyes are a part of the embalming fluids and they could not be removed.

Thus, distinguishing characteristics generally should not be altered or concealed, including, but not limited to, moles, warts, scars, and birthmarks. Surgical scars, scabs, or other health-related deformities can be treated using restorative art only after permission has been obtained by the next-of-kin.

Physiognomy is *the study of the structures and surface markings of the face and features. This includes morphology (the study of size and shape) in combination with natural and acquired facial markings.* As this section progresses, normal facial features will be discussed. **Norm** *is the most common characteristic of each feature, typically common or average.*

Understanding the Basic Terms and Anatomical Position

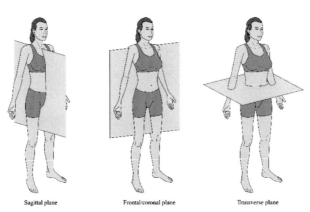

Sagittal plane   Frontal/coronal plane   Transverse plane

There are three Anatomical Planes: **Sagittal Plane** refers to the body divided lengthwise into right and left sides. Sometimes it is called a midsagittal plane if the division is made exactly at the midline. **The Frontal Plane** is also known as the **Coronal Plane**. This plane divides the body into the front (anterior) and back (posterior) portions. The **Transverse Plane** divides the body horizontally into the upper (superior) and lower (inferior) portions.

Understanding the Basic Human Anatomical Terms

1. Anterior and posterior:
   a. **Anterior** - Before or in front of; refers to the ventral or abdominal side of the body.
   b. **Posterior** - Toward the rear or caudal end; toward the back; dorsal.

2. Superior and inferior:
   a. **Superior** - Anatomically towards the head.
   b. **Inferior** - Beneath; lower; the under surface of an organ or indicating a structure below another structure; towards the feet.

3. Medial and lateral:
   a. **Medial** - Middle; nears the medial plane.
   b. **Lateral** - Toward the side.

4. Bilateral, frontal, and profile:
   a. **Bilateral** - Refers to two sides.
   b. **Frontal** - Anterior; the anterior view of the face or features.
   c. **Profile** - An outline of the side view of an object, specifically the human head.

Surface planes:

1. Projection and recession:
   a. **Projection** - The act of throwing forward; a part extending beyond the level of its surroundings.
   b. **Recession** - The withdrawal of a part from its normal position. Sticks out / in.
2. Depression and protrusion:
   a. **Depression** - A hollow or lowered region; the lowering of a part.
   b. **Protrusion** - State or condition of being thrust forward or projecting.

3. Concave and convex:
   a. **Concave** - Having a spherically depressed or hollow surface.
   b. **Convex** - Curved evenly, resembling a segment of the outer edge of a sphere.

4 **Inclination**: A line that is neither horizontal nor vertical. Diagonal slant.

5. **Types of Symmetry:**
   a. **Symmetry-** refers to correspondence in size, shape, and relative position of parts that are on opposite sides of the face.
   b. **Bilateral symmetry** means that the right side of the face looks similar to the left side.
   c. **Asymmetry** means that the face lacks symmetry, balance, and proportion.

6. **Oblique** – means slanted or inclined and neither perpendicular nor horizontal.

Bones in the Skull

A large percentage of restorative art work is completed on the head. The skull bones play a significant function in the foundational work of restoration. Knowing the anatomical structures of the skull and how they correspond to other facial landmarks is important knowledge that embalmers and restorative artists need to know for facial reconstruction. This section will discuss the various parts of the face and head bones. *The cranium consists of 8 bones, and the face consists of 14 bones.*

The geometric form of the normal skull:

1. Oval in form and has three views (front, side, and crown). The most common type is egg-shaped or oval.
2. Variations of form because of enlarged width or length. Seven variations from the front (see Head Shapes, p. 137).
3. Comparison of male, female, and infant skulls regarding: Male bones are larger, heavier, and thicker than a female skull; Infant's bones are small, light brittle.
4. Changes resulting from the loss of teeth: Causes mouth to be sunken and shorter.

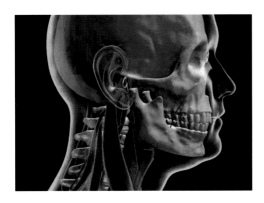

A male skull is:

> Relatively larger than a female skull
> Has a sharper, more angular frontonasal angle
> The supraorbital ridges are more pronounced
> The forehead slopes backward
> Surface of the cheekbone is rough and concave
> Mandible (mental bone or chin) is squarer
> Foramen magnum is larger and longer
> Mastoid process is also larger

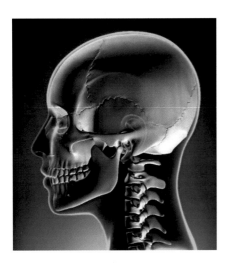

A Female skull is:

> Relatively smaller than a male skull
> Has a smoother curved frontonasal angle
> The supraorbital ridges are poorly developed
> The forehead is nearly vertical
> Surfaces of the cheekbones are smooth and flat
> Mandible (mental bone or chin) is pointed
> Foramen magnum is smaller and rounder
> Mastoid process is also smaller

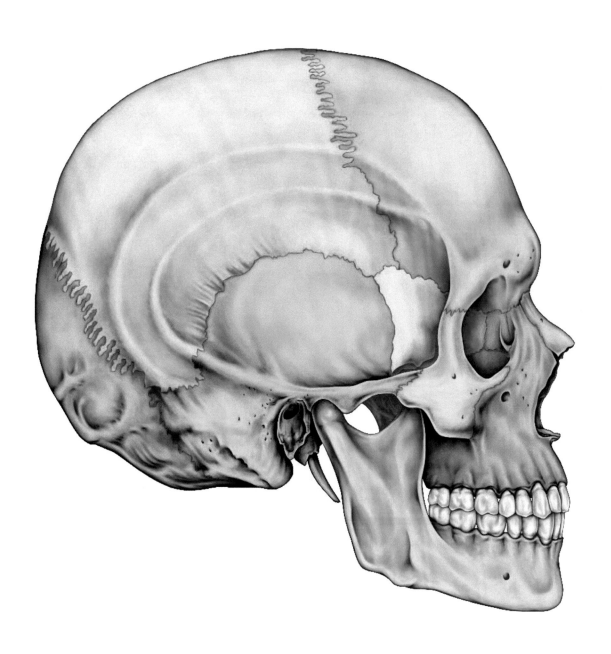

Surface Bones of the Cranium (7 Total)

1. **Occipital Bone** – 1:
    a. Location: The lowest part of the back and base of the skull. Curves under the skull and becomes the cradle for the brain.

    b. **Foramen** (Latin for hole) **magnum** (Latin for large): Opening in the occipital bone through which the spinal cord passes from the brain, and medial to the two mastoid processes.

    c. **Occipital fossa**- 1: a small midline depression on the interior surface of the squamous part of the occipital bone.

    d. **Lambdoid Suture** – (origin is Greek, after the Greek symbol Lambda) (**oid** is Latin for like): superior to the occipital bone, the lambdoid suture is a line of dense fibrous tissue that connects the occipital bone with the parietal bones.

2. **Parietal** – 2: The widest part of the skull.

    a. Location: Superior portion of the sides and back of the cranium, as well as the posterior 2/3 of the roof of the cranium.

    b. Position of the **parietal eminence**: The marked convexity on the outer surface of the parietal bones.

    c. **Parietal eminences (#41) are the widest part of the skull.**
        1) Location anatomically: Superior and posterior to the ears (back top corner of the skull).
        2) Significance physiognomically: From the right parietal eminence to the left parietal eminence is the widest part of the skull. ***Determines the widest part of the cranium*** (Very important on the NBEs)

    d. **Sagittal Suture:** A structure that is medial to the parietal bones and posterior to the frontal bone. It is perpendicular to the coronial suture.

3. **Temporal** – 2 (#46):
    a. Location: Inferior portion of the sides and base of the cranium, inferior to the parietal bones and anterior to the occipital bone.

    b. **Squama** (flat): A recession in the temporal cavity (soft spot on the temple).
    c. Squamosal Suture: This suture is inferior to the parietal bone and superior to the temporal bone.

d. **Anatomical structures used for accurate location of the ear**:
> (1) **External auditory meatus** (#49): External opening to the ear canal. Meatus is Latin for opening.
> (2) **Zygomatic arch** (#54A): Exactly splits ear in half. The temporalis muscle passes underneath this structure.
> (3) **Mandibular fossa**: Place where the mandible articulates with the temporal bone.
> (4) **Mastoid process** (#59): Posterior and inferior to the external auditory meatus. The most inferior part of the temporal bone.

4. **Zygomatic arch – 2 (#54A):**
   a. Location anatomically: Projects from the lower part of the Squama. It is a long, thin-arched process that arises from the skull directly above the ear passage and then extends anteriorly to the cheekbone. The posterior part moves laterally for a short distance; its upper and lower surfaces lie on horizontal planes. Then the process twists inward upon itself, and the two surfaces continue forward on vertical planes. The upper border is long, thin, and sharp; the lower border is short, thick, and arched.

   b. **Temporozygomatic suture** (#54): The suture on the zygomatic arch that joins the temporal bone to the zygomatic bone. In anatomical terms, two parts that are joined together get their name from the point of origination to the point of termination.

   c. Significance physiognomically: ***From the zygomatic arch-to-zygomatic arch*, this determines *the widest part of the face*.** (*Very important on the NBEs*)

   d. **Mastoid process – 2 (#59):**
   > 1) Location anatomically: Creates the posterior and inferior part of the temporal bone.
   > 2) Significance physiognomically: Situated under the lobe of the ear.

5. **Sphenoid Bone – 2:**
   a. Location: Forms the forward part of the base of the skull and contains the depression, or fossa, that houses the pituitary gland.

   b. **Sella Turcica** (Latin for Turkish Saddle) – is a small, bony nook at the base of the brain that holds and protects the pituitary gland. Also known as the Pituitary Fossa.

   c. **Greater Wings of the Sphenoid Bone – 2 (#81A):** The lateral parts of the sphenoid bone that are anterior to the temporal bone and posterior to the zygomatic arch.

6. **Frontal – 1 (#1):**
   a. Location: The anterior 1/3 of the cranium forms the forehead.
   b. Surfaces:
   > 1) Vertical (forehead): The part of the face above the eyes.

2) Horizontal (crown): The topmost part of the head.

3) **Coronal** (Latin for Crown) **Suture** (#81): is located posterior to the frontal bone and anterior to the parietal bone.

   c. Eminences: name and locate anatomically and physiognomically:

      1) **Frontal eminence** – 2: Front corner of skull.

      2) **Supraorbital margin** – 2: Top of the eye socket.

      3) **Superciliary arch** – 2: Located under eyebrows.

      4) **Glabella** – 1 (#3): A small smooth elevation that lies between the Superciliary Arches and joins one to the other. The lateral margins form a part of the orbital margins and converge medially as they descend to the nasal bones.

7. **Ethmoid – 1:**

   a. Location: The ethmoid bone (#17) is a cube-shaped bone located in the center of the skull between the eyes. This bone is posterior to the lacrimal bone and helps to form the eye socket (or orbital cavity) as well as the roof, sides, and interior of the nasal cavity.

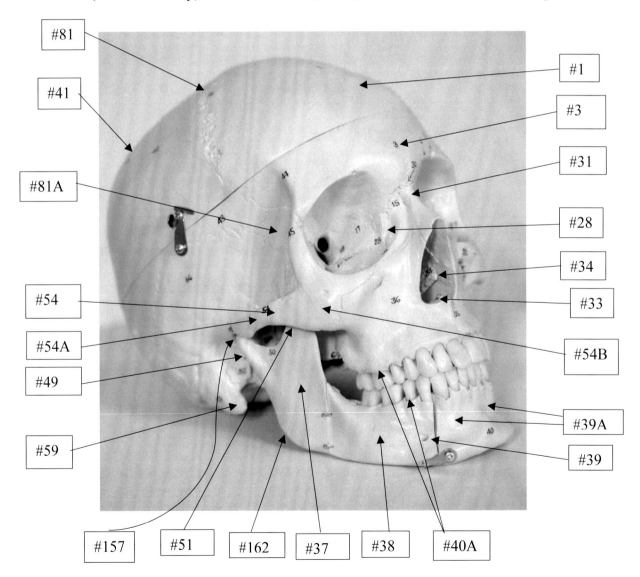

122

Surface Bones of the Face (Total of 14):

1. **Nasal** – 2 (#31):
   a. Location: Directly inferior to the glabella, it forms a dome over the superior portion of the nasal cavity; triangular form.
   b. Formation of the bridge by the articulation of the two nasal bones.
   c. *See the Nose section* (pp. 140-142): for complete anatomical features within the nasal cavity.

2. **Zygomatic** – 2 (#54B): Diamond-shaped surfaces; form the **cheekbones**. The cheekbone creates the prominence of the cheek and the major portions of the inferior and lateral margins of the eye-socket.
   a. Location anatomically: Just inferior to the eye socket. The inferior margins converge to an angle (Zygomatic Tubercle) which is on approximately the same level as the base of the Nasal Cavity. The surface is convex in both directions; the greatest curvature occurs transversely, making the bone lie on both the front and side of the cheek.

   b. Significance physiognomically: Determines the width of the anterior plane of the face.

   c. Surfaces on both frontal and lateral planes of the face.

   d. Value of the bone in cheek rouging: Warm area of the face highlights the natural form of features.

3. **Maxilla** – 2 (#36): Forms the upper jaw.
   a. Location: A paired bone with several processes that form the skeletal base of most of the superior face, the roof of the mouth, the sides of the nasal cavity, and the floor of the orbit.

   b. Eminences:
      1) Nasal spine of the maxilla.
      2) Alveolar processes (#40B). Function: Sockets that holds the teeth in place

4. **Lacrimal** – 2 (#28): A bone that gives structure to the orbital cavity and is an important part of the lacrimal system or tear production.
   a. Lacrimal Fossa – is the dent or groove superior to the lacrimal foramen.
   b. Lacrimal foramen – the opening at the base of the lacrimal bone for the lacrimal sac (tear duct).

5. **Palatine** – 2: The Palatine bones contribute to the posterior part of the roof of the mouth and the floor, and medial wall of the nose, the medial wall of the maxillary sinuses, and the orbital floor.

6. **Inferior Nasal Concha** – 2 (#34): The inferior nasal concha extends horizontally along the lateral walls of the nasal cavity and articulates with the palatines. It also articulates with the ethmoid and lacrimals superiorly.

7.   **Vomer** – 1 (#33): On the midsagittal line, the vomer is *a plow-shaped bone* that helps support the structure of the nasal passage, face and hard palate. This bone is located on the superior and anterior part of the maxilla.

8.   **Mandible** – 1 (#38):
     a. Location: The horseshoe-shaped bone forms the inferior (lower) jaw. It articulates with the skull at the mandibular fossa, which is a cavity at the base of the temporal bone.

Divisions:
     b. **Body** (of the mandible #38):
         (1) **Mental** (Latin for chin) **eminence** (#40): Point of the chin.
         (2) **Mental foremen** (#39): small holes lateral to the mental eminence.
         (3) **Incisive fossa** (#39A): Dent on top of the chin.
         (4) **Alveolar process** (#40A): Sockets that teeth sit in.

     c. **Ramus**: Perpendicular portion of the mandible. Wide, somewhat flattened, and quadrilateral in shape. The posterior border is identifiable with the posterior termination of the cheek.
         (1) **Coronoid** (Latin for crown-like) **process** (#51): Anterior, superior point of the mandible (top front corner of ramus). The Temporalis muscle attaches here.
         (2) **Condyle** (Latin for knuckle) **of the mandible** (#157): Located just posterior to the coronoid process, it articulates with the temporal bone at the mandibular fossa. Jaw hinge.
         (3) **Mandibular notch** (#50): a groove of the ramus on the superior part of the mandible between the coronoid process and the condyle.

     d. **The Angle of the Mandible** (#162): Masseter muscle attaches here.
         (1) Influence on the form of the head from the frontal view.
         (2) Measurement is similar to the distance between the zygomatic bones.

Muscles on the Face

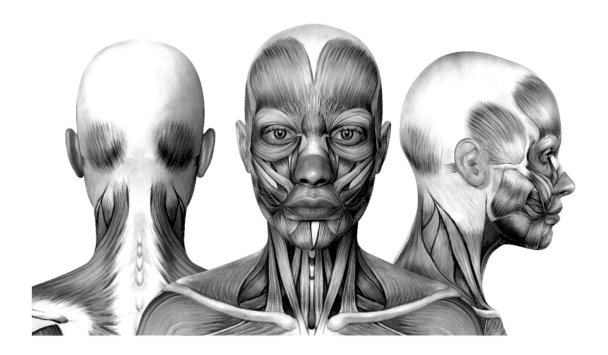

The muscles of the face play an important part in facial features and restorative art. These muscles are an important part of facial expression and, ultimately, a contributing factor to facial features like wrinkles, folds, and grooves. Repetitive use of muscles results in distinct facial characteristics that make every person unique. The location and shape of these facial muscles play an important role in facial reconstruction. The muscles of the face provide the shape, convexity, or concaveness of the facial feature. These are the muscles of the cranium, face, and neck that influence surface forms and expression:

1.   **Occipitofrontalis** (epicranius) – 1. Draws the scalp posteriorly and anteriorly and raises the eyebrows. It can have a line in the forehead after an autopsy that must be filled with mastic compound, latex caulk, or tissue builder.

2.   **Temporalis** – 2: Closes the mandible; mastication and is the **strongest** of the chewing muscles. Attaches to the Coronoid process of the mandible.

3.   **Masseter** – 2: Closes the mandible; mastication. Attaches to the angle of the mandible.

4.   **Orbicularis oculi** – 2: Closes the eyelid; compresses the lacrimal sac.

5.   **Corrugator (the frowning muscle)** – 2: Draws the eyebrows inferiorly and medially.

125

6. **Levator palpebrae superioris** – 2: Raises the superior eyelid. May need to break up rigor with fingers.

7. **Procerus** – 1: Draws the skin of the forehead inferiorly. Bridge of nose.

8. **Orbicularis oris (puckering muscle)** – 1: Surrounds the mouth. Closes the lips. Sphincter muscle.

9. **Quadratus labii superioris** – 2: **3 Heads**. Raises the wings of the nose and deepens the nasolabial sulcus.
    a. **Levator labii superioris alaeque nasi** – 2: Elevates the superior lip, dilates the nostrils.
    b. **Levator labii superioris** – 2: Elevates and extends the superior lip.
    c. **Zygomaticus minor** – 2: Draws the superior lip superiorily and anteriorly.

10. **Levator anguli oris** – 2: Elevates the angle of the mouth. Located near the canine teeth.

11. **Zygomaticus major (laughing)** – 2: Draws the superior lip posteriorly, superiorly, and anteriorly.

12. **Buccinator (trumpeter's muscle)** – 2: Compresses the cheek and retracts the angle of the mouth. Lateral to mouth on the side of the face.

13. **Risorius** – 2: Draws the angle of the mouth anteriorly (pulls mouth back to original position). Runs on top of the buccinator.

14. **Depressor angulus oris** (triangularis) – 2: Depresses the angle (corners) of the mouth.

15. **Depressor labii inferioris** (quadratus) – 2: Draws the inferior lip interiorly and slightly lateral.

16. **Mentalis** – 1: Elevates and protrudes the inferior lip, wrinkles the skin over the chin.

17. **Platysma** – 2: Wrinkles the skin of the neck and chest and depresses the mandible and inferior lip. Broad flat muscle of the neck.

18. **Sternocleidomastoid (SCM)** – 2: Rotates and depresses the head. The widest part of the neck.

19. **Digastricus** – 2: Draws hyoid bone anteriorly and posteriorly. The double-bellied muscle in the floor of the mouth.

Other factors to consider when discussing facial tissue are subcutaneous tissue (under the skin). **Fascia** is a thin casing of connective tissue that surrounds and holds every organ, blood vessel, bone, nerve fiber, and muscle in place. **Glands** are organs in the human body that secrete particular chemical substances into the body. Where glands become a concern for restorative art is when they become enlarged and require reduction through manipulation, excising, or external pressure. Finally, **adipose tissue**, otherwise known as body fat, is a type of connective tissue the extends outward from the body. This becomes a concern in restorative art during the embalming treatment, the cremation process, and in dressing, casketing, and cosmetizing the human remains.

The muscles have a direct effect on the way the integumentary (skin) system forms grooves, wrinkles, and folds. The outermost layer of skin is known as the **epidermis**. It protects the body from infection and keeps the body hydrated. Every seven days, new skin cells are generated, and old cells sluff off. The **dermis** is the inner layer of skin. The dermis is considered connective tissue where blood vessels, oil, glands, nerves, and hair follicles reside. In restorative art, the skin plays a major role in the presentation of a positive memory picture.

Facial Marking

Facial markings are the identifiable characteristics on each person's face. There are several factors responsible for determining the size and shape of various facial markings. Heredity plays a major role in the appearance of facial markings. People tend to exhibit similar facial markings to their parents. As a person grows older, incrementally, their facial marks will change, in part from repetitive use of muscles and facial expressions that will, over time, produce groves and wrinkles in the skin. Striation and action, meaning the alignment of muscle fibers and the more the muscle is used repetily, will impact the formation and definition of facial markings. Also, the environment plays an important role in skin tone and wrinkles. People in southern climates, for example, have a tendency to have drier skin and more wrinkles if they avoid hydration of the skin with moisturizers or lotions. Finally, with age, gravity usually plays a major role in the sagging of tissue, especially when muscle loss happens as a result of the effects of aging.

In Restorative Art, the condition of the human remains can be altered by various events, such as illness and trauma. Blunt force trauma to the face, for example, could result in the formation of scars, scabs, or even malformation of various facial markings. A pathological condition, such as a tumor, could also create the same, if not worse, abnormalities of the facial features. And finally, as a result of age, people have a tendency to gain or lose weight, which could result in the facial tissue either expanding or contracting. Tissue that expands has a tendency to have fewer defined facial wrinkles, while people who become emaciated have a tendency to develop more facial furrows and grooves.

There are three basic physiognomical descriptions that need to be known in order to understand the various facial markings:

> Sulcus or Sulci: A sulcus is a furrow or a wrinkle. Multiple wrinkles near each other are known as sulci. **A sulcus is a linear crevice in the skin accompanied by an adjacent elevation.**

> Groove: A groove is an elongated depression in a relatively even plane or surface.

> Fold: A fold is an elongated prominence that abuts convexly against an adjacent surface.

Natural Facial Markings – There are 9

Oblique Palpebral Sulcus

Philtrum

Nasal Sulcus

Nasolabial Fold

Angulus Oris Sulcus

Angulus Oris Eminence

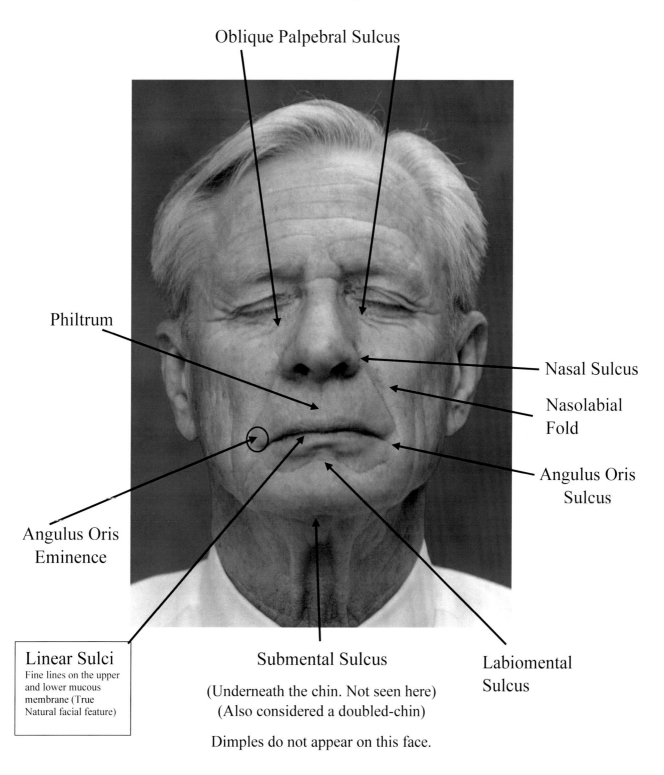

Linear Sulci
Fine lines on the upper and lower mucous membrane (True Natural facial feature)

Submental Sulcus

(Underneath the chin. Not seen here)
(Also considered a doubled-chin)

Dimples do not appear on this face.

Labiomental Sulcus

Classification of Facial Markings – Natural and Acquired

Natural Facial Markings – there are 9, according to the ABFSE Outline.
Natural facial markings are defined *as those furrows, wrinkles, sulcus, grooves, or folds that are present from birth; these are usually hereditary*.

    a.   **Philtrum:** The vertical groove located medially on the superior lip.

    b.   **Nasolabial fold:** The eminence of the cheek and adjacent to the mouth, extending from the superior part of the posterior margin of the wing of the nose to the side of the mouth. Where the cheek meets the upper integumentary lip, it abuts the nasolabial sulcus.

    c.   **Nasal sulcus:** The angular area between the posterior margin of the wing of the nose and the nasolabial fold. The nasal sulcus is located behind the wing of the nose.

    d.   **Oblique palpebral sulcus:** The shallow, curving groove below the medial corner of the eyelids.

    e.   **Angulus oris eminence:** The small, convex prominence lateral to the end of the line of lip closure of the mouth. A small bump.

    f.   **Angulus oris sulcus:** The groove at each end of the line of closure of the mouth.

    g.   **Labiomental sulcus:** The junction of the inferior lip and the chin, which may appear as a furrow.

    h.   **Submental sulcus:** The junction of the base of the chin and the sub-mandibular area, which may appear as a furrow. The fold of a double chin.

    i.   **Dimples:** Shallow depressions located on the cheek or chin; rounded or vertical. Not all people have dimples. Thus, this should not be considered natural facial marking, rather an oddity that appears on some people.

NOTE: Babies have little lines on their mucus membranes or upper and lower lips, as do adults. These sulci should be recognized as **linear sulci** and are a true natural facial marking on all people.

Acquired Facial Markings

Transverse Frontal Sulci

Intercillary Sulci

Superior Palpebral Sulcus

Optic Facial Sulci (Crow's Feet)

Labial Sulci
Acquired lines that extend from the mucous membrane into the integumentary lip.

Inferior Palpebral Sulcus

Linear Sulci
Fine lines on the upper and lower mucous membrane (Natural)

Bucco-Facial Sulcus

Nasolabial Sulcus

Mandibular Sulcus

Platysmal Sulci

Cords of the Neck

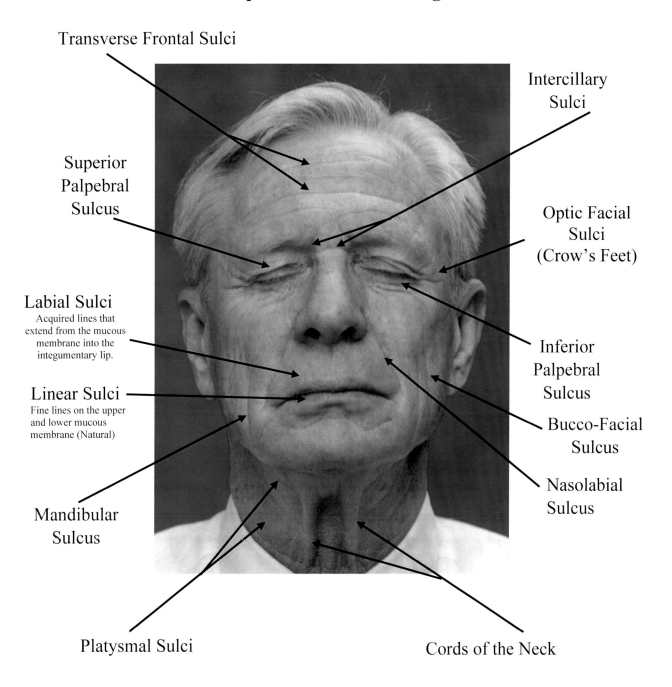

Acquired Facial Markings – There Are 11

Acquired Facial Markings are defined as *those developed throughout your lifetime as a result of the repetitious use of certain muscles. Come with age.*

a. **Nasolabial sulcus**: The furrow originating at the superior border of the wing of the nose and extending to the side of the mouth.

b. **Transverse frontal sulci**: The horizontal furrows (wrinkles) of the forehead.

c. **Interciliary Sulci**: The vertical or transverse furrows (wrinkles) between the eyebrows.

d. **Optic facial sulci (crow's feet)**: The furrows radiating from the lateral corner of the eye.

e. **Superior palpebral sulcus**: The furrow of the superior border of the upper eyelid.

f. **Inferior palpebral sulcus**: The furrow of the inferior border of the inferior eyelid.

g. **Bucco-facial sulcus**: The vertical furrow of the cheek by the corner of the mouth. It is posterior to the mandibular sulcus.

h. **Mandibular sulcus**: The furrow beneath the jawline that rises vertically on the cheek.

i. ***Labial sulci** (furrows of age): The vertical furrows of the lip extending from within the mucous membranes into the integumentary lips.

j. **Platysmal sulci**: The transverse (horizontal), dipping furrow of the neck.

k. **Cords of the neck**: Vertical prominence of the neck.

NOTE: *The labial sulci, are acquired vertical furrows that extend from the upper and lower mucous membranes into the superior and inferior integumentary lips. These wrinkles are usually formed by overuse of the obicularus oris muscle by smokers or in people who pucker their lips excessively, like wind instrument players.

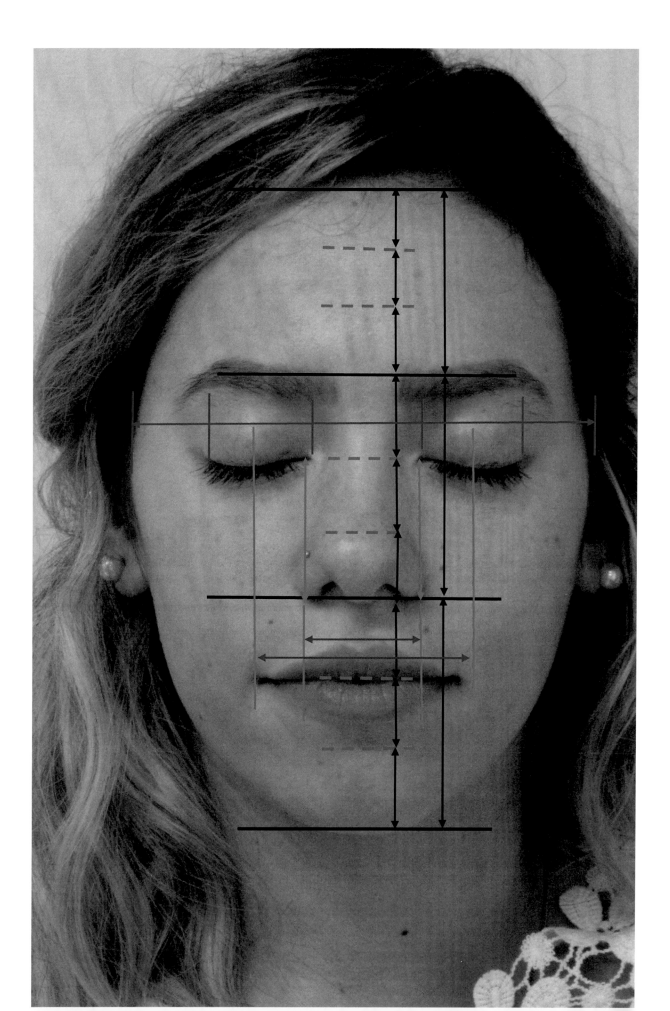

Facial Proportions

1. Applications to restorative art:
    a. To make comparisons between features and photographs and/or between remaining features.
    b. Similarities in the size of features.
    c. Differences in size relationships.
    d. Derivations of size and form in the absence of photographs.

2. Horizontal lines:
    a. The Vertex of the cranium to the line of eye closure is one-half the length of the head.
    b. The base of the chin to the base of the nose is $1/3$ the length of the face.
    c. Line of eye closure: ½ the length of the head, ½ the way between the tip of the nose and the natural hairline.
    d. The normal hairline to the upper border of the eyebrow is $1/3$ the length of the face.
    e. The eyebrow and the top of the ear are on the same horizontal plane.
    f. The base of the nose and the base of the earlobe are on the same horizontal plane.
    g. The line of closure of the lips is ½ the distance from the base of the nose to the labiomental sulcus.
    h. The superior border of the chin is ½ the distance from the line of lip closure to the point of the chin.
    i. Each 1/3 section of the can be divided into 1/3. The total length of the face could be described as $9/9^{th}$, and each individual section can be divided into thirds.
    $3/3 + 3/3 + 3/3 = 9/9^{th}$. The distance from the normal hairline to the Labiomental sulcus, for example, would be $8/9^{th}$.

3. Vertical lines:
    a. The medial end of each closed eye.
    b. Extension from the medial end of each eye to the wing of the nose.
    c. Lateral corner of each closed eye.
    d. Each side of the face, as located in the photograph.
    e. Extension from the middle of each eye to the corners of the mouth.

4. Proportional relationships:
    a. Measurements employing the length from the base of the nose to the eyebrow as a unit of size: Length of the ear, corner of the eye to the external auditory meatus, eyebrow to the natural hairline, and the tip of the nose to the tip of the chin are all the **same length as the base of the nose to the eyebrow**. The face is three noses long.

    b. Measurements employing the width of the close eye as a unit of size: The face is five eyes wide. The wings of the nose are one eye wide. At the inner canthus, the eyes are one eye apart.

    c. Measurements that can be employed in the restoration of a mouth: The mouth is two eyes wide and located $1/3$ the distance from the tip of the nose to the tip of the chin and $2/3$ the distance from the tip of the chin to the tip of the nose. It is ½ the distance from the tip of the nose to the labiomental sulcus.

    d.   All measurements can be employed in the restoration of an eye.

5.   Additional measurements:
      a. Width of the face: $^2/_3$ the length of the face.
      b. The length of the head is divided into equal halves drawn at the line of the eye closure.
      c. Height of an adult measured in head lengths: 7 or 8 heads tall (7 ½).
      d. Supplemental equalities:
         1) Ear-passage to the tip of the nose = $^2/_3$ the length of the face.
         2) Eyebrow to the base of the chin = $^2/_3$ length of the face.
         3) Hairline to the base of the nose = $^2/_3$ length of the face.
         4) Width of the face from ear-passage to ear-passage = $^2/_3$ length of the face.

Using A Photograph:

Compare values of snapshots with professional portraits: A photograph (or painting) in which the subject has been posed and lighted flatteringly by a professional photographer (or artist). Snapshots can be deceiving, especially in the age of Smartphones, which allow the photographs to be manipulated. Sometimes the angle of the camera phone will distort the facial feature. Professional portraits are better because the lighting is controlled. However, even these types of photos can be altered to remove facial features such as wrinkles. Digital images produce high-definition images and are easy to transfer electronically. The advantage of receiving multiple digital images is that the restorative artist can compare and contrast multiple images to develop a basic understanding of similar facial characteristics. Inversion of a photograph is a technique used by embalmers and restorative artists to obtain a different perspective of the subject. This procedure is used in order to detect asymmetry forms that may exist that could be overlooked by just viewing the deceased from the right side. The inversion view allows the restorative artist to determine bilateral symmetry and fix imperfections that could occur when applying wax or cosmetics.

There is value in using a photograph with a three-quarter view image. Such a photo allows us to see the facial view in its fullness with the degree of convexity of the cheeks as it relates to the other facial features. A profile view is ideal for determining projections and depressions of facial features, such as the forehead, chin, nose, and mouth. However, such a profile view lacks determining convexness in proportion to the other facial features. Frontal view photos are ideal for hair style and application of makeup and can be used to determine length and width relationships of facial features.

Lighting is important when using photos because it helps to determine highlights and shadows on the face. The interpretation of these highlights and shadows in a photograph allows the restorative artist to clarify the natural prominences, cavities, and depressions on the face. According to Fritch (2020), "**Normal lighting *[is] a source of lighting from above the head that allows the prominences that have the greatest projections to reflect the greatest amount of light and the deeper areas to reflect little light.* Directional lighting *simply means lighting those travels in a specific direction… it highlights a specific object.*** While considering the human face, directional lighting may misrepresent normal light and dark areas. Flat lighting is lighting that produces minimal contrast in the scene, which means there is very little contrast between highlights and shadows (Fritch, pp.123 &124).

Highlights are defined as surfaces that lie at right angles to the source of illumination that reflect the maximum amount of light, the brighter or whiter part. A shadow, however, is defined as a surface that does not lie at right angles to the source of illumination or is obscured by other surfaces and which reflects little or no light.

Reference to a Photograph:
   a. Compare values of snapshots with professional portraits: A photograph (or painting) in which the subject has been posed and lighted flatteringly by a professional photographer (or artist).
   b. Values of the three-quarter view photograph:
      1) Suggest the form of the profile.
      2) Reveal the degree of fullness of the cheeks.
   c. Value of the profile view.
   d. *Inversion* of the photograph for detection of asymmetry: **Inversion** - Tissues turned in an opposite direction or folded inward. **Asymmetry** - Lack of symmetry or proportion; similarity without identity.
   e. ***Highlight and Shadow***:
      1) Highlight defined: Surface lying at right angles to the source of illumination that reflects the maximum amount of light; the brighter or whiter part.

      2) Shadow defined: Surfaces that do not lie at right angles to the source of illumination or are obscured by other surfaces and which reflect little or no light.

      3) Interpretation of the highlights and shadows of the photograph in their proper relationship to the natural prominences, cavities, and depressions of the face:
         a) Under normal lighting.
         b) Under directional lighting (light source directed up or down).
         c) Under flat lighting (direct lighting from the front).

Basic Facial Profiles

There are three Basic Facial Profiles:
      Convex: Curved evenly; resembling a segment of the outer edge of a sphere. profiles. The forehead recedes posteriorly from the eyebrows, while the chin recedes from the upper lip. ***This is the most common of facial profiles.***

      Concave: Having a spherically depressed or hollow surface. The forehead protrudes beyond the eyebrows and the chin also protrudes beyond the lips. This facial profile is also known as the **infantine retrousse plane** which is ***the least common of facial profiles.***

      Vertical (balanced): Perpendicular to the plane of the horizon, balanced. The chin, forehead and upper lip are all on an even linear plane. No one facial feature is protruded or recedes more than another.

136

Variations of Facial Profiles

Based off the three basic linear profile forms, there are six variations of facial profiles that combine two profiles. These combination profiles always begin at the forehead and end at the chin. Be careful when answering questions regarding variations of facial profiles on the NBE. If the question describes the chin first and the forehead second, remember to always start from the forehead and end at the chin to arrives at the correct answer. There are six variations:

1. **Convex-Vertical:** Forehead recedes from the eyebrows and the chin remains on a balanced or vertical plane.
2. **Convex-Concave:** Forehead recedes from the eyebrows and the chin protrudes beyond the upper lip.
3. **Concave-Convex:** The forehead protrudes beyond the eyebrows and the chin recedes beyond the upper lip.
4. **Vertical-Convex:** The forehead and eyebrows are on an even vertical plane and the chin recedes beyond the upper lip.
5. **Convex-Vertical:** The forehead recedes from the eyebrows while the chin is on a balanced or vertical plane from the upper lip.
6. **Vertical-Concave:** The forehead and the eyebrows are on a balanced or vertical plane and chin protrudes beyond the upper lip.

Frontal View of the Face

There are 7 head shapes from a frontal view. Bone structure, cartilage and other tissue, in addition to the placement of the features, serve to define the general characteristics of each shape.

1. **Oval:** Egg-shaped in form, *this head shape is the most common.* The cheekbones are wider than the cranium and the cranium is slightly wider than the lower jaw. The entire face appears to be soft, rounded and curved.
2. **Round:** *Infantine face.* Short, with full cheeks and rounded appearance. The jawline is slightly fuller and the cranium is rounder.
3. **Square:** Appears to be short and composed of straight lines. The forehead, jawline and cheeks are approximately the same in width. The hairline is often straight.
4. **Inverted Triangle:** This facial form is significantly narrower at the jawline and wider at the cheekbones and the forehead. The forehead is the widest feature on the face. Eyes are wide set.
5. **Triangle:** Of all the head shapes, *this is the least common.* The face appears slightly wider at the jawline than at the cheekbones and forehead. The forehead is the narrowest feature. Eyes are closer together. Some babies, immediately after birth, have this head shape until the frontal and parietal bones relax and flatten out.
6. **Diamond:** Characterized by the wide cheekbones and narrow forehead and jawline, this facial form is widest across the cheeks.

7. **Oblong**: This facial form is like the oval shaped head but it is longer and narrower. The forehead and the chin may be rounded or square in formation. The nose is usually proportionately long.

Facial Shapes	Corrective Contouring to make the Face Appear More Oval
Round	Lighten the cheeks and darken the forehead & jawline.
Inverted Triangle	Lighten the chin & jawline, Darken the sides of the forehead and temples, lighten the cheeks slightly.
Triangular	Lighten the sides of the forehead & darken the sides of the jawline.
Oblong	Darken the chin and top of the forehead & lighten the cheeks slightly.
Diamond	Lighten the sides of the forehead, temples and jawline, & darken the cheeks.
Square	Darken the sides of the forehead & chin and lighten the cheekbones.

Ear (Pinna)

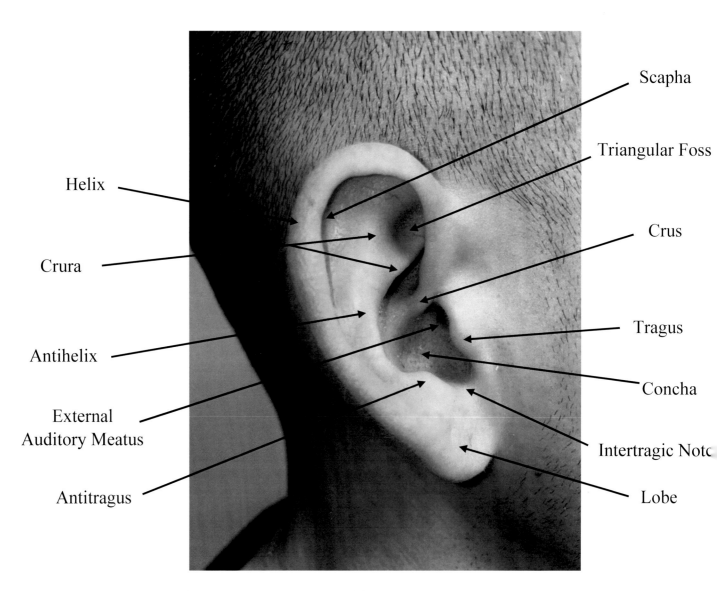

138

The ear, or pinna (the Latin word for wing), is the lateral external features of the face that are a part of the auditory system. The design of the ear is to protect the external auditory meatus. The ear facilitates the collection of sound so that the internal mechanisms of the ear can process the signals as part of the hearing process. The ear is composed of cartilage and is attached to the side of the face with connective tissue.

The ear is on an even horizontal plane with the eyebrow and the base of the nose. Thus, the ear is one-third the length of the face. Also, from ear one passage to the other ear passage is two-thirds the length of the face. The back of the ear is on an even plane with the angle of the mandible. From the tip of the nose to the external auditory meatus is the same distance from ear-to-ear.

Restoration of an ear begins with a firm and dry tissue. The question mark-shaped design should be matched to either a photo or the undamaged ear. The most common restoration for the ear is the treatment of discoloration (post-mortem staining). During the embalming process, most stains can be removed through massage and pinching of the ear tissue. The remaining stained tissue can be treated with a phenol-based compress, secured with plastic stretch wrap. The ear is a warm color area of the face, and during the cosmetizing process, this factor should be taken into account, as well as hair placement.

Parts of the Ear:

a. **Crus of the Helix:** ***The origin of the helix, which is flattened in the concha.***

b. **Helix:** ***the outer most rim of the ear.*** The helix begins at the crus, ascends toward the arch of the helix, then descends and terminates at the lobe of the ear. The helix is a question mark in shape.

c. **Antihelix:** ***the inner rim of the ear.*** The antihelix lies parallel to the descending helix.

d. **Scapha:** ***a fossa between the inner and outer rims of the ear. It is the shallowest depression of the ear.***

e. **Crura of the Helix:** ***the superior and anterior bifurcation branches of the antihelix of the ear.*** The bifurcation forms a triangular depression known as the *triangular fossa.*

f. **Triangular Fossa:** ***depression between the crura of the ear. It is the second deepest depression of the ear.***

g. **Concha:** ***(Latin for shell) the concave shell of the ear. It is the deepest depression of the ear.*** The function of the concha is to funnel sound into the ear canal.

h. **External Auditory Meatus:** ***(meatus is Latin for opening) the opening or passageway of the ear.*** Sound enters the external auditory meatus, which is the beginning of the ear canal.

i. **Tragus:** *an elevation that serves to protect the ear passage (external auditory meatus).*

j. **Antitragus:** *A small eminence obliquely opposite the tragus on the superior border of the lobe of the ear.*

k. **Intertragic Notch:** *the notch between the tragus and the antitragus of the ear.* This is also known as the spillway of the ear. Its shape resembles a spillway.

l. **Lobe:** *The inferior fatty 1/3 of the ear.* Its anterior margin can either be attached or detached from the lateral part of the face.

Nose

The nose is the most anterior part of the face. It projects outward and is the beginning part of the respiratory system. The nose is one of the most identifiable features on the face, and while there are racial similarities, each nose is unique in form, shape, and appearance. There are pathological conditions that will distort the shape of the nose, such as rhinophyma (Greek word for nose growth), which is a common nasal feature in alcoholics.

The Latin word for the nose is rhine and is sometimes spelled rrhine. The nose is classified by the nasal index and the profile classifications. Each nose has a unique racial index that is ancestrally determined based on the family origin (anthropological). The front view determines the racial index, while the side view determines the profile classification. Note: People who are of interracial descent may have a combination of various nasal indexes and profiles.

Nasal Index:
a. **Leptorrhine:** (Lepto is Latin for thin, fine, or slight) *A classification given to a nose that is long, narrow and high bridge.* This nose index is common in people who are Caucasians.
b. **Messorrhine:** (Messo is Latin for middle and the Greek word for between or intermediate) *A classification given to a nose that is medium broad and medium low bridge.* This nose index is common in people of Asian descent.
c. **Platyrrhine:** (Platya is the Latin word for flat or broad) A *classification given to a nose that is short, broad and has a minimum projection.* This nose index is common in people of African descent.

Profile classifications:
a. **Straight Nasal Profile (Grecian):** *A nasal profile in which the dorsum exhibits a straight line from the root to the tip of the nose.* This is the most common of nasal profiles.
b. **Convex Nasal Profile (Roman, Aquiline, or Hooked):** *A nasal profile that exhibits an outward hump or bump on the bridge;* it may appear as a curved or hooked shape in the linear form of the nose.
c. **Concave Nasal Profile** *(snub, pug, infantine, retroussé): A depressed nasal form that may dip concavely from the root to the tip of the nose; dips concavely.* Very common nasal form in infants.

Anatomy of the Nose:
1. **Nasal bones:** Directly inferior to the glabella, they form a dome over the superior portion of the nasal cavity; triangular form.
2. **The nasal spine of the maxilla** – indicates bony length.
3. Major cartilage of the nose –
    a. **Septum:** *Vertical cartilage dividing the nasal cavity into two chambers, responsible for asymmetry of the nose;* the right chamber is slightly larger.
    b. Lateral cartilages: Toward the sides of the nose.
    c. **Cartilage**: *a specialized type of connective tissue: attached to the ends of bones and forming parts of structures, such as the nasal septum and the framework of the ear.*

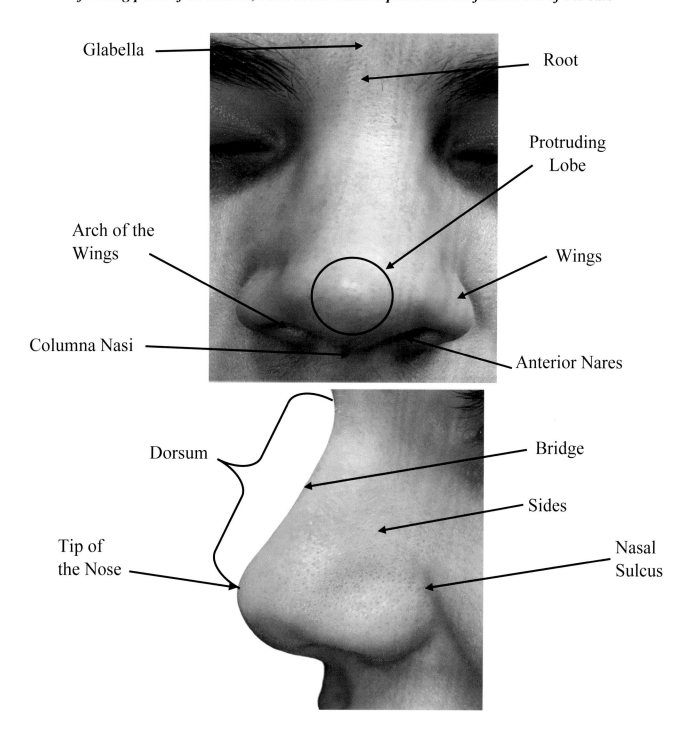

Parts of the Nose:

    a.   **Dorsum:** *Back; the protruding ridge of the nose.* The anterior ridge of the nose, from the root to the tip on the lobe of the nose.

    b.   **The root of the nose:** *The apex (top) of the pyramidal mass of the nose, which lies directly inferior to the forehead; The concave dip inferior to the glabella (profile view).*

    c.   **Bridge of the nose:** *A raised support as the arched portion of the nose which is supported by the nasal bone and 2) is structure or span connecting two parts of a mutilated bone.*

    d.   **Protruding Lobe:** *The rounded, anterior projection of the tip of the nose.*

    e.   **Tip:** *The extremity of anything which tapers (e.g., the tip of the nose termination of the forward projection of the nose).*

    f.   **Wings:** *Lateral lobes of the nose* that lie between the Protruding Lobe and medial to the cheeks.

    g.   **Arch of the wing:** *Inferior margin of the nasal wing, which forms a distinct concave arc superiorly.*

    h.   **Columna nasi:** *The medial partition between the nostrils.* The fleshy termination of the nasal septum at the base of the nose; The most inferior part of the mass of the nose.

    i.   **Sides of the Nose:** *Lateral walls of the nose.* The sides of the nose lie between the wings and the bridge.

    j.   **Nasal Sulcus:** *the angular area between the posterior margin of the wing of the nose and the nasolabial fold;* This is a natural facial marking.

    k.   **Anterior nares:** *The external openings of the nostril.* It is separated by columna nasi.

    l.   **Glabella:** *Located between the superciliary arches and the inferior part of the frontal bone at the root of the nose.*

Restoration of the Nose:

Restoration efforts on the nose need to be done with extreme care and should appear natural. Nasal distortions are the most typical form of restoration that needs to be done. Depending on how the person died, the nose may not be in normal form. Prior to the embalming process, a misshapen nose can be straightened by placing a small amount of absorbing cotton in the anterior nares to reestablish the nasal shape. Massage cream should also be applied prior to embalming to re-hydrate the nasal tissue.

People who have emaciated noses can be filled with tissue builders. This type of restoration needs to be approached with extreme caution because emaciated nasal tissue is very fragile, and if the needle is inserted at the wrong angle, it will puncture through the outer wall of the nose. To fill-out the wings of the nose, insert the needle in the posterior part of the anterior nares and inject it towards the wing of the nose. To fill the lobe of the nose, insert the needle in the tip of the nose and inject upward, smoothing out the tissue builder to the sides and on the bridge. As the needle is withdrawn, pull back on the plunger of the syringe to create a vacuum and prevent leaking from the point of injection. A small ball of cotton with water will stop leaking from the point of injection.

Abrasions or scabs should not be removed until after the embalming process. After embalming, the scabs can be removed, and a phenol or cavity pack should be applied to further dry the tissue. Once cauterized, medium or straw wax mixed with cosmetics (one hue lighter than the skin tone) can be applied to the damaged area. The wax should be smoothed, followed by blending cosmetics to conceal the restored area. **The key to all restoration of facial features is to have firm and dry tissue in order for the wax and cosmetics to adhere to the skin tissue.**

Preventative measures used when shipping human remains to tropical areas, especially during the summer months: Some embalmers soak absorbing cotton with lamp oil and insert it in both nostrils to prevent the invasion of maggots prior to or during the shipping process. Petroleum-based products retard maggot infestation.

Mouth

The mouth is located in the lower one-third of the face. While the eyes are the center of focus for the living, the mouth is the center of focus for the dead. Proper positioning of the mouth and the color of the lips is one of the major factors in customer satisfaction. The shape of the mouth is that of the hunter's bow (p. 12). The mouth is asymmetrical to each person because of the shape and facial markings around the lips. The differences that create the unique characteristics of the mouth are the primary concern of the embalmer and restorative artist. Facial hair, for example, is just as important to create the natural appearance of the mouth as setting the features. For this reason, permission should be obtained before removing facial hair from the deceased.

There are various deviations from normal mouth closure. **Prognathism** *is a term to describe the positional relationship of the mandible and/or maxilla to the skeletal base where either of the jaws protrude beyond a predetermined imaginary line in the sagittal plane of the skull.*

There are five types of prognathism:

a. **Infranasal prognathism:** A form of prognathism in which the base of the nasal cavity project forward abnormally.
b. **Maxillary prognathism:** A form of prognathism in which *the superior jaw protrudes forward abnormally.*
c. **Mandibular prognathism:** A form of prognathism in which *the inferior jaw protrudes forward abnormally.*
d. **Dental prognathism** (buck teeth): A form of prognathism in which *a tooth or teeth protrudes obliquely forward abnormally.*
e. **Alveolar prognathism:** an abnormal protrusion of the alveolar process(es).

Parts of the Mouth

Superior Integumentary Lip

Angulus Oral Eminence

Superior Mucous Membrane

Philtrum

Nasal Labial Sulcus

Labial Sulci

Line of closure

Angulus Oris Sulcus

Inferior Integumentary Lip

Inferior Mucous Membrane

Linear Sulci

Labiomental Sulcus

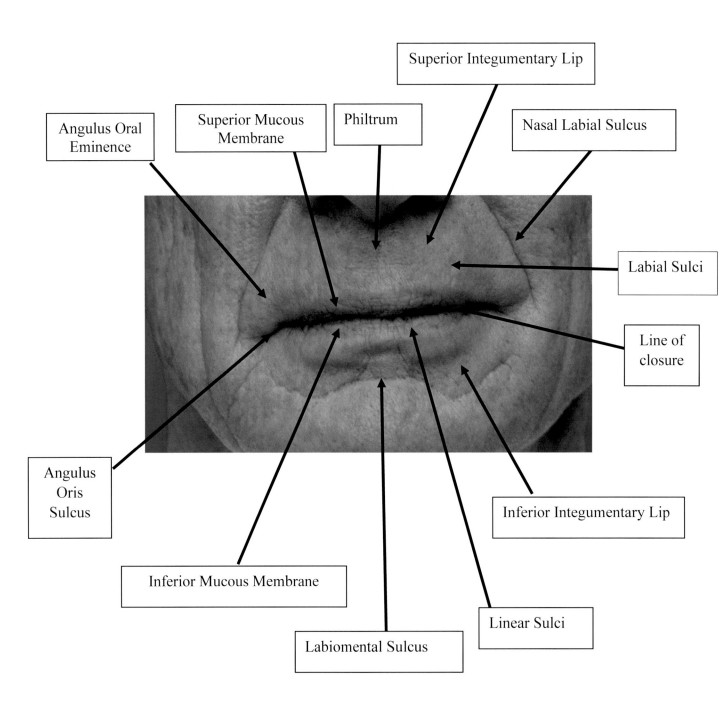

Parts of the Mouth

a. **Mucous membranes:** *The visible red surfaces of the lips; the lining membrane of body cavities that communicate with the exterior.* The superior membrane is "less red" than the inferior.

b. **Medial lobe:** *A tiny prominence on the mid-line of the superior mucous membrane.*

c. **Line of closure** (hunting bow or Cupid's Bow): *The line that forms between two structures, such as the lips, when they are in a closed position and which marks their place of contact with each other.*

d. **Weather lines:** *The line of color changes at the junction of the wet and dry portions of the mucous membranes.*

e. **Superior Integumentary Lip:** *The portion between the base of the nose and the superior margin of the superior mucous membrane.*

f. **Nasal Sulcus:** *The angular area between the posterior margin of the wing of the nose and the nasolabial fold;* a natural facial marking.

g. **Philtrum:** *The vertical groove located medially on the superior lip;* A natural facial marking

h. **Inferior Integumentary Lip:** *The part between the inferior margin of the inferior mucous membrane and the mental eminence.*

i. **Labiomental Sulcus:** *The junction of the inferior integumentary lip and the superior boarder of the chin, which may appear as a furrow.* A natural facial marking.

j. **Surface Planes:** *The central and two lateral surface planes of each Integumentary lip and Mucous Membrane:* Bilaterally repeat the horseshoe curvature of underlying structures.

k. **Angulus Oris Eminence:** *The small, convex prominence lateral to the end of the line of lip closure of the mouth;* A natural facial marking.

l. **Angulus Oris Sulcus:** *The groove at each end of the line of closure of the mouth;* A natural facial marking.

m. **Vertical (Linear) sulci**: The fine linear lines on the mucous membranes (lips). These are natural facial markings.

n. **Labial Sulci:** *The vertical furrows of the lips extending from within the mucous membranes into the integumentary lips.* These are acquired facial markings that develop by excessive pursing of the lips. Common in smokers and people who use wind instruments.

Restoration of the Mouth:

Creating a natural appearance of the mouth begins with setting the features prior to the embalming process. There are various ways of setting features to create the Cupid's bow shape that is convex and properly aligned with other facial features. The mouth will exhibit many concave depressions because of death. While some of these concavities will correct themselves during the embalming process as the fluids swell the integumentary lips, the depressions should be treated pre-embalming with a small amount of cotton strategically placed underneath the lip where the depressions occur. Overfilling the mouth with cotton will distort the normal appearance of the mouth. To bring up the nasolabial fold, insert cotton in the superior and posterior parts of the mouth towards the cheeks. This will give form to the cheeks and define the nasolabial sulcus. The bottom lip is posterior and slightly behind the upper lip.

A missing tooth (or teeth): If a tooth is missing, the use of mastic putty (a/k/a mortuary putty) could fill the gap created by the missing tooth. Some embalmers use cotton or Webril to fill the gap.

When dentures are provided and if they create a natural mouth closure appearance, the dentures should be cleaned and disinfected prior to insertion. The location of the wires should be between the incisor teeth. Attach the closure wires first, with a needle injector (on the left side, if possible), then insert the top denture first, followed by the bottom plate. Close the mouth tightly by holding the mandible while twisting the wires. After snipping the end of the twisted bottom wires, tuck the wire underneath a tooth. Apply cotton over the wires if it creates a line of demarcation on the integumentary lips. If dentures are not present prior to embalming, the use of a mouth former or cotton can be used to recreate normal mouth closure. If the dentures are present post embalming, clean and place the dentures under the pillow of the deceased. Inserting dentures post-embalming will disrupt the natural appearance created during the embalming process.

When creating the natural closure of the lips and creating a normal line of closure of the mouth, stay cream may be used to bring the two mucous membranes together. Stay cream and moisturizer cream will prevent dehydration of the lips post-embalming. Prior to cosmetizing the lips, stay cream or excessive amounts of moisturizer cream should be removed. If a gap is created when removing the creams, a liquid adhesive can be applied at the weather lines, and the lips can them be brought together. For the liquid adhesive to stick, the lips must be clean and dry. Any moisture on the lips will prohibit the adhesive from adhering to the surfaces. Excessive amounts of liquid adhesive, on the other hand, will create a white crustation on the lips and in the corners of the mouth. This crustation needs to be removed prior to cosmetizing the lips.

Distention or swelling of the lips is common in putrefaction cases or in people who have had medical treatment resulting in an over-saturation of the tissue with fluids. Various dehydrating chemicals can be used to reduce the swelling during the embalming process. In addition to using these chemicals, external pressure can be applied to the lips to manipulate the fluid out of the tissue. Channeling with a 16-gauge needle can also assist in pushing the fluids out of the tissue. The insertion of the needle should be done on the lateral corners of the mouth.

Tissue gas will also cause distention and should be treated using various chemicals (such as SanVeino 8 oz per gal or 16oz per gal of DiSpray) as a co-injection.

Treatment of swelling could cause wrinkles. The use of an electric spatula is sometimes used to iron out the wrinkles or dehydrate the liquids in the facial tissue. The key to using an electric spatula is to use copious amounts of massage cream on the face and make even strokes, moving the cream from one point to another. The lack of a sufficient amount of cream on the areas being ironed will result in the burning of the facial tissue, creating a new set of RA problems that will need to be addressed.

Finally, as a last resort, surgical reduction of the distended tissue can be performed. However, the excision of swollen tissue is an invasive procedure and needs to have written permission prior to starting the procedure.

Most Common Lip Restoration

Restoring the lips to a natural appearance requires taking the facial measurements into consideration (See pp. 134-135). The width of the mouth is two eyes wide. A common restoration of the mouth is treating a distended mouth. The corners of the mouth should align with the center of the eyes. Excess width can be reduced by applying small amounts of medium or straw wax to the excessive corners. Cosmetics should be applied to the wax, one skin tone lighter than the complexion of the decease.

If the line of closure is too large, this can be reduced by using small amounts of lip wax (soft wax).

Dehydrated lips can be treated with hypodermic tissue building. The needle should be inserted posterior to the weather line.

Cosmetizing the lips should be adjusted to adhere to personal preferences. Natural lip tone is a soft red for women. Male lip tone is a mixture of red, flesh tone and brown for Caucasians. People of African descent are rose-mocha in color.

Eye

General characteristics of the Eye

The eye is located in the middle one-third of the face. While the eyes are the central focus in humans in life, in death, they are an expression of repose. Improperly placed eye lids, prior to the embalming process, could create a sense of unrest in the deceased. *The upper eyelid is 50% larger than the lower eyelid. Proper closure of the eyelid is in the lower one-third of the eye orbit.* The eye is in the shape of an almond and is roughly the same size from birth. The eye grows during the first two years of development, then again during adolescents, and finally reaches its maximum growth at age 21. The eye is an important tool of measurement for the restorative artist. The width of the eye is equal to the width of the nose. The mouth is two eyes wide. The face, from the zygomatic arch-to-zygomatic arch, is five eyes wide. Two-thirds of the length of the face is five eyes wide. From the normal hairline to the base of the nose is the same distance from zygomatic arch-to-zygomatic arch.

The eye itself is spherical in form. The profile view is triangular in shape. The eye is approximately twice as wide as it is tall. The point of greatest projection for a closed eye is just off-center medially. The lower eye lid is narrower and thinner than the upper eyelid. It follows the curvature of the eyeball and inclines from the line of closure. The upper eyelid overlaps the lower eye lid at the lateral end of the lower eyelid; The upper eyelid has more eyelashes than the lower eyelid. The Latin term for eyelid is palpabrae.

The superior boney margin of the orbital rim, otherwise known as the orbital process, is formed by the frontal bone. The roof of (the superior wall of the eye orbit) is formed primarily by the orbital plate of the frontal bone also the lesser wing of the sphenoid bone near the apex of the eye orbit.

Parts of the Eye

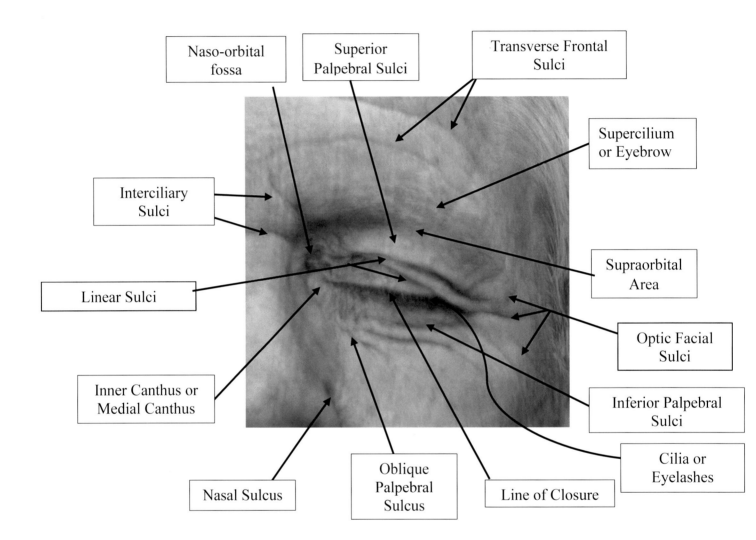

Naso-orbital fossa

Superior Palpebral Sulci

Transverse Frontal Sulci

Supercilium or Eyebrow

Interciliary Sulci

Supraorbital Area

Linear Sulci

Optic Facial Sulci

Inner Canthus or Medial Canthus

Inferior Palpebral Sulci

Cilia or Eyelashes

Nasal Sulcus

Oblique Palpebral Sulcus

Line of Closure

The Latin word for eyelid is *Palpebrum* (*Palpebral* is an adjective and *Palperbrae* is a noun). The upper eyelid is called the Superier Palpebral and the lower eyelid is known as the Inferior Palpebral. The upper eyelid is twice the size as the lower eyelid. The eyelids meet in the lower 1/3 of the eye orbit.

Not shown in this photo is an orbital pouch which is also known as "bags under the eyes." This is a fullness protrusion underneath the inferior palpebral sulcus and oblique palpebral sulcus.

Parts of the Eye

    a. **Nasal orbital fossa:** *A depression superior to the medial portion of the superior palpebrae.*

    b. **Supraorbital area:** *The superior rim of the eye socket.* It is the region between the supercilium and the superior palpebrae.

    c. **Inner canthus:** A *small elevation extending medially and obliquely from the medial corner of the superior palpebrae.* When the eyes are closed, the lips of the "well" at the medial end make contact and form a tiny, oblique eminence. It "seems" to extend from the upper eyelid because it projects more than the lower.

    d. **Cilia:** *Eyelashes; the fringe of hair edging the eyelids*

       1) Characteristics: Come together but do not interlace. Hairs on the upper lid are more numerous, longer, and curve upward. Lower lid curve downward. Very asymmetrical.

       2) Restoration: Various lengths, thick clusters, sparse areas, and non-parallelism. No hair emits from the medial or lateral ends of the eyelids.

    e. *Supercilia: **Eyebrow.***

       1) Characteristics: Diminishes as it moves laterally. Inclines inferiorly as it moves toward the side of the head. The lateral end is pointed toward the ear passage. Eyebrow grows upward and laterally. The head of the eyebrow is on an even vertical plane with the inner canthus and the wing of the nose. The body of the eyebrow has fewer hairs than the head and eventually tapers off towards the tail. The tail has the fewest hairs of the eyebrow.

       2) Restoration: Restoration of missing parts or the entire eyebrow should keep in mind the anatomy of how the eyebrow grows. The recommended procedure for replacing parts or the entire eyebrow is to apply a small layer of surface wax (cosmetize to the skin tone of the individual, and beginning at the head of the eyebrow, apply small amounts of hairs (using spring forceps) for each application. Overlap the hairs and apply fewer and fewer as the restoration develops laterally. Trim excess hairs, if necessary.

    f. Associated facial markings (parts of the closed eye):

       1) **Superior Palpebral and Inferior Palpebral:** *The upper and lower eyelids that recede convexly downward.*

       2) **Superior and Inferior Palpebral Sulcus: a. Superior Palpebral Sulcus:** *The furrow on the superior border of the upper eyelid.* **b. Inferior Palpebral Sulcus:** *The furrow on the inferior border of the lower eye lid.* These are acquired furrows of the attached margin of the upper or lower eyelid.

       3) **Oblique Palpebral Sulcus:** *A shallow curving groove below the medial corner of the inner canthus.* This is a natural marking.

       4) **Optic Facial Sulci:** *The furrows radiating from the lateral corner of the eye.* This is also known as "Crow's feet." This is an acquired facial marking.

       5) **Orbital Pouch:** *bags under the eyes; the fullness between the inferior palpebrae and the oblique palpebrae sulcus.* This is an acquired facial marking.

6) **Linear Sulci:** *Eyelid furrows that are short and broken, which run horizontally on the palpebrae and which may fan from both the medial and lateral corners of the eyes.*

Restoration of the Eye(s)

Sunken eyes:

1) Support of the eyelids. Over extended periods of time, the eyeball will become sunken as a result of the lack of pressure from normal vascular circulation. When treating sunken eyes, in the beginning, less is more. Depending on the amount of time that has lapsed and the pressure and flow of the fluid during the embalming process, sunken eyes could return to their natural form. The first treatment would be to disinfect the eye orbit and exterior eyelids. Then apply eye caps with a small amount of stay cream on the exterior of the cap. After embalming and if the eyes remain sunken slightly, a small amount of cotton or mortuary putty can be applied to the back of the eye cap to raise the form of the eye to an appropriate level.

2) Hypodermic tissue building. This is a procedure by which tissue builder is injected posteriorly in the back of the eye orbit to bring the eyeball forward. The key to doing this procedure is to raise the eyeball without puncturing it, causing leakage of the vitreous humor. With a hypodermic syringe, insert the needle along the lateral margin of the eye socket. Once at the curve of the eye socket, use the needle to push the eyeball medial, then reposition the angle of the needle to continue along the lesser wing of the sphenoid bone. Once the needle is positioned in the posterior and middle of the eyeball, begin to inject tissue fluid slowly until the eyeball is at a proper convexity.

3) Emaciation of the borders of the eye socket can also be treated hypodermically. The objective of this procedure is to provide convexity to the concavity caused by emaciation. As stated above, the concern when doing this procedure is not to puncture the eyeball, which could cause leaking of the vitreous humor fluid. Insert the needle in the lateral part or the eyelid and point it at the medial part of the supraorbital margin. Inject tissue builder slowly while manipulating the fluid around the eye orbit. The same procedure can be applied to the lower eye orbit.

4) Part of the appearance of the eye is the lateral side of the eye, the temporal region. To fill the temporal region with tissue builder, insert the needle at the tail of the eyebrow or in the hairline. Make a series of channels, and then in the middle of the depression, inject tissue builder. As the fluid is being injected, manipulate the fluid outward. This procedure should be done from the top of the head in order to achieve bilateral symmetry. Avoid injecting tissue builder near the lateral part of the eye; this could eliminate the optic facial sulci.

Swollen eyelids:

a.   External pressure: During the embalming process, the eyes and surrounding tissue may begin to distend. Adjusting the rate of flow and applying a water compress (cotton saturated with water) will rectify this issue. External manipulation of the tissue will also reduce swelling in the eyelids.

b.　Cavity fluid compress: Applying a cavity fluid compress will cause dehydration and drying of the eyelids. This is highly recommended in the event of desquamation. The problem with cavity fluid compresses is that they may cause bleaching.

c.　Dehydrating agents: As part of the embalming process, using a dehydrating agent as a pre or co-injection will reduce the amount of excess fluid in the tissue. When using these agents and through a process known as osmosis, the fluid in the tissue is drawn out, which could result in the formation of wrinkles.

d.　Modification of excess wrinkles: Excess wrinkles can either be waxed over or treated with an electric spatula.

e.　Electric spatula: The use of an electric spatula can be used to reduce the swelling of the eye tissue. Caution: copious amounts of massage cream are needed to prevent the burning of the tissue around the eye. In addition, keep the electric spatula away from the eyelids or eyebrows. This device will singe the hair.

f.　Aspiration of blood and serum: Using a 16-gauge needle and a syringe, excess blood or serum can be extracted.

g.　Surgical reduction: Only as a last resort and with expressed written permission from the family, surgical reduction is a way of treating swollen tissue. The process is to remove excess tissue and recreate the natural almond shape of the eye. This process is usually performed in extreme cases with necrotic skin or in severe cases of malformity.

Discolored eyelids:

a. Bleaching: Ecchymosis is a discoloration of the skin resulting from bleeding underneath. This bruising is usually caused by some type of trauma. Pre-embalming, inject a small amount of a bleaching agent subcutaneously and manipulate it outward. During the embalming process, to prevent distension, especially in trauma cases, apply a cavity fluid pack (cover with plastic wrap). The bruised area should turn whitish. This is easier to cosmetize than blueish-purple.

Treatment of protruding eyes:

a. Puncture of the cribriform plate of the ethmoid bone. **Cribriform Plate** - The horizontal plate of the ethmoid bone separates the cranial cavity from the nasal cavity.

b. Aspiration behind the eyeball.

c. Aspiration inside the eyeball.

d. Removal of the vitreous humor of the eyeball. This requires written permission from the family. Vitreous Humor - This liquid or semi-liquid of the body of the eye is known as the aqueous or vitreous humor; it gives shape to the eyeball.

e. Removal of the eyeball. This requires written permission from the family. This procedure requires a skilled and trained eye enucleator. Excessive manipulation of the tissue and muscles around the eye will cause ecchymosis.

Lacerated eyelids:

a. Dry the tissue with a cavity fluid or phenol compress. With liquid adhesive, draw the lacerated area(s) together. Wax over the top of the sealed area(s).

b. Only in extreme cases and with express written permission from the family remove the eyelids and perform the wax restoration. In such cases, if possible, retain the person's eyelashes and reattach them. In most extreme cases, if this procedure needs to be performed, the eyelashes will also need to be reconstructed.

Separated eyelids:

    a.   Liquid adhesives can be applied in small amounts on the posterior margin of the eyelids. Excessive amounts of liquid adhesive will result in a white crusty residue that will need to be removed prior to cosmetology.

    b.   Stretching the eyelids is a manipulation process usually performed with an aneurysm hook underneath the eyelid prior to embalming.

    c.   Incising the levator palpebra superioris (#1). This muscle is located at the top of the eyeball. Incising this muscle will release the eyelid. Over-manipulation of eye muscles could cause ecchymosis.

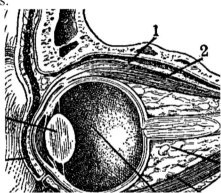

    d.   **Perforated eye cap**: Perforated eye caps have small gripping pieces as part of the cap design. A small amount of stay cream should be placed on the convex part of the eye cap and inserted under the eyelids. A small amount of stay cream should also be placed on the rim of the eyelids and in the inner canthus.

    e.   Total excision and rebuilding with wax: Under very rare circumstances should, the eyelids may be removed, and written permission should be obtained prior to beginning this procedure. If the eyelids are necrotic, they should be removed prior to the application of wax. If the eye is also removed, make sure the eye orbit has been properly cauterized. Rebuild the almond-shape form of the eye with a wound filler (hard wax) in order to establish a foundation for the eyelids. Using very thin layers of medium or straw wax, create overlayments of wax in the shape of the eyelid. Using a lip brush, smooth and shape the eyelids into form. On the final application of wax overlayment, mix a skin tone of color into the wax. Apply the final application; add wrinkles with ligature and the line of demarcation. Synthetic eyelashes should be trimmed prior to installation, remembering that eyelashes don't grow on the medial or lateral ends.

Orbital pouch:

    a.   Reduction by external pressure.

    b.   Aspiration is followed by compresses.

    c.   Electric spatula.

A dehydrated inner canthus can be re-hydrated using an embalming chemical that has humectants. A humectant compress will re-hydrate the inner canthus.

a. Cementing: In the event the inner canthus remains open, apply a small amount of liquid adhesive to the area, and with the back of an aneurysm hook, gently close the gap in the tissue.
b. Waxing: Another way to close the inner canthus gap is by applying a small amount of lip wax to the area and cosmetizing over the top of the application.

Enucleation treatment: There are two types of eye enucleation cases. 1) total eye enucleation, where the entire eyeball is extracted, leaving behind the eye socket, and 2) the extraction of the cornea. This procedure leaves behind the outer shell of the eyeball and the vitreous humor, and other material. This will require the embalmer to remove the vitreous humor and pack the eye with cavity fluid-soaked cotton. Upon completion of the embalming, the eyeball shell is dried and filled with mortuary putty to recreate the shape of the eyeball. An eye cap is placed on top of the eyeball and properly closed.

a. Sealing the cavity: Using a cavity pack in the eye orbit or the eyeball is essential to cauterize the cavity and the small vessels disrupted by the eye enucleation process. During the embalming process, create a normal eye closure with the cavity pack in place.
b. Restoration of contour: Post embalming, remove the cavity pack and use cotton or mortuary putty to reshape the eye contours. Mortuary putty is preferred because cotton has a tendency to wick moisture. An eye cap should also be placed to further aid in the projection of the center of the eye.
c. Closing the eyelids: Apply liquid adhesive to prevent the eye from opening
d. Utilizing prosthetic device: Not recommended. They don't look natural.

General, restorative treatments: The majority of restorative art is the treatment of visible areas of the face and hands. There are other restorative art treatments that are completed to make the human remains presentable for public viewing. This section will discuss various procedures necessary to be taken to create a positive memory picture.

Classification of cases requiring restorative art treatment:
a. Injury: Lacerations, wounds, head trauma, etc.
b. Disease: Cancer tumor, etc.
c. Post-mortem tissue changes: Decomposition, razor burns, etc.

Order of treatments:
a. Pre-embalming treatments: Set features (limbs) in the position desired for viewing, suture any wound. Then inject embalming fluid.
b. Embalming treatments: Use a higher index (astringent) solution for embalming major restorative art cases to fix the tissues in place for further treatment (waxing, etc.). *Only firm and dry tissue can be restored and cosmetized.*
c. Post-embalming treatments: Repair/replace as needed. When cosmetizing, if a procedure such as a liquid opaque is applied to one hand, do the same on the other to keep it bilaterally symmetrical.

Abrasion and laceration treatment:

    a.   Removal of scabs: If a raised scab is present, soften it with Vaseline or massage cream prior to the embalming process. This will moisturize the scab and allow for easy removal after embalming. ***Remove all scabs post-embalming.*** The scab serves as a buffer to fixate surface tissue during the embalming process. A paraformaldehyde pack should be applied post-embalming to dry the surface tissue.

    b.   Creaming unaffected areas: When using astringent solutions, use moisturizer cream on undamaged areas. This will keep as much moisture as possible in the tissues.

    c.   Waxing and reproduction of pores and wrinkles: If present, continue existing sulcus. If not present, replicate the other side of the face.

    d.   Cosmetic application when finished with reconstruction.

Bleaching: Use cavity fluid or Dryene or Phenol base products.

    a.   Discolorations: IV bruises, chemical stains, etc.

    b.   Effect of bleaches:

        1)   On the color of the skin: Lightens. Turns a bruised area from purplish-blue to cloudy white. Bleached tissue is easier to cosmetize than an area with ecchymosis.

        2)   On the moisture content of the skin: Extremely dehydrates the tissue. Moisturizer cream should be applied to re-hydrate the skin tissue. Also, products with high levels of humectants will also hydrate the skin.

        3)   Surface preservation: The use of paraformaldehyde gel or cavity compress will preserve surface tissue. The key in this procedure is to cover the cavity or gel compress with plastic wrap for the chemical to be contained in the area. Excellent preservative qualities. Especially with traumatized areas, these fluids and gels firm surface tissue that may not have received adequate distribution during the embalming process.

    c.   Surface compresses: Cotton soaked with cavity fluid or Dryene or Paraformaldehyde gel. Covering the compress is key to the effectiveness of this procedure.

Hypodermic bleaching: Injecting a bleaching agent subcutaneously under the skin to treat ecchymosis (or bruising) caused by trauma or a medical procedure to an area.

    a.   Reason for possible ineffectiveness: Doesn't uniformly affect tissues, hard and soft spots.

    b.   Caution in using a staining arterial fluid. Don't use an active dye; it will blemish the skin.

    c.   Possible problems: If phenol base products are used, the area needs to be neutralized with 90% isopropyl alcohol, or the bleaching agent area will continue to lighten the bruised area.

    d.   Alternate brush application of phenol (less effective technique).

Burns: There are various reasons that cause burnt tissue. A heat source is the most common thing that causes burns. However, the environment, chemical agents, electrical, and friction also cause burns to human tissue.

Description and characteristics of burns:

      a. 1st Degree: Redness.
      b. 2nd Degree: Blistered skin.
      c. 3rd Degree: Charred skin.
      d. 4th Degree: Exposed bone and muscle tissue.
      e. 5th Degree is total Incineration.

Treatments:

a. **1st Degree Burns:** The **outermost layer of skin is red.** The most common cause of 1st degree burns is the sun. During the embalming process, apply a humectant to the burned area. This will re-hydrate the skin tissue and allow for cosmetics to adhere to the skin. Bleach, if necessary. Subcutaneous injection of a bleaching agent could lighten the severity of the redness; however, it could increase drying of the tissue.

Post-embalming treatment: Use an opaque cosmetic to cover up the redness, followed by a natural skin tone and finishing powder.

b. **2nd Degree Burns:** In addition to **redness, the skin develops a water blister.** This needs to be drained prior to the embalming process, trying to leave the skin attached. Post embalming, the area should be cauterized using a cavity compress. The skin should be reattached with liquid adhesive, if possible. If the skin needs to be removed, the damaged area needs to be sealed with a liquid adhesive, and Derma surgical wax should be applied, followed by cosmetics and finishing powder.

c. **3rd Degree Burns - Deep tissue:** This type of burn damages the dermis tissue. After the embalming process, the burnt tissue needs to be excised, cauterized, and sealed with a liquid adhesive. Derma surgical wax should be applied, followed by cosmetics and finishing powder.

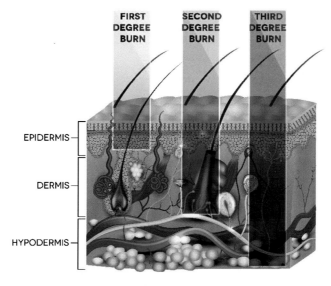

d. **4th Degree Burns Exposes the Muscle and Bone:** This type of burn damages the dermis, muscle and the bone are exposed. After the embalming process, the burnt tissue needs to be excised, cauterized, and sealed with a liquid adhesive. This type of burn may require hard wax or wound filler to be applied prior to the application of surface wax (medium wax), followed by cosmetics and finishing powder. In some cases where the hand is burned to the bone and restoration is not an option, the burned area should still be cauterized, excised, and sealed with a liquid adhesive, then a paraformaldehyde powder should be applied. A latex glove should be applied with shrink wrap on the end. For esthetic reasons, a pallbearer glove should be used to cover up the latex glove.

e. **5th Degree Burns: Total incineration.** The human remains are beyond viewable; however, the remains need to be treated in such a manner that the smell is contained. This procedure is the same procedure for human remains that are non-viewable.

> 1) Most incineration cases will be autopsied. This will alleviate the problem of built-up gases in the abdominal and thoracic cavities. If not autopsied, the abdominal and thoracic cavities will need to be aspirated, followed by injecting 16oz of cavity fluid proximal, and 16oz injected distal, prior to final treatment. Handling of severely incinerated human remains needs to be done with extreme care. Since the organs and integumentary system have been compromised, over-manipulation could result in a biohazard that will need to be contained.
> 2) Place the human remains on a sheet and wrap the remains like a mummy, securing the head and feet with stretch wrap. Pour three bottles of cavity fluid over the remains.
> 3) On another sheet that has paraformaldehyde powder, place the remains on the sheet and put more paraformaldehyde powder on top of the remains. Wrap the remains a second time.
> 4) Place the remains on a large plastic sheet and wrap them again, securing the remains with stretch wrap.
> 5) Place paraformaldehyde powder inside a disaster pouch. Place the human remains in the pouch, followed by more paraformaldehyde powder on top of the remains.
> 6) Zipper the bag: Use liquid adhesive on the zipper to seal the pouch shut.
> 7) Repeat steps 5 & 6.
> 8) Place paraformaldehyde powder on the mattress, then casket the human remains.

Excisions: To remove by cutting out; the area from which something has been cut out.
Incision: A clean linear cut in the tissue or skin.
Laceration: To tear, as into irregular segments.

> a. Temporary suture: Act of sewing; also, the completed stitch. Holds tissue in place for embalming.
> b. Removal of damaged tissue.
> c. Undercutting the edges: Cut deeper than the wax needs to be.
> d. Chemical drying of deep tissues: Hypo injection of the area with cavity fluid.
> e. Sealing: Seal the area with a liquid adhesive.
> f. Deep filling with appropriate materials: Fill a large crater with mortuary putty or wound filler.
> g. Basketweave suture cross-stitching: Weave the stitches in and out of each other.
> h. Wax surfacing and simulation of pores and wrinkles: Match surrounding tissue.

i. Cosmetic adjustments.

Decapitation: The separation of the head from the body; to decapitate is the act of such separation.
- a. Embalming treatment: Embalm the head and torso of the body separately.
- b. Attachment of head to the trunk.
    1) Use of a splint or dowel ($^3/_8$ inch diameter). **Splint** - An appliance of wood, metal, etc., used to keep in place or protect displaced movable parts. Might use a paint paddle held in place with thin wire.
    2) Insertion into foramen magnum: Foramen magnum is much larger than the vertebral column. Drill a hole in the dowel and insert thin wire through the dowel to anchor it in place.
    3) Attachment to spinal column: Insert dowel into the column. Secure with wire.
    4) Alignment of the head.
    5) Suturing muscles.
    6) Deep filling materials.
    7) Surfacing: Wax restoration.

Distensions: Swellings:
- a. Causes:
    1) Embalming.
    2) Decomposition: Tissue gas (*Clostridium perfringens*).
    3) Trauma: A person who has sustained trauma, lives on life supports for a time before they die could result in swelling to the body because of medical intervention.
    4) Pathological condition: Tumors or growths, such as a goiter.

- b. Types:
    1) Liquid: Embalming fluid.
    2) Solid: Tumors.
    3) Semi-solid.
    4) Gaseous: *Clostridium perfringens*. Tissue Gas

- c. Methods of reduction:
    1) External pressure: Carefully pinch the tissue and wrinkle it. Correct with a suture in the posterior surface of the neck.
    2) Other treatments: To kill *Clostridium perfringens* with a chemical (try H_2O_2). 16 oz of Dispray or 8 oz of SanVeino per gallon of arterial fluid will rectify tissue gas (or at least stop it from spreading). Channel the area with a trocar, then apply external pressure to the drain area.
        (a) Lancing and Aspiration: Lance with a scalpel and aspirate with a hypodermic syringe.
        (b) Application of heat: Electric spatula. Be careful not to get too hot.
        (c) Injection of a constricting chemical: Hypo area with cavity chemical.
        (d) Surgical reduction: Excision of tissues must be done before they become firm.

d. Treatment of an un-preserved area: Hypodermic injection of HCHO. May need to excise tissue, but this is not recommended and requires prior approval from the family.

e. Distention in the neck area and be reduced by using a procedure known as channeling and wicking. From the left subclavian to the right subclavian, make a half-moon incision. Separate the connecting tissue with blunt dissection. Using a 16-gauge needle, make channels in the inside neck tissue. Place absorbent cotton in the neck region. Change the cotton every 2 hours or until cotton appears dry. Placing a sand collar around the neck during this process will apply pressure to the area that will further reduce the distention.

Desquamation (skin slip): The separation of the epidermis from the dermis as a result of putrefaction.

a. Preservative treatments: Inject hypodermically, then apply a cavity pack to cauterize the skin back into place.

b. Treatment of exposed and unexposed areas: You may need to remove the skin, and apply adhesive, followed by waxing and cosmetizing.

Neoplasms: Tumors and abscesses, only removed with written permission.

Fracture: Broken bone.

Types of fractured bones:

a. Simple fracture: Fractured bone does not pierce the skin.

b. Compound fracture: Fractured bone pierces the skin.

Treatments: Get bone back under the skin, then suture. Apply plastic and use stretch wrap to hold the bone in place.

a. Resetting: Put everything back into alignment and secure the alignment with a splint and stretch wrap.

b. Wire bridging: The length of wire employed to connect two structures that are undamaged such as the remaining parts of a bone; a wire mesh placed within an aperture to hold other restorative fillers. Use a $1/16$" drill to make holes for wiring.

c. Splinting: You may use paint paddles and stretch wrap.

d. Retraction.

Hair Preparation: At the completion of the embalming operation, wash the hair thoroughly using a quality shampoo and conditioner. Remains with a condition known as cradle cap (dry flakey dead skin on the scalp) is the most common problem in the elderly. Treatment of this condition begins with the application of conditioner at the beginning of the embalming process. After the embalming process is completed, rinse out the conditioner and wash the hair with shampoo. Reapply conditioner and rinse. Hair conditioner is a humectant, and this will re-hydrate the scalp allowing the dead skin flakes to loosen from the hair.

Hair restorations:

a. Sources: Back of the head, beauty supply, barber shops, wigs.

b. Replacement and attachment methods: Glue with rubber cement, liquid adhesive, suturing, wax base, melted wax (candle), and embedding into the skin.

1) Directional growth: Sideburns and beard have vertical hair.
2) Begin at the base of the location of hair replacement. Apply a few hairs at a time to the area. Overlap the next layer and work towards the normal hairline or area where there is normal hair.
3) Trimming and thinning.

c. Scarves, bandages, and wigs: **Bandages**: Sheet, cotton, gauze, or other material used in dressing wounds or wrapping a structure. Place a switch of hair around the edge of the bandage, then cover the rest of the head.
d. Types of hair: curly, straight, light, dark, thick, thin.
e. Sideburns: The growth of hair located anterior of the ears. Directed vertically downward.
f. Mustache: Directed vertically downward. Very irregular. Types: "pencil-line; large, prominent (cookie duster); short, cropped type; curled or "handle-bar."
g. Beard area: The area of the integumentary lips, cheeks, chin, and neck which has hair growth. Types: Goatee, located in the area between the lower mucous membrane and the base of the chin; Vandyke, small beard, confined to the lower part of the face, usually short; Full beard, continues above the short beard, covers the side of each cheek and merges with the sideburn.
h. Eyebrow: *Normal direction is obliquely upward and outward from the lower margin where the hair emerges from the skin* (Very important on the NBE). The "head" lies on the central plane of the forehead; at this position, the hair is only slightly oblique. The "body" lies on both the lateral plane of the forehead and part of the temporal region; the direction becomes more and more oblique as it moves laterally. The "tail" moves obliquely downward and lies on the lateral rim of the eye socket. The tail points to the external auditory meatus.

Hypodermic tissue building:
a. Conditions requiring treatment: Emaciation and sunken tissue.
b. Equipment and materials.
c. Cautions.
d. General procedures.
e. Recommended points of entry: Use a hidden point such as in hair regions, in the nostrils, the corners of the mouth, receded parts of the ears, or the posterior margin in the angle of the jaw.
   1) Sunken eye: Inserted between the lips of the inner canthus at the medial end of the eyelids.
   2) Sunken supraorbital area: Inject tissue filler downward through the eyebrow.
   3) Temples: 5 points: Eyebrow, sideburn, hair of the temple, behind the top of the ear, and behind the anterior part of the helix.
   4) Cheeks: Two opposite points of entry are usually necessary. May use the nostril, corner of the mouth, behind the lobe of the ear, behind the tragus, or behind the upper part of the jaw-line.
   5) Mouth areas: Both ends of the line of closure.
   6) Hands: Points between the knuckles must be deep enough to be hidden from view.
   7) Neck areas.

Severed, missing or twisted limbs: Severed - *To cut or break open or apart; disjoin.* Embalm separately, then reattach the limb.

  a. Treatment of mandibular conditions (dislocation of the jaw):   The TMJ (temporomandibular joint) plays a very important role in this relocation of the jaw.
  b. Penetrating wounds.

Abrasions including razor burn: A darkened, air-dried area on the skin resulting from removal of the epidermis while shaving. **Abrasions**: Antemortem injuries resulting from friction of the skin against a firm object removing the epidermis. Exposure of the dermis to air results in the development of a hard brown surface.

  a. Treatment of scabs: A crust over a sore or wound. Remove scabs post-embalming
  b. Surface stain removers:
      1) Common stain removers.
      2) Solvents for special stains.

Sutures:

  a. Suturing materials: **Ligature: A thread, cord, or wire used for tying vessels, tissues, or bones.** Ligature is used to tie-off (ligate). Suturing thread is used to sew (or bring together) an incision. Thread is commonly used for both.
  b. Reasons for sutures: They may serve one or more purposes:
      1) Hold the borders of an incision together.
      2) Gather and turn under excess tissues.
      3) Hold flaps of skin in position during embalming.
      4) Correct distortion from sagging muscles.
      5) Hold the margin of a deep wound in a fixed position.
      6) Form a mesh to anchor wax.
      7) Anchor deep filler.
      8) Circle and hold the margin of a hole.
      9) Serve as an armature.
      10) Attach a hair switch.

Types of sutures:

  a. The most common suture used among embalmers is the **baseball suture**. The baseball suture provides a very tight and secure closure of an incision if properly created. The suture begins with a locking stitch that secures the thread in place. Then, in a cris-cross fashion, the needle makes suture marks similar to that on a baseball. A double-locking stitch is made at the end of the incision. Finally, the needle is inserted at the base of the suture. pulling the needle through the middle of the incision. This will hide the end of the thread and prevent the wicking of bodily fluids on the clothing.
  b. **Intradermal suture**: A type of suture used to close incisions so that the suture thread remains entirely under the epidermis, a hidden suture.
   1) **Single**: One needle.
   2) **Double**: Two needles, one piece of ligature.
   3) **Purse string**: A series of small stitches through the dermis is made around the circumference of the opening. The ends of the ligature are knotted within the opening, drawing the suture together.

c. **Basketweave suture**: A network of stitches employed to cross the borders of a cavity or excision, used to anchor fillers and to sustain the tissues in their proper position. Interweave the ligature.

d. **Worm suture (inversion, draw stitch):** A method of sewing an incision along the edges without entering the opening whereby the suture becomes invisible and the line of suture becomes depressed, which lends it ease of concealment by waxing.

e. **Bridge or interrupted sutures**: These individual stitches, which are knotted and cut immediately, may be applied before embalming as temporary sutures to hold retracted surface tissues in position.

f. **Loop stitch:** A single, noose-like suture, not pulled taut before knotting, which stands from the skin and anchors restorative materials.

(See Embalming, pp. 24)

Organ and Tissue Recovery Cases: Organ and tissue recovery is a process in which a procurement specialist removes various organs and tissues from deceased human remains. The recovered organs and tissues are then processed and used in transplant cases. This generous donation from the deceased's family saves thousands of lives annually. See embalming section for additional care for Organ and Tissue Recovery Cases (p. 31).

Some of the organs and tissues donated and their use:

a. Blood vessels (usually main arteries like the femoral or brachial) are used in heart-related surgeries

b. Kidneys - Transplant

c. Liver - Transplant

d. Lungs - Transplant

e. Pancreas – Transplant

f. Skin – used in burn cases for skin grafts.

g. Corneas – used in eye surgeries

h. Long Bone. Bone fragments are used in hip and leg replacement surgeries to prevent metallic parts from wearing on bone joints.

i. Others

Restoration after Tissue Recovery: In general, after tissue recovery cases, the human remains should be properly embalmed, as described in the Embalming section of this book. Each organ procurement needs specific treatment to restore the human remains to a viewable condition. In the eye section of this chapter, proper treatment for the eyes was discussed.

Skin Recovery: When skin recovery was first performed several years ago, the epidermis (the outermost layer of skin) was removed with an instrument known as a dermatome. The procurements specialist would remove the skin from the back of the legs, buttocks, and front of the legs. Today, most tissue recovery cases use a process known as deep tissue recovery. This process takes the entire integumentary system down to the peritoneum, and the amount of tissue recovered is now large sections around the abdominal area to the back and large sections of the upper legs.

Restoration Treatment for Tissue Recovery Cases: The human remains should be embalmed as if the skin was intact. There will be some leaking of the embalming fluid during the embalming process. The remains should be aspirated immediately after the embalming process, and 16 oz of cavity fluid should be injected proximal and 16 oz distal. Remains should be placed in a Unionall immediately. Apply cotton to the exposed areas and create a cavity compress. Zipper up the Unionall. Twelve hours later, remove the cotton and apply new cotton with hardened compound and paraformaldehyde powder. Wrap the cotton with absorbent pads and zipper the Unionall. Use liquid adhesive over the zipper to prevent leaking on the clothing.

Cosmetic and Cosmetology

Cosmetology *is the study of beautifying and improving the complexion, skin, hair and nails.* There are several materials and techniques that are used in caring for the dead that utilizes the application of colorants to simulate the natural appearance of the deceased for viewing in the funeral setting. The goal of post-mortem cosmetology is the achievement of a natural, non-cosmetic effect, simulating the appearance of color coming from within the skin. Ornamental cosmetology (beyond the natural skin coloring) applies to the cosmetic embellishment of women (of any age) who wear cosmetics.

Cosmetics are applied to the visible parts of the deceased to achieve the following results:

a. Replace the coloring lost in death, illness or embalming.
b. Compensate for the absorptive effect of funeral illumination.
c. Present a well-groomed appearance consistent with the best characteristics of the deceased.
d. Psychologically ease the grief of the bereaved family by creating a memory picture of peaceful rest, free of pain.
e. Accent or de-emphasize parts of the face or features.
f. Conceal discolorations.
g. Match wax with the color of the complexion.

Coloring methods:

a. Internal: Achieved by arterially injecting an active dye with embalming chemical. An active dye is a colorant that is added to either the fluid or the solution to restore a natural coloring and appearance to the decedent. Typically, a pink/red coloring.
b. External: Achieved by a surface application of the cosmetic by hand, brush, sponge, pad or spray.

Types of external colors that can be applied to the deceased:

a. **Transparent:** *Having the property of transmitting rays of light through its substance so that bodies situated beyond or behind can be distinctly seen.* May be clear or translucent (cloudy) as they appear in the container. Applied thinly, they appear transparent and the skin is visible through them.

b. **Translucent:** *Transmitting light but causing sufficient diffusion to eliminate the perception of distinct images; somewhat transparent.* Appear dense in their container and are capable of hiding faint blemishes. Applied thinly, they present a transparent effect, and the variations of the skin-color are visible through them.

c. **Opaque:** *Not transparent or translucent; not allowing light to pass through a concealing cosmetic.* Employed to conceal discolorations. May create an artificial or "cakey" appearance. Opaque cosmetics are used as a base or foundation that covers up discolorations. Natural color cosmetics are usually applied on top of opaque cosmetics.

Pigments of the skin: The non-technical description of the skin color for Caucasian and light black people is "straw color (faint yellowish tinge) with a pink overtone."

a. **Melanin:** *is the brown to black-brown pigments in the epidermis and hair.* The determinative pigment of all races; the color ranges from tan to brown, too black-brown. True albinos do not have melanin in their skin.

b. **Carotene:** *is the yellow pigment of the skin.* Similar to that found in adipose (fatty) tissue.

c. **Hemoglobin** (Oxyhemoglobin): *Red pigment: the protein coloring matter of the red blood corpuscles which serves to convey oxygen to the tissues forming oxyhemoglobin.* Oxygenated and non-oxygenated blood of the arteries and veins that influences the color of the skin by way of its presence in the superficial capillaries.

Pigment cosmetics necessary to match the skin for all races:

a. Brown (dark): Employed to capture the low range of complexion coloring. It supplies the dark tones of the skin and darkens depressions (especially the eyes).

b. Yellow: Employed to create the sallow component of the skin, to simulate the translucent appearance of the skin on aged persons and to mix with red for the lips of a fair-skinned female in an ornamental makeup.

c. Red: Employed to serve alone as a complexion colorant (plus powder), to heighten the complexion of a ruddy or florid person, to reproduce the warm-color (rouge) areas, and to create minor shadow on receding surfaces.

d. White: Employed to raise the value (lighten) the applied complexion coloring and/or premix with the applied complexion colorant to highlight a prominence. Must be added to the array of cosmetic pigment colors that are counterparts of the pigments of the skin. Reduces the brilliance of yellow, red and brown pigments and also compensates for the diffused appearance of skin pigments being refracted through the epidermis.

Types of External Coloring Media:

a. Liquid Cosmetics: Those that flow and are not solid. Include solutions, lotions, paints, colloids, or suspensions. Many have evaporating vehicles.

b. Cream Cosmetics: Those that are semi-solid. Include pigments supplied in ointments, sticks, pastes, mucilage's, hydrocarbons, or soaps; they have a vehicle of oil, grease, or glycerin that does not evaporate.

163

c. Powder Cosmetics: Those that are solid and composed of extremely fine particles that may be loose or compressed. Usually ground (milled) with talcum, chalk, zinc oxide, or titanium dioxide.

d. Aerosol: Liquid cosmetics that are compressed under pressure and dispensed using a propellant gas. An aerosol cosmetic is dispensed in a mist and is usually used as an undercoating to cover-up skin blemishes.

e. Airbrush Cosmetics: Liquid cosmetics that are dispensed in a fine mist from a reservoir chamber in an airbrush that is attached to an airbrush machine. This mist, if done correctly, will create a natural appearance of the deceased.

f. Emollient: A heavy moisturizer that is creamy, thick and helps to add moisture to the skin. An example of an emollient is moisturizer cream that is applied after embalming. Depending on the quantity placed on the face and hands, the cream can remain, and cosmetics can be applied directly on top of the cream.

Complexions:

1. Types: Classified as light, medium and dark.
2. Variations: Red (ruddy), Brown (Swarthy or dusky), and Yellow (sallow).
3. Deviations: Abnormal skin colorings that mar the countenance. Pathological conditions. *(These are Very Important)*
    a. Bronze: Addison's disease, Hodgkin's disease, TB, uremic poisoning.
    b. Purple: Post-mortem stain, contusions.
    c. Yellow: Jaundice.
    d. Green: Putrefaction or injection of a jaundiced body with an overly strong embalming fluid.
    e. Gray: or "Formaldehyde gray" caused by injection of an overly strong embalming fluid.
    f. Yellow-brown: Extreme dehydration.
4. **Undertones:** *Underlying colors in the skin.* An undertone is the color from underneath the skin surface that affects the overall hue. There are three undertones – cool, warm and neutral. With respect to cosmetics, they are mostly "cool linen" or "warm bisque," which are the most common undertone hues.

Methods of Application – external completion compounds:

a. Hand: or finger.
b. Brush.
c. Aerosol Spray: Atomizer or cosmetics in an aerosol can.
d. Sponge.
e. Puff / Pad.
f. Airbrush.

Mixing techniques: Warm the cosmetics by mixing a small amount in the palm of your hand with a spatula. With a clean hand and clean spatula, remove cosmetic from the container. Adjust the color of the cosmetics to match the skin tone. Apply the cosmetics and discard unused cosmetics. Returning unused cosmetics to the container will contaminate the cosmetics.

Effect of density in the application of cosmetics: As the density of cosmetic is increased, the colorant appears more vivid and changes its value. If a spatula is used to apply cosmetics, it may be too thick. It must be thick enough to cover discolorations, however the thinner the better. Too thick and the cosmetic dries, cracks and appears cakey.

Cosmetic application near hair regions: Apply the cosmetic away from the hair, then use a brush to blend into the hairline. If cosmetics are on the hair, place a comb underneath the hair and with Webril, gently rub the cosmetics off. Avoid using dry-wash shampoo because some people use hair dyes, and this product will strip the hair color.

Highlighting and shadowing with cosmetics: Apply lightest color over the entire face first, then highlight high areas of the face with red tones and shadow low areas with brown.
   a. Eye shadow: Inner canthus of eye (use brown).
   b. Warm color areas: Lips, ears, nose, cheeks, chin and forehead. Applies to both males and females.
   c. Infants: Very pale. Softly flood the entire cheeks and chin in an even coloring.
   d. Children: Pink of the cheeks is located chiefly on the upper part of the front plane of the face; very little, if any, is located on the side of the cheek.
   e. Adolescents: Occupies a triangular space slightly lateral to that of a child. Located a short distance below the eyelids and extends as far as the "middle" of the cheekbone).
   f. Young adults: Area of red is on the upper part of the cheekbone, where the surface recedes inward toward the lower eyelid.
   g. Middle aged adults: Red on the cheek drop to almost the middle of the cheeks. Only the faintest tinge of red should be applied.
   h. Aged adults: Red application to the lower part of the cheeks and occupies an almost triangular space above the jaw line.
   i. Color and shaping of lips: If they have no lips, the restorative artist may have to paint them on. Use lip rouge, not tint. Can make the lips thinner, thicker, wider or narrower.
   j. Variegated: Changing in color; diversified with different colors. Natural irregularity.

Finishing Powder: Removes the high shine on face.
   a. Types: Pigmented or non-pigmented (white). All powders have a tendency to dry. The drying effect of the powder removes the shine from the cosmetics.
   b. Applications: Spray on with an atomizer or apply small amounts of powder with a brush. An atomizer works best because it applies small amounts of powder evenly which can be blended with a finishing or powder brush.
   c. Cautions: Be conscious of caking in corners of the eyes, mouth, nose or ears.

Corrective Cosmetizing: Adjust to lighting where the deceased will be shown. Best to cosmetize human remains under the light source that the deceased will be shown under.
   a. Treatment of small discolorations: Use covering creams. Apply to the area of the discoloration; it will blend in with the rest of the face. If the discoloration is a natural part of the face (e.g. beard shadow, freckles, aging spots, moles or birthmarks), replace them with cosmetics.

b. Effect of funeral lighting on completed cosmetics: Moving from fluorescent to incandescent light will change the appearance of the deceased. Use indirect, filtered light in chapel or visitation room. Direct lighting needs to be adjusted to ensure that the clothing and casket interior will be bright and vibrant. The wrong color of direct lighting will create dull color tones (See p. 175).

c. **Color Rendering Index** (CRI): a measurement of light quality of a light source as compared to sunlight. A color rendering index is a qualitative measurement of the ability of a light source to reveal the colors of various objects faithfully in comparison with a natural or standard light source. Light sources with high CRI are desirable in color-critical applications such as restorative art applications and final placement of the casket and human remains.

Color Theory

Color theory is a critical part of restorative art, body preparation and presentation of human remains for viewing. The improper use of color theory creates an unnatural appearance of the deceased and therefore an unpleasant and unacceptable viewing experience for the family. It is therefore important that a funeral director demonstrates a thorough understanding of color theory.

Color is a visual sensation, perceived by the eye and the mind due to the activity and vibrations of light. When the eye perceives an object, the properties of that object, together with the light source, effects the way the brain perceives the object. What color is perceived is determined by specific wavelengths of light, which enter the eye and stimulate the rods (which respond to various degrees of light) and the cones (which are responsible for the perception of color). Assuming that the individual is not "color-blind" in some way, the brain visually distinguishes colors and the quantities degree of "redness," "brownness," "greenness," "grayness," etc. of the object.

People who have difficulty distinguishing between lightness and darkness or variations of color are known to have either color blindness or night blindness. Most forms of color blindness, an inherited inability to distinguish between certain colors, result from the absence or deficiency of one of the three types of cones. The most common type is *red-green color blindness*, in which red cones or green cones are missing. As a result, the person cannot distinguish between red and green. Prolonged Vitamin A deficiency and the resulting below-normal amount of rhodopsin may cause night blindness or nyctalopia, which is an inability to see well at low light levels.

166

General Characteristics of Color

1. The Spectrum is a visible band of color. This is the original standard of color as it is perceived when light passes through a prism and breaks apart into various colors. The progressive arrangement of these 7 colors are: (**ROY G. BIV**) Red, Orange, Yellow, Green, Blue, Indigo, Violet, and they always appear in this order, known as the **spectrum**. Sir Isaac Newton ran sunlight through a prism in 1666 and the white light dispersed into these individual colors.

2. Absorption and reflection are identified by wavelengths in which light is reflected. Dark colors absorb more light; light colors reflect more light. This is why people wear white on warm days because it reflects the sunlight and makes the person cooler. Light colors have longer wavelengths than dark colors. White objects reflect all the colors in white light equally, with little absorption. Black objects absorb all the colors in the incident light, with little reflection. Pigmentary mixtures deal with the subtraction of wavelengths. A **pigment** *is a coloring matter which can be applied to an object, when combined with some type of vehicle.*

3. Imperfections of Pigments: Narrower than the range of colors in nature. Pigments fade or bleach when exposed to sunlight or air. Many pigments are not pure colors. Pigments are not stable (consistent from tube to tube). Pigments absorb light rays when mixed together.

Dimensions of Color

There are Three Dimensions of Color:

1. **Hue:** *The property of a color by which it is distinguished from other colors.* The hue is the name of the color. Achromatic colors (white, black and gray) have no hue. Pure hues tend to tire the eye, causing visual fatigue and becoming monotonous.

2. **Value:** *Deals with the lightness or darkness of a hue* (how much light it reflects).

   ➢ A **Tint** *is a hue into which various quantities of white are mixed.*

   ➢ A **Shade** *is a hue into which various quantities of black are mixed*; the darkened hue, as contrasted with a whitened hue.

3. **Intensity / chroma:**
   ➢ **Intensity** is the amount of strength of a color due especially to its degree of freedom of a **mixture with** its complementary color or gray; equivalent to its brightness or dullness.

   ➢ **Chroma** is a synonym for intensity. Chroma is the intensity or purity of the color.

   ➢ **Tone**: A hue mixed with either a small quantity of gray or the complement of the hue, resulting in dulling the hue. All tones are tertiary colors.

Pigment Theory *is also known as the Prang System.* Pigment theory theorizes that all visible colors originate from three basic colors, red, yellow and blue. These are known as the 3 primary colors. Within the Prang system there are also 3 secondary hues, and 6 intermediate hues. Together, these 12 colors form the color wheel. Tertiary colors are adulterations of these three classes.

Classes of hues: Each hue can be identified as belonging in the class of primary, secondary, or intermediate colors.

   a. **Primary: Three hues (Red, Yellow and Blue)** produce all other chromatic pigment colors by their mixtures. Mixtures of other hues cannot produce these three. By mixing pairs of primary hues in equal and unequal proportions, those hues in the spectrum and those intermittent between them are produced. The mixture of the three primary hues in equal proportions produces gray.

   b. **Secondary: Three hues** are produced by a mixture of equal parts of two primary pigment hues producing **Purple, Green and Orange**. A second equilateral triangle (inverted) depicts the relationship of the primary and secondary hue. Lie midway between the two primary hues that produce it and directly opposite of its complementary color.

   c. **Intermediate:** Produced when a primary and its adjoining secondary hue are mixed in equal strengths. The **six intermediate hues** are located midway between the primary and secondary hues that produce them. Intermediate hues are always named by their primary color first, followed by the secondary color in which a small amount of the primary color was added to, resulting in the new color (with a few exceptions). The intermediate colors are: **Yellow-Orange, Yellow-Green, Red-Orange, Violet (mixing more red with purple), Blue-Green, and Indigo (mixing more blue with purple).**

   d. **Tertiary:** A hue which results from the mixing of two-secondary pigmentary hues or an unbalanced proportion of complements with warm hue or cool hue predominating. This results in dulled **gray** hues.

1. Chromatic and achromatic colors: **Chromatic colors** *are comparable to the colors of the Spectrum plus those produced by their mixtures.* These colors are called pure in that they are unadulterated with black, white or gray.

Achromatic *are colors not found on the Spectrum*. These are the neutral hues: white, black, and gray, also, silver and gold (for decorative purposes).

2. Warm hues / Cool hues: **Warm Hues** (Orange predominates): A color which appears in the spectral band, characterized by long wave lengths; a color which makes an object appear closer and larger; a color which reflects warmth; i.e. **red, orange, yellow, and** other **colors in which they predominate**. These colors have **long wavelengths.**

   Cool Hues (Blue predominates): A color that creates the impression of coldness such as **blue, greens, purple, or any intermediate pigmentary hue in which they predominate**; a receding color, absorb heat rays. These colors have **short wavelengths.**
   Warm and cool colors are not harmonious, they are contrasting.

3. Changing the **value** of a hue: **Value** *deals with the lightness or darkness of the color*.

Tints and **Shades**

   Tints: *A hue into which various quantities of white are mixed (add white to hue).*
   Shade: *A hue into which various quantities of black are mixed; the darkened hue.*

4. Changing the **intensity** of a hue **tone**: A hue mixed with either a small quantity of **gray or the complement of the hue**, resulting in dulling the hue. Intensity deals with the degree of purity or dullness (grayness) of the chromatic hue.

5. **Color harmony**
   a. **Monochromatic** *is a variation of one color which includes its tones, tints and shades.*
   b. **Analogous colors** *are two or more hues that have the same hue in common.* Examples of these analogous colors are: Red-Orange, Red, Violet or Yellow-Green, Yellow, Yellow-Orange
   c. **Complementary** *colors are directly opposite hues on a color wheel*; any two pigmentary hues which, by mixture equal quantities togethers will **produce gray**. Equal strengths are necessary. Blue and Orange are complements. Red and Green are complements.
   A method to determine complementary hues quickly: The complement of a primary hue is a secondary hue made by combination of the two remaining primary hues. The complement of a secondary hue is the remaining primary hue not involved in its mixture.
   d. **Juxtaposition** is a frequent question asked on the NBEs. The principle of juxtaposition occurs when *any two colors seen together modify each other in the direction of their complements; if they are complements, they enrich each other; if they are not complements, they dull each other.*

e. **After-image** is a psychological perception. *After-image is a visual impression remaining after the stimulus has been removed.* Eyes have become over stimulated. For example, if you look at the sun (not recommended) for a period of time then look away, the afterimage of the sun remains because the brain was over stimulated by the brightness of the sun.

6.   Value Contrasts: Lightness or darkness of a color.

Effect on the hue against a white, black or gray background will create different effects in perception. Depending on the background, color is perceived in different ways.
   a. **White Background**: A pure hue appears richer and more vivid against a white background. This background seems to strengthen the appearance of the hue.
   b. **Black Background**: A pure hue appears less vivid and lighter (higher in value) against a black background. This background seems to rob the strength of the hue as it makes it appear paler.
   c. **Gray Background**: A pure hue appears to lose its vividity against a gray background…especially if the values of the gray and the hue are alike. Gray backgrounds have a neutralizing effect on the hue.

Monotony may occur when closely related colors are used in an arrangement because of the constant repetition of the high value motif. A small amount of a single contrasting value (or a very contrasting hue) introduced within the heart of the area will supply the accent that is needed.

7.   Utilization of Value Contrasts:
   a. Strong value contrasts: Have a tremendous ability to attract attention. A beautiful object should be placed against a background of a very different value.
   b. Close value contrasts: Helpful when it is desirable to draw the least possible attention to an object. Object may be visually subdued against a similar environment.

8.   Hue Contrasts: Visually, complementary colors placed in juxtaposition produce a balanced stimulation on the nerve endings in the retina of the eye. They eliminate eye-fatigue that results from over-stimulation by one hue. Only a small quantity of one complement is necessary to balance a large amount of the other and still bring all the nerves of the eye into action.

9.   After-Image: If a hue is held in the line of vision and the eyes become over-stimulated, the complement will be seen when the stimulus is removed.

10. Casket Selection Room: Avoid any atmosphere of depression. This can best be achieved by a suggestion of the out-of-doors. A subdued scenic wallpaper depicting a landscape in various gray-greens may be used on the longest wall. Pale gray-green on the other walls repeats the idea of greenery without being too

monotonous. Avoid bright colors and bold patterns or very warm wall colors such as rose or deep gold.

11. Clothing and Casket Interior Harmony: Garment colors and casket interior colors should be selected to blend harmoniously and flatter the appearance of the deceased. If most of the attention is drawn to the casket interior or to the garment, it can be assumed that the *wrong colors* have been selected.

12. Color Harmonies - Two types:
    a. Related Hues: Include the monochromatic and the analogous types of color schemes.
    b. Contrasting Hues: Include complementary, triad, split-complementary, double complementary, tetrad, and non-complementary-contrast types of color schemes.

13. Harmonies of Related Hues:
    a. Monochromatic: A color scheme that involves one hue only. It is a harmony of self-notes of the same hue. It includes all values and intensities of this single hue, i.e., red, pink, cherry, burgundy, maroon, and dusty rose are all red in hue.
    b. Analogous: Involves two or more hues which lie adjacent to each other on the color-wheel and contain the same hue in each of the colors.
    c. Complementary: Involves any two hues that are opposite each other on the color-wheel.
    d. Triad: A triad involves three hues; as nearly as possible they should be at least three hues from each other on the color-wheel. The primary hues (red, yellow, and blue) are a perfect triad, as are the secondary hues (orange, green and purple). See color wheel (p.168) to demonstrate a triad.
    e. Split Complementary: Split compliments also involves three hues. The complement of the primary hue is not included; the two hues on either side of the direct complement are employed. The complementary color of Red is Green. A split complement would be Red and Blue-Green and Yellow-Green. Notice how both Blue-Green and Yellow-Green are analogous hues of green. That is what makes them a split complementary color scheme.
    f. Double complements: Involves four hues… two adjacent hues on the color-wheel and their complements. Example: Red and Green and Yellow and Violet
    g. Tetrad: Also involves four hues… two separated hues and their complements.
    h. Contrast Non-complementary: Involves two hues… include both a warm and a cool hue.
    Examples: red and blue, yellow and blue, yellow and green, orange and green, or orange and purple.

14. Color Schemes in Room Interiors: Color in the funeral home conveys a message; it has something to say. Every funeral home room interior and funeral setting should reflect a mood and be associated with its purpose. The colors should be

171

appropriate to the goal desired, e.g. the chapel should express peaceful dignity. The wake room should have a living room atmosphere and reflect the comfort of a homelike environment.

15. Development of a Color Scheme: A rug is often the initial source in the development of a color scheme because it covers such a large area. The harmony of any room begins with the floor.

16. Dominant Hue: In every room there should be one outstanding hue. All others are subordinated. The dominant hue may be repeated more vividly in smaller areas.

17. Patterns in Textiles and Wall Coverings: "Tone on tone" of the same hue in textiles (upholstery, draperies, and rug) softens and mutes the fundamental hue; a solid color appears much more vivid. Interwoven threads of different hues also reduce the vividity of the major hue.

18. Advancing and Receding Hues: Cool hues, which are the colors of distance in nature, seem to recede and make an object appear smaller and, therefore, more distant. Warm hues seem to advance and make an object appear larger and closer. An upholstered chair in a cool hue seems smaller than an identical chair in a warm hue.

19. Law of Areas: "Large areas of color should be quiet in effect, while small areas should show strong contrasts". The larger the amount of the hue used, the more subdued it should be, the smaller the amount used, the more vivid it should be.
    a. The hue on the largest area (wall, etc.) should be weak.
    b. The hue occupying a small area should be approximately one-half subdued. It may be a little more vivid but still fairly weak.
    c. The remaining hue should be vivid but limited to very small accents.
    d. **Feng shui: (*fung-shway or fung-shwee*)** the art of placement, creates perfect balance in offices, building and other human environment simply by the placement of the items in that environment.

20. **Color Schemes in Floral Arrangements**:
    a. Floral offerings from members of the family must be given preference in the arrangement. The floral piece from the closest survivor is placed at the head end of the casket.
    b. Other family offerings should be located at the foot-end of the casket.
    c. These priorities should not be violated.
    d. When the floral offerings are exceptionally plentiful, the arrangement may be extended into the foyer or an adjacent room.
    e. **Mass Arrangement of Non-Family Pieces**: Mass grouping of the floral offerings of similar hues should be in such a fashion to create a color-scheme that is visually appealing. Every floral offering has a dominant hue. The accents supplied by the florists are negligible when seen *in masses* (in a group

or all together) with no background visible between them. No need to remove a piece from one position to substitute one which arrived late.

    f. **Repetition in Floral Offerings**: Mass arrangements require groupings of each hue to reinforce their beauty. Alternating complementary colors in a mass arrangement should be avoided; alternating them neutralizes them and erases their integrity.

    g. **Symmetrical and Asymmetrical Balance**: Symmetrical balance refers to the placement of similar floral offerings in the same position at each side of the casket. Asymmetrical balance refers to the balance of dissimilar floral offerings at each side of the casket.

    h. **Activities of Hues**: Chromatic colors exhibit different degrees of aggressive activity. These activities are associated with the illusions of force and weight.

    i. **Force**: Some hues seem to strive for attention while others seem passive, retiring and quiet. Pure hues (Red and Orange) appear most aggressive and forceful. Blue, green and purple exhibit less force; each may "carry as a dark area but its color identity does not seem to be as clear." A pure warm hue has more force and "carries" better than the same hue lightened, darkened, or grayed. A tint "carries" better than a shade or tone.

    j. **Weight**: Various hues differ in regard to the illusion of weight; some give the impression of heaviness while others seem light-weight. A pure hue seems heavier than the same hue grayed. It seems heavier than its tint or a gray of equal value. A darkened hue (shade) seems heavier than the same hue lightened (tint). A cool hue appears heavier than a warm hue. In nature the eye is accustomed to seeing dark colors low and the mind associates this with the idea of strength and solidity. The darker the "color" the less of it is required to sustain a large amount of a lighter (paler) "color" above the area.

21. **Color in Light** (illumination: Giving or casting of light). The color of an object depends upon the hue it reflects, and also upon the illumination it receives. If the illuminating light does not contain the same hue, the color will either be converted or destroyed. Colored illumination may completely change the hue of the object or make it appear drab or ugly (See p. 175). The hue of objects should be selected under the same conditions that they will be seen.

   1. **Types of lights**:

    a. Incandescent: Glowing filament. Gives off a warmer appearance but does not have yellowing impact. High heat production.

    b. Fluorescent: Gas tube with electrons (electrical current) passing through it. Low heat production, cool. *Note*: Do not use this type of light in a funeral home, especially when cosmetizing human remains. The light that this lighting source produces will cause the facial features to appear flat and distorted.

    c. Selective Transmission and Absorption: A great deal of the wattage of a white bulb is lost (absorbed) in passing through a coloring agent.

    d. LED (light-emitting diode). LED light is energy-efficient lighting that produces very bright lighting. The problem with using LED lighting to illuminate human remains is that it could produce too much lighting which will affect the colors and shadows on the remains. When using LED lighting, using a rheostat to adjust the intensity of the lighting is recommended.

2. **Direct vs indirect lighting**: Direct lighting illuminates directly on the object, such as overhead lighting that shines on the casket or human remains. Indirect lighting is lighting that reflects illumination on an object. A torchiere is an example of indirect lighting. The lighting from the torchiere projects outward and upward illuminating the object around the light source.

3. **Dimensions of color illumination**: Hue, chroma, and saturation:
   a. **Hue**: The property of a color by which it is distinguished from others.
   b. **Chroma**: Color intensity of purity; synonym for intensity.
   c. **Saturation**: A visual aspect indicating the vividness of the hue in the degree of difference from a gray of the same lightness.

4. **Methods of mixing colored illumination**: White light produced by mixing three primary colors.
   a. **Additive**: The primary hues are red, blue and green. They are said to parallel the three sets of receptors in the eye. Correct mixtures of primary hues can form every other hue. By alternating the brightness of different pairs of the primaries (by means of a dimmer switch) intermediate hues can be obtained. By projection of equal strengths of pairs of primary hues, the secondary hues result (yellow, blue-green and magenta). Red and Green produce Yellow. Blue and Green produce Blue-Green. Red and Blue produce Magenta. Red, Blue and Green produce white.

   b. **Subtractive**: Involves the diminution of the wavelengths of light. Reduction can be gradually extended to a point where a complete blackout (absence of any illumination) results. Accomplished in filtering out the transmitted coloring by superimposing two or more color-media upon one light source. When white light passes through a color media, only the color of the media is transmitted; all other hues in white light are absorbed. When white light passes through a blue color media, only blue light is transmitted. Then, if a red coloring media is placed in the path of the blue rays, no illumination will pass through. The result will be black (absence of light). The only hue that will be transmitted through two or more superimposed transparencies is the hue they have in common.

5. **Primary hues of the Subtractive Method**: Yellow, magenta and blue-green.
   a. Yellow superimposed upon magenta transmits red.
   b. Yellow superimposed upon Blue-green transmits green.
   c. Magenta superimposed upon blue-green transmits blue.
   d. If all the subtractive primaries are superimposed over one light source, there is complete subtraction, and no light is transmitted.

6. **Effects of colored lights on colored objects**: The color is identifiable by virtue of the reflection of the light rays.
   a. Emphasis: The hue of an object appears more vivid when seen under the same hue of illumination.
   b. Absorption: When two values or intensities of the same hue are present (and the same hue in illumination strikes them), the larger area appears more vivid while the smaller appears more "washed out".
   c. Conversion: If the hue of an object and the illumination differ, the color of the object will either be converted into a different color or be obliterated.
   d. Illumination of complementary hue (or nearly so) grays the color of the object while illumination of the same (or similar) hue as the object enhances its beauty. On objects of more than one hue, it is usually much safer to employ unsaturated illumination.

According to Klicker (2003) the perception of color is greatly influenced by the lighting on the object. Various lighting on colors of clothing and casket interiors will produce different color tones. In a funeral home, overhead direct lighting is usually three lights: pink, soft white and yellow. Soft white light illuminates the color of the object. Some funeral homes also indirect lighting, such as torchieres with redneck bulbs. Lighting on various clothing colors will produce different effects. See chart below:

COLORS	Lighting		
	Red	**Yellow**	**Blue**
Red	Color fades out	Color stays red	Darkens the red
Orange	Lightens the orange	Fades the orange slightly	Darkens the orange
Yellow	Turns yellow white	Yellow fades out	Turns orchid
Green	Darkens the green	Turns to a dark gray	Lightens the green
Blue	Turns to a dark gray	Turns to dark gray	Depending on the shade of blue, the lighting could turn to pale blue
Violet	Darkens to black	Darkens to almost black	Turns to orchid

7. **Types of Illumination**:
   a. Point Lighting: Refers to the movement of the light rays in a straight line from the light source. Known as direct lighting.
   b. Semi-diffused Lighting: When a diffusing apparatus (e.g. a lamp shade) is placed upon a point light, the light rays are bounced against it and the direct path is altered to become semi-diffused. Modifies the contrasts of light and dark areas, minimal shadows.
   c. Diffused Lighting: The light rays are scattered in all directions from the light source. Known as indirect lighting; the light rays bounce from the ceiling (or adjacent wall) and flood the area generally.

8. **Lighting Fixtures**:
   a. Torchiere Lighting: Two types of floor lamps (or torchieres) employed for funeral settings. Usually uses a redneck light bulb to produce a warm glow effect.
   b. Totally Indirect: Bowl is opaque; all light rays are thrown toward the ceiling to be reflected downward into completely diffused illumination. Doesn't give off enough light.
   c. Semi-Indirect: Torchiere has a translucent bowl that transmits direct rays as will as indirect. The indirect rays greatly exceed the direct ones. More open at the top, and light passes through the glass.
   d. Cove Lighting: Box-like fixture extending around the walls of the room interior several feet from the ceiling. Contains lamps (incandescent or fluorescent) that throw the illumination upward.
   e. Alcove Lighting: Recess in the wall for the casket. Behind the side and top walls, the light fixtures can be hidden from sight.
   f. Trough Lighting: Long, narrow receptacle (usually metal) with a reflecting surface within. Usually hidden behind a ceiling joist or an arch to be inconspicuous. Direct illumination.
   g. Dome Lighting: Relatively large, luminous light fixture submerged in the ceiling and provides direct illumination.
   h. Flood (or spot) Lighting: Incandescent bulbs used as accent lights to illuminate the casket or floral offerings. May be recessed in the ceiling with the light rays directed through circular apertures. Usually used outside for sidewalks and landscaping.
   i. Chandelier, Candelabra, and Candle Lighting: A hanging chandelier may beautify an interior but may (or may not) provide adequate illumination for the funeral setting. Supplies a semi-diffused illumination.
   j. Table and Floor Lamp Lighting: Lamps with direct and indirect illumination. These lamps are supplementary lighting.

Removal of Stains

According to Klicker (2003), stains are caused by various things such as dirt, grease or other materials such as cigarettes or man-made materials like paint. All rectifying remedies to remove stains, should always be first tested, on a section of the material that will be non-visible to the public. Some materials will react to the chemical or treatment product and cause an after stain that may be more noticeable than the original stain. Here are some of the ways to treat some stains:

Adhesive Tape	Rubbing alcohol, white vinegar or a product known as GooGone
Blood	Cold Water or Ammonia
Paint	Turpentine, Paint Thinner, or Dry Wash (First test on an area of the material not visible to the public). GooGone. Keytone based products.
Nicotine	Lemon Juice
Tar	Acetone or GooGone
Grease or Oil	Ether, Acetone, carbon tetrachloride, or a degreaser product. GooGone. Keytone based products.
Lipstick	Dry Wash
Ink	Lemon Juice or Petroleum Jelly

Glossary for Restorative Art

Abrasion – antemortem and/or postmortem injuries resulting from friction of the skin against a 4 firm object resulting in the removal of the epidermis.

Abscess – a localized accumulation of pus.

Absorption – the process of taking in, as in a colored object which absorbs certain rays of light and reflects other rays giving the object its recognizable color. (e.g., An apple is called red if the 10 red rays are reflected and the other rays in the light are absorbed.)

Abut – to bluntly adjoin another structure; for example, the line of eye closure.

Acetone – dimethyl ketone; a colorless liquid which is used to soften and remove scabs; a solvent for restorative wax, or a stain remover.

Achromatic color – a color not found in the visible spectrum; a neutral color such as white, black, gray, and silver and gold (for decorative purposes).

Acquired facial markings – facial markings that develop during one's lifetime, primarily as a result of repetitious use of certain muscles.

Additive method – a process of mixing colored lights on a surface on which the wave lengths of each are combined; adding two or more colored lights together to create another color of light.

Adhesive – sticking to or adhering closely; substances which may be applied in order to sustain contact of two surfaces.

Aerosol – a colloidal solution dispensed as a mist.

After-image – psychological; a visual impression remaining after the stimulus has been removed.

Airbrush – a pressured atomizer utilized for spraying liquid paint or cosmetic upon a surface.

Alveolar processes – a bony ridge found on the inferior surface of the maxilla and the superior surface of the mandible which contains the sockets for the teeth.

Alveolar prognathism – an abnormal protrusion of the alveolar process(es).

Analogous – in color harmony, two or more hues which have the same hue in common.

Angle of the mandible – a bony angle formed by the junction of the posterior edge of the ramus of the mandible and the inferior surface of the body of the mandible; marks widest part of lower 1/3 of face.

Angulusoris eminence (a/k/a Angulus oris eminence) – the small convex prominence found lateral to the end of the line of closure of the mouth; a natural facial marking.

Angulusoris sulcus (a/k/a Angulus oris sulcus) – the groove found at each end of the line of closure of the mouth; a natural facial marking.

Anterior – before or in front of; an anatomical term of position and direction which denotes the front or forward part.

Anterior nares – the external openings of the nostrils.

Antihelix – the inner rim of the ear.

Antitragus – a small eminence obliquely opposite the tragus on the superior border of the lobe of the ear.

Aquiline – curved, as the beak of an eagle; as viewed from the profile, a nasal profile which exhibits a "hook" or convexity in its dorsum.

Arch of the wing – the inferior margin of the nasal wing which forms a distinct concave arc superiorly.

Armature – framework; a material, commonly of pliable metal or wood, employed to provide support for a wax restoration.

Aspiration – to draw out liquids or gases by means of suction.

Asymmetry – lack of symmetry, balance, or proportion.

Base – (1) in cosmetology, the vehicle in a cosmetic (oil base); the initial application of cream or cosmetic; (2) the lower part of anything, the supporting part.

Basic pigment – four hues which correspond to the pigments of the skin.

Basket weave suture – a network of stitches which cross the borders of a cavity or excision to anchor fillers and to sustain tissues in their proper position.

Bilateral – two sides.

Bilateral differences – dissimilarities existing in the two sides or halves of an object.

Bilateral view – an inferior or superior viewpoint which permits the comparison of the two sides or halves of an object or facial feature.

Blanch – to whiten by removing color; to make pale.

Bleaching – the act of lightening a discoloration by hypodermic means or by surface compress.

Bleaching agent – a chemical which lightens or blanches skin discolorations

Body of the mandible – the horizontal portion of the lower jaw.

Bridge – a raised support; the arched portion of the nose which is supported by the nasal bones; a structure or span connecting two parts of a mutilated bone.

Bridge stitch – (interrupted suture) a temporary suture consisting of individually cut and tied 5 stitches employed to sustain the proper position of tissues.

Brilliance – brightness; in colored illumination, the quantity of illumination passing through a color transparency.

Buccal cavity – the space between the lips and the gums and teeth; the vestibule of the oral cavity.

Buccal depressions – natural, shallow concavities of the cheeks which extend obliquely downward from the medial or lateral margins of the cheekbones.

Buccinator – the principle muscle of the cheek which compresses the cheeks and forms the lateral wall of the mouth.

Bucco-facial sulcus – the vertical furrow of the cheek; an acquired facial marking.

Burn – to oxidize or to cause to be oxidized by fire or equivalent means; a tissue reaction or injury resulting from the application of heat, extreme cold, caustic material, radiation, friction, or electricity.

Burns by Degree:

First-degree burn: usually limited to redness (erythema), a white plaque, and minor pain at the site of injury. These burns only involve the epidermis. Sunburns can be included as first-degree burns.

Second-degree burn: manifest as erythema with superficial blistering of the skin. Involve the superficial (papillary) dermis and may also involve the deep (reticular) dermis layer.

Third-degree burn: occur when the epidermis is lost with damage to the subcutaneous tissue. These burns will result in scarring and may require grafting.

Fourth-degree burn: damage to muscle, tendon, and ligament tissue, thus resulting in charring and catastrophic damage of the hypodermis, leaving exposed bone tissue. Often resulting in death.

Fifth-degree burns: Total incineration. The gross (meaning overall) incineration of the human remains, that are non-viewable and need to be treated in such a manner to prevent burnt odors from emanating.

Carmine – purple-red in coloration; (aka crimson).

Carotene – the yellow pigment of the skin.

Cartilage – a specialized type of dense connective tissue; attached to the ends of bones and forming parts of structures, such as the nasal septum and the framework of the ear.

Cauterizing agent – a chemical capable of drying tissues by searing; caustic.

Cement – a substance used to promote the adhesion of two separated surfaces, such as the lips, the eyelids, or the margins of an incision.

Channeling – creation of dermal and subdermal passageways , through a single entry point in the tissue, in order to allow for the removal of watery fluids and gasses.

Charred – reduced to carbon; the state of tissues destroyed by burning.

Chroma (Intensity) - brightness or dullness of a color.

Chromatic color – a color having hue; a color of the visible spectrum.

Cilia – the eyelashes.

Collodion – a clear syrup-like liquid which evaporates, leaving a contractile, white film; a liquid sealer.

Color – a visual sensation perceived by the eye and the mind due to the activity and vibration of light.

Color corrective – a category of concealer that neutralizes discoloration and pigmented 8 blemishes by using opposing colors from the color wheel.

Color Rendering Index (CRI) – a measurement of light quality of a light source as compared to sunlight.

Colorant – in cosmetology, a substance used to impart color to an object; dye, pigment, ink, or 14 paint.

Colored filter – colored glass, gelatin, or other substances which transmit light of certain wave lengths while absorbing the others.

Colored light – illumination of an identifiable hue.

Color wheel – a circle in which the primary, secondary, and intermediate hues are arranged in orderly intervals.

Columna nasi – the fleshy termination of the nasal septum at the base of the nose; located between the nostrils; the most inferior part of the mass of the nose.

Complements – directly opposite hues on the color wheel; any two pigmentary hues which, by their mixture in equal quantities, produce gray.

Complexion – the color and texture of the skin, especially that of the face.

Compound fracture – a broken bone which pierces the skin.

Compress – gauze or absorbent cotton saturated with water or an appropriate chemical and placed under or upon tissues to preserve, bleach, dry, hydrate, constrict, or reduce swelling.

Concave – exhibiting a depressed or hollow surface; a concavity.

Concave-convex profile – a facial profile variation in which the forehead protrudes beyond the eyebrows while the chin recedes from the plane of the upper lip.

Concave nasal profile – a depressed profile form which may dip concavely from root to tip (also see retrousse and infantine).

Concave profile – a basic facial profile form in which the forehead protrudes beyond the eyebrows while the chin protrudes beyond the plane of the upper lip (e.g. infantine, retrousse, and least common).

Concave-vertical profile – a facial profile variation in which the forehead protrudes beyond the eyebrows while the upper lip and chin project equally to an imaginary vertical line.

Concha – the concave shell of the ear; the deepest depression of the ear.

Concurrent – treatments of a restorative nature performed during the embalming operation.

Condyle – a rounded prominence at the end of a bone forming an articulation; on both the mandible and occipital bone.

Contour – the outline or surface form.

Contusion – a bruise often accompanied with distention.

Convex – curved evenly; resembling a segment of the outer edge of a sphere.

Convex-concave profile – a profile variation in which the forehead recedes from the eyebrows while the chin protrudes beyond the plane of the upper lip.

Convex nasal profile – (Roman, aquiline) a nasal profile which exhibits a hump in its linear form. e.g. Roman, aquiline.

Convex profile – a basic profile form in which the forehead recedes from the eyebrows while the chin recedes from the plane of the upper lip (most common).

Convex-vertical profile – a profile variation in which the forehead recedes from the eyebrows while the chin and upper lip project equally to an imaginary vertical line.

Cool hue – blue, green, purple, or any intermediate pigmentary hue in which they predominate; a receding hue which creates the illusion of distance from the observer; a color of short wavelengths.

Cords of the neck – vertical prominences of the neck; an acquired facial marking.

Coronal plane – anatomical plane dividing the anterior of the body from the posterior.

Coronoid process – the anterior, non-articulating process of the ramus of the mandible which serves as the insertion for the temporalis muscle.

Corpulence – having an abnormal amount of fat on the body.

Corrective shaping – a cosmetic technique which consists of highlighting those parts of the face or individual features to enlarge or bring them forward or shadowing them to reduce the appearance of size or deepen a depression.

Corrugator – a pyramid-shaped muscle of facial expression which draws the eyebrows 47 inferiorly and medially.

Cosmetic – a media for beautifying the complexion and skin, etc.

Cosmetic compound – a cosmetic medium composed of two, three, or all four basic pigments.

Cosmetizing – the process of applying cosmetics to a surface.

Cosmetology – the study of beautifying and improving the complexion, skin, hair, and nails.

Cranium – that part of the human skull which encloses the brain.

Cranial sutures – non-moveable joints that connect the bones of the cranium together.

Cream cosmetic – a semi-solid cosmetic.

Cribriform plate – the horizontal plate of the ethmoid bone separating the cranial cavity from the nasal cavity.

Crown (Vertex) - the topmost part of the head.

Crow's feet – **(Optic facial sulcus)** the furrows radiating from the lateral corner of the eye; acquired facial markings.

Crura of the antihelix – the superior and anterior bifurcating branches of the antihelix of the ear.

Crus of the helix – the origin of the helix which is flattened in the concha.

Decapitation – separation of the head from the body; to decapitate is the act of such separation.

Decomposition – separation of compounds into simpler substances by the action of microbial or autolytic enzymes.

Deep – below the surface, or toward the central part of a structure.

Dehydration – the loss of moisture from body tissue.

Density – the thickness of the applied cosmetic.

Dental prognathism – oblique insertion of the teeth.

Dental tie – ligature around the superior and inferior teeth employed to hold the mandible in a fixed position.

Depression – a hollow or shallow concave area in a surface.

Depressor angulioris – a muscle of facial expression which depresses the angle of the mouth.

Depressor labii inferioris – a muscle of facial expression which draws the lower lip inferiorly 2 and slightly lateral.

Derma (dermis, skin) – the corium, or true skin.

Desquamation (Skin slip) – the separation of the epidermis from the dermis as a result of 7 putrefaction.

Desiccation – extreme dehydration often resulting in post-embalming discolorations.

Diamond – a facial shape in which the cheeks are the widest point accompanied by a narrowing forehead and chin.

Digastric – a double bellied muscle which draws the hyoid bone superiorly.

Dimples – shallow depressions located on the cheek or chin in a rounded or vertical form; e.g. one of the natural facial markings.

Discoloration – any abnormal color in or on the human body; may be removed by arterial injection.

Distal – away from the center of the body or point of attachment. 23 24 Distention – a state of stretching out or becoming inflated.

Distortion – a state of being twisted or pushed out of natural shape or position.

Dorsum – top; the anterior protruding ridge of the nose from the root to the tip of the lobe.

Dusky – swarthy; somewhat dark in color; when used to describe the complexion color.

Edema – abnormal accumulation of fluids in tissues or body cavities.

Electric spatula – an electrically-heated blade used to dry moist tissues, reduce swollen tissues, and restore contour to natural form.

Emaciation – a wasted condition resulting in sunken surfaces of the face.

Embed – to fix or fasten in place.

Eminence – a prominence or projection.

Emollients – heavy moisturizer; creamy, thick, helps to retain moisture.

Enucleation – the removal of an entire mass or part, especially a tumor or the eyeball, without rupture.

Epicranius (Occipitofrontalis) – the muscle that draws the scalp posteriorly and inferiorly and raises the eyebrows.

Epidermis – the outermost layer of skin; the cuticle or scarf skin.

Excise – to remove as by cutting out.

External auditory meatus – the opening or passageway of the ear.

External pressure – weight applied to a surface.

Eyebrows (Supercilia) – superficial hairs covering the superciliary arches.

Eyebrow pencil – a cosmetic in pencil form for coloring the hairs of the eyebrow, or creating an eyebrow where the hairs were removed.

Eye cap – a thin, dome-like shell made of hardened cloth, metal, or plastic placed beneath eyelids to restore natural curvature and to maintain the position of posed eyelids.

Eyelids (Palpebrae) – two movable flaps of skin which cover and uncover each eyeball.

Eye shadow – a cosmetic color applied to the upper eyelid.

Eye socket – the bony region containing the eyeball; the orbital cavity.

Face – anatomically, the region from the eyes to the base of the chin; physiognomically, the region from the normal hairline to the base of the chin.

Facial markings – the "character" lines of the face and neck; wrinkles, grooves, cords, and dimples.

Facial profiles – the silhouettes of the face from the side view.

Facial proportions – mathematical relationships of the facial features to one another and/or to the head and face.

Feather – to reduce gradually to an indistinguishable edge; to "taper."

Feature builder (tissue builder) – a substance used to elevate sunken (emaciated) tissues to normal level by hypodermic injection.

Fifth degree burns – The gross (meaning overall) incineration of the human remains that are non-viewable.

Firmness – the degree of rigidity or stability; a condition of the tissues necessary for the application of wax.

Firm wax – the densest and least adhesive type of wax; a putty-like material used to fill large cavities or model features.

First degree burn – an injury caused by heat which produces redness of the skin.

Florid – flushed with red, when describing a complexion; not as vivid as ruddy.

Fluorescent light – the illumination produced by a tubular electric discharge lamp; the fluorescence of phosphors coating the inside of a tube.

Fold – an elongated prominence adjoining a surface.

Foramen magnum – an opening in the occipital bone through which the spinal cord passes from the brain.

Forehead – that part of the face above the eyes.

Form – external shape; a mold for casting; produce a certain shape; to constitute existing elements.

Foundation – the complexion cosmetic in ornamental cosmetology.

Fourth degree burn – total evacuation (absence) of tissue.

Fracture – broken bone.

Frenulum – the vertical restraining fold of mucous membrane on the midline of the inside of each lip connecting the lip with the gum.

Frontal – anterior; the anterior view of the face or features.

Frontal bone – the anterior third of the cranium, forming the forehead and the anterior portion of the roof of the skull.

Frontal eminences – paired, rounded, unmargined prominences of the frontal bone found approximately one inch beneath the normal hairline.

Frontal plane – see Coronal plane.

Frontal process of the maxilla – the ascending part of the upper jaw which gradually protrudes as it rises beside the nasal bone to meet the frontal bone; the ascending process of the upper jaw.

Funeral lighting – the quality and quantity of illumination used for presentation of casketed remains.

Furrow – a crevice in the skin accompanied by adjacent elevations.

Geometric – the shape of a plane figure determined by its outline.

Glabella – a single bony prominence of the frontal bone located between the superciliary arches in the inferior part of the frontal bone above the root of the nose.

Grecian – a nasal profile form in which the dorsum exhibits a straight line from the root to the tip; a straight nasal profile.

Groove – an elongated depression in a relatively level plane or surface.

Hairline – the outline of hair growth on the head or face; the lowest centrally located part of the hair of the cranium.

Hard palate – the anterior portion of the roof of the mouth.

Height – the vertical measurement of a feature or part of a feature; the distance above the base.

Helix – the outer rim of the ear.

Hemoglobin – red pigment; the protein coloring matter of the red blood corpuscles which serves to convey oxygen to the tissues forming oxyhemoglobin.

Hidden stitch (Intradermal suture) – type of suture used to close incisions in such a manner that the ligature remains entirely under the epidermis.

Highlight – a surface lying at right angles to the source of illumination which reflects the maximum amount of light; the brighter part.

Horizontal – parallel to the plane of the horizon.

Hue – the property of a color by which it is distinguished from other colors.

Hunting bow – shaped as a bent wood weapon with a central belly; resembling a "cupid" bow; the five arcs in the line of the lip closure resemble the design of the classic hunting bow.

Hypodermic injection – the insertion of chemicals directly into the tissues through the use of a syringe and needle.

Hypodermic tissue building – the injection of special creams or liquids into the tissues through the use of a syringe and needle to restore natural contour.

Illumination – giving or casting of light.

Incandescent Light – the illumination resulting from the glowing of a heated filament.

Incision – a clean cut into tissue or skin.

Incisive fossa – the depression between the mental eminence and the mandibular incisors.

Incisor teeth – the four teeth located anteriorly from the midline on each jaw.

Inclination – slope; deviation from the horizontal or vertical; oblique.

Infantine – babyish, childlike in regard to much adipose tissue; also refers to a facial shape or nasal profile.

Inferior – beneath; lower in plane or position; the undersurface of an organ or indicating a structure below another structure; toward the feet.

Inferior palpebral sulcus – the furrow of the lower attached border of the inferior palpebra; an 8 "acquired" facial marking.

Infranasal prognathism – a form of prognathism in which the base of the nasal cavity protrudes abnormally.

Inner canthus – eminence at the medial corner of the closed eyelids.

Integumentary lips – superiorly, the skin portion of the upper lip from the attached margin of the upper mucous membrane to the base of the nose; and inferiorly, the skin portion of the lower lip from the attached margin of the lower mucous membrane to the labiomental sulcus.

Intensity – see Chroma.

Interciliary sulci – the vertical or transverse furrows between the eyebrows; "acquired" facial markings.

Intermediate hue – a pigmentary hue produced by mixing, in equal quantities, a primary hue with its adjacent secondary hue on the color wheel.

Internal decapitation – trauma that occurs when the skull base separates from the spine.

Interrupted suture – see Bridge stitch.

Intertragic notch – a notch or opening between the tragus and the antitragus of the ear.

Intradermal suture – see Hidden stitch.

Inversion – turned in an opposite direction or folded inward.

Inverted triangle – a facial shape with a wide angular forehead, angular jaw, and pointed chin.

Jawline – the inferior border of the mandible.

Juxtaposition – any two hues seen together which modify each other in the direction of their complements.

Labia – lips.

Labial sulci – the vertical furrows of each lip extending from within the mucous membranes into the integumentary lips; acquired facial markings.

Labiomental sulcus – the junction of the lower integumentary lip and the superior border of the chin, which may appear as a furrow; a natural facial marking.

Laceration – an irregularly torn or jagged wound.

Lanugo – the downy hair of a fetus, children, or women.

Lateral – a position or direction away from midline; to the side.

LED lighting – light emitting diode lighting; a semiconductor device that converts electricity into light; noted for its high energy savings and long-lasting durability.

Length – a vertical dimension.

Leptorrhine – a nasal index having a long, narrow, and high-bridge.

Levatorangulioris – a muscle of facial expression which elevates the angle of the mouth.

Levator labii superioris alaeque nasi – a muscle of facial expression which elevates the upper lip and dilates the nostril opening; the common elevator.

Levator labii superioris – a muscle of facial expression which elevates and extends the upper lip.

Levator palpebrae superioris – a muscle of facial expression which raises the upper eyelid.

Ligature – thread, cord, or wire used for tying vessels, tissues, or bones.

Light – to shine; a form of electromagnetic radiation that acts upon the retina of the eye to make sight possible.

Line of closure – the line that is formed between two structures, such as the lips or the eyelids when in a closed position, which marks their place of contact with each other.

Linear sulci – eyelid furrows which are short and broken, extending horizontally on the palpebrae themselves and which may fan from both the medial and lateral corners of the eyes.

Lip brush – a small, flat brush having soft hairs of uniform length.

Lip wax – a soft restorative wax, usually tinted, used to surface the mucous membranes or to correct lip separations.

Liquid cosmetic – a fluid, colorant in which pigments are dissolved or suspended.

Liquid sealer – a quick-drying fluid adhesive.

Lobe – the inferior part of the ear or the projection of the nose overlying the lower lateral cartilages.

Loop stitch – a single, noose-like suture, not pulled taut before knotting, which stands from the skin and which anchors restorative materials.

Major restoration – restorative art procedures with greater time requirements, higher skill level, and authorization.

Mandible – the horseshoe-shaped bone forming the inferior jaw.

Mandibular fossa – the small oval depression on the zygomatic process of the temporal bone into which the condyle of the mandible articulates, just anterior to the external auditory meatus.

Mandibular notch – a relatively deep indentation between the condyle and coronoid process of the mandible.

Mandibular prognathism – jaw protrusion of the inferior jaw.

Mandibular sulcus – the furrow beneath the jawline which rises vertically on the cheek; an acquired facial marking.

Mandibular suture – type of mouth closure that utilizes the mandible for the inferior anchor and the nasal septum for the superior anchor.

Margins – the boundaries or edges.

Mascara – a cosmetic preparation used to darken the eyelashes.

Mask – anything that hides or conceals, as cosmetics.

Massage cream – a soft, white, oily preparation used as a protective coating for external tissues; a base for cream cosmetics and a wax softener; an emollient.

Masseter – muscles of mastication which close the mandible.

Mastoid process – the rounded projection on the inferior portion of the temporal bones just posterior to the lobe of the ear.

Matte – having a dull finish; created by the application of loose powder, lack of sheen.

Maxilla – a paired bone with several processes that form the skeletal base of most of the superior face, roof of the mouth, sides of the nasal cavity, and floor of the orbit.

Maxillary prognathism – superior jaw protrudes.

Medial – nearer to the midline; opposite of lateral direction.

Medial lobe – tiny prominence on the midline of the superior mucous membrane.

Median plane (mid-sagittal plane) – situated or placed in the middle of the body dividing it into the right and left halves.

Melanin – the brown to black-brown pigment in the epidermis and hair.

Mental eminence – a triangular projection on the inferior portion of the anterior mandible.

Mentalis – the muscle which elevates and protrudes the inferior lip, wrinkles the skin over the chin.

Messorrhine – a nasal index which is medium broad and medium-low bridged.

Mid-sagittal plane – see Median plane.

Minor restoration – restorative art procedures that require minimal time and basic skill.

Modeling – constructing a form with a pliable material such as wax or clay.

Monochromatic – variations of one hue; tints, tones, and shades of one hue.

Mottle – to diversify with spots or blotches of a different color or shade.

Mouth former – a device used in the mouth for shaping the contour of the lips.

Mucous membranes – the visible red surfaces of the lips; the lining membrane of body cavities which communicate with the exterior.

Musculature suture –type of mouth closure that utilizes the mentalis muscle for the inferior anchor and the nasal septum for the superior anchor.

Mutilated – disfigured by a loss of a natural part by force.

Nasal bones – directly inferior to the glabella and forming a dome over the superior portion of the nasal cavity.

Nasal cavity – the orifice in the bony face bounded by the margins of the nasal bones and the maxilla.

Nasal index – the ratio of nasal width to nasal height multiplied by 100.

Nasal spine of the maxilla – the sharp, bony projection located medially at the inferior margin of the nasal cavity.

Nasal sulcus – the angular area between the posterior margin of the wing of the nose and the nasolabial fold; a natural facial marking.

Nasolabial fold – the anterior fold of the cheek which descends laterally along the upper lip 48 from the wing of the nose; a natural facial marking.

Nasolabial sulcus – the furrow lying medial and adjacent to the nasolabial fold; an acquired facial marking.

Naso-orbital fossa – the concavity superior and medial to the inner corner of the eye.

Natural facial markings – those that are present at birth, hereditary.

Natural shadows – areas of color in the tissues normally darker than the adjacent areas.

Needle injector – an instrument used to impel specially designed metal pins (with wire attached to each pin) into bone.

Neoplasm – a new and abnormal formation of tissue, as a tumor or growth.

Norm – the most common characteristics of each feature; typical, common, average.

Oblique – slanting or inclined, neither perpendicular nor horizontal.

Oblique palpebral sulcus – the shallow, curving groove below the medial corner of the eyelids; a natural facial marking.

Oblong – a facial shape in which the head is long and narrow throughout.

Occipital bone – lowest part of the back and base of the cranium, forming a cradle for the brain.

Occipital protuberance – the prominence at the center of the external surface of the occipital bone.

Occipitofrontalis – (see Epicranius)

Opaque – not transparent or translucent; not allowing light to pass through a concealing cosmetic.

Optic facial sulci – see Crows feet.

Oral cavity – the mouth; the orifice containing the teeth and tongue.

Orbicularis oculi – the muscle that closes the eyelids; compresses the lacrimal sacs.

Orbicularis oris – the muscle that closes and puckers the lips.

Orbital cavity – see Eye socket.

Orbital pouch – bags under the eyes; the fullness between the inferior palpebrae and the oblique palpebral sulcus.

Ornamental – an adornment or embellishment; to artificially beautify the face.

Oval – a facial shape with a rounded forehead, cheeks, and chin and is longer than it is wide; most common geometric head form.

Palatine bone – one of the bones forming the posterior part of the hard palate and lateral nasal wall between the interior pterygoid plate of the sphenoid bone and the maxilla.

Palpebrae – see Eyelids.

Parietal bones – two bones that form the posterior 2/3 of the vault of the cranium and part of the sides of the skull.

Parietal eminence – the rounded peak of the external convexity of the parietal bones; determines the widest part of the cranium.

Pathological condition – diseased; due to disease.

Penetrating wounds – wounds that cause a puncture of the skin, a cavity, or an organ.

Phenol – disinfectant employed to dry moist tissues and to bleach discolored tissues.

Philtrum – the vertical groove located medially on the superior lip; a natural facial marking.

Physiognomy – the study of the structures and surface markings of the face and features.

Pigment – a coloring matter which can be applied to an object, when combined with some type of vehicle.

Pigment theory – the Prang system; system which theorizes that all visible colors originate from 30 three primary colors or hues.

Planes – surfaces having very little curvature.

Plaster of Paris – calcium sulfate; a white powdery substance which forms a quick-setting paste when mixed with water.

Platyrrhine – a nasal index which is short and broad and has the minimum of projection.

Platysma – thin layer of muscle covering anterior aspect of neck.

Platysmal sulci – the transverse, dipping furrow of the neck; an acquired facial marking.

Point of entry – point of insertion for hypodermic injection or channeling.

Pores – minute depressions in the surface of the skin, as in the openings of the sweat glands.

Post-embalming – treatments of a restorative nature performed after the embalming operation.

Posterior – position of direction; toward the back.

Powder – any solid substance in the state of fine, loose particles as produced by crushing or grinding.

Powder atomizer – a device used to blow powder onto a surface.

Powder brush – a device containing hairs or bristles set in a handle; used to apply and/or remove powder.

Pre-embalming – treatments of a restorative nature performed before the embalming operation.

Primary hue – one of three pigmentary hues (red, yellow, and blue) which can be combined to make all other hues; in light color theory the hues red, blue, and green can be combined to make all other hues.

Procerus – the muscle that draws the skin of the forehead inferiorly.

Professional portrait – a photograph or painting in which the subject has been posed and lighted flatteringly by a professional photographer or artist.

Profile – the side view of the human head.

Prognathism – projection of the jaw(s) beyond the projection of the forehead.

Projection – the act of throwing forward; a part extending beyond the level of its surroundings.

Proportions – the relationships of the size of one feature as compared with another feature or 29 with the width or length of the face.

Protruding lobe – the rounded, anterior projection of the tip of the nose.

Protrusion – the state or condition of being thrust forward or projecting.

Proximal – a structure that is closer to the center of the body or point of attachment.

Puncture – a hole or wound resulting from piercing.

Purse string suture – a suture made around the circumference of a circular opening or puncture to close it or to hold the margins in position.

Radiate – to spread out from a common point.

Ramus – the vertical portion of the mandible.

Razor burn – a darkened, air-dried area on the skin resulting from removal of the epidermis while shaving.

Recession – a type of surface formed by the withdrawal of a part from its normal position.

Rectangle – a facial shape with a flat forehead, cheeks, and jaw that are all the same width, and the length is longer that it is wide.

Reflection – the return of light waves from surfaces; the bending or folding back of a part upon itself.

Restorative art – the care of the deceased to recreate natural form and color.

Retrousse – a nose which is turned up superiorly at its tip; a concave nasal profile.

Risorius – the narrow superficial band of muscle which pulls the angle of the mouth laterally.

Rods of the eye – the long, rod-shaped sensory bodies of the retina of the eye responsive to light but not color.

Roman – the aquiline profile of the nose.

Root – the apex (top) of the pyramidal mass of the nose which lies directly inferior to the forehead; the concave dip inferior to the forehead (profile view).

Round (infantine) – a facial shape in which the vertical distance and the width between the cheekbones are equal and the cheeks and chin are rounded.

Ruddy – red complexion; having a healthy reddish color, said of the complexion, more vivid than florid.

Sagittal – anatomical plane dividing the body into right and left sides.

Sallow – a yellowish, sickly color of the complexion.

Saturation – a visual aspect indicating the vividness of the hue in the degree of difference from a gray of the same lightness.

Scapha – fossa between the inner and outer rims of the ear; the shallowest depression of the ear.

Sealer – a quick-drying material which leaves a hard, thin transparent coat or layer through which moisture cannot pass.

Second degree burn – those resulting in acute inflammation of the skin and blisters.

Secondary hue – equal mixture of two primary light colors that will produce pigmentary hues (orange, green, and purple); a mixture of yellow, magenta, and cyan (green-blue).

190

Septum – vertical cartilage dividing nasal cavity into two chambers, responsible for asymmetry of the nose.

Severed – to have been cut or broken apart; disjoined.

Shade – a hue into which various quantities of black are mixed; the darkened hue.

Shadow – surfaces which do not lie at right angles to the source of illumination or are obscured by other surfaces and which reflect little or no light.

Sheen – shine; as of the reflection of natural oils of the skin.

Sides of the nose – the lateral walls of the nose between the wings and the bridge.

Simple fracture – fractured bone which does not pierce the skin.

Skin slip – see Desquamation.

Soft wax – wax that is softer and more pliable than modeling wax; less adhesive than lip wax.

Spatula – a flat, blunt, knife-like instrument used for mixing cosmetics and modeling; a palette knife.

Spectrum – visible band; the original standard of color; the progressive arrangement of colors (ROYGBIV) seen when a beam of white light is broken down into its component colors.

Sponge – an elastic, porous mass of interlacing horny fibers which are permanently attached; remarkable for its power of absorbing water and becoming soft when wet without losing its toughness.

Squama – the vertical surface of the temporal bone.

Square – a facial shape in which the vertical and horizontal measurements are equal, the hairline is straight, and the jaw is angled.

Stain – to discolor with foreign matter; an area so discolored.

Stain removers – any substances or agents which will cause an external discoloration to be removed or lessened.

Sternocleidomastoid – a muscle of the neck that is attached to the mastoid process of the temporal bone and by separate heads to the sternum and clavicle; marks the widest part of the neck.

Stipple brush – a small, rounded, stiff brush, all bristles the same length, used to simulate pores on wax; stencil brush; could be used for cosmetic application.

Straight nasal profile – a nasal profile in which the dorsum exhibits a straight line from the root to the tip; the most common nasal profile.

Subcutaneous – situated or occurring beneath the skin.

Sublingual suture – type of mouth closure that anchors inferior to the tongue and utilizes the nasal septum for the superior anchor.

Submandibular – describing those portions which lie immediately inferior to the mandible.

Submental sulcus – the junction of the base of the chin and the submandibular area, which may appear as a furrow, a natural facial marking.

Subtractive method – method of diminishing the wavelengths of light by superimposing two or more color transparencies over the same light source; the light is gradually reduced by absorption of colors in the light.

Sulcus – a furrow, wrinkle, or groove.

Superciliary arches – the inferior part of the forehead just superior to the median ends of the eyebrows.

Supercilia – eyebrows.

Superficial – closer to the surface.

Superior – more elevated in place or position; higher; upper; anatomically towards the head.

Superior palpebral sulcus – the furrow of the superior border of the upper eyelid; an acquired facial marking.

Supraorbital area – region between the supercilium and the superior palpebrae.

Supraorbital margins – the superior rim of the eye sockets.

Surgical reduction – restoration to a normal position or level through surgical excision.

Suspension – a substance in which particles of ground pigments are mixed with a fluid but are undissolved.

Suture – act of sewing; also the completed stitch.

Swarthy – dark-colored complexion, as a face made swarthy by the tropical sun.

Symmetry – correspondence in size, shape, and relative position of parts that are on opposite sides of the face.

Taper – a form which receded away from a given point; a form which becomes gradually smaller toward one end; to reduce gradually from the center.

Temporal bones – inferior portion of the sides and base of the cranium, inferior to the parietal bones and anterior to the occipital bone.

Temporal cavity – the concave surface of the head overlying the temporal bone.

Temporalis – muscles of mastication which help to close the mandible.

Tertiary hue – the hue which results from the mixture of two secondary pigmentary hues or an unbalanced proportion of complements with the warm hue or cool hue predominating.

Texturizing brush – a brush with a relatively large tuft of good quality, fine bristles, such as black sable or finch; used to blend and stipple cosmetics or powder into the applied (cream) cosmetic and clean out deposits impacted in pores.

Third degree burn – destruction of cutaneous and subcutaneous tissues; seared or charred tissue.

Three quarter view – in reference to a photograph, a view which reveals the fullness of the cheeks.

Tint – a hue into which various quantities of white are mixed.

Tip – the extremity of anything which tapers (e.g. the tip of the nose; the termination of the forward projection of the nose).

Tissue builder – see feature builder.

Tone – a hue mixed with either a small quantity of gray or the complement of the hue, resulting in dulling the hue.

Toupee – a small wig or patch of false hair covering a bald spot; a hairpiece.

Tragus – elevation protecting the ear passage (external auditory meatus).

Translucent – transmitting light but causing sufficient diffusion to eliminate perception of distinct images; somewhat transparent.

Transparent – having the property of transmitting rays of light through its substance so that bodies situated beyond or behind can be distinctly seen.

Transverse frontal sulci – furrows which cross the forehead; acquired facial markings.

Trauma – a physical injury or wound caused by external force or violence.

Triangle – a facial shape in which the forehead is pointed, the sides widen inferiorly, and the jaw is the widest point;(least common geometric head form).

Triangular fossa – depression between the crura of the ear; the second deepest depression of the ear.

Tumor – a spontaneous new growth of tissue forming an abnormal mass.

Undercut – the angled cut of the borders of an excision, made so that the skin surface will overhang the deeper tissues.

Undertones – underlying colors in the skin.

Value – the lightness or darkness of a hue.

Vehicle – a material combined with pigments so they may be applied more easily.

Vertex – see Crown.

Vertical – perpendicular to the plane of the horizon; balanced.

Vertical-concave profile – one in which the forehead and the eyebrows project equally to a vertical line and the chin protrudes more than the upper lip.

Vertical-convex profile – one in which the forehead and the eyebrows project equally to a vertical line and the chin recedes from the projection of the upper lip.

Vertical (balanced) profile – one in which the forehead, upper lip and chin project equally to an imaginary vertical line; e.g. balanced.

Vomer – bone of the nasal cavity situated between the nasal passages on the median plane; it forms the inferior and posterior portion of the septum of the nose.

Warm color areas – areas of the skin surface which, during life, are naturally reddened; places where cosmetics will be applied to restore the appearance of warmth that red hemoglobin will give.

Warm hue – a color which appears in the spectral band, characterized by long wave-lengths; a color which makes an object appear closer and larger; a color which reflects warmth; i.e. red, orange, yellow, and other colors in which they are predominate.

Wax – a restorative modeling or surfacing material composed of beeswax, spermaceti, paraffin, starch, and a coloring pigment which will soften at body temperature and will reflect light in a manner similar to normal skin.

Weather line – the line of color change at the junction of the wet and dry portions of each 41 mucous membrane.

White light – a ray of light which contains all the hues of the visible spectrum, in such proportion that the light appears colorless or "natural"; as daylight or sunlight.

Width – the dimension of an object measured across from side to side.

Wings of the nose – lateral lobes of the nose.

Wire bridging – the length of wire employed to connect two structures which are undamaged such as remaining parts of a bone; a wire mesh placed within an aperture to hold other restorative fillers.

Worm suture – (a/k/a inversion suture, draw stitch); a method of sewing an incision along the edges without entering the opening whereby the suture becomes invisible, and the line of suture becomes depressed, which lends it ease of concealment by waxing.

Zygomatic arch – the process on the temporal and zygomatic bones; determines the widest part of the face.

Zygomatic arch depression – one of the lesser concavities of the face located on the lateral portion of the cheek inferior to the zygomatic arch.

Zygomatic bones – bones of the cheeks.

Zygomaticofrontal process – the lateral rim of the eye socket formed by a process of the frontal bone and a process of the zygomatic bone.

Zygomaticus major – muscles of the face which draw the superior lip posteriorly and superiorly.

Zygomaticus minor – muscles of the face which draw the superior lip superiorly and anteriorly.

Domain III

Preparation for Final Disposition

Preparation of Human Remains for Final Disposition

Preparation for disposition is the entire purpose of funeral services. Helping families to take leave of their loved ones with respect and dignity should be in the mission statements of all funeral firms. The funeral director is responsible for caring for the dead while helping the bereaved begin their grieving process. However, there is much more to operating a funeral home, such as personnel management, facilities maintenance, community outreach, financial management, and advertising which are not directly involved with the preparation of remains. This section focuses on the variety of methods that must be applied to suit society's needs for the different types of dispositions which exist today.

Each of the potential dispositions begins either with a body that has been embalmed in a typical or common way or with remains that have not been embalmed, thus presenting different challenges for disposition.

1. Long-Term Storage Prior to Viewing

Death happens at the most inconvenient time. In the practice of funeral directing, more and more families are unable to travel to the location of the visitation for a week or two, requiring a delay in viewing and services. If the situation is known at the time of embalming, extra arterial injection with a specialty fluid, supplemented by a humectant co-injection (ex. Sorbitol or Lanolin), could retard decomposition and maintain the appearance of the fullness of the tissues. Water will evaporate from the body tissues over time, resulting in shrinkage and darkening of the tissues; humectants should prevent dehydration. Additionally, the use of massage cream on all exposed surfaces delays dehydration. If the potential need for extra arterial injection is not known at the time of first embalming, a six-point injection may be utilized to re-embalm the areas that the embalmer feels are not entirely preserved. Hypodermic injection could be used to address difficult areas of distribution. Sacrificing the natural feel of the tissues and losing the flexibility of extremities for easier dressing are tradeoffs for a higher level of preservation. This is an unusual situation; atypical treatment with paraformaldehyde gel may be necessary to firm flaccid tissue.

The signs to look for that indicate the problems associated with dehydration include separation of eyes and lips, shrinking of tissues, discoloration of different areas, pockets of gas under the skin, flies or maggots, shrinking of fingertips, and foul odor.

The remains should not be dressed, cosmetized, or casketed until shortly before the actual viewing will occur. Moisture evaporating from the body could absorb into the clothing and casket interior, supporting mold and bacterial growth, with the potential for reversal of embalming by excess moisture or humid conditions. This will re-hydrate the muscles and protein tissues. Cooling to normal room temperature is preferred; embalmed remains kept in a cooler close to the freezing point (32° Fahrenheit) leak excess embalming fluid through the skin, resulting in moisture or condensation of bodily fluids. The refrigerated human remains require a daily inspection to determine the condition of the remains and, if necessary, corrective measures should be taken to deal with small problems (such as mold development or dehydration) as they arise. The human remains placed in a cooler should be properly labeled with a toe tag or wrist band and placed in the cooler, head-first. A cooler manifest should be posted on the outside of the cooler identifying the proper location of the human remains in the cooler. The remains should be covered for dignity and privacy.

Dignity and respect should be given to the human remains at all times. The remains should be dressed in a hospital gown and wrapped in a sheet when placed in a cooler for extended periods of time. The sheet will draw moister away from the remains and towards the material. The sheet will also serve as an indicator of points that need to be treated post-embalming, such as IV holes or bodily fluid discharge. Plastic garments should be placed on the human remains shortly before dressing for visitation or services.

The FTC allows a storage fee to be charged for each day that the remains are on the funeral home premises and no other funerary treatments (such as embalming) were performed. Custodial care fees can be charged to the consumer only on days of waiting to engage for services. For example:

Day 1: Mr. Thompson dies on Monday, and the funeral director makes the removal and embalms the remains;

Day 2: On Tuesday, the family makes arrangements, and the funeral director arranges for the service a week away.

Day 3: On Wednesday, the funeral director files the death certificate, publishes the obituary, and finalizes all the plans for the visitation Monday afternoon.

Day 4-7: The remains are in the prep room, covered on the embalming table.

Day 8: The hairdresser and the funeral staff dress, casket, and cosmetize the remains for visitation. Family viewing is from 1:15 PM to 2:00 PM.

Day 9: Church service followed by committal service at a local cemetery.

In the above scenario, only on Days 4-7 can the funeral director charge a custodial fee because the funeral home was storing the remains and not engaged in the practice of funeral directing during those days.

Human remains that have not been embalmed can only be held in a mortuary cooler as a means of delaying decomposition. The FTC requires the funeral director to offer the "use of the cooler" as an alternative to embalming, if a cooler is on the premises. Some state regulations require the funeral firm to have a cooler on the funeral home premises as a condition for charging for the use of a cooler. Charging for the use of the cooler and charging a custodial fee is considered "double-dipping" and is frowned upon by most state regulatory agencies.

Assuming embalming or other chemical treatment is not allowed by family preference, the best that can be done is to treat the surfaces of the face, neck, and hands with a very thick layer of massage cream (which contains a humectant such as lanolin), adding more when necessary. Posing the features is important, but if permission has not been given, it is mutilation to use an invasive technique like injector needles or mandibular sutures. The mouth may be kept closed by placing a strip of cloth around the chin and tying it on top of the head towards the back. A chin rest positioning device may also be used.

The use of a mortuary cooler requires careful documentation. Each time human remains are placed in or removed from the cooler, the time, date, and employee performing the task is documented on the Refrigeration Log. Remains should be placed in the cooler, head-first, so the ankle ID can be quickly and easily observed. No matter how many calls a firm makes annually, all human remains in a cooler should have an identification tag on the remains and on the body bag. The longer and more often the door is open, spilling out cooled air, the more expensive the cooler is to operate. It is legal to charge for refrigeration as long as no other service was performed on the remains during that day.

In order to identify the remains, it is necessary for the family (or a family agent) to visually inspect the human remains. To prepare for visual identification, The funeral director should ask for permission to do minimally invasive procedures, such as shaving, closing the jaw and mouth with injector needles (wires), closing the eyes with adhesive, and injecting cavity fluid. Be certain that the permission for limited treatment is specific to avoid legal jeopardy.

Can a funeral director charge for this limited invasive procedure? Identification is considered part of the cremation or direct burial process and is incorporated in the package fee. If, for example, the family does not choose to embalm but would like to view their loved one's remains prior to direct burial, with permission, the funeral director could charge for topical disinfection and a preparation fee.

2. Mausoleum and Entombment

The general idea for proper mausoleum entombment is to allow the slow evaporation of moisture from the remains as well as control any leakage. Modern mausoleum crypts are built to allow liquids to drain into a type of gutter system, as well as bodily gases to escape through a roof vent. Well-prepared human remains will allow evaporation to occur easily and control the amount of leakage. Cemeteries with mausoleums have entombment rules which need to be followed.

Remains that will be entombed in a mausoleum should be embalmed with a more concentrated arterial solution than normal to reduce the amount of water introduced into the body tissues. Regional injection to address areas of deficiency may be required.

Prior to casketing human remains, a leakproof pouch should be placed in the casket to collect any leakage that may occur over time. The pouch can be concealed underneath the human remains during visitation and services, and prior to final disposition, the remains are zippered into the pouch. It is not recommended to use an adhesive around the zipper in this situation because this will prohibit off-gassing. Bodily fluids that accumulate in the pouch will evaporate over time in wooden caskets. Some wooden caskets have a plastic tray in the base of the casket to accumulate bodily fluids. Metal caskets with a gasket are designed to off-gas when the internal gas pressure reaches maximum capacity. Non-gasketed caskets will off-gas similar to wooden caskets. A mold-inhibitor chemical that will prevent mold growth, often paradichlorobenzene, should be placed in the casket. Local requirements, usually promulgated by the Department of Health, may vary. Some cemeteries require that the casket be wrapped in a membrane that will maintain a hermetic seal over the long term. Some cemeteries place casketed remains on a plastic tray before entombment. Allowing moisture to evaporate is generally a better method for long-term storage. After all, some Egyptian mummies have lasted for thousands of years just from pure desiccation (removal of moisture).

3. Transportation by Common Carrier

Common carriers are companies that are hired to transport goods. Examples: buses, trains, trucks, and airlines. Generally, human remains are transported long distances by airlines because they travel faster than land-based carriers. Human remains that will be transported by airplane must have certain preparations made in order to have a safe journey to their final destination. Most airlines require that the body be embalmed. In some cases, religious practice prohibits embalming, and some airlines will transport those cases. Unembalmed remains must be placed in a leakproof container with gel packs applied for cooling. Two packs go on the front of the body, two packs on the back, one pack under the head, and one pack goes under each leg. Hands should be bound over the abdomen. Dry ice is prohibited for shipping human remains because the off gassing (release of CO_2 gas) was causing live animals stored next to the human remains to perish. Human remains that start to exhibit beginning or advanced stages of decomposition, should be transported using private carriers, such as a removal van or contracted removal service. Creating a biohazard in an airport could result in hazmat cleaning fees for the shipping funeral director. This could cause unnecessary delays and layovers in shipping.

Different types of containers can be used to transport the remains by common carrier. If the remains are not in a casket, they can be transported in a **combination unit**. *This unit has particle board sides and top, a plywood base, and a cardboard cover over the entire unit.* The remains are stabilized by straps built into the unit and usually have padding to protect the remains. This is the most cost-effective container for common carrier transportation due to weighing the least. If the remains are already in a casket, then an **air tray** is utilized. *This system uses a plywood base to which the casket is attached with straps, and the unit is covered with a plastic casket sheet and a cardboard cover.* Be sure to check with the airlines regarding weight limits. Due to the extra weight of a casket, this is the more expensive method of shipping. Air trays are used properly when there are services at the forwarding funeral home prior to shipping the human remains for final disposition. If the forwarding funeral home does not have public or private services prior to shipping, ethically, the casket should be sold by the receiving funeral home. This keeps shipping costs down (ethical treatment of the family) and allows the receiving funeral home to care for the family's needs as if the person died near home to provide the full service (ethical treatment of other funeral directors).

When shipping by a common carrier, it is necessary to affix the Burial Transit Permit and shipping information to the outside of the combination unit or air tray. The receiving funeral home's name, address, and telephone number must be displayed on the combination or air tray unit. Air freight may be paid by either the shipping or the receiving funeral home. Air trays and combination units are single-use items and must be destroyed after one use.

When shipping internationally, it is necessary to have additional documentation. The process begins by contacting the consulate for the country where the human remains will be sent. This will ensure that the requirements, policies, and procedures are adhered to prior to shipping.

Most countries have similar rules about what documentation is required for shipping human remains to another country. These are some of the most common documents required:

1. Burial Transit Permit.
2. Copy of the Death Certificate.
3. A statement from a Department of Health official stating that the human remains are not infectious, contagious, or communicable.
4. Citizenship information, such as the passport.
5. The destination funeral home receiving the remains needs to be declared.
6. Embalming report
7. Caskets might have to be inspected by Customs and sealed before they can be placed on the airplane. Transportation Safety Administration (TSA) regulations need to be followed at all times.

Some countries have a consulate fee that needs to be paid prior to shipping. Trade services should be utilized to process shipping human remains out of the United States. There are too many varying factors to consider, and professional trade services seem to know each of these requirements and they have a system for processing these types of air transports.

Since 9/11/2001, the Transportation Security Administration (TSA) has imposed rules and regulations on shipping human remains via common carrier. For a funeral home to send human remains on a common carrier, they must become a Known Shipper prior to shipping human remains. Each airline has an application that needs to be processed with TSA for a Known Shipper ID to be assigned to a funeral home. Each airline will issue a separate Known Shipper ID.

When sending casketed remains on an airplane, it is necessary to account for severe changes in cabin pressure. Wooden caskets do not seal, so they may be latched in their usual fashion. Metal caskets that seal present a unique problem. The gasket and locking mechanisms on sealer caskets are designed to relieve pressure from the inside - out. This gasket mechanism is designed to allow gases produced by decomposing remains to escape when the internal pressure increases, potentially causing the casket to rupture. For burial purposes, this is necessary. If the cargo hold of an airplane loses its pressure, the air inside the casket will flow out. However, when pressure is restored in the cargo hold or when landing the aircraft, the air pressure cannot go back into the casket, because the gaskets prevent airflow inward. The result is that the casket top itself will be crushed by atmospheric pressure. Metal caskets can be locked; however, the plug over the key chamber needs to be placed in the document envelope affixed to the top of the shipping unit. This opening will allow easy airflow in and out of the casket regardless of pressure change, preventing damage. If this procedure is not done, the forwarding funeral home could be liable for replacing the damaged casket.

When possible, air transportation needs to take into consideration various routes to avoid extremes of weather conditions. During summer months, use a northerly route to avoid high temperatures at airports. Conversely, during winter months, use a more southerly route, if possible, to avoid freezing temperatures and weather delays. Sometimes using airports that are in areas of extreme weather conditions cannot be avoided.

Another concept with shipping during high-temperature seasons or shipping to tropical countries is to prepare the remains by using cotton soaked in lamp oil inserted into each nasal cavity. This would prevent the development of maggots if there were flies present previously or upon arrival of the remains. Prior to public viewing or prior to shipping human remains, the best funeral practice is to always keep the face covered to prevent a fly from using the nasal cavity as a receptacle for laying their eggs.

Another factor to consider in common carrier transportation is unembalmed remains or a decomposing case in which embalming has failed to retard the natural decomposition of the remains. Human remains in advanced stages of decomposition can be shipped using a container known as a Ziegler case. This is an eight-sided (octagonal-shaped) metal casket that is welded and used for extreme conditions or cases. A Zieglar case is a one-piece lid with a rubber gasket. The lid is placed on top of the container and is screwed down, then soldered or welded shut. Once properly closed, it is completely sealed. The strength of the seal prevents the outflow of air if there is a pressure drop (discussed above), so when pressure is restored, the container will not collapse. The Ziegler case can be placed in a regular burial casket with the interior removed. The corners are tapered diagonally to allow the removal of straps or other devices used to lower it into the casket.

4. Green Burial

Green burial refers to human remains which are interred in the ground, without any chemical treatment, and usually in a biodegradable burial unit or wrapped in a burial shroud. This concept of human remains disposal is based on the notion that it allows the remains to naturally decompose fully back to the earth. The general tenets of green burial are that there will be no synthetic chemicals introduced into the ground, that the burial container can fully decompose, and that there is minimal marking of the gravesite. Most green cemeteries use latitude and longitude coordinates to locate the grave. There are hybrid cemeteries which are traditional cemeteries that have a green section in addition to their regular areas for burials. Generally, there is no embalming, no vaults, no metal caskets, and no wood caskets with finish. The strength of green cemeteries is that they are an ecologically sensible alternative to cremation, where a large amount of fossil fuels are used during the cremation process.

Green cemeteries in the northern portion of the country have a problem with winter burial. When the frost is too deep in the ground to open a grave, the body must be stored until spring. This requires embalming because an unembalmed body would have to be kept in a cooler for a long time. That would be expensive, as well as defeating the conceptual idea of reducing the *carbon footprint*. There are fluids manufactured by at least two chemical companies which are approved for green burial. These fluids contain naturally occurring chemicals that break down completely into harmless molecules, thus meeting the requirement for full decomposition in a green cemetery. Some of the green embalming chemicals are supplied in their fully diluted form and can be used in the embalming machine with no further dilution. Preservation of the cellular tissue is minimal; firming and long-term preservation is noticeably different from conventional embalming with formaldehyde or glutaraldehyde-based chemicals.

5. Preparation for Cremation

The Burial Transit Permit is obtained from the Registrar in the locality where the death occurred after the death certificate has been filed. Cremation is a means of final disposition which uses intense heat to incinerate the human remains and reduce them to their calcium and carbon components. A Burial Transit Permit is issued and needed prior to cremation. Once the cremation has been completed, the crematory operator will file the completed Burial Transit Permit with the Registrar where cremation occurs. The cremated remains from that point forward are not considered a legal entity. They may be treated in any way that is legal, which mostly means not littering and scattering cremated remains in public or private areas where doing so is prohibited. Crematories will provide a Certificate of Cremation (that authenticates the cremated remains as being those of the person brought to the crematory), which can be taken to a cemetery to prove that the cremated remains in that urn are a particular person. The Certificate of Cremation replaces the body transit permit required by cemeteries for the burial of cremated remains. This certificate is needed for shipping cremated remains, as well as traveling with an urn on a common carrier. Burying cremated remains is not considered the final disposition; the cremation process is the final disposition of the human remains.

The most important aspect of cremation is being absolutely certain that the proper person is being cremated. *Identification of all human remains begins at the point of removal when an ID bracelet is affixed to the wrist and ankle.* In some states, like Ohio, this is a state regulation. Each time that the remains are moved for various treatments (such as embalming or cosmetology), the ID bracelets should be checked and verified. Human remains need to be identified by the family (or their appointed representative) prior to cremation in the container selected by the family during arrangements. A family member needs to sign a statement declaring that they identified the remains of their loved one. No human remains should be cremated prior to proper identification by the next-of-kin or person making the funeral arrangements.

The direct cremation package price for cremation includes the treatment of the remains for sanitary purposes, and there is no additional charge allowed for this preparation. Prior to having the family identify the human remains, the following procedures should be implemented to prepare the remains for positive identification by the person making the arrangements:

1. The deceased hair should be combed.
2. The face should be disinfected and sanitized.
3. Orifices should be swabbed with a disinfectant spray, and any visible signs of bodily fluids should be removed.
4. The oral cavity should be secured to the closed position
5. Eye caps with stay cream on top should be inserted under the eyelids.
6. The deceased should be prepared and placed in the cremation unit selected by the family during the arrangements.
7. The remains should be in a state of repose that presents a positive memory picture.
8. Human remains placed in an alternative container should be covered from the chest down with clothing, a hospital gown, a blanket, or a quilt.

Preparing the human remains for an identification session is included in the direct cremation package price. If the family wishes for a private viewing session with immediate family and the funeral home has a policy in place for viewing unembalmed remains in such a setting, the funeral home can charge for such viewing, provided that such a session appears on their General Price List.

Crematories have a capacity that cannot be exceeded. Capacity is the measure of how large a person may fit in the retort. The common capacity of a retort is 450 pounds, meaning that a larger person needs to be taken to a crematory that can accommodate excessive weight limits. A similar term to capacity is burn rate which is a measure of how fast the body is consumed by heat and flame. When more than one human remains are being cremated during the day, larger remains are cremated first because the retort needs to be set at a low temperature to burn off the adipose tissue (body fat) gradually. Cremating large human remains, too fast, could cause the retort to catch fire, creating damage to the retort and possibly the crematory. The person with the least amount of weight is cremated last and poses minimal threat to crematory operations.

Sample question:

A crematory had human remains that weighed 375lbs. When was it cremated?

    A. 8:00 a.m.
    B. 11:00 a.m.
    C. 3:00 p.m.
    D. 4:00 p.m.

Answer: 8:00 a.m.

Tooth extraction is Prohibited.

Tooth extraction at the request of the family can only be performed by a dentist. A funeral director is not trained to remove teeth, and doing so could cause a liable situation and be considered a form of mutilation. Dental gold is not the same as jeweler's gold. Dental gold has little resale value…it is made mostly of various alloys in order to be durable and withstand oral acids.

Preparation of the human remains for cremation includes:

1. Removal of any pacemaker, defibrillator, or device that has a cell battery as a component. The small pill size pacemaker embedded in the heart poses little risk and may be left in place. Only remove subcutaneous battery units. Battery cells that are not removed will explode in the retort and could cause damage to the retort. In addition, shrapnel from a battery-operated device could be life-threatening to the crematory operator.
2. To remove a battery-operated device that is subcutaneous, an incision is made over the device to expose the device. Connective fascia tissue might have to be removed to expose the unit. Using an aneurism hook, the device should be extracted from the body and pulled tight. The leads that are attached to the heart can be snipped with wire cutters. The device should be disposed of properly and not in the biohazard waste container because usually, this material is incinerated and will pose the same hazard as previously stated.
3. The funeral home may charge an extra fee to remove pacemakers because it is not done for each and every case. This fee should be nominal and must be on the GPL.
4. All belongings should be documented on an inventory sheet and signed by the family. Remove all personal items that should be returned to the family, such as hearing aids or jewelry.
5. The human remains should be placed in a leakproof pouch specially designed for the cremation process. Note: Disaster pouches will emit toxic chemicals such as benzopyrene (BAP) and polyaromatic hydrocarbons (PAH); both are a violation of the Environmental Protection Act (EPA).
6. Radioactive implants, active or inactive, need to be removed by a trained surgeon prior to cremation. An embalmer is not licensed to remove such an implant. Knowingly cremating human remains with radioactive implants is also a violation of the EPA. If a surgeon is unwilling to remove the implants, the family should be counseled on other options of final disposition.
7. The human remains should be dressed in a minimal garment, such as a hospital gown or clothes brought in by the family. If the deceased is wearing the clothes from the removal, the pockets should be checked prior to cremation and any contents should be documented and returned to the family.
8. The cremation container should have the head end clearly marked with the decedent's last name and the name of the funeral home written on the exterior.
9. A numbered metal medallion that can withstand the temperatures during the cremation process is placed on the cremation container prior to being placed in the retort and remains through the cremation process.

10. After the cremation process is completed, the medallion should be attached to a plastic bag containing the pulverized cremated remains. If possible, that medallion should be included in the urn when presented to the family.

Recap: All human remains should be identified by the person making the arrangements (or designated representative). The remains need to be checked for a pacemaker or other device with a battery pack; the remains should be checked head-to-toe for jewelry; and finally, the remains should be in a leakproof pouch acceptable for cremation.

Documents required for cremation include:
1. Burial Transit Permit.
2. Authorization for Cremation form or Cremation Authorization forms specific to state regulations, which authorizes the crematory to perform the cremation.
3. In some cases, a cremation permit is issued by a coroner, medical examiner, or Department of Health. This requirement varies from state-to-state.
4. Further documentation includes a statement about what will happen to those cremains if they are not retrieved within a certain period of time. This, too, varies among the states, ranging from 60 days to four years (Customer Designation of Intention form).
5. If, for religious reasons, the family requires an intact bone fragment, a written notarized statement from the family must accompany the authorization form. The bone fragment should not exceed 3" in length.
6. The family should be informed that cremation is an irreversible process by which intense heat is used to reduce the human remains to their calcium deposits. This disclosure should be a part of the informed consent section on the cremation authorization form and should be reviewed with the family at the end of the arrangement process.

A funeral home should not retain cremated remains for an extended period of time. Cremated remains may be buried in the ground (interment), placed in a niche or columbarium (inurnment), placed in a common receptacle for many different cremated remains (ossuary), or returned to the family for their retention. There is no law specifying that they need to be disposed of in any specific way or time frame. Some states have provisions within the law that allows the funeral director to properly dispose of unclaimed cremated remains in a prescribed manner. In New York State, for example, a Customer Designation of Intention form is used during the arrangements to identify the consumer's wishes for the cremated remains after the cremation process has been completed. This form also indicates that after 120 days, if the cremated remains are unclaimed, the funeral home has the right to dispose of the cremated remains in a prescribed manner.

A funeral director may transfer the cremated remains from a temporary container to a final container, such as an urn selected during arrangements, as a service to the family. A funeral director may not comingle the ashes of two or more people in the same container. There are companion urns that have two sections but do not mix the cremains. Inurnment may be in one urn or several small ones; it is allowed to divide into smaller units for burial in different places. When the urn has been filled, it is important to be certain the outside is clean, showing no dust or other indication of what is inside. If transporting cremains on an airplane, it is requested that the content material must be transparent to X-Ray so it can be checked by TSA.

Human remains with radioactive implants cannot be cremated unless the radioactive implant has been removed. Knowingly cremating human remains with radioactive implants is a violation of EPA standards and could result in a federal violation for the crematory operator and the funeral director. Removal of radioactive implants can only be done by a trained medical professional who can properly dispose of the radioactive material. If no medical professional is willing to remove the radioactive implants, the funeral director needs to counsel the family on alternative means of final disposition. Radioactive implants whose shelf-life has expired are also covered under this rule.

Sending Cremated Remains via Mail
Cremated remains can only be sent via United States Postal Services Priority Mail Express. The postal service has a specific box marked "Cremated Remains," in which the cremated remains must be packaged for shipping and can be obtained without charge from the Post Office. The package needs to be sent by registered mail, and a signature receipt is required. A tracking number will be issued.

Funeral Directing and Preparation for Disposition

First Call:
Funeral directors are not able to proceed with a case until they receive an official notification of death, generally known as the "first call." With the rise of cell phones, almost all notifications of death are made via telephone (at least 98%). The notification of death is most commonly made by the family, an agency, such as a nursing home or hospice center, a hospital, a medical examiner's office, a police agency, or even a friend. Gathering important preliminary information regarding the caller and their relationship to the decedent is the essential part of the first call.

The person answering phones on behalf of the funeral home must use an appropriate tone of voice and proper language. Neutral language should always be used to ensure that respect is given to every person equally. When answering phones, the person's tone and diction should be clear, crisp, moderate volume, and slightly slower than normal speech, and use appropriate enunciation and pronunciation. The person should sound understanding and empathetic, not too cheerful or somber. The person should also not sound bored, annoyed, or angry. This is the first interaction the funeral home and director may have with the family and will set the tone for any future interactions.

When gathering first call information, the person receiving the call needs to **determine the nature of the call:** That is, is the caller calling regarding an "at-need" case in which someone has died or "pre-need" case in which someone wants to pre-arrange their funeral services, but death has not occurred yet, or death is imminent (very close).

Acquiring Vital Information: The removal process begins by **obtaining vital information**. The preliminary information obtained on the *first call* must be accurate and informative. This information, if wrong, will affect other information obtained during the conference arrangements. Misinformation could cause delays, cost the firm money to correct errors, and is unprofessional.

The person taking the call needs to obtain the following information:
1. The name of the decedent.
2. The location of the deceased. If an institution, has the deceased been transferred to the morgue, and the remains been released?
3. If the caller is a representative of an institution, the question should be asked if the deceased is ready for the funeral home to make the removal.
4. If the person dies at home and the death is attended by an agency (such as Hospice or Home Healthcare), usually the representative from the agency calls the funeral home. During this conversation with the healthcare worker, the funeral director obtains the majority of the information:
   a. Address where the removal will take place
   b. Who will be signing the death certificate
   c. Time of Death (TOD)
   d. Name of the next-of-kin or contact person who will be making the arrangements.
   e. Contact person's phone number and possibly an alternative phone number
   f. Obtain pertinent information about the location of the removal.
      1) If there are stairs, sharp corners, multiple floors,
      2) The decedent's weight, state (decomposition, rigor mortis), and cultural/religious beliefs needs to be obtained to ensure that appropriate removal measures are taken.

5. If the caller is a family member and the death was an unattended death, the funeral director will inform the caller to call 911 and notify the authorities that a death occurred. This could be alarming for some family members. The funeral director should inform the caller that calling the authorities is a normal procedure when a person dies without medical personnel attending the death. The funeral director should explain the process of involving the authorities:
   a. After the caller calls 911, a uniformed officer, such as a police officer or sheriff, will show up at the house and take some preliminary information.
   b. The coroner/medical examiner official will come to the home and authorize the removal.
   c. The coroner/medical examiner or police officer will then call the funeral home and authorize the removal. If the death was suspicious or no doctor would sign the death certificate, the coroner/medical examiner personnel could require the human remains to be taken to the ME's office or local morgue.
   d. At that time, the funeral home personnel will come to the home and bring the deceased back to the funeral home or do as directed by the authorities.
   e. Reassuring the family that the funeral home is always there for them, the funeral director's cell phone number (optional) should be offered, or the funeral director should provide the best number for the funeral home. Reassure the family that the authority will be expeditious, and if no one replies within 30 minutes, the next-of-kin should call the funeral home.

Medical Facility Notification: If the caller is the next-of-kin, and the decedent is at a medical facility or other agency, additional information may need to be obtained, such as:

1. Medical Record Number (obtained from the institution)
2. Date of Admission
3. Location of facility or room where the patient is residing
4. The physician who will be signing the death certificate
5. The next-of-kin contact information

Most medical institutions will provide a face sheet that has this information. Some institutions are reluctant to provide this information because of HIPPA (Health Insurance Portability and Accountability Act) regulations. Unfortunately, such institutions are misguided regarding the information that funeral directors can obtain information about the deceased. The following is the **HIPPA regulation** *with respect to disclosing information to the funeral director:*

Standard: Uses and disclosures about decedents.

> (1) **Coroners and medical examiners.** A covered entity may disclose protected health information to a coroner or medical examiner for the purpose of identifying a deceased person, determining a cause of death, or other duties as authorized by law. A covered entity that also performs the duties of a coroner or medical examiner may use protected health information for the purposes described in this paragraph.

> (2) **Funeral directors.** A covered entity may disclose protected health information to funeral directors, consistent with applicable law, as necessary to carry out their duties with respect to the decedent. If necessary for funeral directors to carry out their duties, the covered entity may disclose the protected health information prior to, and in reasonable anticipation of, the individual's death.

Source:

http://www.hipaasurvivalguide.com/hipaa-regulations/164-512.php

Occasionally, funeral homes will receive calls from "price shoppers," a person who will call many funeral homes to compare and contrast pricing for funeral services. Under Federal Trade Commission (FTC) Funeral Rule, firms are required to disclose current pricing information to the consumer, both in-person and over-the-phone inquiries. While accurate pricing over the phone is a triggering event for pricing disclosure, under the Funeral Rule, the funeral director is not required to mail or email a General Price List (GPL). The key to these types of inquiries is to provide accurate information while engaging in a conversation as to what types of services are available and how the firm can best serve their needs.

The Removal: After the first call information has been obtained and authorization has been granted, the decedent can be removed from the residence/institution. Funeral home personnel should not be dispatched until proper authorization has been obtained. However, the funeral director should begin the removal process by notifying additional staff of the pending removal. Coordinating and preparing the removal vehicle with the proper equipment and organizing personnel in the midst of other scheduled events, like funerals and visitations, may require freeing up personnel in order to comply with state regulations governing removals.

Once the first call has been received and permission to remove the human remains has been granted, the removal can be made from the place of death. **The removal** is *the transfer of human remains from the location of death to the funeral home.*

Various vehicles may be used for removals. Some firms solely use a hearse for all removals and funeral services. Some firms utilize a removal vehicle which is usually a minivan or SUV that has the space for a removal cot. The choice of vehicle may depend on factors such as availability, location of the removal, number of decedents, and the family's wishes (some families are adamantly against a hearse coming to the house). Most states require that a removal vehicle has tinted windows to impede the view from the public.

Vehicles should be properly maintained, including necessary inspections, registrations, and oil changes. The removal vehicle should have an adequate supply of gas, especially in the event of midnight removals when gas stations may not be available. The vehicle should also be cleaned, both interior and exterior, to maintain a professional appearance and a clean environment. The vehicle should also be equipped with the proper removal equipment, which includes, but is not limited to:

1. A mortuary cot to carry the decedent, a pillow or head block, sheets,
2. Alternative moving devices like Reeves Carrier or a MedSled First Call,
3. Mortuary/body bags (a/k/a, disaster pouch). This is a regulation in some states,
4. Hand sanitizer/wipes,
5. Relevant paperwork (General Price List, Embalming Authorizations, Business Cards, Information sheets),
6. Appropriate PPE (disposable gloves, masks, shoe covers, disposable gown).

Mortuary bags vary in size and thickness and should be chosen based on the conditions and location of the decedent. Severely obese or decomposing decedents should be placed in a Disaster Pouch, which is thicker with reinforced straps.
Depending on the age of the decedent, a different removal device may be used. A baby or infant will be too small for a standard cot; therefore, the funeral home may use a bassinet or infant carrying container.

The removal staff should be trained in proper ergonomics and lifting techniques to ensure proper lifting occurs without injury. Lifting in the funeral industry is an occupational hazard, and under OSHA regulations, removal personnel need to be briefed on each various removal situation to ensure the deceased is being handled with care and respect while maintaining employee safety. At least one removal personnel should be appropriately licensed (unless state regulations don't require a licensed funeral director). Some states require a licensed funeral director to be present to sign discharge paperwork. Additional non-licensed removal personnel may be utilized for additional help, especially on removals when the deceased is obese. The general rule of thumb is there should be at least two people for each removal if the deceased is under 250 lbs. In some cases, police agencies and fire departments may be called to do lift assists with difficult removals. All removals should be completed, caring for the human remains with the utmost dignity and respect.

All removal personnel should be neat and professionally presentable because they are the first representation of the funeral home to have contact with the family. Their attire should conform to the standards of the funeral home. The social norms established by the community will influence funeral home policy regarding proper attire. For example, a rural farming community may not want removal staff to wear suits. In this situation, dress pants and a dress shirt with the funeral home logo affixed may be appropriate.

Home Removals:

Once at the removal site, the funeral director should first speak with the family to introduce the staff and discuss the removal process. If there is only one person making the removal, the deceased should be removed last after the family has been briefed by the funeral director. Before the removal occurs, the deceased needs to be properly identified and checked for personal belongings. The funeral director should confirm with the family their wishes with these personal effects. A wedding ring or other jewelry should be removed at the next-of-kin's request. Other items, such as clothing, glasses, dentures, and personal mementos, should be taken only at the next of kin's request. All items should be appropriately documented in the file, with instructions on what is to happen with each.

If there are two funeral home personnel on the removal (which should be in the majority of cases), the removal should be done first after the initial contact with the family. Universal precautions should be used on all removals. The remains should be shrouded in a bed sheet (with the face covered) for a smooth transition from the bed to the removal cot. **Someone should always remain with the decedent to ensure safety and confidentiality**.

If the furniture is moved during the removal, the furniture should be moved back after the human remains have been secured in the removal vehicle. If the decedent is in a bed, the best practice is to either fold up the bedding or re-make the bed for the family. If a bed sheet was used for the removal, the sheet should be washed and given back to the family at the time of arrangements. If the sheet is badly stained and is deemed a biohazard, the family needs to be informed that the sheet was properly disposed of because it was a biohazard.

Once the removal has been completed and the deceased is secured in the removal vehicle accompanied by another removal person (**never leave the human remains unattended**), the funeral director returns to the resident and discusses with the next-of-kin the following information:

1. What type of services are desired?
2. If services include public viewing or a public funeral with the human remains present, verbal permission is needed for embalming. A simple nod of the head is not considered permission.

3. If the family chooses cremation as a means of final disposition, the funeral director should ask, "Is that before or after public or private visitation?" Presenting options to the family is a way to allow the family an opportunity to choose the type of services that best fits their understanding of how to honor the life accomplishments of the deceased. A family that chooses cremation doesn't always mean direct cremation without services. Most family's welcome options to make an educated decision.

4. The next-of-kin may inquire about pricing information. A GPL is required to be available during the removal process. This is a triggering event (under the Funeral Rule) and requires the funeral director to physically hand the next-of-kin, for their retention, a copy of the GPL that explains the cost for such services:

    > For example: "Mrs. Thompson, you asked me how much embalming costs. In order to be in compliance with state and federal regulations, I must present to you a copy of the General Price List which lists all the funeral goods and services we provide at the Jones Funeral Home. (Open the GPL and point to the charge in question). You asked me how much embalming costs. Our cost for embalming is $750.00."

5. Establish a meeting time for the arrangement conference.

6. Some funeral homes present the family with a cloth or canvas garment bag that has a laminated card attached, with instructions on what to bring to the arrangements. Each side is gender specific, with information that may be required during the arrangement conference and the appropriate clothing necessary for public visitation and services.

Institutional Removals:

The decedent needs to be appropriately identified, tagged and labeled. If the decedent is in a mortuary pouch, the best practice is to open the bag and check the toe tag or hospital bracelet that may be affixed to the decedent. The name on the ID tag should match the name on the mortuary pouch. Be sure to complete all required paperwork at the institution to ensure that there are records of the removal.

A Registered Resident/Apprentice or Licensed Funeral Director may have to provide their Resident/Apprentice/Funeral Director License as well as Driver's License to the institution. Licensed personnel should also be the ones signing any agency documents during the removal process.

➤ *Who may sign for removal may vary from state-to-state.*
➤ *Some Veteran Administration Hospitals have their own registrar and death certificates are completed at the time of removal. In these cases, only a fully licensed funeral director could sign for the removal, as residents/apprentices cannot sign death certificates.*

Arrangement Conference:

The purpose of the arrangement conference is to obtain vital statistical information for the death certificate, coordinate and plan the preferred method of disposition and services desired by the family, fill out the necessary paperwork and authorizations, and review the financials.

Traditionally, arrangements are held in the funeral home shortly after the death. However, as more and more people live away from their families, arrangements may be made in a variety of formats, including both in person and virtually through phone, email, and fax. Arrangements may also be held in other locations besides the funeral home, such as the family's house or in an institution, such as Hospice or nursing home.

Arrangements should be a form of client-centered counseling in which the client helps guide the arrangement conference with encouragement from the funeral director. The funeral director should allow the client family to tell them stories about their loved ones to learn more about their life and details that could be pertinent to the funeral services. The funeral director should use open-ended questions to guide the conversation.

Arrangements should be made by the legally appointed person. The hierarchy of who is entitled to make arrangements varies from state-to-state. Traditionally, the first in line is a legally appointed agent, followed by a legal spouse.

➢ *Health-Care-Proxy and Power of Attorney cease after the death occurs.*
➢ If the decedent has pre-arrangements that are pre-funded, the wishes of the deceased should be honored.

The death certificate is a legal document containing vital statistics, dispositions, and final medical information pertaining to the deceased. The death certificate contains vital statistical information about the decedent, as well as the manner and cause of death provided by a medical professional and is certified by the registrar where the person passed away. Most death certificates in the United States are filed on the Database Application for Vital Events (DAVE) system. Most states use the DAVE system; however, there are some municipalities that still utilize paper filing of death certificates.

The funeral director provides the following information for the death certificate. Required information may vary from state-to-state:

1. Name of decedent
2. Date of birth of the decedent
3. Date of death
4. Time of death
5. Last known address of the decedent
6. Address of death
7. Decedent's race
8. If the decedent is of Latino/Hispanic background
9. Decedent's highest education
10. Decedent's occupation and last known workplace
11. Decedent's parent one birthname
12. Decedent's parents' two birthname
13. Decedent's veteran status
14. If a decedent is a veteran, years that they served in the military
15. Name of informant (person giving the information)
16. Address of informant
17. Method of disposition
18. Name and location of the place of disposition (crematory, cemetery, medical facility)

19. Funeral Home name, address, and registration number
20. Funeral Director's name and registration number

Vital statistics are entered and electronically signed by the funeral director. The cause and manner of death are signed by the licensed medical professional. Once the local registrar receives the signed death certificate electronically, the document is processed, and a burial transit permit is issued.

An important concept to know: What is the difference between a Death Certificate and a Burial Transit Permit? A ***Death Certificate is filed*** by the funeral director, and a ***Burial Transit permit is issued*** by the registrar.

Some states may need additional information for their death certificates. Some municipalities also require a medical clearance to be obtained before cremation can occur. If information is not known, "unknown" may be written on the line requesting the information (check state requirements). Don't leave blank spaces on a death certificate. Cause of death is how the person actually died. Example: myocardial infarction. Manner of death is the broad classification of the mode of death: natural, homicide, suicide, accidental, and unknown.

With the DAVE system, the voluntary filing of the **SSA-721** Statement of Death by the funeral director is no longer required. Once the death certificate is filed with the Registrar's Office, Social Security is immediately notified that the decedent's social security number is no longer active. If the death certificate is paper filed, the funeral director will need to complete form SSA-721 and file it with the local Social Security office. A surviving spouse or child, under the age of 18, may be eligible for the lump-sum death benefit of $255, which utilizes form **SSA-8**, Application for Lump-Sum Death Payment. SSA-8 is a form completed by a case worker at Social Security.

Once the funeral director has the vital statistical information, the **Death Certificate** *is filed with the local registrar* to obtain certified copies for the decedent's family, as well as obtain the **Burial Transit Permit**, *which is issued by the registrar allowing the disposition to take place.* Most death certificates are filed with the local registrar using the Database Application for Vital Events (DAVE) system. Certified copies of the Death Transcript can be ordered on DAVE, and the Burial Transit Permit can be downloaded and printed by the funeral director at the funeral home. Certified copies of the death certificate are needed for any property or assets that are in the name of the decedent. Including but not limited to titles, deeds, insurance policies, retirement, bank, and utility accounts.

Methods of Final Disposition

The first service detail that needs to be selected is the method of disposition. The methods of disposition are:

1. Burial- when the body is placed in a casket and buried in a cemetery or entombed in a mausoleum.
   a. Traditional burial - will have a funeral service before burial.
   b. Direct burial – will not have any services before burial.
2. Cremation- when the body is incinerated in a retort.
   a. Services with cremation after- the body is present for the services, and the cremation takes place afterward.
   b. Services after cremation- a memorial service will be held after the body has been cremated, with or without the cremated remains present.
   c. Direct cremation- the body will be cremated, and there will not be any services.
   Legalities of scattering cremated remains vary from locality-to-locality.
3. Body Donation - in which the decedent is donated to a medical institution for research. (Note: many medical facilities cremate the decedent when they are finished with their body).
4. Burial at Sea – this may be a full body in a casket or cremated remains.
5. Alternative disposition - sustainable "green" forms of disposition.
   a. Green burial – no casket or vault and no carcinogenic embalming fluids.
   b. Alkaline hydrolysis (not available in most states) – water cremation is a process in which the human remains are placed in a pressure chamber that is filled with a mixture of water and potassium hydroxide and heated to a temperature around 160° C or 320°F. The soft tissue is dissolved, and the bone fragments remain. The remaining bones are processed similarly to the manner used in the cremation process.
   c. Natural Organic Reduction (NOR), a/k/a Human Composting, is a process of the final disposition of human remains in which microbes convert the human remains into compost material (not available in most states). This process requires the body to be wrapped in a biodegradable shroud. The remains are placed in a reusable container and organic material is placed on top of the remains. Microbes, overtime (30 to 60 days), will dissolve the human remains, depending on several factors. After this time, much of the human remains will decompose and become compostable material, leaving behind the bones.

214

There are a wide range of services that could be selected. These include but are not limited to:

1. Calling hours or visitation - to allow friends and family to come and give condolences
2. Home funerals - Services at the decedent's or family's house
3. Memorial Service - These are services without the body present may or may not have cremated remains present.
4. Funeral Service – These are funeral services with the body present.
5. Humanistic service - in which there is no religious connotation.
6. Adaptive service - non-traditional services but may have spiritual or religious connections.
7. Graveside service – The services only take place at the gravesite.

When selecting services, various items should be discussed, including but not limited to

1. Date and time
2. Location of services
3. Cemetery name and lot/plot location, if applicable
4. Desired clergy, celebrant, or speaker
5. Pallbearers (casket bearers) - will the family provide pallbearers, or will the funeral home provide this service?
6. Desired merchandise: casket, vault, urn, alternative container, memorial packages, prayer cards (See Merchandising section in the Art's Review Manual)
7. Use of hearse if applicable or desired
8. Military honors, if eligible and requested
9. Order of the procession vehicles
10. Desired restoration, cosmetics, hairstyle of decedent-may obtain a photo for reference.
11. Clothing wishes for the decedent
12. Ways to personalize the services

The family may also desire a death notice or an obituary. A death notice is a short publication stating someone has passed away and may include service information. An obituary is a longer publication containing a biographical sketch of the person's life, including information about the person and the service details. Families may wish to write the obituary on their own but may also want input from the funeral director or may wish to have it written completely by the funeral director. Grammar and proper sentence structure is the responsibility of the funeral director since the name of the funeral home will be publicized. Obituaries will vary from family-to-family, but many include surviving relatives, deceased relatives, school/work/activities/organization involvement information, and donation requests.

Once the disposition of the decedent and the service information has been discussed and decided, it is important to complete all required and relevant paperwork.

Death Certificate	A legal document containing vital statistics, disposition, and final medical information pertaining to the deceased.
Cremation Authorizations	Forms authorizing the cremation of the decedent.
Embalming Authorizations	Form authorizing embalming of the decedent.
Right to Control Disposition	Identifies the person who has the legal authority to handle funeral arrangements. Usually, it is the next-of-kin.
Designation of Intentions	Designates what is to happen with cremated remains after the cremation (return to next of kin, burial, etc.)
Identification Authorization	Obtains signature identifying the decedent.
Itemized Statement of Goods and Services	Itemized costs of services and merchandise selected. Includes payment contract.

Financials:

After the paperwork has been completed, the financial information may be reviewed. The pricing should be taken from the General Price List following Federal Trade Commission (FTC) guidelines (See FTC section in the Art's Review Manual), and *the selected goods and services should have their itemized prices recorded* on the **Statement of Goods and Services**. The Statement of Goods and Services should be prepared during the arrangement session and reviewed with the client's family. As the charges are being reviewed, the funeral director should use the statement, "You selected ___, and this is the charge for that service or merchandise." Explaining all the services and merchandise selected with the corresponding charges will give the consumer one last opportunity to determine if these are the services they choose for their love-one.

During this explanation, the family should understand which charges are declinable and which are non-declinable, also known as the Basic Arrangement Fee. On the Statement of Goods and Services, there are two sections with funeral home charges, that is, Services and Merchandise and Additional Services and Merchandise. Cash Advances are third party payments for services rendered, such as a cemetery or crematory. The practice of charging for cash advances is a convenience for the family so that the consumer only pays one bill for all the services. The disadvantage is that the final amount appears to be higher, and the consumer could perceive that the cash advances are funeral home charges when they are fees that are passed on to third-party vendors. Only the amount charged by a third-party vendor is the amount that can be charged to the consumer. Charging a fee for cash advances is a violation of FTC and some state regulations.

The Statement of Goods and Services form should be signed by the client's family, acknowledging that they are being charged for the goods and services they selected, and they assume financial responsibility for services rendered. Payment for services rendered should be discussed at the end of the arrangements. The funeral home payment policy will dictate the terms and conditions of the contract. Sometimes arrangements need to be made for a third party, such as Social Services, the Veterans Administration, a charity, or a life insurance company, to pay for the funeral expenses.

If the person is on Medicaid, Social Services, or disability services, they may be eligible for public assistance (sometimes referred to as indigent burial funds through the county in which they reside). The eligibility requirements and the documentation requirements vary from municipality to municipality. The amount that is covered by social services also varies.

Military and Veteran Benefits

If the decedent is a veteran or active-duty Service Member, they may be entitled to Military Honors and benefits. Veteran benefits generally must go through the Department of Veterans Affairs to ensure and verify status and qualifications. These would include burial allowances and interment costs.

To be eligible, veterans must meet the VA's criteria:
1. Veterans with an honorable or other than-honorable (general) discharge are entitled to a burial flag.
2. To obtain the burial flag, a copy of the **DD214** (a/k/a Separation Papers from the military) or another discharge form must be present. The discharge form must state the type of discharge.
3. A burial flag may be obtained using **VA form 27-2008** (*Application for United States Flag for Burial Purposes*) from the United States Postal Service.
4. Veterans are also entitled to a Military Marker. There are a few different marker and medallion options, which may be selected by the family using form, **VA 40-1330** *Application for Headstone or Marker* (marker) or **VA 40-1330M** (medallion), usually affixed to a headstone or mausoleum crypt. On the marker application forms, there is a box to indicate if the family would like a Presidential Memorial Certificate.
5. If a person was dishonorably discharged from the military, they are usually not eligible for military honors or benefits. Verification of questionable eligibility for Veteran benefits can be made with the local Veterans Affairs Office.
6. **VA form 21-530** *is used for Veteran Burial Allowances,*
7. **VA form DD 1375** *is the request for payment for funeral expenses and interment expenses.*

Request for Military Honors

The family may also wish to have Military Honors rendered at the end of the funeral or committal services. Military Honors vary depending on the status of the Veteran (veteran, retiree, rank, etc.). Honors may include the playing of taps, three-volley salutes, folding and presenting of the flag, and casket bearing. Coordinating with the Casualty Affairs Unit or Military Honor Team on what items the decedent is eligible for is the best way to determine the type of honors.

Arranging for Military Honors varies depending on branch and location, as honors are rendered by the branch in which the decedent served. The branches of the military and armed forces include the Army, Navy, Air Force, Marines, and Coast Guard. For example, in New York State, Army Honors are rendered through Fort Drum's Casualty Affairs Department, and Navy Honors are rendered out of a Reserve Unit located in Syracuse, NY. Each branch and location have different paperwork that needs to be filled out, and the DD214 (discharge form) must accompany the request for honors.

If the decedent dies while on Active Duty, the military may handle the preparation and arrangements. Active-Duty deaths may be prepared at Dover Air Force Base in their Mortuary Affairs Unit in Dover, Delaware. When a death occurs out of the country on deployment or rotation, 95Ms (Mortuary Affair Specialists) are tasked with retrieval and examination of the body, along with preparation to return their remains to the United States. The military also has specific embalming requirements and standards that must be followed in the event of an Active-Duty death.

Burial may take place in a military, veteran, or National Cemetery. The decedent or their dependent must meet eligibility requirements for burial in a National Cemetery. To establish eligibility and arrange for the burial, the funeral director will need to contact the National Cemetery Scheduling Office and submit the proper documentation. There are additional eligibility and scheduling requirements for Arlington National Cemetery and Airman's Home National Cemetery.

In some instances, a veteran organization, such as a VFW or an American Legion, may ask to be part of the funeral services. They generally have their own short service that is given after the celebrant or clergy has concluded. If the decedent was only eligible for the folding of the flag and the playing of taps, or the military lacks the personnel for a full honor team, the VFW or the American Legion may assist with the three-volley salute and other honors. Generally, the funeral director will coordinate these details with the organization commander or leader on behalf of the family.

When a full twenty-one honor team is provided, the general order of personnel is:

1. Chaplain – Military, religious speaker *Chaplains may be of different faiths
2. Bugler – to play taps *Generally, they hold the bugle and play a recording
3. Color Bearers
4. Color Guard - Carry the flags
5. Casket bearers – (Carry the casket, also known as pallbearers)
6. Firing detail
7. Commander of the firing detail
8. Detail Commander

Burial at Sea:

Some personnel may be eligible for a burial at sea. These include members and former members of the Armed Forces, US Civilian Marine Personnel of the Military Sealift Command, dependents, and United States citizens deemed eligible by their notable service to the United States. There are specific burial requirements for casketed remains and cremated remains.

To set up a burial at sea, the director, along with the next-of-kin, must complete and file a request form with Naval Affairs. The DD214 and a VA copy of the death certificate must accompany this request. Note: A VA copy of the Death Certificate is provided free of charge for all veterans by the local Registrar. If cremated remains are being scattered at sea, the Certificate of Cremation must be presented to the Naval Base of Choice (Norfolk, VA; Jacksonville, FL;

San Diego, CA; Bremerton, WA; and Honolulu, HI). Once the paperwork has been received, the Commanding Officer will contact the funeral home to ensure the human remains are properly encased, according to military regulations.

Casketed remains require the following:
- ➢ Casketed remains must have 150 lbs. of extra weight added to the casket with the following:
- ➢ 6 - 1" nylon bands placed around the casket. Two on the head end, two on the foot end, one lengthwise, and one around the sides.
- ➢ Twenty holes (4 in the head cap, 4 in the foot cap, 8 in the bottom, 2 in the foot end, and 2 in the head end) must be drilled into the casket as well to ensure the remains sink.
- ➢ Casketed remains can be placed in water at least three nautical miles from shore, as long as the water is 600 feet (100 fathoms) deep.

Cremated remains require the following:
- ➢ Cremated remains need to be sealed in a bio-degradable container.
- ➢ Cremated remains can be placed in water at least three nautical miles from shore.

Upon approval for burial at sea or scattering at sea, the funeral home will be contacted, and a time will be scheduled for the casketed remains (or cremated remains) to the base. Along with the human or cremated remains, copies of the paperwork and the burial flag should be given to the Commanding Officer.

The Burial at Sea Ceremony Procedure:

- ➢ Once the remains are with the Navy, they will bring the decedent onto the ship or aircraft for the burial at the sea ceremony.
- ➢ Generally, these burials take place during a deployment or rotation; therefore, families are not able to be present.
- ➢ On the request form, the next-of-kin designates a particular religion for the service, if desired.
- ➢ The Navy will then record and take photos of the service and take GPS coordinates of the final disposition.
- ➢ The Office of the Naval Commander will send the next-of-kin the folded flag and shell casings.
- ➢ This process can take 6-12 months, depending on the deployment or rotation length.

Pre-Arrangements

Pre-arrangements will have similar conversations as at-need arrangements; however, they are more geared toward the future. The same attention to detail needs to be given to pre-arrangements as if they were for an at-need case. Pre-arrangements may be made anywhere; at the funeral home, the family's house, an agency, or other locations. Many people opt to set up pre-arrangements for a variety of reasons, including:

> ➢ imminent death,
> ➢ diagnosis of a terminal illness,
> ➢ aging,
> ➢ traveling,
> ➢ living in two different places,
> ➢ lack of family,
> ➢ applying for Medicaid (which requires people to spend down their assets),
> ➢ social service allotments, rehabilitation center allotments, and
> ➢ moving into a nursing home or hospice facility.

Pre-arrangements generally allow people to make their own wishes known and recorded to ease the financial and planning burden on the family. This allows the funeral director to make an initial connection with the client and their family. Pre-arrangements may just be **pre-planned,** in *which the service and disposition details are discussed and recorded in a file,* or maybe **pre-funded,** in which *the beneficiary or other relevant person (caretaker, next-of-kin, power of attorney) begins funding a pre-need account.*

Pre-funding a funeral account should determine if the client qualifies for a revocable contract or an irrevocable contract.

A **revocable contract** *is a legally binding contract that can be terminated by the purchaser at any time prior to the death of the beneficiary with a refund of the money paid on the contract as prescribed by state law.* Depending on the type of pre-need revocable contract, if there are funds in excess of the cost of the at-need services rendered, these funds are returned to the estate of the deceased. Depending on how the funds are deposited in a fiduciary (a third-party entity, like a bank or credit union) and depending on state or federal regulations, upon the request of the purchaser, the funds can be withdrawn at any time prior to death. All principle and interest should be returned to the purchaser upon request, barring any contractual penalties for early withdrawal.

An **irrevocable contract** *is an agreement for future funeral services that cannot be terminated or canceled prior to the death of the beneficiary.* The funds, however, are portable and can be moved from one funeral home to another; however, they can never be refunded to the purchaser. Excess funds after the services have been rendered must be surrendered to the governmental agency from whom the purchaser was receiving public assistance. Only individuals spending down or who are on Medicaid/SSI benefits can establish an irrevocable trust account. This type of account is created to prevent Medicaid fraud.

If a person wishes to create a pre-need contract that cannot be changed or canceled by a family member prior to death, a written instrument, such as a Designation of Agent form, should be created to outline the pre-need arrangements and also to designate an agent to handle the at-need affairs of the purchaser when death occurs.

Pre-funded funeral contracts may be guaranteed or non-guaranteed. **Guaranteed funeral contracts** *are agreements where the funeral firm promises that the services and the merchandise will be provided at the time of need for a sum not exceeding the original amount of the contract plus any accruals, regardless of the current prices associated with providing the services and merchandise at the time of the funeral/services rendered.*

Non-guaranteed funeral contracts *are agreements in which the funeral firm promises to apply the amount of pre-paid funds plus any accruals to the balance due at the time services are rendered. However, the cost of the funeral will be based on the current price for the services and merchandise at the time the death occurs.*

Many funeral firms will guarantee the prices for the funeral services and merchandise; however, non-guarantee cash advance items. This practice is common because funeral homes cannot guarantee third-party vendors' costs for providing their services in the future.

Some states have Pre-Need Insurance policies that can be purchased as a means of funding funeral arrangements. Such policies must be sold by a licensed insurance agent and are regulated by the insurance laws within the state. Some states, such as New York, prohibit the sale of such policies because they are not consumer friendly. If, for example, a policyholder misses a payment (a/k/a premium), the policy lapses, thus voiding the policy and forfeiture of all the premiums paid to date. In a pre-need contract established with a funeral home where the funds are set aside in an interest-bearing account, if a payment is missed, the funds that are set aside are still the asset of the beneficiary until death occurs.

Preparing for Services

Upon completion of the arrangements, the funeral director coordinates and implements all the necessary paperwork and personnel for the services selected by the client's family. This includes contacting the clergy or celebrant, church or another venue, cemetery or crematory, merchandise manufacturer if not in-house, vault company, military or fraternal organization, musicians, cosmetic/hair personnel if not done by the director, and funeral home staff (including funeral attendants, drivers, and cleaners).

The decedent should also be appropriately prepared with desired clothing and restoration if necessary. Merchandise will also need to be ordered or created for the services. If the firm prints its own memorial items (such as prayer cards or register books), it is important to be sure they are printed correctly and timely. Most funeral homes use computer software that generates these items; however, accuracy when the data is entered, is essential; an error in the initial data entry will cause errors throughout all the documents and sundry items.

The funeral home should also be cleaned and set up for the services. This would include being mindful of which religious and cultural items are in the service room. If the firm is decorating for a themed or personalized service, all items are placed in the desired location for display. Flowers should also be appropriately arranged, keeping in mind who sent the piece and the relationship to the deceased.

The exits should be in compliance with the state fire code with illuminated emergency exit signs. Accessibility services, such as ramps, elevators, and restrooms, should be cleaned and in ADA (Americans with Disabilities Act) compliance. The funeral establishment should be in compliance with the local building code. The establishment should have appropriate safety measures such as proper fire extinguishers, fire alarms, carbon monoxide detectors, and labeled exits.

During the Services

The family should be escorted into the facility or service room for their first viewing of the decedent to ensure their satisfaction with the preparations and setup. The funeral director should answer any questions the family may have and make any changes that are desired. If adjustments need to be made to the deceased, the funeral director should ask the family to step out of the room and make the necessary corrections in private. Witnessing the adjustment of the deceased could be traumatizing to some family members.

During the services, funeral home personnel should be visible and available to assist patrons with opening doors, answering questions, navigating the funeral home, as well as beginning and dismissing services. Personnel should be clean and dressed appropriately as they are a representation of the image of the firm. The staff should be knowledgeable and familiar with the service details and the facilities.

The Procession

The funeral director ideally should have cars parked and lined up for the procession before the start of the services. The pallbearers should be identified and briefed as to what is expected prior to the services. They should possibly be seated together for an easy exit after the conclusion of the service. Once the service has concluded, the pallbearers should be gathered and organized accordingly to move and carry the casket to the hearse.

A traditional funeral procession:

1. Escort- Law enforcement vehicle and personnel, if desired and available
2. Lead Car
3. Clergy's Car – clergy may ride in the lead car
4. Pall Bearers if they are not riding with their family
4. Hearse/coach
5. Family
6. Friends

In a funeral procession, the family and funeral coach (hearse) should never be separated. Funeral flags or funeral placards need to be visible. Four-way flashers and headlights should be on during the procession and turned off once at the cemetery. The hearse and lead car should have a purple hazard strobe light on top of the vehicle to indicate the funeral procession. Without an escort or proper traffic controls, all traffic laws must be obeyed.

The Committal

After the funeral service is the committal service at the gravesite, funeral personnel should be at the head and foot of the casket during the casket carry to the grave. The funeral director should ask the pallbearers if anyone has any lifting or health concerns that would restrict them from carrying the casket to the grave. The funeral director should maintain proper decorum while the casket is being carried to the grave and inform the pallbearers of any obstructions, hazards, or obstacles that need to be avoided. The clergy should lead the casket to the grave. The funeral director directs the proper movement of the pallbearers to ensure their safety and the smooth transition of the human remains to their place of rest.

Once at the gravesite, the casket should be placed on the lowering device, and the pallbearers should be thanked for their service. The clergy or celebrant should be positioned at the head of the casket for the short committal service. Once the committal service concludes, the funeral director thanks the attendees and provides them with directions, such as a request from the family for the participants to join them for a reception (repass) and its location. Usually, the vault lid is placed on the base after the family has left the burial site. The funeral director must stay at the cemetery until the lid is placed on the vault.

After the Services

Once services have concluded, the funeral director should meet with the family to give them copies of the paperwork, certified copies of the death certificate, relevant merchandise that may not have been taken from the funeral (prayer cards, register books, cards), and flowers requested by the family.

Aftercare

After services have concluded and all documents have been given to the family, checking in on the client's family is an essential part of providing quality services. After the funeral services, some families may have questions about settling their loved one's final affairs. The funeral director could serve as a resource to direct the family to various services and community resources. This may be in the form of a phone call to see how the family is doing or a drop-in visit to the client if they are in the area. Follow-up could also be through email, letters, or cards. Many firms send cards on holidays or after the first year of death. This allows the family to feel that the funeral home truly cares about them and that their loved one was not just another case. Aftercare is a great way to maintain a positive reputation and possibly gain more client families through positive word of mouth.

Funeral homes can also organize community activities such as events, gatherings, and seminars to invite and connect with the general public. Some firms host holiday remembrance events, information sessions, and support groups. Some firms may also have an aftercare pamphlet or booklet to give clients at the end of services that contain information about grief and other resources, such as counselors in the area or literary suggestions on grief.

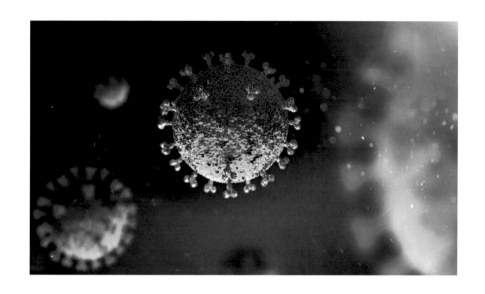

Domain IV

Pathology
Microbiology
Anatomy

Prefixes and Suffixes

Prefixes

a - without or not
acro-extremity
adeno-gland
an-without
ante-before
anti-against
arthro-joint
auto-self
bio-life
chol-bile
cyst-bladder
dia-through
dys-difficult
en-in
endo-within
entero-intestine
epi-upon
ex-out

hem, hemo-blood
hetero-dissimilar
homo-similar
hydro-water
hyper-above or excess
hypo-deficiency, beneath
hyster-uterus
infra-below
inter-between
intra-within
leuko-white
macro-large
mal-bad
mast-breast
mega-great
melan-thick
men-mouth
micro-small

myo-muscle
myx-mucus
necro-death
neo-new
nephr-kidney
oligo-few
osteo-bone
peri-around
phago-to eat
phleb-vein
polio-grey
poly-many, excess
post-after
pro-before
pseudo-false
pyo-puss
syn-together with
xantho-yellow

Suffixes

algia-pain
angio-vessel
ase-enzyme
cele-portrusion
centesis-perforating
chole-bile
ectasis-dilate
ectomy- removal of
emesis-vomit
emia-blood
esthesia-sensation
genesis-generation of

iasis-a process
itis-inflammation
lith-stone
malacia-softening
megaly-large
odynia- pain
oid- like
oma-tumor
osis-full of
ostomy- mouth
otomy-cut
pathy-disease

penia-poverty or decrease
phila-affinity for
plasia- to form
plegia-paralysis
pnea-breath
ptosis-falling
rhagia-bursting forth
rhea-flow
sclerosis-hardening
stasis-standing still
trophy-to nourish
uria-relating to urine

Selected Word Parts

Knowing how to dissect word parts is an important part of preparing for the National Board Exam. These word parts and their meanings and examples will help create a foundation and understanding of words on the NBEs.

A- or an- means not or without. Ex. If the face is asymmetrical, that means the facial features are not the same.

Acute – sudden onset, short term - The patient, all of a sudden, had a pain in his chest. The patient had acute pain in his chest. The common cold is an example of an acute illness. The cold typically comes on abruptly and lasts a few days.

Athero - means gruel or paste - When combined with the root word **sclero** - it means hardening. Together the words mean the hardening of the paste.

Arteriosclerosis – means the hardening of the arteries. The gruel-like matter in the arteries becomes hardened.

Card - coro- or coron - means heart. Cardiac tissue means the tissue of the heart. Coronary heart disease is when the coronary artery on the surface of the heart is affected either by a blockage or the thickening of the artery (see arteriosclerosis).

Myo - muscle. For example, Rhabdo**myo**sarcomas are malignant (cancerous) tumors of the muscle tissue.

Infarct – is the formation of an area of necrosis in a tissue caused by an obstruction.
Utilizing three-word parts (card, myo, infarction), we generate the term: Myocardial Infarction. Breaking down this term, we see Myocardial: muscle and heart infarction: necrosis due to a blockage. This means that the person has necrosis in the muscle tissue of the heart. This typically occurs due to a blockage in the coronary artery, killing the heart tissue and often leading to a heart attack.

Bi - or di-, dipl - two. **Bi**lateral symmetry means that the same features are on both the left and right sides of the face. On the typical human face, there are two eyes exhibiting bilateral symmetry on either side of the nose. **Di**chlorobenzene is a benzene ring with two chlorines attached.

Chole - bile. Bile is secreted by the liver and stored in the gallbladder to assist with digestion.
Lith- stones. Tonsillo**lith** is the presence of tonsil stones.
    Cholelithiasis is when a person has gallstones, in which bile hardens.

Chronic = long term. Typically, chronic refers to something (like an illness) that develops slowly over time and lasts for a long duration. An example would be Kidney Disease. In which the disease takes years to develop and generate symptoms, and the person has the disease for a long period of their life, if not the rest of their life.

Colo- large intestine. The most well-known term for the large intestine is the **colo**n. A **colo**noscopy is a procedure in which medical professional looks inside the rectum and colon to determine if there are any abnormalities or to make a diagnosis.

Congenital- present at birth. Congenital diseases are those that someone is born with. One congenital defect is spina bifida, in which the spine does not close properly in-utero. A congenital illness might be HIV/AIDS if the disease was spread in-utero from mother to child.

Cyst - sac, pouch-type structure, bladder. A sac within or on the body surface containing air or fluid. Dermal cysts are present on the face and may have exudate inside the sac. **Cyst**itis is inflammation of the bladder.

-cyt- cell. An erythro**cyt**e is a red blood cell. A leuko**cyt**e is a white blood cell.
      eryth- red. An **eryth**rocyte is a red blood cell.
      leuk- white. A **leuk**ocyte is a white blood cell.

Dia - across. **Dia**meter is the distance if a straight line passing from side to side through the center of a circle. **Dia**lysis is the process of diffusing blood across a semi-permeable membrane for filtration.

Dys - abnormal. When an organ is **dys**functional, it does not work properly. Bowel **dys**function is when the intestine is not operating correctly.

-eme, - emia blood. Hyper**emia** is when there is excess blood in the vessels. An**emia** is when the body lacks red blood cells (erythrocytes), or there is red blood cell dysfunction.

Endo - inside. The **endo**thelial lining of organs is the innermost lining typically made up of epithelial tissue.

Gast - stomach. **Gast**ritis is the inflammation of the stomach. **Gast**ric juices are the acids within the stomach.

Gen - beginning, start. Angio**genesis** is the start of a new blood vessel.

Heme - blood. **Hem**ophilia is a clotting disorder of the blood. **Hem**aturia is when blood is present in urine.

Hepat - liver. **Hepat**itis is an inflammatory disease of the liver. **Hepat**omegaly is the enlargement of the liver.

Hyper-upper, higher, above. When a limb becomes **hyper**extended, it has moved past its normal range of motion. **Hyper**tension is when the body's blood pressure is too high. **Hyper**thyroidism is when there is an overproduction of hormones.

Hypo - lower. Less, below. Hypo is the opposite of hyper. **Hypo**tension is when the body's blood pressure is too low. **The hypo**dermic injection is an injection right below the skin. **Hypo**thyroidism is when there is a lack of hormone production.

Isch - decreased. **Isch**emia is decreased blood flow to an area. **Isch**emic strokes are when there is decreased blood flow to the brain.

-Itis-inflammation of the act of being inflamed. Gastr**itis** is the inflammation of the stomach. Hepat**itis** is inflammation of the liver. Laryng**itis** is inflammation of the larynx.

-Lys, -lyt, -lyst- cutting, breaking down, decomposing, splitting. Auto**lys**is is the breakdown of the body by its own enzymes. Hydro**lys**is is the splitting of water.

Micro - small. **Micro**biology is the branch of science that studies **micro**organisms, organisms that are too small to be seen by the naked eye, including bacteria. A **micro**scope helps to view very small items, such as microbes.

Necro - death. **Necro**sis is the pathological death of cells, causing areas of tissue death. This can lead to gangrene.

Neo - new. A **neo**plasm is a new abnormal growth of tissue. Causing a tumor that may be benign or malignant.

-osis condition of. . . also excess. Diag**nosis** is the recognition and naming of a disease or illness. Symbi**osis** is the interaction between two different organisms.

Path-, pathy- disease, suffering. **Path**ology is the branch of science that studies the cause and effects of disease. **Path**ogenicity is the ability of a **path**ogen to cause disease.

Peri- around. **Peri**meter is the length around an object or area. Ex. A fence is around the perimeter of a yard. The **peri**toneum is the membrane lining the cavity around the internal organs.

Phago - eating. **Phago**cytes are cells that perform **phago**cytosis (engulfing particles and microorganisms) during the immune response.

Phleb - veins. A **phleb**otomist performs blood draws from the vein of patients. **Phleb**itis is the inflammation of the veins.

Pneu - air. **Pneu**monia is an infection of the lungs that may restrict airflow.

Pulm -, pleural- lungs. The **pulm**onary artery brings blood from the lungs to the heart. **Pulm**onary circulation is blood flow throughout the lungs. The **pleural** cavity contains the lungs.

Rhag, rrhage- flow, burst forth. Hemo**rrhag**ing is excessive bleeding.

Sten - small, narrow. **Sten**osis is the narrowing of a structure. Arterial **sten**osis is the narrowing of the artery.

Stom -, stoma-, -stome- opening and mouth. An o**stom**y bag is a pouch outside of the body used to collect waste from those who have had surgery on the colon and have a resulting **stoma** (hole) in the abdomen.

Taph - or tapho = graves, tombs, death art. An epi**taph** is an inscription on a headstone or tombstone.

Thanato - death. **Thanato**logy is the study of death. **Thanato**chemistry is death chemistry.

Thromb - clot. A **thromb**us is a stationary clot that has formed on the interior wall of a vessel. This clot may cause vascular stenosis (narrowing) and decreased blood flow. This clot may break free to become an embolus.

Vasc- vessels. The **vasc**ular network is the network of blood vessels in the body.

Pathology

This section will discuss the study of disease processes and their impact on the human body, with an emphasis on those conditions that relate to or affect the handling of human remains. As funeral directors and embalmers, it is important to understand how to properly handle human remains with diseases to prevent the spread of these illnesses to professional caregivers or to their families.

Overview of Pathology

Pathology can be defined as *the science that entails the study of disease and abnormal conditions of the body.* Pathology can either be general, with no reference to a particular body system, or special, in relation to a particular organ or system. In the 1800s, Rudolph Virchow proposed the cellular doctrine of pathology, in which he stated that if individuals are sick, it is because their cells are sick, describing an abnormal cellular function as a result of the disease. The field of pathology can be broken down into five sections of study that include pathology anatomy, the study of structural changes in the body caused by disease (including gross pathology, changes seen with the naked eye, or histo-pathology, the study of tissues under a microscope); surgical pathology, the study of tissue specimens excised surgically in a major or minor operation; clinical pathology, the study of disease by means of body secretions, excretions, and other bodily fluids in a laboratory; physiological pathology, the study of changes in bodily functions as a result of disease; and **medicolegal (forensic) pathology**, *the study of disease to ascertain cause and manner of death.*

Medicolegal pathology is of great importance to us as funeral directors and embalmers, for it is part of the autopsy process. Autopsies (also known as necropsies and postmortem exams) can be performed for a variety of reasons. They can be clinical, educational, or forensic/legal. Autopsies are performed by pathologists, who are trained and licensed medical professionals and can be used to confirm or alter clinical diagnoses and accepted treatments, advance medical knowledge and research, and assist in medicolegal cases. Autopsies can pose a vast number of issues for the embalmer and the embalming process (See the Embalming section for more information regarding embalming autopsy cases pp. 28 - 30).

Diseases are often diagnosed (*denoting the name of a disease or syndrome*) by medical professionals after the client experiences signs (*measurable objective disturbances produced by disease, e.g., rapid pulse*) and symptoms (*subjective, non-measurable disturbances felt or experienced by a patient, e.g., headache*).

A syndrome is *a set of signs/symptoms associated with a particular disease.* Diseases can be congenital (*existing at the time of birth or shortly thereafter*) or acquired (*presenting after birth*). Illnesses can be classified in duration as acute (*rapid onset, short duration*), fulminant (*rapid and severe onset, usually fatal*), or chronic (*slow onset, long duration*). After a diagnosis is made, the patient may be given a prognosis (*prediction of the outcome of the disease*), and a treatment plan may be established.

During the treatment plan, the disease could become:
- exacerbated (*increasing in severity*),
- abated (*lessening of signs and symptoms*),
- or go into remission (*temporary cessation of symptoms*).

Note that diseases that go into remission could become:
- recurrent (*reappearance after a period of remission*).

Diseases can also have **complications** (*unfavorable secondary conditions arising during the course of the disease*), and iatrogenic issues can arise from the adverse activity of physicians.

The following three different classifications of disease prevalence (*number of cases of a disease in a specified population at a given time*):

Term	Definition	Example
Endemic	A disease that is continuously present in a community	flu
Epidemic	A disease that is currently in higher-than-normal numbers	obesity
Pandemic	A worldwide, widespread epidemic	COVID-19

When discussing pandemic and epidemic diseases, two concerns are the **morbidity rate** (*relative incidence of disease in the population or number of cases in a given time at a given population*) of that illness and the **mortality rate** (*number of deaths in a given time or place in proportion to deaths of a population*). Funeral professionals should pay attention to both rates as well. The high mortality rate of the COVID-19 pandemic alerted the funeral professional to be aware of increasing deaths and increasing workloads. The morbidity rate demonstrated that personal protection needed to be a high priority when caring for decedents who died from this disease and their family members who may have been exposed.

Etiology

Etiology is *the study of the cause of disease.* People may have predisposing conditions that could make them more susceptible to various diseases and illnesses, which include but are not limited to age (immune system development), race/ethnicity, nutritional status, biological sex, occupational exposures, environment, emotions, stress levels, economic status (health care affordability and accessibility), and genetics (**heredity**: *genetic characteristics transmitted from parent to offspring*).

The **pathogenesis** (*how a disease develops*) of diseases may also be caused by trauma, injuries, **physical agents** (heat, cold, radiation), **chemical agents** (poisons, drugs), **infectious agents** (plants, parasites, animals, bacteria, viruses), **deficiencies** (*disease due to lack of essential dietary or metabolic substances like vitamins*), **allergens** (*hypersensitivity to a substance that does not normally cause a reaction*), **sporadic conditions** (*occurring separately or apart from others of its kind*), **nosocomial conditions** (*infections acquired in a hospital*), or possibly **idiopathic conditions** (*of unknown cause*).

Changes and Abnormalities

Diseases, injuries, and trauma can all affect our cells in a variety of ways, such as **degeneration** (*the deterioration of tissues with corresponding functional impairment due to disease or injury*). Cellular degeneration can be seen by cellular swelling, **fatty degeneration** (*the abnormal accumulation of fat in cells, i.e., obesity*), or amyloid disease, where the cells become cartilage-like and rigid. Another type of cellular change is **infiltration**, *the process of seepage or diffusion into tissues of substances that are not ordinarily present.* This infiltration can present itself as **exogenous pigmentation** (*discoloration outside of the body*), **endogenous pigmentation** (*discoloration inside of the body*), **calcification** (*calcium and salt deposits in the body*), and **gout** (*excess uric acid causing deposits in joints*).

Cells can also **regenerate** (*the replacement of damaged cells with identical new cells*). Regeneration happens in a physiological way when skin cells are replaced after flaking off. Tissues can also become **atrophied** (*wasting or decreasing in size*) or **hypertrophied** (*increasing in size*). These size changes can occur for both physiological and pathological reasons. Atrophy can occur as a normal physiological response after enlargement (e.g., a uterus shrinking after childbirth). Atrophy can also be pathological, such as the shrinkage of muscles accompanying febrile diseases like tuberculosis. Hypertrophy can occur for physiological reasons, such as breast enlargement for milk production; for pathological reasons, such as gallbladder enlargement with the presence of gallstones; and for compensatory reasons, such as one kidney becoming larger as the other kidney fails or is missing and is doing the job of both.

Necrosis (*the pathological death of tissues*) is a cellular change that is extremely important to funeral directors and embalmers. This should not be confused with **necrobiosis** (*physiological death of cells, i.e., cellular life cycle*), necrosis is often seen by the naked eye as gangrene, which results from insufficient blood supply in the body, physical agents like radiation, and various chemical agents. A classic example of necrosis is seen as "diabetes foot" in patients with uncontrolled diabetes. Necrotic gangrene can be seen in three forms: wet, dry, and gas. Wet gangrene results from venous blockages and disruptions; in this type of gangrene, the area will be moist and fleshy with a green/black discoloration. Dry gangrene is the result of arterial blockages and will be dry to the touch but may also be green/black in color. Gas gangrene, also known as tissue gas, is a result of *Clostridium perfringens,* a bacterium that rapidly spreads through the body. Bodies with gas gangrene will become very discolored and bloated, causing a variety of issues such as purge.

Necrosis can also be seen as caseation, a soft cheese-like substance seen in patients with tuberculosis and syphilis. When blood flow is disrupted, coagulative necrosis can be seen as blood clots, and as those clots begin to putrefy, **hemolysis** (*the breakdown of red blood cells*) will result in liquification.

There are a variety of defects and body abnormalities that can be present in the body. Many of these structural abnormalities are birth defects, deformities, or malformations that occur during development.

The following are some examples of birth defects:

Defect Name	What it is
Spina bifida	A congenital defect in which a part of the vertebral column is absent or has an incomplete closure.
Hypoplasia	Underdevelopment of tissue organs or body part.
Aplasia	Failure of a tissue or an organ to develop normally.
Polydactylism	Extra toes or fingers.
Phocomelia	A congenital condition in which the proximal portions of the limbs are poorly developed or absent. Hands or feet attached to the trunk or poorly formed limbs.
Amelia	Congenital absence of one or more limbs.
Cleft palate and lip	Cleft Palate and lip.
Color blindness	Inability to metabolize beta-carotene; hereditary, passed from mother to son.
Vascular Nevus	Superficial blood vessels are enlarged and show through the skin; a **nevus** is a congenital discoloration of a circumscribed area of the skin due to pigmentation.
Down Syndrome	Trisomy 21 (an extra chromosome on pair 21); a variety of congenital problems that cause moderate/severe mental disabilities.

Inflammation

Inflammation (*a tissue reaction to irritation, infection, or injury marked by localized heat, swelling, redness, pain, and sometimes loss of function; inflammation is a normal response to an abnormal situation*) is a common non-specific immune response to abnormalities in the body. The function of inflammation is to isolate injuries, destroy invading microorganisms, and inactivate toxins to promote healing. Inflammation can be the result of physical trauma, chemical irritants, microorganisms, and autoimmune disorders (such as allergic reactions).

The cardinal signs of inflammation include heat, redness, swelling, pain, and altered functions, which are due to the increase in blood flow and **inflammatory exudates** (a *fluid that oozes through the tissues into a cavity or to a surface*) in the area. Exudates can include purulent (pus), hemorrhagic (red blood cells), and serous (clear blood serum).

Lesions (*specific pathological structural or functional changes brought about by disease*) are often seen as a result of various pathological issues. Lesions can be categorized in the following ways:

Abscess	Localized accumulation of pus walled off in a pocket.
Ulcer	An open sore or lesion of the skin or mucous membrane accompanied by **sloughing** of inflamed necrotic tissue.
Vesicle	Blister-like elevation of the skin containing serous fluid.
Carbuncle or furuncle	A **furuncle** is an abscess or pyogenic infection of a sweat gland or hair follicle. A **carbuncle** consists of several boils of the skin and subcutaneous tissues with the production and discharge of blood and dead tissues (multiple furuncles together).
Pustule	A small elevation of the skin containing pus.

These pathological changes and responses can result in tissues needing repair by physical methods such as surgery, regeneration, or resolution, in which the inflammatory response stops, and the tissues go back to a normal state.

Pathological Issues Related to the Circulatory System

- **Edema or dropsy:** An abnormal accumulation of fluid in tissues or body cavities, while **dropsy** is an excessive accumulation of fluid in tissues or cavities of the body.
  - Cause: **Edema** comes from increased permeability of capillary walls, while **dropsy** involves increased capillary pressure due to venous obstruction or heart failure as well as inflammatory conditions in addition to fluid and electrolyte disturbances.
  - Effect: **Edema** causes swelling in tissues, and **dropsy** results in purge and embalming difficulties
  - Other Information:
    - **Anasarca** is a generalized massive edema in subcutaneous tissue, and **ascites** mean an accumulation of free serous fluid in the abdominal cavity.
    - **Hydrothorax** is an abnormal accumulation of fluid in the thoracic cavity.
    - **Hydropericardium** is an abnormal accumulation of fluid within the pericardial sac.
- **Hyperemia:** Excess of blood in an area of the body.
  - Cause: Physiological in exercise or g-forces; pathological involving obstruction.
  - Effect: In active hyperemia, arterial flow in the area is increased, while in passive hyperemia, there is an obstruction of venous outflow.

- **Ischemia:** Reduction in arterial blood supply to an area or body part.
  - Cause: The buildup of plaque in the artery.
  - Effect: Necrosis.

- **Thrombosis:** The formation or presence of an attached blood clot (stationary).
  - Cause:
    - Injuries to blood vessels.
    - Reduced rate of blood flow, and if blood is stationary, it will clot.
    - Alterations in blood composition in a buildup in blood platelets.
    - Blood diseases.

- o Effect:
  - Ischemia is a reduction in arterial blood supply to an area or body part.
  - Passive hyperemia involves an excess of blood in an area of the body caused by venous obstruction.
  - Gangrene: Ischemic necrosis plus putrefaction.
  - Infarction: The formation of an area of necrosis in a tissue caused by an obstruction in the artery supplying the area.
- o Other Information:
  - Location of thrombi: Attached to walls of arteries or veins.
  - Changes in thrombi: Continue to build up, or chunks can break off (embolism)

- ➢ **Embolism:** Free-floating objects in the bloodstream.
  - o Cause:
    - Fragments of thrombi (most common).
    - Bacteria.
    - Tumor cells/**metastasis**: Spread of disease from primary focus to distant parts of the body; in malignant tumors, the appearance of secondary growths in parts of the body at a distance from primary growth.
    - Animal parasites.
    - Fat: Very common.
    - Gas: Air embolism (CO_2 or O_2).
    - Foreign bodies, e.g., a splinter of wood, etc.
  - o Effect:
    - Ischemia: Reduction in arterial blood supply to an area or body part.
    - Infarction: The formation of an area of necrosis in a tissue caused by an obstruction in the artery supplying the area.
    - Spread of infection.
    - Necrosis: Pathological death of tissue still a part of the living organism.

- ➢ **Hemorrhage:** Escape of blood from the blood vascular system.
  - o Cause:
    - Trauma: Wound or injury (could be caused by blunt force trauma).
    - Vascular diseases.
    - Hypertension: Heart pumping too hard due to blockage.
    - Blood diseases.

  - o Effect:
    - Petechia: Antemortem, pinpoint, extravascular blood discoloration visible as purplish hemorrhages of the skin.
    - Ecchymosis: Small non-elevated hemorrhagic patch; extravasation of blood into the tissue; no swelling.
    - Hematoma: Tumor-like **swelling** of blood. Raised.
    - Epistaxis: Bleeding from the **nose.**
    - Hemoptysis: Blood in **sputum.**
    - Hematuria: Blood in the **urine.**
    - Hematemesis: **Vomiting** of blood.

- Melena: Blood in the stool (**feces**).

A variety of postmortem conditions can also occur as a result of these issues, including but not limited to **poor circulation, abscesses, hemorrhages, emaciation (*excessive wasting away of the body*), dehydration (*loss of moisture from body tissues*)**, decomposition, and discolorations. All of these conditions can create problems for the embalmer that may require specific embalming chemicals and techniques.

Oncology

Oncology is *the study of neoplasms or tumors*. Neoplasms are formed as a result of abnormal and uncontrolled cell division and multiplication, forming masses or new tissue growths that can be classified clinically, in which medical professionals look at the course of the disease, the type of growth, and what tissue holds the origination.

Neoplasms can be studied histologically through their tissues and morphology. Benign neoplasms are mild in character and are generally harmless. These types of neoplasms grow by expansion and do not migrate; do not return after surgical removal; do not cause extensive tissue damage; do not cause whole body changes; resemble normal tissues and are generally not fatal (but can be in rare circumstances such as in the brain or those that put pressure on vital organs).

Benign Neoplasms

Benign neoplasms usually have the suffix "oma."

Benign Epithelial Neoplasms:

Adenoma	Benign tumor of glandular origin
Papilloma	Circumscribed outgrowth from skin or mucous membrane, e.g., wart
Nevus	A congenital discoloration of a circumscribed area of the skin due to pigmentation (brown), like a mole
Polyp	Growth or mass of tissue that protrudes from a mucous membrane

Benign Connective Tissue Neoplasms:

Osteoma	Nonmalignant tumor of the bone
Chondroma	Nonmalignant tumor of the cartilage
Lipoma	Nonmalignant tumor of the fat
Angioma	Nonmalignant tumor of vascular origin (cardio or lymph)
Fibroma	Nonmalignant tumor of fibrous connective tissue

Benign Muscle Tissue Neoplasms:

Rhabdomyoma	Nonmalignant tumor of striated or skeletal muscle tissue
Leiomyoma	Nonmalignant tumor of smooth muscle tissue (involuntary)

Benign Nervous Tissue Neoplasms:

Neuroma	Benign tumor of nervous tissue.

Malignant Neoplasms

Malignant or harmful neoplasms grow by infiltration (penetrating surrounding tissues), metastasize (***transfer of a disease from its primary site to a distant location***) via the vascular system, reoccur after surgical removal, cause extensive tissue damage, cause whole body changes, do not resemble surrounding tissues, and are generally lethal without treatment.

Malignant epithelial neoplasms usually have the suffix "carcinoma."

Melanoma	Epithelial tissue, when it spreads known as multiple melanomas
Squamous cell carcinoma	Epidermis
Adenocarcinoma	Malignant tumor of glands
Transitional cell carcinoma	Between the layers of skin
Basal cell carcinoma	A discolored bump on the skin caused by excessive exposure to the sun

Malignant connective tissue neoplasms usually have the suffix "sarcoma":

Osteosarcoma	Malignant tumor of the bone
Chondrosarcoma	Malignant tumor of the cartilage (very rare)
Liposarcoma	Malignant tumor of the fat
Angiosarcoma	Malignant tumor of vascular origin (cardio or lymph)
Fibrosarcoma	Malignant tumor of fibrous connective tissue
Lymphoma	Malignant tumor of lymphatic tissue (an exception to the rule)

Malignant muscle tissue neoplasms:

Rhabdomyosarcoma	Malignant tumor of striated or skeletal muscle tissue
Leiomyosarcoma	Malignant tumor of smooth muscle tissue (involuntary)

Malignant nervous tissue neoplasms:

Glioma	Malignant tumor of the brain

Neoplasms can also be in the form of **cysts** (*sacs within or on the body surface containing air or fluid*), which can be seen in areas such as the ovaries or sebaceous cysts such as pimples.

Neoplasms and cancer can cause a variety of postmortem conditions that we, as embalmers, should be aware of during the embalming process. These conditions include but are not limited to emaciation, discolorations, hemorrhages, tissue deformation, extravascular obstruction, **cachexia** (a *severe form of malnutrition*)*,* and dehydration.

Two terms of note regarding oncology are **hyperplasia**, *the increase in the size of an organ or part due to an excessive but regulated increase in the number of cells,* and **metaplasia**, *the replacement of one type of tissue into a form in which it is not normally found.*

Diseases
(See Anatomy Section for review on systems and structures)

Diseases of the blood (-cytosis = increase; – penia = decrease)

Leukocytosis	**Increase** in the number of white blood cells. The normal response to an abnormal situation
Leukopenia	**Abnormal** reduction (**decrease**) in the number of white blood cells in the blood
Anemia	A decrease in the number of erythrocytes (RBCs), hemoglobin, or both. Primary: Caused by a disease itself. Secondary: Result of another disease
Leukemia	A disease characterized by the appearance of **great numbers** of **immature** and **abnormal** white blood cells (hematopoietic disorder). Blood cancer
Polycythemia Vera (erythrocytosis)	An **abnormal increase** in total red blood cell mass (**RBCs**; hematopoietic disorder)
Hemophilia	An inherited hemorrhagic disease characterized by a tendency toward excessive and sometimes spontaneous bleeding; inability to metabolize Vitamin K
Purpura	A condition in which spontaneous bleeding occurs in the subcutaneous tissues, causing the appearance of purple patches on the skin
Thrombocytopenia	Deficiency of platelets in the blood; having this **causes** purpura

Diseases of the Heart and Blood Vessels

There are many predisposing factors to these types of diseases, which include but are not limited to heredity, obesity, diabetes, elevated cholesterol levels, smoking, substance abuse, stress, and diet.

Dilatation	The condition of the heart being enlarged, normally occurring, artificially, or as a result of disease; hypertension is the worst cause.
Hypertrophy	The enlargement of an organ, or partly due to the increase in the size of cells composing it, maybe transitory due to exertion.
Endocarditis	Inflammation of the endocardium or lining membrane of the heart, including that of the valves.
Insufficiency (incompetence)	Failure of a heart valve to close.
Stenosis	Abnormal constriction (narrowing) of a channel or orifice.
Prolapse	Falling or sliding of an organ from its normal position in the body; valves won't close, allowing the blood to go back through the valve.
Pericarditis	Inflammation of the pericardium, which is a sac-like structure surrounding the heart.
Myocarditis	Inflammation of the myocardium (muscle tissue of the heart)
Rheumatic Heart Disease	Results from a streptococcal infection in the ears or throat, although organisms are no longer present when the disease presents itself.
Coronary Artery Disease	Diseases affecting the coronary arteries: a. Arteriosclerosis b. Atherosclerosis c. Thrombosis d. Spasms: Cardiac arrhythmia/tachycardia/bradycardia e. Embolism
Cardiac Failure	a. Acute: Cardiac arrest; very quick b. Chronic (congestive): The heart is pumping inadequately to meet the needs of the body. Congestive heart failure causes edema.
Myocardial Infarction	When an area of the myocardium is deprived of blood due to occlusion of the coronary artery, that tissue dies, and the dead muscle is called an infarct.
Cardiomyopathy	A disease of the myocardium due to primary disease of the heart muscle (see myocarditis).
Carditis	Inflammation of the heart.
Arteritis	Inflammation of the arteries.
Arteriosclerosis	A disease of arteries resulting in thickening and loss of elasticity of the arterial walls.

Atherosclerosis	A form of arteriosclerosis marked by the deposition of lipids in the inner layer of arterial walls.
Aneurysm	A localized dilatation of a blood vessel; dilatation is the condition of being enlarged. May burst due to pressure.
Phlebitis	Inflammation of a vein.
Varicose Veins	The vein becomes swollen and painful and appears knotty under the skin. It may cause itching.

Diseases of the Digestive System

Review: The alimentary canal begins at the mouth and includes accessory organs. The gastrointestinal tract begins at the stomach.

Stomatitis (oral mucositis)	Inflammation of the mouth.
Glossitis	Inflammation of the tongue.
Gingivitis	Inflammation of the gums.
Pharyngitis	Inflammation of the pharynx.
Esophagitis	Inflammation of the esophagus.
Gastritis	Inflammation of the stomach.
Peptic ulcer	Ulcers of the stomach and small intestine; **peptic** refers to digestion, and an **ulcer** is an **open sore** accompanied by **sloughing of inflamed** necrotic **tissue.**
Enteritis	Inflammation of the intestines.
Colitis	Inflammation of the colon (a type of enteritis).
Appendicitis	Inflammation of the appendix.
Hemorrhoids	Varicose veins of the rectum near the anus known as "**piles.**"
Hepatitis	Inflammation of the liver, of which **jaundice** is a sign.
Cirrhosis	A disease of the liver, progressive destruction of liver cells is associated with the regeneration of cells and an increase in fibrous tissue **hardening** caused by overworking liver.
Cholecystitis	Inflammation of the gallbladder.
Cholelithiasis	Presence or formation of gallstones (**choleliths**).
Cholangitis	Inflammation of the bile ducts (Biliary tract).
Pancreatitis	Inflammation of the pancreas in which insulin production is compromised.
Proctitis	Inflammation of the rectal lining.
Peritonitis	Inflammation of the peritoneum (lining of the abdominal cavity).
Diverticulosis	**A diverticulum** is a sac opening out from a tubular organ (inside the intestines); a little pouch of the sac that forms in the intestine as the mucosal lining pushes through the muscle.
Pyloric stenosis	Abnormal constriction of the pyloric sphincter valve of the stomach.

Anomalies	Abnormality in development (growth) but usually doesn't get large enough.
Hernias	Abnormal protrusion of part of an organ through an abnormal opening in the wall that normally contains it; abnormal outpouching or protrusion.
Carcinoma of stomach	Cancer of the stomach
Polyps	A growth or mass of tissue that protrudes from a mucous membrane. It may be benign or malignant.
Colon/rectal carcinoma	Cancer of the colon/rectum.
Stenosis	Abnormal constriction of a channel or orifice.
Paralysis	**Peristalsis** is when the wavelike contractions that push the food along stop.
Volvulus	**Twisting** of the intestine on itself.
Intussusception	Enfolding or **telescoping** of one segment of the intestine into another.
Adhesions	Adherence or **knitting together** of two surfaces. Typically happens during the healing process after an injury or surgery.

Diseases of the digestive system can lead to many postmortem conditions, which include but are not limited to ascites, dehydration, decomposition, coagulation of the blood, jaundice, edema, hemorrhage, purge, and distention.

Diseases of the Respiratory Tract

Review: Air enters the nasal cavity before passing through the throat (pharynx) to the windpipe (trachea). The larynx (voice box) is the entrance to the trachea. The trachea then branches to the two bronchi that lead to the lungs. These bronchi continue to branch into smaller tubes called bronchioles. The bronchioles then terminate at the alveoli, the small air sacs.

Rhinitis	Inflammation of the nose; common cold.
Sinusitis	Inflammation of the sinus; next step after rhinitis.
Pharyngitis	Inflammation of the pharynx.
Laryngitis	Inflammation of the larynx.
Common cold	Coryza is caused by the rhinovirus; not systemic and affects the head only.
Tracheitis	Inflammation of the trachea.
Bronchitis	Inflammation of the bronchi.
Bronchial asthma	Allergic reactions in the bronchi cause swelling in the tube, blocking airflow.
Pneumonia	Inflammation of the lung. 1. Lobar: One lobe of the lung only. Double pneumonia is in both lungs (one or more lobes each). 2. Bronchial (bronchitis); in bronchi. 3. Viral: Caused by a virus instead of bacteria or fungi.
Pleurisy	Inflammation of the pleural membranes of the lungs.
Empyema	When the pleural cavity contains pus; **pye = pus.**

Tuberculosis	*Mycobacterium tuberculosis*; plugs up lungs; consumption.
Pneumoconiosis	A general term used to denote any prolonged inhalation of mineral dust, such as silica.
Atelectasis	The collapse of lung tissue; airless condition of the lung.
Emphysema	Over distention of pulmonary air sacs with air; the presence of air in tissues, so alveoli can't contract and push CO_2 out of the sac, and alveoli get stretched out.
Lung abscess	As the bronchi dilate, pockets are formed where infectious material collects; abscesses develop, which cause pus to be coughed up in the sputum.
Fungal disease	*Histoplasmoses capsulatum*; fungus "love" moist, dark areas
Cleft lip/cleft palate	Genetic/developmental malformation of lip and/or palate. It may be unilateral or bilateral.
Cystic fibrosis	A disease of the exocrine glands produces thick mucus, causing blocked airways.
Respiratory polyps	Mucus membranes of the nose.
Respiratory Carcinomas / Sarcomas	Respiratory system cancer.
COPD (chronic obstructive pulmonary disease)	When airflow is reduced or blocked.

Diseases of the respiratory system can lead to many postmortem conditions that include but are not limited to cyanosis (***blue coloring due to lack of oxygen***), emaciation, dehydration, hydrothorax (***edema of the thoracic cavity***), edema, and cavitation (***formation of cavities in an organ or tissue***).

Diseases of the Urinary System

Review: When discussing the urinary system, it is important to remember the is the vital organ. The functional unit of the kidney is known as the nephrons, which consist of Bowman's capsules, proximal convoluted tubules, loops on Henle, and distal convoluted tubules that lead to the collecting tubules. Nephrons are where filtration occurs to form urine for excretion.

Nephritis	Inflammation of the functional unit of the kidney (nephron)
Uremia	A toxic condition caused by retention in the blood of waste products normally excreted in the urine; caused by kidney failure. Hematuria = Blood (RBCs) in urine.
Glomerulonephritis	Kidney disease (inflammation) affecting glomeruli; **Glomerulus**: Small tuft of capillaries in a Malpighian body of the kidney in which blood filtration occurs.
Pyelonephritis	Suppurative (pus) inflammation of the kidney and pelvis
Pyelitis	Inflammation of the kidney pelvis at the **junction between** the **ureter** and the **kidney.**
Hydronephrosis	Distention of one or both kidneys with urine as a result of an **obstruction** such as a kidney stone (nephrolithiasis or urinary calculi); **fluids build up** in the kidneys.
Nephrolithiasis	Kidney stones (urinary [renal] calculi).
Urethritis	Inflammation of the ureters, which are a pair of urinary tubes connecting kidneys to the bladder.
Cystitis	Inflammation of the urinary bladder.
Urethritis	Inflammation of the Urethra.
Polycystic kidneys	Congenital anomaly, error in development associated with **multiple cyst** formation.
Hypoplasia	Underdevelopment of tissue organs or body.
Dysplasia	Abnormal development of tissue; **dys** = pain
Pyuria	Pus in urine.
Carcinoma of kidney Carcinoma of bladder Prostate carcinoma	Cancer.
Acute renal failure	A sudden and severe onset, failure of kidneys to function properly.
Chronic renal failure	Slow and moderate onset, failure of kidneys to function properly.
Oliguria	Diminished amount of urine formation.
Anuria	Absence of urine formation.
Dysuria	Painful or difficult urination.

Diseases of the urinary system can lead to many postmortem conditions, including but not limited to edema, uremia, jaundice, dehydration, and odor (especially due to excess ammonia).

Diseases of the Nervous System

Review: The nervous system is responsible for stimulus-response in the body. The central nervous system is made up of the brain and spinal cord. The peripheral nervous system is made up of nerve branches that extend throughout the body.

Meningitis	Inflammation of the meninges: **pia mater** and **arachnoid mater.**
Hydrocephalus	Excessive accumulation of cerebrospinal fluid in the ventricles of the brain.
Encephalitis	Inflammation of the brain and meninges caused by a virus; **Cephalus = brain.**
Myelitis	**Poliomyelitis**: Inflammation of gray matter of the brain/spinal cord caused by a virus.
Neuritis	Inflammation of a nerve.
Epilepsy	A chronic neurological disease marked by sudden alterations in consciousness, frequently through convulsions (seizures). Brain impulses are temporarily disturbed. There are various types of seizures, including petit and grand mal.
Rabies	Fatal **viral** disease of the brain and spinal cord transmitted by a rabid animal's saliva
Multiple sclerosis	The chronic, progressive **demyelinating disease of the central nervous system**; **myelin**: lipid sheath on neuronal fibers destroyed in multiple sclerosis and of unknown origin.
Parkinson's disease	A disease of the brain that appears gradually and progresses slowly; a degenerative disease of the **basal ganglia**. Resulting in involuntary movement like **shaking palsy.**
Alzheimer's disease	Brain abnormality due to buildup of protein deposits, resulting in premature **senility**; unknown origin, but there is some familial tendency to develop.
Creutzfeldt-Jakob disease	Mad cow disease is caused by a **prion** (misfolded protein); very slow, taking 17-20 years to develop. Typically acquired through contaminated meat. No cure, and it is extremely contagious through the cerebrospinal fluid.
Cerebral palsy	A muscular disorder caused by **brain damage at** or near the time of **birth**. Typically, motor and mental disabilities become apparent before the age of three.
Cerebrovascular accident (stroke)	Disruption in blood flow to the brain due to cerebral hemorrhages and blood clot formation leading to permanent brain damage.
TIA (transient ischemic attack)	Brief/critical periods of reduced blood flow in the cerebral artery. Typically, the symptoms last less than an hour and does not result in permanent damage.
Concussion	The immediate and temporary disturbance of brain function resulting from a violent blow to the head, causing the head and brain to move back and forth rapidly.
Contusion	A bruise, often accompanied by swelling, without breaking the skin.

Intracranial hemorrhage	1. Extradural (epidural): On the outside of the dura mater, between the dura mater and the skull, **dura mater** is the outer membrane (meninx) covering the brain.
	2. Subdural: Beneath dura mater.
	3. Subarachnoid: Beneath arachnoid mater; the surface of the brain torn, usually by a **skull fracture.**

Diseases of the nervous system can lead to many postmortem conditions, including but not limited to brain purge, hemorrhage, atrophy, and poor circulation.

Diseases of the Female Reproductive System

Review: the female reproductive system is comprised of the vagina, the uterus, the cervix, the fallopian tubes, and the ovaries. The purpose is to release an ovum every month during ovulation for fertilization.

Endometritis	Inflammation of the endometrium, the inner lining of the uterus, carried by blood/lymph to other locations or doesn't stop growing and expands out of the uterus.
Endocervicitis	Inflammation of the mucous lining of the cervix uteri or the neck, which is any constricted portion of an organ, such as the inferior cylindrical part of the uterus.
Salpingitis	Inflammation of the fallopian tube (**salpinx**).
Oophoritis	Inflammation of the ovary.
Vaginitis	Inflammation of the vagina.
Gonorrheal and chlamydia infections	**Gonorrhea** is an infectious STD caused by the bacterium *Neisseria gonorrhoeae*; **Chlamydia** is a prevalent STD caused by *Chlamydia trachomatis* characterized by burning on urination, frequent and painful urination, and low back pain, which may spread to uterine (fallopian) tubes.
Syphilis	An STD caused by the bacterium *Treponema pallidum*; spirochete, anaerobic. Lesions: -Primary = **chancre** (on the surface of the skin). -Secondary: rash. -Tertiary = **gumma** (gummy lesion, usually on the spinal cord)

Herpes infection (Herpes Simplex Type II)	A form of vesicles appearing in clusters on an inflammatory base but with no tendency to rupture; in *Herpes zoster,* they are distributed along the nerve trunks, which leads to an inflammatory skin disease characterized by the formation of groups of vesicles. Typically Type II is found on the genital region, but it may also be in/on the mouth. Type I may also be found in both places as well.
Ectopic pregnancy	The implantation of the fertilized ovum (zygote) in a site other than the normal one in the uterine cavity.
Eclampsia	Convulsions of toxic origin occurring during the latter part of pregnancy or during labor; **toxemia of pregnancy** resulting in convulsions (seizures).
Dermoid cysts	Nonmalignant cystic tumors in which are found elements derived from the ectoderm, such as hair, teeth, or skin; they frequently occur in the ovary but may develop in other organs, such as the lungs. **Tumors of the ovary: dermoid**: Resembling the skin; **teratoma**: Complex tumor whose substance represents several different tissues.
Cervical cancer	Cancer of the **cervix**, which is the inferior cylindrical part of the uterus.
Breast cancer	Cancer of the breast/mammary tissue.

Diseases of the female reproductive system can lead to many postmortem conditions; these include but are not limited to rapid blood coagulation, ascites, edema, and infections.

Diseases of the Male Reproductive System

Review: The male reproductive system is comprised of the testes, the scrotum, the seminiferous tubules, the epididymis, the vas deferens, seminal vesicles, the prostate, prostate gland, urethra, which is where spermatogenesis occurs to form sperm for fertilization of the female ovum.

Orchitis	Inflammation of the testes.
Prostatitis	Inflammation of the prostate gland.
Hydrocele	A fluid-containing sac or tumor; a collection of fluid formed in the space along the spermatic cord and in the scrotum (**edema**). Painless enlargement of the tunica vaginalis.
Cryptorchism (cryptorchidism)	Condition in which the descent of a testis stops at some path in its normal path into the scrotum.
Hernia	Abnormal protrusion of part of an organ through an abnormal opening in the wall that normally contains it; intestines may follow the same path as testicles used to descend.

Benign enlargement of the prostate (hyperplasia)	Common in men over 50.
Carcinoma of prostate	Common in old age, the tumor may be small and asymptomatic.
Testicular carcinoma	Testicular cancer is an extremely rare, highly malignant
Breast cancer	Cancer of the breast/mammary tissue.

Diseases of the male reproductive system can lead to many postmortem conditions, including but not limited to rapid blood coagulation, ascites, edema, infections and discolorations.

Diseases of the Bones and Joints

Review: The bones and joints are important in the framework of the body. They assist with structure and support. The axial skeleton contains 80 bones, and the appendicular skeleton has 126 bones. Both skeletons create the full body that contains 206 bones.

Osteoporosis	Osteo = bone and porosis = porous; loss of bone density.
Osteomyelitis	Inflammation of bone and bone marrow.
Osteomalacia / rickets	A disease marked by softening of the bones due to faulty calcification in adulthood.
Arthritis	Inflammation of a joint.
Bursitis	Inflammation of a **bursa**, which is a sac or pouch of synovial fluid located at friction points, especially around the joints.
Fractures	Any break in the bone; types: **simple** does not penetrate the skin, and **compound** does penetrate the skin. **Comminuted** is splintered, crushed bone; **greenstick** is cracked on one side, bent on the other; and **pathological** are spontaneous fractures due to disease.
Scoliosis (scolios = twisted)	An abnormal **lateral** curvature from the normal vertical line of the spine, usually in the thoracic region. 1. **Kyphosis** (kyphos = a hump), known as a hunchback, is an exaggeration of the thoracic curve of the vertebral column. 2. **Lordosis** (lordos = bent backward), known as swayback, is an exaggeration of the anterior lumbar curve of the vertebral column.
Achondroplasia	Defective cartilage formation resulting in improper bone development and achondroplastic dwarfism.
Paget's disease (osteitis deformans)	Irregular thickening and softening of the bone; overgrowth of bone.
Osteosarcoma	Bone cancer.

Diseases of the bones and joints can lead to many postmortem conditions, including but not limited to malformations, positioning problems, and bone procurement for study.

Diseases of the Endocrine Glands

Review: The endocrine system works to maintain and secrete hormones to the body through the bloodstream. The system is made up of various glands and structures, such as the pituitary gland, thyroid, adrenal glands, parathyroid, and pancreas.

Pancreas (Islets of Langerhans, Pancreatic islets): Produces insulin	Diabetes mellitus (meli = honey)	Disease caused by hyposecretion of insulin. Glucose in the urine. Type I is when the pancreas does not produce insulin, and Type II is due to insulin resistance.
	Pancreatic Cancer: Carcinoma of the Pancreas	Usually fatal within six months to one year.
Pituitary Gland	Acromegaly	Hyperfunction of the pituitary gland after ossification (after puberty-adulthood) has been completed resulting in too much human growth hormone (hGH).
	Giantism (gigantism)	Caused by hypersecretion of human growth hormone (hGH) during childhood.
	Dwarfism	Result of endocrine dysfunction. Hyposecretion of hGH during childhood.
	Diabetes insipidus (insipidus = tasteless)	Hyposecretion of antidiuretic hormone (ADH) or nonfunctional ADH receptors. Profuse urination is the most common problem with dysfunction of the pituitary gland.
Thyroid Gland: Controls metabolism and produces thyroxine	Cretinism	A congenital condition due to **hypo**thyroidism in which thyroxine is not synthesized, resulting in mental disabilities and a smaller stature.
	Myxedema	Caused by severe **hypo**thyroidism during the adult years.
	Grave's disease	**Exophthalmic goiter,** marked by the protrusion of the eyeballs, increased heart action, **enlargement of the thyroid gland**, weight loss, nervousness, **and hyperthyroidism.**
	Goiter	Enlargement of the thyroid gland. Hyperthyroidism. Large nodule in the neck from lack of iodine.
Parathyroid Glands: 4 glands on the back of the thyroid gland.	Hypoparathyroidism	Insufficient secretion of the parathyroid glands; Tetany is sustained muscular contraction of the hands and feet.
	Hyperparathyroidism	Condition due to increased activity of the parathyroid glands.
	Hypercalcemia	Abnormally high levels of circulating calcium in the bloodstream; comes from the bones.

249

Adrenal glands on top of the kidney	Addison's disease	Resulting from deficiency (hypofunction) in the secretion of adrenocortical hormones. Steroid hormones cause adrenals to atrophy with **bronzing of the skin.**
	Cushing's disease	Hypersecretion of glucocorticoids secondary to hypersecretion of adrenocorticotropic hormone from the pituitary; causes hyperglycemia.
	Waterhouse-Friderichsen syndrome	**Acute** adrenal insufficiency due to hemorrhage into the adrenal gland caused by meningococcal infection (same source of meningitis).

Diseases of the endocrine system can lead to many postmortem conditions, including but not limited to edema, discolorations, deformities, and poor circulation.

Diseases of the Integumentary System

Review: The integumentary system is comprised of the skin. It is the body's largest organ and a major line of defense against microorganisms. The skin has three main layers: the epidermis, dermis, and hypodermis.

Acne	Inflammation of sebaceous (oil) glands that usually begins at puberty; blackheads, pimples, blocked, clogged, or plugged-up glands.
Abscess	A localized collection of pus and liquefied tissues in a cavity.
Syphilis	An STD caused by the bacterium *Treponema pallidum*; spirochete, anaerobic. Lesions: -Primary = **chancre** (on the surface of the skin). -Secondary: rash. -Tertiary = **gumma** (gummy lesion, usually on the spinal cord).
Seborrheic dermatitis	Dandruff
Melanocytic nevus	A **melanocyte** is a melanin-forming cell; a **nevus** is a congenital discoloration of a circumscribed area of the skin due to pigmentation; a **mole** is a circumscribed vascular tumor of the skin due to hyperplasia of the blood vessels.
Malignant melanoma	A type of skin cancer.
Squamous cell carcinomas	Cancer of the flat, scaly, epithelial cell.

Diseases of the integumentary system can lead to many postmortem conditions, including but not limited to discolorations, dehydration, scaling, lesions, and swelling.

Diseases of the Lymphatic System

Review: The major function of the lymphatic system is filtration. It consists of the organs and lymph nodes that work to filter body fluid and fight infection. The lymph nodes are small filtering stations that help fight an infection that produces certain white blood cells, lymphocytes, monocytes, and plasma cells to destroy invading organisms. Organs such as the spleen, tonsils, and adenoids (**adenoids**: lymphoid; having the appearance of a gland) are comprised of lymphoid tissue and function in the body's internal defense.

Tonsillitis	Inflammation of the large lymphatic nodules embedded in the mucous membrane of the throat (tonsils).
Lymphangitis	Inflammation of the lymph vessels.
Splenomegaly	Enlargement of the spleen due to an accumulation of RBCs.
Lymphedema	Edema due to obstruction of the lymphatic system.
Lymphoma (Hodgkin)	Solid tumor of the lymphoreticular system that can have its origin in any lymphoid tissue but usually begins in the lymph nodes of the supraclavicular, high cervical, or mediastinal areas.
Lymphoma (non-Hodgkin)	A group of solid malignant tumors of lymphoid tissues, T-cell lymphomas that arise directly from the thymus.

Diseases of the lymphatic system can lead to many postmortem conditions, including but not limited to edema, emaciation, metastasis, and swelling.

Glossary for Pathology

Abscess - Localized accumulation of pus.

Acquired - A disease, condition, or abnormality that is not hereditary on innate (present at birth).

Acromegaly - Hyperfunction of the pituitary gland after ossification has been completed.

Acute - A disease with a rapid onset and short duration.

Allergy - A hypersensitive immune response to a foreign substance.

Amelia - Congenital absence of one or more limbs.

Anaplasia - Condition of neoplastic cells indicating their loss of differentiation or their reversion to more primitive forms.

Anasarca - Generalized edema in subcutaneous tissue.

Anemia - A decrease in the number of erythrocytes, hemoglobin, or both.

Aneurysm - A localized dilatation of a blood vessel.

Aplasia - Failure of a tissue or an organ to develop normally.

Arteriosclerosis - Disease of the arteries resulting in a thickening and loss of elasticity of the arterial walls.

Ascites - Accumulation of free serous fluid in the abdominal cavity.

Atherosclerosis - A form of arteriosclerosis marked by the deposition of lipids in the inner layer of arterial walls.

Atrophy - A wasting decrease in the size of an organ or tissue.

Autopsy (Postmortem Examination) - A postmortem examination of the organs and tissues of a body to determine the cause of death or pathological condition.

Cachexia - A general state of ill health associated with emaciation.

Carbuncle - Several communicating boils of the skin and subcutaneous tissues with the production and discharge of pus and dead tissues.

Carcinoma - Malignant neoplasm of epithelial origin.

Chronic - A disease with a more or less slow onset and long duration.

Cleft Palate - Congenitally malformed palate with a fissure along the midline.

Communicable - A disease that may be transmitted either directly or indirectly between individuals by an infectious agent.

Complication - An unfavorable condition arising during the course of the disease.

Concussion - The immediate and temporary disturbance of brain function as a result of trauma.

Congenital - Present at birth.

Congestion - Accumulation of an excess of blood or tissue fluid in a body part.

Contusion - A bruise, often accompanied by swelling.

Cretinism - A congenital condition due to hypothyroidism resulting in developmental disabilities.

Cryptorchism (Cryptorchidism) - failure of the testicles to descend into the scrotum.

Cyanosis - bluish discoloration of the skin or mucous membranes (lips) due to lack of oxygen.

Cryobiology - Science that treats the effects of low temperatures on biological systems.

Cyst - a closed sac or pouch with a definite wall that contains fluid, semi-fluid, or solid material.

Deficiency - A condition due to lack of dietary or metabolic substance.

Definitive - Final; ending.

Degeneration - The deterioration of tissues with corresponding functional impairment as a result of disease or injury.

Dehydration - Loss of moisture from body tissue.

Diagnosis - The term denoting the name of the disease or syndrome; to recognize the nature of a disease.

Dilatation (Dilation) - The condition of the heart being enlarged due to stretching as a result of the disease.

Dry Gangrene (Ischemic Necrosis) - necrotic tissue due to reproduction in the arterial blood supply due to the body part that remains aseptic.

Dysplasia - Abnormal development of tissue.

Ecchymosis - Superficial bleeding under the skin or mucous membrane; a bruise.

Ectopic pregnancy - The implantation of the fertilized ovum outside the uterus.

Edema - Abnormal accumulation of fluid in tissues or body cavities.

Emaciation - Excessive wasting away of the body.

Embolism - A sudden obstruction of a blood vessel by debris.

Emphysema - Over distension of pulmonary air sacs with air; the presence of air in tissues.

Empyema - a collection of pus in the body cavity, especially in the pleural space.

Endemic - A disease that is continuously present in a given population.

Epidemiology - the study of the distribution and determinants of disease and wellness in populations and the use of this data to enhance public health.

Epilepsy - A chronic neurological disease marked by sudden alterations in consciousness and frequently by convulsions.

Epistaxis - Bleeding from the nose.

Erythrocytosis (polycythemia vera) - An increase in the number of red blood cells.

Etiology - The study of the cause of disease.

Exacerbation - Increase in severity of the disease.

Exogenous - Originates outside a cell, organ, or organism.

Exsanguination - Loss of blood to the point where life can no longer be sustained.

Exudate - Any fluid released by the body with a high concentration of proteins, cells, or solid debris.

Febrile - pertaining to or characterized by fever.

Fulminating - Having rapid and severe onset, usually fatal.

Furuncle - An abscess or pyogenic infection of a sweat gland or hair follicle.

Gangrene - Ischemic necrosis plus putrefaction.

Gas gangrene - Necrosis of tissue by *Clostridiumperfringens*

General pathology - Deals with the study of the widespread processes of disease, such as inflammation, degeneration, necrosis, cellular death, repair, etc., without reference to particular organs or organ systems.

Goiter - Enlargement of the thyroid gland due to iodine deficiency.

Gross pathology - Study of changes in the structure of the body that are readily seen with the unaided eye as a result of the disease.

Hematemesis - Vomiting of blood.

Hematoma - Tumor-like swelling of blood.

Hematuria - Discharge of red blood cells in the urine.

Hemophilia - a hereditary bleeding disorder marked by a deficiency of blood-clotting proteins.

Hemoptysis - Blood in the sputum.

Hemorrhage - Escape of blood from the blood vascular system.

Hereditary - Genetic characteristics transmitted from parent to offspring.

Hernia - Abnormal protrusion of part of an organ through an abnormal opening in the wall that normally contains it.

Hydrocele - Abnormal collection of fluid in any sacculated cavity in the body, especially tunica vaginalis.

Hydrocephalus - Excessive accumulation of cerebrospinal fluid in the ventricles of the brain.

Hydronephrosis - Distention of the pelvis and calyces of one or both kidneys with urine as a result of obstruction.

Hydropericardium - Abnormal accumulation of fluid within the pericardial sac.

Hydrothorax - Abnormal accumulation of fluid in the thoracic cavity.

Hyperemia - Excess of blood in an area of the body.

Hyperplasia - The increased size of an organ or part due to the excessive but regulated increase in the number of its cells.

Hypertrophy - The enlargement of an organ or part due to the increase in the size of cells composing it.

Hypoplasia - Underdevelopment of tissue, organ, or the body.

Iatrogenic - any injury or illness that occurs as a result of medical care

Idiopathic - Of unknown cause (example: essential hypertension).

Infarction - the death of tissue due to lack of blood supply.

Infection - A disease caused by microorganisms, especially those that release toxins or invade body tissues.

Infestation - The presence in or on the body of macroscopic organisms.

Infiltration - The passage and accumulation of a substance into cells, tissue, or organs.

Inflammation - A tissue reaction to irritation, infection, or injury marked by localized heat, swelling, redness, pain, and sometimes loss of function.

Intoxication - State of being intoxicated, especially of being poisoned by a drug or toxic substance.

Ischemia - Reduction in arterial blood supply.

Jaundice - yellowish discoloration of the tissue due to the presence of bilirubin in the blood. Microorganisms can be considered the cause of a certain disease.

Lesion - A circumscribed area of pathologically altered tissue; an injury or a wound.

Leukemia - a malignancy of the hematopoietic tissue characterized by a massive increase in the number of white blood cells present in the body.

Leukocytosis - An increase in the number of white blood cells in the blood.

Leukopenia - abnormal reduction in the number of white blood cells in the blood.

Lymphadenitis - Inflammation of lymph node.

Lymphedema - an abnormal accumulation of tissue fluid in the interstitial space due to lymphatic disturbances.

Lymphoma - Malignancy of lymphoid tissue.

Malformation (anomaly) - A defect or deformity.

Medicolegal (forensic) pathology - Study of disease to ascertain cause and manner of death.

Melena - Blood in stool.

Metaplasia - Conversion of one kind of tissue into a form that is not normal for that tissue.

Metastasis - The Transfer of a disease from its primary site to a distant location.

Microscopic pathology (histopathology) - Study of microscopic changes that cells, tissues, and organs undergo as a result of the disease.

Moist (wet) gangrene - Necrotic tissue that is wet as a result of inadequate venous drainage; may be accompanied by the invasion of saprophytic bacteria.

Morbidity rate - The number of cases per year of certain diseases in relation to the population in which they occur.

Mortality rate - The number of deaths in a given time or place or population of death to the population.

Necrosis - Pathological death of cells, tissues, and organs while still a part of the living tissue.

Neoplasm (tumor) - The abnormal, excessive, and uncontrolled multiplication of cells with the formation of a mass or new growth of tissue.

Nosocomial - Infections acquired in a healthcare setting.

Nosology - Science of classification of disease.

Nuclear medicine - Use of radioisotopes in medicine.

Occupational disease - A disease with an abnormally high rate of occurrence in members of the workforce.

Osteomalacia - An abnormal softening of the bones in adults.

Osteomyelitis - Inflammation of bone and bone marrow.

Osteoporosis - Loss of bone density.

Pandemic disease - Epidemic widespread, even to a worldwide extent.

Pathological anatomy - Study of structural change in the body caused by disease.

Pathology - The science that deals with the study of disease.

Pathogenesis- the origin and development of a disease

Petechia (pl., **petechiae**) - Antemortem, pinpoint, extravascular blood discoloration visible as purplish hemorrhages of the skin.

Phocomelia - Congenital condition in which the proximal portions of the limbs are poorly developed or absent.

Physiological pathology - Study of changes in body functions due to disease.

Pigmentation - Normal and pathological coloration of skin or tissues.

Pneumoconiosis - General term used to denote any prolonged inhalation of mineral dust.

Pneumonia - Inflammation of the lungs due to an infection.

Pneumonitis - Inflammation of supporting framework of the lung.

Poliomyelitis - An inflammation of the gray matter of the spinal cord as a result of a viral infection.

Polyp (polypus) - A growth or mass of tissue that protrudes from a mucous membrane.

Prevalence - Number of cases of disease present in a specified population at a given time.

Prognosis - Prediction of the outcome of the disease.

Prostatitis - Inflammation of the prostate gland.

Purpura - A condition in which spontaneous bleeding occurs in the subcutaneous tissues, causing the appearance of purple patches on the skin.

Pus - Fluid product of inflammation, consisting of leukocytes, bacteria, dead tissue cells, foreign elements, and fluid from the blood.

Pustule - A small elevation of the skin containing pus.

Putrefaction - Decomposition of proteins.

Recurrent - Reappearance of symptoms after a period of remission.

Regeneration - The replacement of damaged cells with normal cells of the same type.

Regurgitation - Backward flowing.

Remission - A cessation of symptoms of the disease.

Repair - The replacement of damaged tissue with fibrous connecting tissue.

Resolution - The termination of the inflammatory response with the affected part returning to its normal state (hemostasis).

Rickets - A disease of infants and young children caused by a deficiency of vitamin D, resulting in defective bone growth.

Sarcoma - Malignant neoplasm of non-epithelial origin.

Signs - Objective disturbances produced by disease; observed by physician, nurse, or person attending patient (example: pulse, fever, heart rate).

Special pathology - Deals with the specific features of the disease in relation to particular organs or organ systems.

Spina bifida - Congenital defect in which a part of the vertebral column is absent or incomplete closure.

Stenosis - Abnormal constriction of a pathway or orifice.

Symptoms - Subjective indication of the presence of disease.

Syndrome - Set of signs and symptoms associated with a particular disease (example: Down's Syndrome).

Teratoma - a congenital tumor formed by various types of tissues.

Thrombocytopenia - An abnormal decrease in the number of platelets in the blood.

Thrombosis - The formation or presence of an attached blood clot.

Ulcer - An open sore or lesion of the skin or mucous membrane accompanied by sloughing of inflamed necrotic tissue.

Uremia - A toxic condition caused by retention in the blood of waste products normally excreted in the urine.

Valvular insufficiency (incompetence) - Failure of a heart valve to close tightly, thus allowing regurgitation of blood.

Vesicle - blister-like elevation of skin containing serous fluid.

Microbiology

This section will discuss the basic principles of microbiology as it relates to the practice of funeral directing. Sanitation, disinfection, and protecting public health are all fundamental elements utilized in the embalming practice. By developing personal and professional hygiene practices, the spread of infectious diseases can be minimized.

Microbiology *is the scientific study of microorganisms under a microscope and their effect on other living organisms.* These microorganisms cannot be seen by the naked eye.

The field of microbiology was developed after spontaneous generation was disproved by scientists like Louis Pasteur and replaced with **germ theory** (which *states that microorganisms cause disease).* By the late 1800s, Robert Koch had established Koch's postulates, the steps needed to determine the specific causative microorganism for particular diseases. Building upon both the work of Koch and Pasteur, Ferdinand Cohn would become the founder of the field of bacteriology.

Microorganisms are either eukaryotes or prokaryotes. Eukaryotes are larger, more complex microorganisms that have a true nucleus with membrane-bound organelles (ex., plants and animals). Prokaryotes are smaller, less complex, and do not have a nucleus (ex., Bacteria, and Archaea).

Microorganisms can cause **infections** (*a group of microorganisms living and growing)* through the transportation of the microorganism through a **vector** (*a way to get from point one to point two).* These vectors include **carriers** *(a person/animal that has an organism and transmits it to you)* or **reservoir hosts** (*animals who can harbor or carry a disease without becoming infected).* One example would be the bubonic plague. This disease was transmitted through fleas (vectors/carriers) that were on rodents (reservoir hosts). This disease spread rapidly and killed one-third of Europe's population in the Middle Ages.

Note: Infections should not be confused with infestations (***macroorganisms living and growing).*** An example of an infection would be contracting the flu virus from sharing a water bottle with a friend. An example of an infestation would be contracting lice (pediculosis) through sharing a hat. Lice larvae can be seen with the naked eye. However, the flu virus is microscopic and cannot be viewed with the naked eye.

Microbiology can be broken down into five subsections:

1. **Bacteria:** *(Bacteriology is the science that studies bacteria)*
Bacteria are prokaryotic one-celled microorganisms of the Kingdom Monera, existing as **free-living organisms** or as parasites, multiplying by binary fission and having a large range of biochemical properties. Bacteria are comparatively large organisms. Bacteria are considered eukaryotes because they do not have a nucleus. However, they do have a cell wall.

2. **Mycoplasmas:** Mycoplasmas are a type of bacteria of the genus Mycoplasma that are found in humans. Most *do NOT* have a cell wall. They are the smallest free-living organisms. They are larger than viruses and smaller than other bacteria cells.

3. **Rickettsia**: *(Rickettsiology is the area of science that studies rickettsia)*
Rickettsia is a genus of Gram-negative, pathogenic, intracellular parasitic bacteria. They are not free-living organisms; they are obligate intracellular parasites, meaning they must take over a host cell to exist.

4. **Viruses**: *(Virology is the study of viruses and viral diseases)*
Viruses are intracellular, infectious parasites capable of living and reproducing only in living cells. **Not a free-living organism**. They are the smallest microorganism, comprised of only one strand of genetic material.

5. **Protozoa**: *(Protozoology is the science that deals with the study of protozoa)*
One-celled large free-living organisms of the Kingdom Protista. Most are unicellular, although some are colonial. They are single-cell animals/plants with a true nucleus.

6. **Fungi**: *(Mycology is the branch of science concerned with the study of fungi)*
Fungi are a group of diverse and widespread eukaryotic unicellular and multicellular organisms lacking chlorophyll, usually bearing spores and often filamentous. Reproduce by forming spores. Yeast – unicellular, molds – multicelullar.
Note: The following are **two groups of infectious organisms** that are of importance to embalmers and funeral directors:

Prion: *A small proteinaceous infectious particle that is resistant to most procedures that modify nucleic acids. They are incredibly small.* Prions infect brain tissue, denaturing it until death occurs. This type of disease may lay dormant for a lengthy period of time before displaying symptoms. Examples of prions are mad cow disease and Creutzfeldt-Jakob Disease (CJD). CJD is a special case when it comes to embalming. The embalmer should use the highest levels of sanitation possible to ensure no transmission occurs. CJD is typically spread through ingestion of contaminated meat and cerebrospinal fluid.

Chlamydia: A large group of nonmotile, Gram-negative intracellular bacteria.

Taxonomy

Taxonomy is the classification and scientific naming of organisms. This system shows the relationship between organisms as the result of evolution.

DOMAIN	Eukarya	
KINGDOM	Animalia	
PHYLUM	Chordata	
CLASS	Mammalia	
ORDER	Carnivora	
FAMILY	Canidae	
GENUS	*Canis*	
SPECIES	*Canis lupus*	

WOLF

Domain: The broadest classification. There are three domains: Eukarya, Bacteria, and Archaea.
Kingdom: Most classification systems have four kingdoms within the three **domains:** Monera, Fungi, Plantae, and Animalia.
Phylum: Within kingdoms
Class: Within phylums
Order: Within classes
Family: Within orders
Genus: Within families
Species: Within genuses. Identifies individual types of organisms. The most specific. Ex. Sapiens (humans).

The following example is for humans:
Domain: Eukarya
Kingdom: Animalia
Phylum: Chordata
Class: Mammalia
Order: Primates
Family: Hominidae
Genus: Homo
Species: Sapiens

Scientific naming uses both genus and species. The genus is capitalized, and the species is lowercase. Both the genus and species are italicized. The genus may also be shortened to the capital first letter.

Ex. Humans: Genus- Homo, Species: Sapiens.
Scientific name: *Homo sapiens or H. sapiens*

Bacteria

Reproduction:

Bacteria multiply by a process known as binary fission. **Binary fission** is *a method of asexual reproduction in which the cell splits into two parts which individually develop into two complete cells.* See the diagram below:

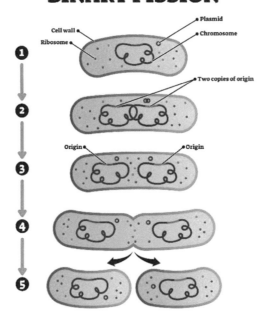

At optimal conditions, new generations of bacteria will form every 20 minutes. *A visible group of bacteria growing on a solid medium, presumably arising from a single microorganism, is a bacterial colony.*

Bacterial growth can be affected by a variety of factors. **Autotrophic** *(self-nourishing)* bacteria can grow and thrive without organic compounds. They can obtain carbon through by-products such as carbon dioxide. These types of bacteria do not attack humans. In contrast, heterotrophic bacteria require complex organic food from a direct carbon source. Heterotrophic bacteria can be further broken down into three categories:

1. Strict (obligate) saprophytes feed on dead or decaying organic matter.
2. Strict (obligate) parasites depend on a living host to feed on living organic matter.
3. Facultative bacteria are a bit more complex as they can adapt to the conditions presented to them. Due to their ability to adapt, they can survive adverse living conditions.

Bacteria also have varying oxygen requirements:

1. Strict (obligate) aerobes need an abundance of free oxygen to survive.
2. Microaerophilic bacteria need minimal amounts of free oxygen to survive.
3. Strict (obligate) anaerobes, on the other hand, do not need oxygen to survive. They actually need an absence of oxygen to survive.
4. Facultative bacteria, again, can adapt to their conditions regarding oxygen needs, allowing them to survive in a variety of environments.

Temperature is another factor that can affect bacterial activity. The lowest temperature that bacterial growth can occur is called the *minimum temperature.* The highest temperature that bacterial growth can occur is called the *maximum temperature.* The sweet spot, or best temperature for bacterial growth, is called the *optimum temperature.* These temperature ranges vary depending on the type of bacteria; however, like all organisms, certain species thrive in the extremes. Psychrophiles thrive in cold temperatures between 0 - 25°C (32 - 77°F). Mesophiles prefer moderate temperatures between 25 - 40°C (77-104°F). Thermophiles are best suited for high-temperature ranges of 40 - 70°C (104 -158°F), which is well above 140°F, the usual temperature at which proteins coagulate.

Bacterial cells can be affected by **osmotic pressure** (*pressure developed when two solutions of different concentrations are separated by a semipermeable membrane, such as a cell membrane*). See the Thantochemistry section (pp. 72 & 73) and Embalming section on concentration (pp. 19 & 20).

1. Plasmolysis *(bacterial cells shriveling/shrinking)* is caused when the cell is exposed to hypertonic environments in which the environment has a **higher** concentration of the solute, drawing excess fluid **out** of the cell to create equal concentrations. Think about when you eat a bag of chips; you get thirsty from the salt. The salt draws water out of your mouth and throat to balance out the salt concentration.

Note: *Crenation* is when the red blood cells shrivel and shrink, causing formaldehyde grey during the embalming process.

2. Plasmoptysis *(bacterial cells swell and burst)* is caused when the cell is exposed to hypotonic environments in which the environment has a **lower** concentration of the solute, drawing excess fluid **into** the cell to create equal concentrations. Think about blowing up a balloon. When the balloon becomes too full, it pops.

3. Isotonic solutions occur when the cell and environment have equal concentrations of solute and solvent. This does not affect the cell.

Morphology (shape):

A micron (μ) is 0.001 millimeters, or 10^{-6} meters. A micrometer (μm) is also known as a micron. The average size of a bacteria cell is 1-2 micrometers wide and 1-20 micrometers long.

The actual shape of bacterial cells can vary.

Classification	Shape	Arrangement	Example
Coccus	Spherical/ball shaped	Diplococci: Gram-positive bacteria occurring in pairs (Dyad/Diplo=2) Staphylococci: Gram-positive, nonmotile, opportunistic bacteria that tend to aggregate in irregular grape like clusters Streptococci: Gram-negative rods, which form a chain like colony.	
Bacillus	Rod shaped	Diplobacilli: A double bacillus, two being linked end to end to each other. Streptobacilli: Gram- negative rods, which form a chain like colony.	
Spirillum	Spiral shaped	Vibrio: Comma shaped. Spirillum: Corkscrew shaped. Spirochete: Ribbon shaped.	

Structure and function of Bacteria:

Bacteria have rigid cell walls to keep their shape. Note: That mycoplasmas do not have rigid cell walls. In some bacteria, outside of the cell walls are capsules, which are gelatinous shells created by the bacteria as a form of protection. The cell wall also serves to contain the cell membrane, a permeable substance that surrounds the cell. Within the cell membrane is the gooey liquid material called cytoplasm.

When viewing bacteria under a microscope, the results of staining will be different based on whether the bacteria are gram-negative or gram-positive.

1. Gram-positive bacteria: Lack an outer membrane but have thick layers of peptidoglycan in the cell wall.

2. Gram-negative bacteria: They have an outer lipopolysaccharide membrane and a thin peptidoglycan cell wall.

Bacteria also have tails called flagella, used as a means of transportation and movement, similar to a propeller on a boat. They also have pili, which look like whiskers on the side of the bacterial cell to latch onto other cells and organisms.

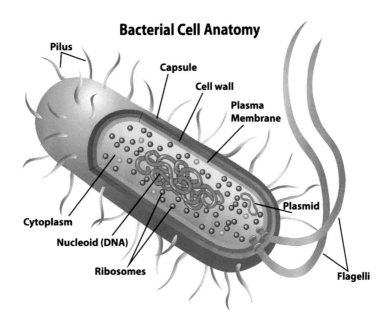

Bacterial Cell Anatomy

Some bacteria can create endospores if they are in an active and alive state. To be considered active and alive, they must be in a vegetative state. If they are in the sporulating state, the bacteria are considered dormant. Bacterial spores are highly resistant and difficult to kill.

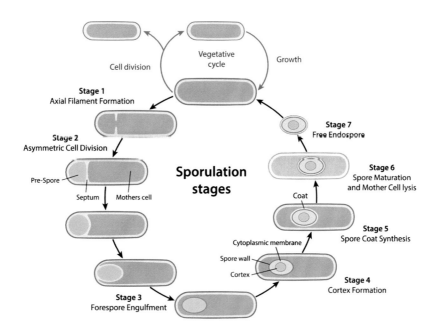

Associations:

Bacteria are able to associate with other species in three different ways. The first way is through symbiosis. **Symbiosis** *is species living together in close association.* Symbiosis can be further broken down into three types.

1. **Mutualism** is when two species live in close association, and both benefit each other. The oxpecker is an example of this. Oxpeckers are birds that sit on the backs of rhinoceroses and zebras. They eat bugs and pests that are attracted to the rhinos and zebras. This interaction benefits both species, as the birds get food while helping the zebras and rhinos not get infestations.
2. **Commensalism** is when two species live together, but only one is benefited, and the other is unharmed. One example would be jackals that follow tigers. The tiger kills its prey and eats the majority of the meat. The jackal waits until the tiger is done and feeds on the carcass. This benefits the jackal while the tiger remains unharmed.
3. **Parasitism** is when two species are associated, and one benefits while the other is harmed. One example would be getting bit by a tick. The tick benefits by feeding on your blood, while you may be infected with Lyme Disease, thus harming the host.

The second way that bacteria interact with other species is through **synergism**. This is *the harmonious action of two microorganisms producing an effect that neither could produce alone.* One example of synergism is the treatment of cancer in patients. Many times, patients need to combine more than one type of medication to create the desired result. This desired result could not occur with only one of the medications.

The third way is **antagonism**. This is the *inhibition of one bacterium by another in a mutual opposition/contrary action.* This could be seen through the destruction of one type of bacteria that has been ingested by bacteria in your gastrointestinal tract, keeping you from getting sick.

Microbial Control and Elimination

Funeral directors and embalmers are exposed to a variety of risks. Therefore, there are appropriate ways to minimize or eliminate all hazards in the workplace. Microorganisms are of particular interest to embalmers because they are present when handling human remains. Since microorganisms are not visible to the naked eye, embalmers need to use various PPEs and techniques to create a barrier between the deceased and the handler.

The best level of microbial control is sterilization. **Sterilization** is *the process of completely removing or destroying all life forms, or their products, on or in a substance.* The second-best level is disinfection. **Disinfection** is *the destruction of infectious agents by chemical or physical means directly applied to the inanimate object. This method only kills pathogenic organisms.* Disinfection does not destroy all life forms, only pathogenic (illness-causing) ones. The least effective level of control is antisepsis. **Antisepsis** *prevents sepsis by preventing or inhibiting the growth of the causative microorganisms.* Antiseptic treatment only prevents the reproduction of the microorganism, limiting its growth. It does not kill the microorganism.

To actually achieve one of these three levels of control, there are a variety of physical and chemical methods. See the Embalming section (pp. 5, 35) for the proper use of PPE during the embalming process.

Physical Control

Physical means of control can include scrubbing a decedent while washing the body.

Another physical or mechanical way to control microorganisms is using heat (one of the best methods). Utilizing excessive heat with an open flame will kill microorganisms. An example would be passing a needle through a flame to sterilize it. Dry heat could be used in the form of an oven. Moist heat can also be utilized through boiling, free-flowing steam, or steam under pressure. The best way to achieve steam under pressure is through the use of an autoclave. Autoclaves or pressure cookers apply 15 pounds of pressure for 15 minutes at 121.5°C, resulting in the elimination of the microorganisms. Many schools have autoclaves to clean instruments from biology labs.

Unlike heat, cold temperatures will only inhibit bacterial growth. This is a form of antiseptic control in which the bacteria become dormant. Meaning they will be dormant when cold but will start reproduction again when the temperatures rise. This is why coolers do not work to kill bacteria on decedents.

Ultraviolet (UV) light can be used to kill bacteria. However, too much exposure can be harmful to embalmers and funeral directors.

Chemical Control

When learning about chemicals, the suffix **"ICIDE"** *means to kill.* These types of chemicals are known as **disinfectants** or *chemical/physical agents that kill disease-causing microorganisms. Generally used on inanimate objects.* When most people think of disinfectants, they think of Sodium hypochlorite, more commonly known as bleach, a household cleaning agent. Bleach has great disinfectant properties but should not be used around formaldehyde compounds. Bleach and formaldehyde create a gas known as bismethylchloride or Bis(chloromethyl) ether, which is a deadly carcinogen (cancer-causing agent).

There are a few different types of disinfectants used in funeral services:

(1) Germicide: A substance that destroys microorganisms. This is a broad range type of chemicals used for a variety of microorganisms. However, this type is not effective against bacterial spores (spores are very resistant and difficult to kill).
(2) Bactericide: An agent that destroys only bacteria, but not necessarily their spores.
(3) Fungicide: An agent that kills fungi and their spores.
(4) Viricide: An agent destructive to viruses. It works by preventing the virus from entering the host cells.
(5) Insecticides: Are used to kill insects. These do not kill microorganisms, solely the insect or vector that may be harboring/transporting them.
(6) Larvacide: Used to kill insect larva. This is extremely important in cases where maggots are present, as maggots are not affected by formaldehyde.

There are many factors that affect the effectiveness of these disinfectants. These factors include but are not limited to the natural state of the disinfectant (solid, liquid, gas), the concentration of the chemical, the surface that needs to be disinfected (wood, steel, cloth), the number of microorganisms present, the kind of microorganisms, the exposure time after the chemical is applied, the temperature during disinfection (an increase in temperature is ideal), and the pH of the disinfectant (7.35-7.45 is ideal for microorganisms that can affect us).

There are particular disinfectants that are more suitable for the embalming room.

1. Halogens: These are chemicals that utilize halogens (group 7 elements on the periodic table- See Thantochemistry section, p.70). Halogens are classified as having 7 valence electrons in their outer electron shells. This means they only need 1 additional electron to have a stable octet. They are extremely poisonous. These include F, Cl, Br, and I. One example would be iodophors: Iodine containing compounds (for example, Prepodine).

2. Hypochlorites (bleaches): OCl- (NaOCl = Household bleach). Although bleach should not be used with formaldehyde, it can be used to wash and disinfect equipment after embalming has taken place.

3. Alcohols (OH) can also be used as disinfectants. These would include Isopropyl or Methyl alcohols (Methanol). For example, CH_3CHCH_3. Note: Ethyl alcohols (ethanol) should not be used.

4. Aldehydes are common disinfectants as well as preservatives utilized during the embalming process. Although formaldehyde is the most commonly used chemical during embalming, many people are familiar with formalin (formaldehyde solution containing a max solution of 40% by volume and 37% by weight).
   Note: **Methanal** is the IUPAC name for formaldehyde and may be used interchangeably (not to be confused with Methanol, which is a type of alcohol). Glutaraldehyde ($C_5H_8O_2$) is another type of aldehyde that is commonly used in embalming as a preservative and a disinfectant.

5. Phenolic compounds are also used as disinfectants and preservatives in embalming solutions. Examples include phenol (a carbolic acid), which is commonly seen in cavity fluids or as a bleaching agent; cresols (Lysol); and hexachlorophenes.

6. The last group is quaternary ammonium compounds such as benzalkonium chloride. These can be used in the presence of formaldehyde and are often used to clean surfaces. **Remember that ammonium-based compounds will neutralize formaldehyde and should be used in the event of a spill.**

Microorganisms and Disease

When discussing microorganisms and disease, these are important basic terms that need to be mastered:

1. **Infection:** The state or condition in which the body or a part of it is invaded by pathogenic agents that, under favorable conditions, multiply (growth and reproduction) and produce injurious effects.

2. **Contamination:** The act of introducing disease, germs, or infectious material into an area or substance. Organisms are present but not necessarily growing. If you introduce microorganisms onto an inanimate object (i.e., touching a doorknob after coughing into

your hands), it becomes contaminated. Decontamination is the process of removing hazardous material from an object/area, making it safe to handle.

3. **Pathogenic organisms.**
   a. True pathogens: Infectious agent that is naturally disease-producing. An example is *Bacillus anthracis*.
   b. Opportunistic pathogen: An organism that exists as part of the normal flora but may become pathogenic under certain conditions. Usually indigenous to the body. Can't produce disease without help, such as an injury or other organism. An example is Candida overgrowth in the body due to the overuse of antibiotics which disrupts normal Candida levels.

4. **Pathogenicity:** The state of producing or being able to produce pathological changes and disease. Disease-producing capability. The name of the disease it causes is its pathogenicity. For example, *Bacillus anthracis* causes anthrax.

5. **Virulence:** Relative power and degree of pathogenicity possessed by organisms to produce disease. How pathogenic is it? How fast will it make me sick? How sick will it make me?

6. **Attenuation:** Dilution or weakening of virulence of a microorganism, reducing or abolishing pathogenicity. Virulence takes away; examples are vaccinations with a low dose or with dead/non-viable vaccine (safest version but not as effective). It might also heat up an organism to weaken it but not kill it.

7. **Indigenous flora:** microorganisms that are naturally found in or on the body.

8. **Drug-Fast:** Resistant to the action of a drug or drugs. They are very difficult to remove and kill.

There are various types of infections that can occur due to microorganisms. Infections can be **exogenous** *(originating outside of a cell or organism)*, or they can be **endogenous** *(produced or arising from within a cell or organism)*. This indicates whether the organism came from outside or inside of the body. Infections can also be classified as **acute** *(a short duration of sudden severe symptoms)* or **chronic** *(a long duration of less severe symptoms, slowly arising over time)*. An example of an acute infection would be a head cold picked up during the winter that lasts a week. An example of a chronic infection would be reoccurring bronchitis that lasts over a year. Infections may also be **local** *(infection caused by germs multiplying in one location)*, **general** *(infections that are systemic or seen across the body)*, or **focal** *(starts in one location and then spreads to other parts of the body)*.

A mixed infection is when ***two or more organisms cause an infection in the body.*** When multiple microorganisms create infections, one may cause a **primary infection *or the original infection,*** which could then pave the way for a secondary infection by another microorganism. A classic example would be contracting a head cold (primary infection) and, while you are sick and susceptible, picking up an ear infection (secondary infection).

These are important types of blood infections that need to be known:
   a. **bacteremia** *(bacteria are present but not growing in the blood)*
   b. **septicemia** *(the multiplication of bacteria in the blood)*
   c. **toxemia** *(distribution of poisonous waste through the circulatory system, creating generalized symptoms)*.

These are important to embalmers as they utilize the circulatory system during arterial embalming and are exposed to blood and bodily fluids through the injection and drainage process. Embalmers need to be aware of possible microorganism exposure.

Infections may also be **communicable** *(able to be transmitted between people either directly or indirectly)* or **non-communicable** *(not able to be transmitted between people)*. Communicable diseases are considered contagious, as they can be spread easily. Communicable diseases can be classified in the following ways:

a. **Endemic:** Disease that occurs continuously (never-ending) in a particular region but has low mortality. Malaria in sub-Saharan Africa is considered an endemic disease as it is always prevalent, but the mortality rate is much lower due to a rise in education and prevention.

b. **Epidemic:** Appearance of an infectious disease or condition that affects many people at the same time in the same geographical area (generally 30% of the population or more). One major example that affected the funeral industry was the rise of HIV/AIDS in the United States between 1980s-1990s.

c. **Pandemic:** A disease affecting the majority of the population of a large region or one that is epidemic at the same time in many different parts of the world. The most common example in the 2020s is the COVID-19 pandemic, affecting the entire globe.

d. **Sporadic:** A disease that occurs occasionally or in scattered instances. This could be the plague, which is still seen in various countries at different times.

Virulence *(relative power and degree of pathogenicity possessed by organisms to produce disease)* can also be affected by a variety of factors. The first factor is **toxin production** or the *amount of poisonous substance* that is created. **These toxins may be exotoxins or endotoxins.**

1. **Exotoxins** *(toxins produced by a microorganism and excreted into its surrounding medium, the waste product of microorganisms, generally a protein substance)*

2. **Endotoxins** *(bacterial toxin confined within the body of gram-negative bacterium, released only when the bacteria are broken down)*.

The virulence may also be increased with the addition of an **enzyme** or **catalyst** *(a substance that decreases the activation energy and increases the rate of a chemical reaction)*. Bacterial cells sometimes have **capsules** *(a polysaccharide layer with small protein attachments)*, which creates a protective buffer between the cell and the environment. This buffer allows for the bacterial cell to survive in more hostile environments. Endospore production can also enhance virulence as the spores are able to protect themselves in dormancy and survive in harsh environments.

Infections can be acquired from infected people and animals through vectors, reservoir hosts, and through the environment (water sources, dirt, etc.). These infections can be contracted through direct or indirect methods. Direct methods would include physical contact (sexual contact, shaking hands), droplets (sneezing, coughing), or congenitally (born with it or acquired through development and birth). Indirect methods would include fecal-oral transmission (ex., fecal particles in food preparation from unsanitary conditions), milk (not pasteurized or treated, spoiled), water (drinking infected water, swimming, sewage leaks), **fomites** *(inanimate objects harboring microorganisms, such as doorknobs and cellphones)*, soil, or **vectors** *(person/animal that harbors* *microorganism and carries it to the human host)*. Vectors could be biological, in which the organism multiplies within the vector before becoming infectious and typically transmit the microorganism through a bite (mosquitos), or mechanical, in which the microorganism is simply externally carried by the vector and is transmitted through contact (if bacteria are on the feet of flies).

There are many **portals of entry and exit** *(ways for microorganisms to enter or leave the body)* for pathogens and microorganisms in the body. These pathogens can enter the body through various ways, including the skin, mucous membranes (mouth, nose), respiratory tract (coughing), digestive tract, genitourinary tract (STIs), and the placenta. These pathogens can also leave the body through feces, urine, semen, vaginal excretions, **sputum** *(thick, expectorated matter from the lungs)*, saliva, blood, pus/lesions, vomit, and tears.

However, just because a person comes in contact with a pathogen does not necessarily mean they will become sick. Too few microorganisms may have entered the body to actually create an infection, the microorganism may have low virulence, and the person may have resistance to that particular pathogen. Along with mechanical methods such as washing hands and using proper hygiene, the body also has natural defenses to combat infections. Physiological defenses include **inflammation** *(heat and swelling as a result of blood movement to the infected area)*, **fever** *(increase in body temperature aimed to stop microorganism growth and reproduction)*, and **phagocytosis** *(white blood cells that multiply and attack microorganisms)*. There are also natural chemical defenses that the body uses. These include **lysozymes** *(protect the eyes through the production of tears)*, gastric juices in the stomach, **antibodies** *(glycoprotein substances that interact with antigens of the invading pathogen as an immune response to infection)*, and **interferon** *(substances that coat the outside of a cell to prevent the penetration of cells by viruses)*.

Immunology

Immunology is the study of the immune system. Understanding immunology requires knowing the difference between antigens and antibodies. **Antigens** are *foreign substances that stimulate the formation of antibodies in the immune system of the body.* **Antibodies** are *glycoprotein substances that interact with antigens of the invading pathogen as a response to infection.* Antigen/antibody reactions are specific to each other in a lock-and-key type of mechanism. Antibodies for one particular pathogen will not react to the antigens of a second pathogen. There are antibodies through natural or innate immunity, which are born within the human system. Also, humans can acquire immunity through natural methods (active: having and recovering from a disease or passive: through placenta or colostrum) or artificial methods (active: vaccines or passive: immune serums containing the antibodies which require boosters). For example, those who became infected with COVID-19 and recovered acquired antibodies naturally, which will allow them to fight the pathogen if re-infection occurs. Those who wish to be protected but have not acquired the pathogen may opt for the vaccine, which triggers the production of antibodies to use as a defense if the infection does occur in the future.

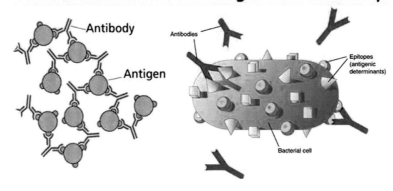

Differences Between Antigen and Antibody

Pathogens and Diseases

Universal precautions (*acting as if everybody is infectious)* are important to preventing the embalmer or funeral director from contracting illnesses from the deceased. Personal protective equipment (PPE) such as gloves, face shields, and gowns should always be used when handling remains.

Bacterial Infections

The following are common bacterial infections that may be present in decedents:

Disease	Info	Pathogenicity	Portal of entry/exit	Modes of Transmission
Staphylococcus aureus	Gram-positive grape-like cluster of cocci One of the most virulent staphylococcus infections Are generally penicillin-resistant; some are multidrug resistant (MDR)	Staph infections, Skin abscesses, food poisoning (enterotoxin), nosocomial infections, toxic shock syndrome, MRSA (methicillin-resistant *S. aureus*)	Compromised mucus membranes, skin, upper respiratory tract	Person to person, droplet spray boils/abscesses, reservoir hosts
Streptococcus pyogenes	Gram-positive chain of cocci, pus generator	Strep throat, scarlet fever (exotoxin A), septic sore throat, puerperal sepsis (childbed fever), rheumatic fever	Soft tissue in back of nasopharynx	Droplet spray (coughing/ sneezing)

272

		Exotoxin A can lead to Toxic Shock Syndrome		
Streptococcus pneumoniae (pneumococcus)	Gram-positive chain of cocci Note: is a capsule forming bacteria	Bacterial pneumonia, lobar pneumonia, meningitis, otitis media (middle ear inflammation)	Respiratory system	Person to person, droplet spray
Neisseria gonorrhea (gonococcus)	Gram-negative bacterial diplococcus Maybe MDR	Gonorrhea, ophthalmia neonatorum (blindness in newborn), gonococcal ophthalmia (blindness at any age)	Genital/urinary tract	Sexual contact, mother to baby, through the birth canal
Neisseria meningitidis (meningococcus)	Gram-negative bacterial diplococcus, non-spore-forming, obligate aerobe	Epidemic meningitis, meningococcemia (may cause death within 2 hours)	Respiratory, airborne	Person to person, droplet spray, reservoir hosts
Clostridium tetani	Gram-positive anaerobic endospore-forming rod Note: produces exotoxin (gives off toxin disrupting the nervous system)	Tetanus (lockjaw)	Deep puncture wounds	Through wound by a contaminated object (rusty nail, etc.) *non-communicable
Clostridium perfringens	Gram-positive anaerobic spore-forming rod Note: produces exotoxins (gas), enzymes break down host tissue	Gas gangrene (antemortem), Tissue gas (postmortem), food intoxication	Compromised skin, cut or tear in the mucus membrane	Normal inhabitants of soil, contaminated hands, contaminated instruments

Clostridium botulinum	Gram-positive anaerobic spore-forming rod, creates exotoxin	Botulism	Digestive tract	Ingestion of contaminated food
Clostridium difficile	Gram-positive anaerobic spore-forming rod	Nosocomial infection, extreme gastrointestinal distress and diarrhea	Gastrointestinal tract	Medical facilities, contamination, and contact
Corynebacterim diphtheriae	Gram-positive club-shaped bacterial rod Note: exotoxin production causes lesions in the throat called a pseudomembrane	Diphtheria	Upper respiratory tract: localization in the pharynx	Person to person, droplet spray
Salmonella typhi	Gram-negative bacterial rod	Typhoid fever	The gastrointestinal tract, digestive tract	The indirect fecal-oral route, mechanical vectors (flies)
Francisella tularensis	Gram-negative rod displays bipolar staining	Rabbit fever, tularemia	Unbroken skin-pores	Handling infected animals
Mycobacterium tuberculosis	Acid-fast bacterial rod, has a natural waxy outer coating, high lipid content, forms tubercles, may be MDR.	Tuberculosis	Respiratory tract	Airborne, environment
Mycobacterium avium	An acid-fast bacterial rod that causes lung infection in immunocompromised people	Opportunistic form of tuberculosis in AIDS patients	Respiratory tract	Birds, the pigeon is normal host. Airborne
Treponema pallidum	Spirochete	Syphilis Lesions: Primary = **chancre** (on the surface of the skin).	Genitourinary tract	Sexual contact

		Tertiary = **gumma** (gummy lesion, usually on the spinal cord) Congenital syphilis: infants		
Borrelia burgdorferi	Spirochete It may be dormant for long periods of time.	Lyme disease	Tick bites through skin	Vectors: Ticks. Also spread through animals and urine.
Vibrio cholera	Spirochete, gram-negative curved bacterial rod. Enterotoxin	Asiatic cholera (severe diarrhea)	Gastrointestinal tract, digestive system	Contaminated food and water
Yersinia pestis	A gram-negative rod that displays bipolar staining	Plague	Skin through bites	Vectors (fleas), reservoir hosts (rats)
Klebsiella pneumoniae	Gram-negative encapsulated bacterial rod, club-shaped	Lobar pneumonia	Respiratory tract	Droplet spray
Bacillus anthracis	Spore forming, exotoxin producer	Anthrax causes severe dehydration from diarrhea and hemorrhaging	Digestive tract, respiratory tract	Airborne, food/water
Hemophilus influenza	Gram-negative bacterial rod	Influenzal meningitis	Respiratory tract	Droplet spray
Proteus sp. (sp. = species) *Pseudomonas sp.*		Secondary infection of burns		
Shigella sp.	Gram-negative bacterial rods	Shigellosis (bacillary dysentery)	Digestive tract	Foodborne and waterborne
Leptospira interrogations	Spirochete	Leptospirosis		Soil-borne cat litter
Escherichia coli	Gram-negative bacterial rod	E-coli, traveler's diarrhea, enteritis	Digestive system	Food and waterborne
Campylobacter jejune	Gram-negative curved bacterial rod	Campylobacteriosi, diarrhea	Digestive system	Food and waterborne

Mycoplasma Infections

The following are common mycoplasma infections that may be present in decedents.

Disease	Info	Pathogenicity	Portal of entry/exit	Modes of transmission
Mycoplasma pneumonia	Penicillin will not work, no rigid cell wall	Primary atypical pneumonia (walking pneumonia), bronchitis, pharyngitis	Respiratory tract	Droplet spray

Rickettsia infections

The following are common rickettsia infections that may be present in decedents.

Disease	Info	Pathogenicity	Portal of entry/exit	Modes of transmission
Rickettsia prowazekii	Short, nonmotile Gram-negative, bacilli, obligately intracellular pathogens, typically transmitted to humans by arthropod vectors.	Epidemic (louse-born) typhus	Insect (lice) bites	Insect vectors, reservoir hosts (rodents)
Rickettsia typhi	Short, nonmotile Gram-negative, bacilli, obligately intracellular pathogens, typically transmitted to humans by arthropod vectors.	Epidemic (flea-born) typhus	Insect (flea) bites	Insect vectors, reservoir hosts (rodents)
Rickettsia rickettsii	Short, nonmotile Gram-negative, bacilli, obligately intracellular pathogens, typically transmitted to humans by arthropod vectors. Most commonly spread through dog and wood ticks	Rocky Mountain spotted fever (tick born)	Tick bites	Insect vectors, Reservoir: Deer, elk, bears

Coxiella burnetii	Short, nonmotile Gram-negative, bacilli, obligately intracellular pathogens, typically transmitted to humans by arthropod vectors.	Q fever (flu-like)	Respiratory tract, digestive tract	Food, water, arthropods, airborne Animals can carry it and can be spread through the dust.

Chlamydia infections

The following are common Chlamydia infections that may be present in decedents.

Disease	Info	Pathogenicity	Portal of entry/exit	Modes of transmission
Chlamydia psittaci	Bacteria only grow intracellularly, obligate intracellular parasites. Infectious stage (elementary body) of growth and non-infectious stage (reticulate body) of growth	**Psittacosis** – Parrot fever. **Ornithosis** = Birds	Respiratory	Dust, Droplet spray Humans get from feathers and bird droppings
Chlamydia trachomatis	Bacteria only grow intracellularly, obligate intracellular parasites. Infectious stage (elementary body) of growth and non-infectious stage (reticulate body) of growth STD	Trachoma: Inflammation of the eye. Lymphogranuloma venereum: Inguinal region (lymph nodes). NGU (non-gonococcal urethritis) or NSU (non-specific urethritis)	Genito-urinary tract	Sexual contact

Fungal infections

The following are common fungal infections that may be present in decedents.

Disease	Info	Pathogenicity	Portal of entry/exit	Modes of transmission
Microsporum sp., trichophyton sp., epidermophyton sp.	Recurring and typically chronic	Cause **Dermatomycosis** general name for all fungal diseases Dermatropic diseases. Ringworm, athlete's foot, jock itch, etc.	Skin contact	Touching, coming in contact with the spores/molds/yeasts
Coccidiosis immitis	Infects lungs after breathing in spores	Valley Fever	Respiratory system	Spores in soil
Candida albicans	Typically, overgrowth due to an imbalance of normal flora	**Candidiasis:** Yeast Vaginal Thrush ***Monilia albicans***- White fungus	Endogenous microorganism	Imbalance in the normal flora
Histoplasma capsulatum	Dimorphic fungus (mold in soil, yeast in humans and animals)	**Histoplasmosis:** Lungs Pneumonia It can also cause fungal meningitis.	Respiratory system	Opportunistic infection Inhalation Contaminated soil, bird droppings
Cryptococcus neoformans	A yeast	**Cryptococcosis:** Lungs Lung infection that spreads via blood to the brain	Respiratory tract	Pigeon droppings, contaminated soil Not spread human to human or animal to a human directly

| Aspergillus sp. | A mold common among gardeners and farmers Affects eyes, heart, kidneys, skin | **Aspergillosis** | Respiratory tract | Found in decaying vegetation and manure |
| Pneumocystis jiroveci | The opportunistic pathogen, multi-drug resistant | **Pneumocystosis** Interstitial plasma cell pneumonia | Respiratory system | Animals or may be carriers, air droplets |

Protozoa infections

The following are common protozoa infections that may be present in decedents.

Disease	Info	Pathogenicity	Portal of entry/exit	Modes of transmission
Entamoeba histolytica	Amoebas	amoebiasis (amebic dysentery): Montezuma's revenge	Gastrointestinal tract	Fecal-oral, water, flies, food, sexual contact (anal-oral)
Plasmodium malariae	Intraerythrocytic sporozoan infection (within red blood cells)	malaria (Plasmodium vivax)	Skin	Mosquitos
Toxoplasma gondii	Systemic sporozoan infection, opportunistic infection affects immune-compromised. *While pregnant, women should not handle litter boxes	toxoplasmosis	Digestive tract, respiratory tract	Undercooked food, contaminated food/water, cat feces, rodents, birds, farm animals, sandboxes
Giardia lamblia	Infection of the small intestine	Waterborne illness Giardiasis	Fecal-oral	Contaminated water, sexual contact, food, daycares, swimming pools

Prion infection

The following are common prion infections that may be present in decedents.

Disease	Info	Pathogenicity	Portal of entry/exit	Modes of transmission
Creutzfeldt-Jakob Disease	Very slow, may take 10+ years to show symptoms	Mad cow disease		Infected brain matter and spinal cord fluid

Viral infections

The following are common viral infections that may be present in decedents.

Disease	Info	Pathogenicity
Dermatropic (skin) diseases	Obligate intracellular parasites – smallest that can be studied	Smallpox – variola: Eradicated Measles – (a thermotropic viral disease known as) rubeola. German measles–rubella. Chickenpox (children) – shingles (adult) – *Varicella zoster*: Same organism in kids as adults. Hides in myelinated sheaths around nerves. Activated by stress or lowering resistance. Herpes simplex I and II. I = around the mouth. II = genital area (generally)
Pneumotropic (upper respiratory tract) diseases		Influenza: Symptoms manifested throughout the body – aches, diarrhea, vomiting, etc. Common cold: Coryza–Rhinovirus attacks through the nose and face area. Localized in the head. Hantavirus: Spread by mouse droppings. Influenza like symptoms with blood hemorrhaging.
Neurotropic (central nervous system) diseases		Rabies: Animal bites, saliva. Poliomyelitis: A gray matter of the brain – fecal-oral route. Viral encephalitis. Inflammation of the brain by a virus, vectored by insect bite (mosquito).

Viscerotropic (visceral) diseases		Hepatitis – A (infectious). Fecal oral route. Hepatitis – B (serum). Bodily fluids were transferred. Hepatitis – C (non-A, non B): Deadly. Infectious mononucleosis: **Epstein-Barr virus**. Kissing disease. Mouth-to-mouth contact. Cytomegalovirus: **Cells** of **great size**. Cloudy swelling. Fever, malaise (tired/sleepy), enlarged spleen/liver. Epidemic parotitis – mumps: Swollen/inflamed parotid glands. MMR shot: Mumps, measles, rubella.
Immunological	T-cells are the major group of cells affected	HIV/AIDIS Kaposi's sarcoma-blotchy skin in AIDS patients

Glossary for Microbiology

Acute – an infection with rapid onset and short duration

Antagonism - the inhibition of one organism by another.

Antibodies - A substance developed by the body in response to, and interacting specifically with, an antigen, also known as immunoglobulin.

Antigen - Any substance that stimulates an immune reaction.

Antisepsis - The prevention or inhibition of the growth of causative microorganisms on live tissue.

Attenuation - reduction of the virulence of a microorganism.

Autotrophic bacteria - Self-nourishing bacteria that are capable of growing in the absence of organic compounds.

Bacillus (pl. Bacilli) - Any rod-shaped bacteria

Bacteria - A prokaryotic one-celled microorganism of the Kingdom Monera, existing as free-living organisms or as parasites, multiplying by binary fission.

Bacterial colony - A visible group of bacteria, presumably arising from a single microorganism.

Bactericide - An agent that destroys bacteria, but not necessarily their spores.

Bacteriology - Science that studies bacteria.

Binary fission - A sexual reproduction in prokaryotic cells resulting in two individual cells with genetic consistency.

Biological vector - An infected arthropod in which the disease-causing organism multiplies or develops within the arthropod prior to becoming infective.

Capsule - A gelatinous coating that surrounds some bacterial cells that help to prevent phagocytosis.

Cell wall - A ridge layer outside the cell membrane of plants, fungi, and bacteria.

Chronic - An infection with slow onset and long duration

Coccus (pl. Cocci) - A type of bacteria that is spherical.

Commensalism - The symbiotic relationship of two organisms of different species in which one gains some benefit, such as protection or nourishment, and the other is not harmed or benefited.

Communicable - disease that may be transmitted directly or indirectly from one individual to another.

Contamination - The act of introducing disease germs or infectious material into an area or substance.

Disinfectant - A chemical or physical agent that kills disease-causing microorganisms generally used on inanimate objects.

Disinfection - a chemical or physical agent that kills vegetative forms of microorganisms on inanimate objects.

Drug-fast - A biological resistance to the reaction of drugs.

Endemic disease – A disease that occurs continuously in a particular region/population.

Endogenous infection - A form of infection caused by pathogens or an agent normally present in the body.

Endospore - A thick-walled body produced by a bacterium to enable it to survive unfavorable environmental conditions.

Endotoxin - A bacterial toxin that is liberated only when the cell producing it disintegrates.

Epidemic - A disease or condition that is currently in higher-than-normal numbers in a given population.

Exogenous infections - A form of infection caused by a pathogen or agent not normally present in the body.

Exotoxin - A toxin produced within a living cell and secreted into its surrounding medium.

Facultative aerobe - A microorganism that prefers an environment devoid of oxygen but has adapted so that it can live and grow in the presence of oxygen.

Facultative anaerobe - an organism that prefers the presence of oxygen but is capable of living and growing in its absence.

Facultative parasite - prefers dead organic matter as a source of nutrition but can adapt to the use of living organic matter under certain conditions.

Facultative saprophyte - Prefers living organisms as a source of nutrition but can adapt to the use of dead organic matter under certain conditions.

Focal infection - An infection originally confined to one area but may spread to other parts of the body.

Fomite - Any inanimate object to which infectious material adheres and can be transmitted.

Fungicide - An agent that kills fungi and their spores.

Fungus (p1. fungi) - A group of diverse and widespread unicellular and multicellular organisms, lacking chlorophyll, usually bearing spores and often filamentous.

Germicide - A substance that destroys microorganisms.

Heterotrophic bacteria - An organism that must obtain its nourishment from complex organic matter.

Hypochlorites - chlorine-containing compound.

Infection - a condition in which the body, or a part thereof, is invaded by a pathogenic agent that can multiply and produce injurious effects.

Iodophores - a compound that contains iodine.

Local infection - An infection that is contained in one area of the body.

Maximum temperature - Temperature above which bacterial growth will not take place.

Mechanical vector - A vector in which growth and development of the infective agent do not occur.

MRSA (Methicillin-resistant Staphylococcus aureus - A strain of *Staphylococcus aureus* that is resistant to a large group of antibiotics called the beta-lactams, which include the penicillins and the cephalosporins.

Mesophile - Bacteria that prefers moderate temperature and develops best at temperatures between 25°C and 40°C.

Microaerophilic - A microorganism that grows best in an oxygen-reduced environment.

Microbiology - Scientific study of microorganisms and their effect on other living organisms.

Minimum temperature - Temperature below which bacterial growth will not take place.

Mixed infection - Infection caused by two or more organisms.

Mutualism - A relationship in which organisms of two different species live in close association for the mutual benefit of each.

Mycology - The branch of science concerned with the study of fungi.

Mycoplasmas - a group of bacteria that lack cell walls and are highly pleomorphic

Normal flora - a microbial population that lives within or under the host in a healthy condition.

Opportunist - An organism that exists as part of the normal flora but may become pathogenic under certain conditions.

Optimum temperature - Temperature at which organisms grow best.

Osmotic pressure - Pressure that develops when two solutions of different concentrations are separated by a semipermeable membrane.

Pandemic - A disease affecting the majority of the population of a large region or an epidemic that has become very widespread or is worldwide.

Parasitism - An interactive relationship between two organisms in which one is harmed and the other benefits.

Pathogenicity - The state of producing or being able to produce pathological changes and disease.

Primary infection - An infection that develops in an otherwise healthy individual.

Prion - An infectious self-replicating protein involved in human and animal diseases of the central nervous system. This misfolded form of the prion protein has been implicated in a number of diseases in a variety of mammals, including bovine spongiform encephalopathy (BSE, also known as "mad cow disease") in cattle and Creutzfeldt-Jakob disease (CJD) in humans.

Protozoa - eukaryotic, animal-like, unicellular organisms.

Protozoology - Science that deals with the study of protozoa.

Psychrophile - Bacteria that prefer cold, thriving at temperatures between 0°C and 25°C.

Sanitation - to reduce microbe population to a safe level as determined by public health.

Secondary infection - An infection made possible by a primary infection that lowers host resistance.

Septicemia - Growth and spreading of bacterial cells in the bloodstream.

Spirillum - Spiral-shaped bacteria having a ridge cell wall.

Spirochete - Spiral-shaped bacteria having a flexible cell wall.

Sporadic - A disease that occurs occasionally in a random or isolated manner.

Staphylococcus - A genus of gram-positive, nonmotile, opportunistic bacteria which tend to aggregate in irregular grape-like clusters.

Sterilization - Process of completely removing or destroying all life forms and their products, including endospores.

Streptobacilli - rod-shaped bacteria occurring in chains.

Streptococci - spherical-shaped bacteria occurring in chains.

Strict (obligate) aerobe - A microbe that can only live in the presence of oxygen.

Strict (obligate) anaerobe - A microbe that can only survive in an area without oxygen present.

Strict (obligate) parasite - A parasite that is completely dependent on its living host for survival.

Strict (obligate) saprophyte - An organism that can survive on dead or decaying organic matter.

Symbiosis - The living together in close association with different species.

Synergism - The relationship between two or more microorganisms of different species in which they grow better together but can survive alone.

Thermophile - Bacteria that thrive best at high temperatures, between 40°C and 70°C.

Toxemia - the presence of toxins in the blood.

Toxin - A poisonous substance of plant, animal, bacterial, or fungal origin.

True pathogen - An organism that, due to its own virulence, is able to produce disease.

Vibrio - Spiral bacteria that are curved or bent rods that resemble commas.

Viricide - An agent destructive to viruses.

Virology - The study of viruses and viral diseases.

Virulence - Relative power of an organisms to produce disease.

Virus - An intracellular pathogen limited to replicating only in living cells, containing only one form of nucleic acid.

Anatomy

This section will explain the 11 biological systems of the human body. This is not an all-encompassing guide for anatomy but rather an overview of each system. Some of the concepts are further explained in detail in other sections of this book (Microbiology, Pathology, Embalming, Restorative Art) as they relate to their function and how they are an important part of the process of Embalming and Restorative Art.

Anatomy is the branch of science dealing with the study of the structure of the body (in the glossary), and the relationship among structures. Anatomy can be broken down into seven subdivisions:

Gross anatomy	That branch of anatomy that deals with structures that can be studied without using a microscope, using only the unaided eye
Microscopic anatomy	Branch of anatomy dealing with structures that can only be studied using a microscope. a. Cytology: Chemical and microscopic study of cells. b. Histology: Microscopic study of the structure of tissues
Systemic anatomy	Study of specific systems of the body, such as the nervous or respiratory system, without regard to region
Regional anatomy	Study of a specific region of the body, such as the head or chest, without regard to the system.
Pathological anatomy	Sometimes referred to as abnormal anatomy. Study of structural changes (from gross to microscopic) associated with disease.
Topographical anatomy	Study of surface forms. The use of a known and identifiable surface marking or structure to locate some deeper-lying structure.
Physiological anatomy	Study of functions of the parts of the body and how they work.

Anatomical Directions and Positions

Anatomical Position:

(See Restorative Art Section for diagram pp.116 & 117)

1. Statement and explanation of this position: The subject stands erect (upright position) facing the observer, with feet flat on the floor, arms placed at the sides, and palms turned forward.
2. The rationale supporting the use of the concept: Having one standard anatomical position allows directional terms to be clear; any body part or region can be described relative to any other part.

Bilateral symmetry is when both sides of the body (right and left) are the same. Bilateral refers to the two sides of the body. Symmetry refers to items exactly the same on either side of an axis. Ideally, the body should have bilateral symmetry. However, this is not always the case.

Body Regions and Anatomical Position

(Located in the Restorative Art section p. 117-119 & Embalming p. 25 – 26)

Body Cavities

The body has multiple cavities that are separated and created by body walls:

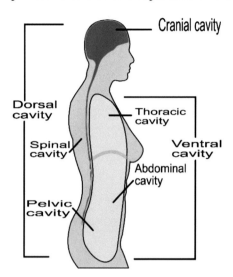

> ➤ Cranial Cavity: Part of the dorsal (back) cavity. Formed by the cranial bones and contains the brain.
> ➤ Spinal Canal: Part of the dorsal cavity. Formed by the vertebrae of the backbone and contains the spinal cord and roots of the spinal nerves. The vertebral column: The 26 vertebrae of an adult and 33 vertebrae of an infant; encloses and protects the spinal cord and serves as a point of attachment for the ribs and back muscles. Also called the **backbone, spine,** or **spinal column.**
> ➤ Thoracic/ventral cavity: This is the superior portion of the ventral body cavity. Contains:
>   • 2 pleural cavities: Space between visceral and parietal pleurae (the serous membranes that surround the lungs and lines the walls of the chest and diaphragm).
>   • Mediastinum: the broad, median partition between the pleurae of the lungs, extending from the sternum to the vertebral column and containing the heart.
>   • pericardial cavity: surrounds the heart.
> ➤ Abdomino-pelvic cavity. This is the inferior portion of the ventral body cavity. A line drawn across the right and left anterior iliac spines subdivides this cavity into the superior abdominal cavity and the inferior pelvic cavity.
> ➤ Peritoneal cavity: between the visceral peritoneum and the parietal peritoneum (abdominal wall).
> ➤ The pelvic cavity is in the ventral cavity.

Cells, Tissues, and Organs

The human body is made up of cells. **Cells *are the basic structural and functional unit of all organisms and are the smallest structures that can sustain life.*** Cells are comprised of chemicals and organelles to carry out specific functions. There are different types of cells, such as animal cells, plant cells, and bacterial cells. They each have different unique aspects and functions that differentiate them.

A group of cells creates a tissue. There are various types of tissues in the body, including:

1. Epithelial: Tissue that forms glands or the superficial part of the skin. Also, the tissue that lines organs and passages within the body.
2. Connective: The most abundant in the body. Works to bind and support the body. Includes tendons, ligaments, cartilage, bones, and blood.
3. Muscles: Used for motion, contractility, extensibility, elasticity, and excitability. There are 3 types:
   ➢ Skeletal
   ➢ Cardiac: (heart)
   ➢ Smooth
4. Nervous: Works to initiate and transmit nerve impulses. Transport electrical messages.

A group of tissues comprises an organ. **Organs *perform specific body functions*.** For example, the lungs function for respiration and gas exchange.

A ***group of organs of similar functions creates an organ system***. There are 11 organ systems in the human body. They are the following:

1. Integumentary system - skin, works for protection, support, and movement.
2. The skeletal system - comprised of the skeleton, works for protection, support, and movement.
3. Muscular system - comprised of the muscles, works for protection, support, and movement.
4. The nervous system- comprised of the brain and nerves, works in response to stimuli.
5. Endocrine system - works for hormone transport, production, and secretion.
6. Circulatory system - works for blood and fluid transport.
7. Lymphatic (immune) system - works for fluid transport and filtration.
8. Respiratory system - works for gas exchange.
9. Urinary system -works to excrete waste and filter fluids.
10. Digestive system - works to breakdown food and energy.
11. Reproductive systems - work to share genetic information through the production of offspring.

INTEGUMENTARY SYSTEM

STRUCTURE OF THE HUMAN SKIN

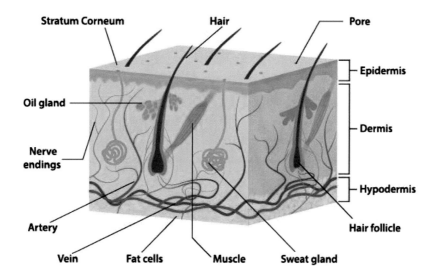

The integumentary system involves the network of skin and nails used for the structure and protection of the body. Nails are comprised of a protein called keratin. The skin is comprised of three layers. The most superficial layer is the epidermis, which is comprised of keratinized stratified squamous epithelium, and is the thinnest layer. The middle layer is the dermis, a dense layer of connective tissue that contains hair follicles, exocrine glands such as sebaceous glands, which secrete oil for lubrication, and sudoriferous (apocrine) glands that produce sweat and blood vessels. The deepest layer is the hypodermis, where we see blood vessels and adipose tissue.

Skeletal System

The human skeletal system

The skeletal system consists of bone tissue (osteocytes=bone cells), cartilage, red and yellow bone marrow, and periosteum (membrane around the bones). This system works to give structure and protection to the body. It also assists the body in movement. Bone marrow, within the bones, is also the site of blood cell production. Osteology is the scientific study of bones. The adult human body has 206 bones, excluding the sutural (extra bone pieces that form within a suture) and sesamoid (a bone embedded within a tendon or muscle) bones. 80 bones comprise the axial (skull, neck, back, and ribs) skeleton, and 126 bones comprise the appendicular (extremities, shoulder girdle, pelvis) skeleton.

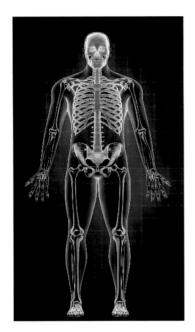

Axial Skeletal System

The longitudinal axis, or center, of the body, is a straight line that runs through the body's center of gravity. This imaginary line extends through the head and down to the space between the feet. The axial skeleton consists of the bones that lie around the axis.

a. **Skull** (22 bones and six ear ossicles): The skeleton of the head consisting of the cranial and facial bones.
b. **Cranium** (8 bones): The skeleton of the skull that protects the brain and the organs of sight, hearing, and balance. Includes the frontal, parietal, temporal, occipital, sphenoid, and ethmoid bone.

Important notes:

c. **Calvaria**: Dome-like superior portion of the cranium, composed of the superior portions of the frontal, parietal, and occipital bones. Also called the skullcap.
d. **Orbit**: The bony pyramid-shaped cavities of the skull that contains and protects the eyeball.

e. **Cranium**: The part of the skull that encases the brain

Neck and the Spinal Column:

f. **Hyoid** (1 bone): Located in the neck between the mandible and larynx. Supports the tongue and provides attachment for some muscles of the neck and pharynx. The hyoid bone does not articulate with any other bone.
g. **Vertebral column**: Spinal column. Vertebrae are named by region:
   1) Cervical = Neck.
   2) Thoracic = Chest.
   3) Lumbar = Lower back.
   4) Sacrum = Pelvic Girdle.
   5) Coccyx = Tailbone.
- **Cervical** (# 1 = atlas; # 2 = axis) (7): First seven bones of the spinal column.
- **Thoracic** (12): 12 vertebrae between the base of the neck superiorly and the diaphragm inferiorly. Point of posterior attachment for the 12 pairs of ribs.
- **Lumbar** (5): 5 bones of the spinal column between the sacrum and thoracic vertebrae.

- **Sacrum** (1): Fused vertebrae forming the sacrum. Formed of united vertebrae and is wedged between the two innominate (hip) bones. Forms the base of the vertebral column and, with the coccyx, forms the posterior boundary of the true pelvis.
- **Coccyx** (1): Small bone at the base of the spinal column, formed by four fused rudimentary vertebrae.

Sternum and Ribs
➢ Sternum: Breastbone. Flat, narrow bone located in the middle of the anterior thoracic wall.
    a. Manubrium: Superior portion.
    b. Body: Middle, largest portion.
    c. Xiphoid process: Inferior, smallest portion.

➢ Ribs (12 pair, 24 total): Make up the sides of the thoracic cavity.
    a. True ribs (7 pair, 14 total): Direct anterior attachment to sternum by a strip of hyaline cartilage.
    b. False ribs (3 pair, 6 total): Costal cartilages attach indirectly to the sternum. The 8th, 9th, and 10th pairs of ribs attach to each other, and then to the cartilages of the seventh pair of ribs.
    c. Floating ribs (2 pair, 4 total): Anterior ends do not attach to the sternum. They terminate in the abdominal muscles. Only attached posteriorly to the thoracic vertebrae.

Appendicular Skeleton: 126 bones

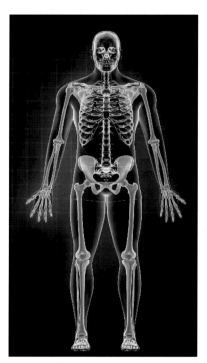

Contains the bones of the upper and lower limbs (extremities) and the bones called girdles, whose function is to connect the limbs to the axial skeleton.

- Upper extremities and pectoral girdle (64 bones).
- Lower extremities and pelvic girdle (62 bones).

THE UPPER EXTREMITIES AND PECTORAL GIRDLE

Arms and shoulders. 64 Bones. The pectoral girdle consists of the Clavicle and Scapula.

➢ **Clavicle** (2): Collarbone. Long, slender S-shaped bone with two curves, one convex, and one concave. The anterior portion of the pectoral girdle articulates with the sternum at the sternoclavicular joint.
➢ **Scapula** (2): Shoulder Blade. Large triangular, flat bone situated in the posterior part of the thorax between the levels of the second and seventh ribs.
➢ **Humerus** (2): Longest and largest bone of the upper limb. Articulates proximally with the scapula and distally with both the ulna and radius.
➢ **Ulna** (2): Located on the medial aspect (little finger side) of the forearm and is longer than the radius. At the proximal end of the ulna is the olecranon process which forms the prominence of the elbow. The coronoid process is an anterior projection that, together with the olecranon, receives the trochlea of the Humerus.
➢ **Radius** (2): Located on the lateral aspect (thumb side) of the forearm.
➢ **Carpals** (16): Joined to one another by ligaments. Arranged in two transverse rows, with four bones in each row.
➢ **Metacarpals** (10): Constitute the palm of the hand. Bases articulate with the distal row of carpal bones, and the heads articulate with the proximal Phalanges of the fingers.
➢ **Phalanges** (28): Bones of the fingers. 2 in each thumb and 3 in each finger.

THE LOWER EXTREMITIES AND PELVIC GIRDLE

62 Bones. Pelvic Girdle – Legs and hips.

➢ **Os coxa** (2): Hipbones
➢ **Ilium** (Flank): Largest of the three subdivisions. The superior aspect of hip
➢ **Ischium** (Hip): Inferior and posterior portion
➢ **Pubis** (Pubic): Inferior and anterior portion
➢ **Femur** (2): Thighbone. The longest, heaviest, and **strongest bone in the body**. The proximal end articulates with the hipbone. The distal end articulates with the tibia and patella.
➢ **Patella** (2): Kneecap. Small triangular bone located anterior to the knee joint. A sesamoid bone that develops in the tendon of the quadriceps femoris muscle
➢ **Tibia** (2): Shinbone. The larger medial bone of the leg. Articulates at its proximal end with the femur and fibula and at its distal end with the fibula and talus bone of the ankle. **Medial malleolus**: Medial surface of the distal end of the tibia. Articulates with the talus bone of the ankle and forms the prominence that can be felt on the medial surface of the ankle.
➢ **Fibula** (2): Parallel and lateral to the tibia. Considerably smaller than the tibia. The proximal end articulates with the inferior surface of the lateral condyle of the tibia inferior

to the level of the knee joint. The distal end of the fibula has a projection called the lateral malleolus. **Lateral malleolus**: Articulates with the talus bone of the ankle. Forms the prominence on the lateral surface of the ankle.

> **Tarsals** (14): Collective term for the seven tarsal bones of the ankle. The talus, the most superior tarsal bone, is the only bone of the foot that articulates with the fibula and tibia.

> **Metatarsals** (10): Bones of the foot. Articulate proximally with the first, second, and third cuneiform bones and with the cuboid. Distally, they articulate with the proximal row of Phalanges.

> **Phalanges** (28): Bones of the toes. The great (or big) toe has two phalanges; all others have three.

JOINTS

The scientific study of joints is known as **arthrology**. *A* **joint or articulation** *is any place in the body in which two adjacent bones or bones and cartilage come together, creating a connection.* Some joints are held together by connective tissue, and some are held together with a fluid-filled sac called a joint cavity. Joints can be classified structurally (how they are held together) or functionally (how they move). Functionally joints can be freely moveable, known as diarthrosis; slightly moveable, known as amphiarthrosis; or immobile (not moveable), known as synarthrosis.

> **Synarthrosis:**
> - **Suture**: A fibrous joint composed of a thin layer of dense fibrous connective tissue that unites the bones of the skull. Ex. Cranial sutures (fontanels): Coronal suture between the frontal and parietal bones of the skull.
>
> - **Gomphosis**: A fibrous joint in which a cone-shaped peg fits into a socket (e.g., roots of the teeth with the sockets).
>
> - **Synchondrosis**: A cartilaginous joint in which the connecting material is hyaline cartilage. Temporary joint replaced by synostosis or symphysis. Ex. Sternocostal joint: Joint connecting the sternum and ribs.

> **Amphiarthrosis:** Fibrous joint in which there is considerably more fibrous connective tissue than there is in a suture. As a result, the fit between the bones is not as tight. This permits some degree of flexibility and movement.

> Examples:
> a. Pubic symphysis: Anterior, inferior part of hipbone. The joint between the two hipbones consisting of a pad of fibrocartilage.
> b. Sacro-iliac articulation: Articulation between the sacrum and the innominate bone of the pelvis

➤ **Diarthrosis:** Contains a space called a synovial joint that separates the articulating bones. They contain articular cartilage that covers the surfaces of the articulating bones but does not bind the bones together. Articular cartilage reduces friction at the joint when the bones move and help absorb shock.

    Examples:
      a. Shoulder: The region of the proximal humerus, clavicle, and scapula; a part of the shoulder girdle complex.
      b. Hip: Upper part of the thigh, formed by the femur and innominate bones.
      c. Elbow: Joint between the arm and forearm.
      d. Knee: Anterior aspect of the leg at the articulation of the femur and tibia. The articulation itself is covered anteriorly with the patella or kneecap.

DIGESTIVE SYSTEM

The digestive system works to break down foods eaten to release and absorb nutrients into the body. The digestive system begins at the mouth and ends at the rectum/anus. The digestive system does work with many other body systems, including the cardiovascular system, endocrine system, and nervous system.

The organs of the digestive system are divided into two categories: alimentary canal organs and accessory structure organs. Alimentary canal organs are those in the continuous tube that originates in the mouth, and terminates at the anal opening, known as the alimentary canal or gastrointestinal tract (alimentary comes from the root word "aliment," which means to nourish). The alimentary canal is 25 feet long during life and 35 feet long postmortem and includes the mouth, pharynx, esophagus, stomach, large and small intestines, and rectum. Accessory structures and organs aid in digestion and include the teeth, tongue, salivary glands, liver, gall bladder, and pancreas.

The Digestive System

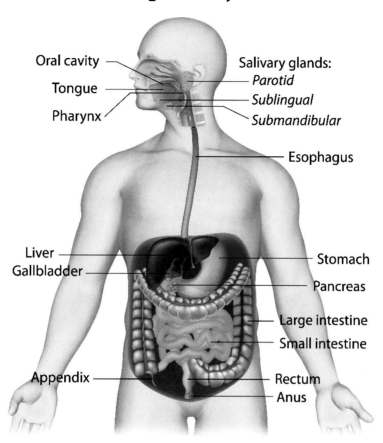

- ➤ **Mouth:** The oral or buccal cavity is formed by the cheeks, hard and soft palates, and tongue.
  - Mouth (oral or buccal) divisions: The cavity within the cheeks, containing the tongue and teeth and communicating with the pharynx.

  - Teeth: Dentin and enamel that projections in jaws and serves as devices for mastication. There are 32 permanent teeth, 16 in each jaw. They include the following types: incisors, canines (cuspids), premolars (bicuspids), and molars.

  - Tongue: A freely movable muscular organ lying partly on the floor of the mouth and partly in the pharynx. Its function is the manipulation of food in mastication and deglutition, speech production, and taste. Its surface is covered with mucous membranes. Accessory organ of digestion and mastication.

- **Salivary glands**: The glands of the oral cavity that secrete saliva. Accessory organs of digestion.

  o **Location:**
    - Parotid: Inferior and anterior of the ears between the skin and the masseter muscle.
    - Submandibular: Below the posterior floor of the mouth, medial to the body of the mandible.
    - Sublingual: Below the tongue in the anterior floor of the mouth.

  o **Structure:** (tubuloalveolar): Consisting of tubes and alveoli, as in a tubuloalveolar salivary gland.

  o **Function:** Secrete saliva. Helps cleanse the mouth and teeth. Lubricates dissolve and begin the chemical breakdown of food.

➢ **Pharynx:** Passageway for air from the nasal cavity to the larynx and food from the mouth to the esophagus.
  o **Location:** Extends from the base of the skull to the level of the 6th cervical vertebra, where it becomes continuous with the esophagus. Communicates with the posterior nares, eustachian tube, mouth, esophagus, and larynx.
  o **Structure:**
    - Nasopharynx: Part of the pharynx situated above the soft palate (postnasal space).
    - Oropharynx: Central portion of the pharynx lying between the soft palate and upper portion of the epiglottis.
    - Laryngopharyx: Lower portion of the pharynx that extends from the cornu of the hyoid bone or vestibule of the larynx to the lower border of the cricoid cartilage.
  o **Function:** Passageway for air and food.

➢ **Esophagus:** Muscular, collapsible canal, essential for carrying swallowed foods and liquids from the mouth to the stomach. Length = 9 to 9.75 in.
    Location: Begins at the inferior end of the laryngopharynx, passes through the mediastinum anterior to the vertebral column, pierces the diaphragm through an opening called the esophageal hiatus, and ends in the superior portion of the stomach. Lies posterior to the trachea.

  o **Structure:**
    - Gross: Fibromuscular tube.
    - Microscopic:
      a. Mucosa: Consists of nonkeratinized stratified squamous epithelium, lamina propria (areolar connective tissue), and muscularis mucosa (smooth muscle). Near the stomach, the mucosa also contains mucous glands.

b. Submucosa: Contains areolar connective tissue, blood vessels, and mucous glands.

c. Muscularis: Superior third is skeletal, the intermediate third is skeletal and smooth, and the inferior third is smooth muscle.

d. Serosa: Known as the adventitia because the areolar connective tissue of this layer is not covered by epithelium and because the connective tissue merges with the connective tissue of the surrounding structures of the mediastinum through which it passes.

- o **Function**: Carrying swallowed foods and liquids from the mouth to the stomach.

➢ **Stomach (gaster):** A J-shaped enlargement of the GI tract.
Location: Directly inferior to the diaphragm in the epigastric, umbilical, and left hypochondriac regions of the abdomen.

- o **Structure**:
  - ▪ Gross:
    - a. Cardia: Surrounds the superior opening of the stomach.
    - b. Fundus: Rounded portion superior to and to the left of the cardia.
    - c. Body: Large central portion of the stomach inferior to the fundus.
    - d. Lesser curvature: Superior edge of the stomach, the concave medial border.
    - e. Greater curvature: Inferior edge of the stomach, the convex lateral border.
    - f. Pyloris: Region of the stomach that connects to the duodenum.
    - g. Pyloric sphincter: Communicates with the duodenum.

  - ▪ Microscopic: Composed of the same four basic layers as the rest of the GI tract, with certain modifications.
    - a. Mucosa: Layer of simple columnar epithelial cells called mucous surface cells.
    - b. Submucosa: Composed of areolar connective tissue, it connects the mucosa to the muscularis.
    - c. Muscularis: Three layers of smooth muscle. Outer longitudinal, middle circular, and inner oblique.
    - d. Serosa: Squamous epithelium and areolar connective tissue, part of the visceral peritoneum.

➢ **Small intestine:** Major events of digestion and absorption occur in the small intestine. About 2.5 cm (1") in diameter and 3 meters (10') long in a living person (6.5 meters or 21' long in a cadaver).
- o Location: Abdomen inferior to stomach and liver and superior to the urinary bladder.

- o **Structure**:
  - ▪ Gross:
    - a. Duodenum: Shortest segment and is retroperitoneal. Starts at the pyloric sphincter and extends 25 cm (10") until it merges with the jejunum. Means "12" (12 fingers breadth long).
    - b. Jejunum: About 1 meter long and extends to the ileum. Means "empty" (found empty at death).
    - c. Ileum: Final portion of the small intestine. About 2 meters long and joins the large intestine at the ileocecal sphincter valve.

  - ▪ Microscopic:
    - a. Brunner's (duodenal) glands: Compound glands of the duodenum and upper jejunum. Embedded in the submucous tissue and lined with columnar epithelium. Similar to the pyloric glands of the stomach and secretes a clear alkaline mucinous solution.
    - b. Peyer's patches (aggregation of lymph nodules): Found in the ileum near its junction with the colon. Circular or oval about 1 cm wide and 2 to 3 cm long. Lie in the mucosal and submucosal layers and always occur on the side of the intestine opposite to the attachment of mesentery.

  - o **Function**: Digestion and absorption of food/nutrients.

- ➤ **Large intestine:** About 1.5 meters (5') long and 6.5 cm (2.5") in diameter. Divided into four regions Location: Extends from the ileum to the anus and is attached to the posterior abdominal wall by is mesocolon, which is a double layer of peritoneum.
  - o **Structure**:
    - a. Cecum: Hanging inferior to the ileocecal valve, it is a blind pouch about 6 cm (2.5") long.
    - b. Vermiform appendix: Attached to the cecum is a twisted, coiled tube about 8 cm (3") long.
    - c. Colon: Large intestine from the end of the ileum to the rectum. 1.5 meters (59") long.
      - 1) Ascending: Begins at the cecum and passes upward to the liver.
      - 2) Transverse: Turns across the body, passing ventral to the liver and stomach.
      - 3) Descending: Turns downward at the spleen and continues to the brim of the pelvis.
      - 4) Sigmoid: Begins near the left iliac crest, projects medially to the midline, and terminates at the rectum at about the level of the third sacral vertebra.

  Rectum: The last 20 cm (8") of the GI tract. Lies anterior to the sacrum and coccyx. Anal canal: Terminal 2-3 cm (1") of the rectum. Mucous membranes are arranged in longitudinal folds and contain a network of arteries and veins (where hemorrhoids develop). The opening of the anal canal to the exterior is the anus.

- o **Function:** Completion of absorption, manufacture of certain vitamins, formation of feces, and the expulsion of fecal matter from the body.

- ➢ **Liver (hepar** *is Greek for liver*)**:** Heaviest gland in the body (3 lb.) and second largest organ of the body (after the skin).
  - o **Location:** Inferior to the diaphragm and occupies most of the right hypochondriac and part of the epigastric regions of the abdominopelvic cavity.

  - o **Structure:** Covered by visceral peritoneum, divided into two principal lobes, right and left.

  - o **Function:** Metabolizes carbohydrates, lipids, and proteins and maintains normal glucose levels. Also removes drugs and hormones from the blood, excretes bilirubin, synthesizes bile salts, stores vitamins and minerals, and activates vitamin D. Phagocytosis of worn-out red and white blood cells and some bacteria.
    - ▪ Production of bile (a digestive enzyme). Plays a role in emulsification (breakdown of fat).
    - ▪ Detoxification of the blood.

- ➢ **Gall Bladder:** Pear-shaped sac about 7-10 cm (3-4") long.
  - o **Location**: In a depression on the posterior surface of the liver and hangs from the inferior anterior margin of the liver.

  - o **Structure**: Simple columnar epithelium arranged in rugae resembling those of the stomach.

  - o **Function**: Stores and concentrates (up to tenfold) bile until it is needed in the small intestine.

- ➢ **Biliary Tract:** Organs and ducts that participate in the secretion, storage, and delivery of bile into the duodenum.
  - o **Location**: From the liver/gallbladder to the duodenum.
  - o **Structure**:
    - ▪ Hepatic ducts: Canal that receives bile from the liver. Unites with the cystic duct to form the common bile duct.
    - ▪ Cystic duct: Duct of the gallbladder. Unites with the hepatic duct to form the common bile duct.
    - ▪ Common bile duct: Duct carrying bile to the duodenum and receiving it from the cystic duct of the gallbladder and the hepatic ducts.
    - ▪ Hepato-pancreatic duct (papilla of Vater): Duodenal end of the drainage systems of the pancreatic and common bile ducts.

  - o **Function**: Delivers bile into the duodenum from the gallbladder.

> ➤ **Pancreas:** Retroperitoneal gland about 12-15 cm (5-6") long and 2.5 cm (1") thick.
>   **Location**: Lies posterior to the greater curvature of the stomach and is connected by two ducts to the duodenum.
>
>   o **Structure**:
>   ▪ Gross: 12-15 cm (5-6") long and 2.5 cm (1") thick, divided into head, body, and tail. The head is the expanded portion near the C-shaped curve of the duodenum. Located superior to and to the left of the head are the central body and the tapering tail.
>   ▪ Heterocrine:
>   1. Endocrine portion: 1% of cells organized into clusters called pancreatic islets (islets of Langerhans). Secretes the hormones glucagon, insulin, somatostatin, and pancreatic polypeptide.
>   2. Exocrine portion: Small clusters of glandular epithelial cells, about 99% of which are arranged in clusters called acini. Cells within acini secrete a mixture of fluid and digestive enzymes called pancreatic juice.
>
>   o **Function**: Produce pancreatic juice, a clear, colorless liquid consisting of water, some salts, sodium bicarbonate, and several enzymes.

The Urinary (Excretory) System

Overall, the urinary system works to excrete waste from the body through the excretion of urine. However, the urinary system has many other functions, including filtering the blood and regulating the pH of the body. The kidneys need to produce a minimum of 500 mL of urine a day to release waste. Urine production below these levels could indicate bodily problems such as dehydration or kidney disease. The kidneys and the abilities of the urinary system may be affected by diseases such as diabetes.

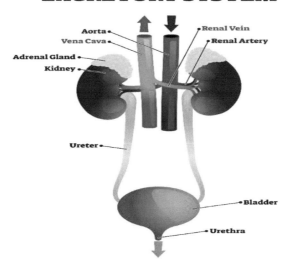

300

Kidneys: Paired reddish organs shaped like kidney beans. They are **retroperitoneal,** meaning they lie outside of the peritoneal cavity.

- o **Location**: just above the waist between the peritoneum and the posterior wall of the abdomen.
- o **Structure**:
  - ▪ **Gross**
    a. Shape: 10-12 cm (4-5") long and 5-7.5 cm (2-3") wide. Its concave medial border faces the vertebral column.
    b. Perirenal fat pad and capsule.
    c. Cortex (renal): Superficial reddish area. The smooth textured area extending from the renal capsule to the bases of the renal pyramids. Together the renal cortex and renal pyramids constitute the functional area (parenchyma) of the kidney. Within the parenchyma are about 1 million microscopic structures called nephrons, which are the functional units of the kidney.
  - ▪ **Microscopic**
    a. Tubules: A small tube or canal. The convoluted tubules of the nephron unit of the kidney, along with the loop of Henle, the distal convoluted tubule, and the collecting tubule, provide a passageway for the glomerular filtrate to reach the renal pelvis.
    b. Glomeruli: Small structures in the Malpighian body of the kidney made up of capillary blood vessels in a cluster and enveloped in a thin wall. A group of twisted capillaries.

- ➤ **Ureters (2):** The tube that carries urine from the kidney to the bladder. Retroperitoneal.
  - o **Location**: Originates in the pelvis of the kidney and terminates in the base of the bladder. Connects the renal pelvis of each kidney to the urinary bladder.
  - o **Structure**: 25-30 cm (10-12") long. The right is slightly shorter than the left. As they descend, their thick walls increase in diameter from 1 mm to a maximum of about 1.7 cm (.7").
    - ▪ Gross: Urine drains through papillary ducts into the minor calyces. They join to become major calyces that unite to form the renal pelvis. From the renal pelvis, urine drains into the ureters and then into the urinary bladder.
      a. Calyces: A cup-like division of the kidney pelvis.
      b. Pelvis: The expanded, proximal portion of the ureter, lying within the kidney and into which the major calyces open.

- ➤ **Urinary bladder:** Receptacle for urine excreted by the kidneys.
  - o **Location**: A hollow muscular organ situated in the pelvic cavity posterior to the pubic symphysis.

○ **Structure**:
- **Gross**: On the floor of the urinary bladder is a small triangular area called the trigone. The two posterior corners of the trigone contain the two ureteral openings, whereas the opening into the urethra, the internal urethral orifice, lies in the anterior corner.
- **Microscopic**: Two coats make up the wall of the urinary bladder.
  a. Epithelium: The deepest is the mucosa, a mucous membrane composed of transitional epithelium and an underlying lamina propria similar to that of the ureters.

  b. Muscularis: Muscular layer of the urinary bladder. Surrounding the mucosa is the intermediate muscularis, called the detrusor muscle. It consists of three layers of smooth muscle tissue.

➢ **Urethra**: A canal for the discharge of urine extending from the bladder to the outside. A small tube leading from the internal urethral orifice on the floor of the urinary bladder to the exterior of the body. In the female, its orifice lies in the vestibule between the vagina and clitoris; in the male, the urethra traverses the penis, opening at the tip of the glans penis. In the male, it serves as the passage for semen as well as urine.
○ **Location**: In females, the urethra lies directly posterior to the pubic symphysis. Its length is approximately 4 cm (1.5"). The female urethra is directed obliquely, inferiorly, and anteriorly. The opening of the urethra to the exterior is located between the clitoris and the vaginal opening. The male urethra is about 15-20 cm (6-8") long. From its origin, it first passes through the prostate gland, then through the urogenital diaphragm, and finally through the penis.
○ **Structure**:
- Male: Consists of a deep mucosa and a superficial muscularis. It is subdivided into three anatomical regions: (1) The prostatic urethra passes through the prostate gland. (2) The membranous urethra (the shortest portion) passes through the urogenital diaphragm. (3) The spongy urethra (longest portion) passes through the penis. The epithelium of the prostatic urethra is continuous with that of the urinary bladder. The lamina propria of the male urethra, like that of the female, is areolar connective tissue with elastic fibers and a plexus of veins.
- Female: Consists of a deep mucosa and superficial muscularis. The mucosa is a mucous membrane composed of epithelium and lamina propria (areolar connective tissue with elastic fibers and a plexus of veins). The muscularis consists of circularly arranged smooth muscle fibers and is continuous with that of the urinary bladder.
○ **Function**: Terminal portion of the urinary system. Serves as the passageway for discharging urine from the body. In the male, it also serves as the duct through which various reproductive secretions are discharged from the body.

THE REPRODUCTIVE SYSTEM

This system is used for sexual reproduction. The male reproductive system contains gametes (specialized sex cells containing 23 chromosomes) in the form of sperm cells. The female reproductive system contains gametes in the form of egg cells or oocytes. During fertilization, the sperm cell combines with the egg cell to start the process of fetal development over the nine- month human gestation period.

The reproductive system also contains sex organs and is affected by various sex hormones (estrogen for the female reproductive system and testosterone for the male reproductive system).

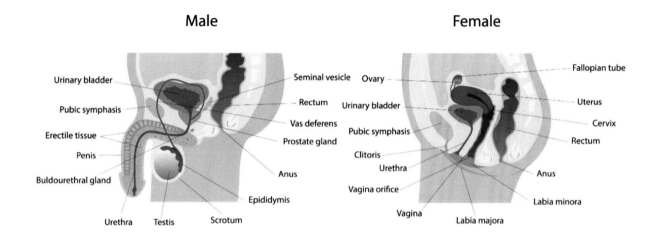

THE MALE REPRODUCTIVE SYSTEM

Scrotum: A sac that hangs from the root (attached portion) of the penis and consists of loose skin and superficial fascia. The sac of skin that holds the testes.

- ➤ **Testes:** Paired oval glands measuring about 5 cm (2") in length and 2.5 cm (1") in diameter.
  - o **Location**: In the scrotum.
  - o **Structure**: Covered by a serous membrane called the tunica vaginalis. Internal to the tunica vaginalis is a dense white fibrous capsule (tunica albuginea) that extends inward, forming septa that divides each testis into a series of internal compartments called lobules. Each lobule contains one to three tightly coiled tubules, the seminiferous tubules. A process called spermatogenesis produces sperm here.
  - o **Function**: Produce sperm and testosterone.
- ➤ **Spermatic ducts:**
  - o **Location**: Ascends along the posterior border of the epididymis (a small oblong body resting upon and beside the posterior surface of the testes, consisting of a convoluted tube 3.97-6.1 meters [13-20 ft.] long, enveloped in the tunica vaginalis, ending in the ductus deferens), penetrates the inguinal canal and enters the pelvic cavity. It loops over the ureter, over the side, and down the posterior surface of the urinary bladder.

- o **Structure**: About 45 cm (18") long, is lined with pseudostratified columnar epithelium and contains a heavy coat of three layers of muscle.
- o **Function**: Canal for passage of semen, esp. the ductus deferens and the ejaculatory duct.
- ➤ **Urethra:** Shared terminal duct of the reproductive and urinary systems.
  - o **Location**: Passes through the prostate gland, the urogenital diaphragm, and the penis.
  - o **Structure**: Divided into three parts: The prostatic urethra is 2-3 cm (1") long and passes through the prostate gland. It continues inferiorly, and as it passes through the urogenital diaphragm, a muscular partition between the two ischial and pubic rami is known as the membranous urethra. The membranous urethra is about 1 cm (1/2" in length. As it passes through the corpus spongiosum of the penis, it is known as the spongy (penile) urethra. This portion is about 15-20 cm (6-8") long. The spongy urethra ends at the external urethral orifice.
  - o **Function**: Terminal portion of the urinary system. Serves as the passageway for discharging urine from the body. In the male, it also serves as the duct through which various reproductive secretions are discharged from the body.
- ➤ **Prostate gland:** A single, doughnut-shaped gland about the size and shape of a chestnut
  - o **Location**: Inferior to the urinary bladder and surrounds the prostatic urethra.
  - o **Structure**: Partly muscular and partly glandular. Consists of a median lobe and two lateral lobes. It is enclosed in a fibrous capsule containing smooth muscle fibers in its inner layer. Muscle fibers also separate the glandular tissue and encircle the urethra.
  - o **Function**: Secretes a thin, opalescent, slightly alkaline fluid that forms part of the seminal fluid. Also closes the urethra during sexual intercourse.
- ➤ **Penis:** The male organ of copulation and urination.
  - o **Location**: Suspended from the front and sides of the pubic arch.
  - o **Structure**: Cylindrical in shape and consists of a body, root, and glans penis. The body of the penis is composed of three cylindrical masses of tissue, each bound by fibrous tissue called the tunica albuginea. The smaller midventral mass, the corpus spongiosum penis, contains the spongy urethra and functions in keeping the spongy urethra open during ejaculation. All three masses are enclosed by fascia and skin and consist of erectile tissue permeated by blood sinuses.
  - o **Function**: Contains the urethra, a passageway for the ejaculation of semen and for the excretion of urine.

THE FEMALE REPRODUCTIVE SYSTEM

- ➤ **Ovaries: Female gonads**
  - o **Location**: Lie in the superior portion of the pelvic cavity, one on each side of the uterus.
  - o **Structure**: Resemble unshelled almonds in size and shape, 4 cm long, 2 cm wide, and 8 mm thick. Consists of two parts, an outer portion or cortex, which encloses a central medulla. Contains the germinal epithelium, the tunica albuginea, the stroma, ovarian follicles, a mature (Graafian) follicle, and a corpus luteum.
  - o **Function**: Produce the reproductive cell, the ovum (ova), and two known hormones, estrogen and progesterone.

- ➢ **Uterine** (fallopian) tubes: 2 tubes extending laterally from the uterus.
  - ○ **Location**: Attached to either side of the uterus and leading from the region of the ovary.
  - ○ **Structure**: 10 cm (4") in length. The open, funnel-shaped portion of each tube, called the infundibulum, is close to the ovary. It ends in a fringe of finger-like projections called fimbriae, one of which is attached to the lateral end of the ovary. From the infundibulum, the uterine tube extends medially and inferiorly and attaches to the superior lateral angle of the uterus. The ampulla of the uterine tube is the widest, longest portion, making up about the lateral two-thirds of its length. The isthmus of the uterine tube is the more medial, short, narrow, thick-walled portion that joins the uterus.
  - ○ **Function**: Transport secondary oocytes and fertilized ova from the ovaries to the uterus.
- ➢ **Uterus: Womb.**
  - ○ **Location**: Situated between the urinary bladder and the rectum.
  - ○ **Structure**: Size and shape of an inverted pear. In a female who has never been pregnant, it is about 7 ½ cm (3") long, 5 cm (2") wide, and 2 ½ cm (1") thick. It is larger in females who have recently been pregnant and smaller (atrophied) when female sex hormone levels are low, as occurs while taking birth control pills or after menopause.
    - ▪ **Gross**:
      - (a) Fundus: Dome-shaped portion superior to the uterine tubes.
      - (b) Body: Major tapering central portion.
      - (c) Cervix: Inferior narrow portion opening into the vagina.
    - ▪ **Microscopic**: 3 layers of tissue.
      - (a) Endometrium: Inner layer of the uterus and is highly vascular.
      - (b) Myometrium: Middle layer that forms the bulk of the uterine wall. Consists of three layers of smooth muscle fibers and is the thickest in the fundus and thinnest in the cervix.
      - (c) Perimetrium: Outer layer (serosa) is part of the visceral peritoneum.
  - ○ **Function**: Serves as part of the pathway for sperm to reach the uterine tubes. It is also the site of menstruation, implantation of a fertilized ovum, development of the fetus during pregnancy, and labor.
- ➢ **Vagina**: Female organ of copulation.
  - ○ **Location**: Situated between the urinary bladder and the rectum, the vagina is directed superiorly and posteriorly, where it attaches to the uterus.
  - ○ **Structure**: Tubular, fibromuscular organ lined with mucous membrane and measures about 10 cm (4") in length.
  - ○ **Function**: Serves as a passageway for the menstrual flow and childbirth. It also receives semen from the penis during sexual intercourse.
- ➢ **External genitalia**: The genitalia are collectively termed the vulva (or pudendum) and include the mons pubis, labia majora, labia minora, and clitoris.
  - ○ **Location**:
    - ▪ Mons Pubis: Anterior to the vaginal and urethral openings.
    - ▪ Labia Majora: From the mons pubis, two longitudinal folds of skin extend inferiorly and posteriorly. Homologous to the scrotum and is covered by pubic hair.

- Labia minora: Medial to the labia majora are two smaller folds of skin. The labia minora is devoid of pubic hair and fat.
- Clitoris: A small, cylindrical mass of erectile tissue and nerves. Located at the anterior junction of the labia minora. A layer of skin called the prepuce (foreskin) is formed at the point where the labia minora unite and covers the body of the clitoris.
- Vestibule: The region between the labia minora. Within the vestibule are the hymen (if still present), vaginal orifice, external urethral orifice, and the openings of several ducts.
- The vaginal orifice (opening of the vagina to the exterior) occupies the greater portion of the vestibule and is bordered by the hymen. Anterior to the vaginal orifice and posterior to the clitoris is the external urethral orifice, the opening of the urethra to the exterior.
  - **Structure**: The perineum is the diamond-shaped area medial to the thighs and buttocks that contains the external genitals and anus. It is bounded anteriorly by the pubic symphysis, laterally by the ischial tuberosities, and posteriorly by the coccyx.
- **Breast** – Mammary glands: Modified sudoriferous (sweat) glands that produce milk.
  - **Location**: Lie anteriorly on the pectoralis major and serratus anterior muscles and are attached to them by a layer of dense irregular connective tissue.
  - **Structure**: Each breast has one pigmented projection, the nipple that contains external openings called lactiferous ducts where milk emerges. Each lobe contains grape-like clusters of milk-secreting glands termed alveoli embedded in connective tissue.
  - **Function**: Synthesis, secretion, and ejection of milk.

THE RESPIRATORY SYSTEM

The respiratory system works to perform gas exchange within the body through the respiration process. Respiration works to remove waste products such as carbon dioxide to maintain homeostasis in the body and maintain pH balance. It also works to bring vital oxygen into the bloodstream, which is used to produce ATP (energy) for cells.

External respiration includes the exchange of gases between the air spaces of the lungs and blood in the pulmonary capillaries. Internal respiration includes the exchange of gases between blood in the systemic capillaries and tissue cells.

The Respiratory System

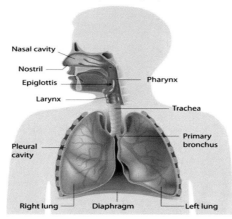

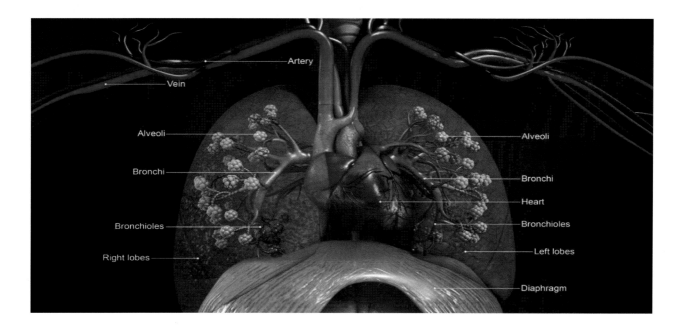

> **Nose**
>   o **Location**: Projection in the center of the face.
>   o **Structure**:
>   ▪ Anterior (external) nares [or nostrils]: External opening into the nose.
>   ▪ Nasal cavities:
>   (a) Paranasal sinuses: Accessory nasal sinuses that open into the nasal cavities. The are the frontal, ethmoidal, sphenoidal, and maxillary. All are lined with ciliated mucous membranes continuous with that of the nasal cavities.
>   (b) Nasal septum: A wall or septum between the two nasal cavities.
>   (c) Nasal conchae: One of the three scroll-like bones that project medially from the lateral wall of the nasal cavity; a turbinate bone. The superior and middle conchae

are processes of the lateral mass of the ethmoid bone; the inferior concha is a face bone.

- Posterior nares or choanae: The opening between the nasal cavity and the nasopharynx.
  - o **Function**: The organ of olfaction and the entrance that warms, moistens and filters the air as it passes through the respiratory tract.
- ➤ **Pharynx:** Throat.
  - o **Location**: Starts at the internal nares and extends to the level of the cricoid cartilage, the most inferior cartilage of the larynx (voice box). Lies posterior to the nasal cavity and oral cavity, superior to the larynx, and just anterior to the cervical vertebrae.
  - o **Structure**: A somewhat funnel-shaped tube about 13 cm (5") long.
    - Nasopharynx: Superior portion of the pharynx extends to the plane of the soft palate.
    - Oropharynx: Intermediate portion of the pharynx lies posterior to the oral cavity and extends from the soft palate inferiorly to the level of the hyoid bone.
    - Laryngopharynx: Inferior portion of the pharynx begins at the level of the hyoid bone and connects the esophagus (food tube) with the larynx (voice box).
  - o **Function**: Respiratory/digestive function, the common passageway for air, food, and drink.
- ➤ **Larynx:** Voice Box. This short passageway connects the laryngopharynx with the trachea.
  - o **Location**: Lies in the midline of the neck anterior to the fourth through sixth cervical vertebrae (C4-C6).
  - o **Structures**: Thyroid cartilage (Adam's apple), Epiglottis (leaf-shaped lid), Glottis (vocal cords), and the cricoid cartilage (a ring of hyaline cartilage that forms the inferior wall of the larynx).
  - o **Function**: Epiglottis: Covers the glottis during swallowing, closing it off. Glottis: Voice production.
- ➤ **Trachea:** Windpipe. Tubular passageway for air about 12 cm (5") long and 2 ½ cm (1") in diameter.
  - o **Location**: Anterior to the esophagus and extends from the larynx to the superior border of the fifth thoracic vertebra (T5), where it divides into the right and left primary bronchi.
  - o **Structures**:
    - Epithelial: Mucosa: deepest layer.
    - Fibro-muscular: Trachealis muscle/elastic connective tissue holds open ends of cartilage rings.
    - Cartilaginous: Submucosa: 16-20 incomplete rings of hyaline cartilage that look like the letter C.
  - o **Function**: Passage for air from the buccal cavity to the right and left primary bronchi.
- ➤ **Bronchi**
  - o **Location**: Travels from the superior border of T5 into the lungs.
  - o **Structures**: Same basic makeup as the trachea.

    a. Epithelial:

    b. Fibro-muscular:

    c. Cartilaginous:

d. Degrees of branching: Trachea divides into right and left primary bronchus at the superior border of T5. On entering the lungs, the primary bronchi divide to form smaller bronchi, the secondary (lobar) bronchi, one for each lobe of the lung (the right lung has 3 and the left lung has 2). The secondary bronchi continue to branch, forming still smaller bronchi called tertiary (segmental) bronchi, which divides into bronchioles. Bronchioles, in turn, branch repeatedly, and the smallest bronchioles branch into even smaller tubes called terminal bronchioles. This extensive branching from the trachea resembles a tree trunk with its branches and is commonly referred to as the bronchial tree. From the trachea to the alveolar ducts, there are about 25 orders of branching of the respiratory passageways.

- o **Function**: Passageway for air from the trachea to lungs.
- ➢ **Lungs**: Paired cone-shaped organs lying in the thoracic cavity. The heart and other structures in the mediastinum separate them from each other. Two layers of serous membrane, collectively called the pleural membrane, enclose and protect each lung.
  - o **Location**: Thoracic cavity bi-lateral to the heart. The lungs extend from the diaphragm to just slightly superior to the clavicles and lie against the ribs anteriorly and posteriorly.
  - o **Structure**: Right lung has 3 lobes, and the left lung has 2 lobes.
    - ▪ **Gross**:
      - (a) Lobes: Each lung is divided into lobes by one or more fissures. Both lungs have an oblique fissure, which extends inferiorly and anteriorly. The right lung also has a horizontal fissure.
      - (b) Bronchopulmonary segments: There are ten tertiary bronchi in each lung. The segment of lung tissue that each supply is called a bronchopulmonary segment.
    - ▪ Pleura: Two layers of serous membrane called the pleural membrane enclose and protect each lung. The superficial layer lines the wall of the thoracic cavity and is called the parietal pleura. The deep layer, the visceral pleura, covers the lungs themselves. Between the visceral and parietal pleurae is a small potential space, the pleural cavity, which contains a lubricating fluid secreted by the membranes. This fluid reduces friction between the membranes and allows them to slide easily onto one another.
    - ▪ **Microscopic**: Respiratory bronchioles subdivided into several (2-11) alveolar ducts. Around the circumference of the alveolar ducts are numerous alveoli and alveolar sacs. An alveolus is a cup-shaped out-pouching (air sac). Alveolar sacs are two or more alveoli that share a common opening.
  - o **Function**: Exchange of respiratory gases (O_2 and CO_2) between the lungs and blood.

THE CIRCULATORY SYSTEM

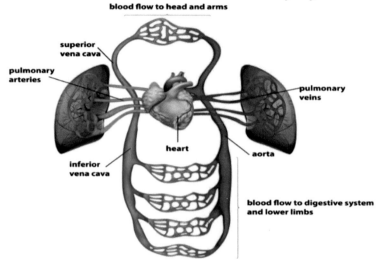

Blood Flow in Human Circulatory System

Angiology is the study of the cardiovascular system, and cardiology is the study of the heart and blood vessels.

The cardiovascular system works to circulate blood, oxygen, hormones, and blood components throughout the body through a network of blood vessels and the heart.

Path of blood-flow through the heart:

Superior/Inferior Vena Cava--> Right Atrium --> Tricuspid Valve --> Right Ventricle --> Pulmonary Semilunar Valve --> Pulmonary Trunk --> Pulmonary Arteries (Only arteries to carry deoxygenated blood) --> Lungs --> Alveoli (gas exchange) --> Pulmonary veins (Only veins to carry oxygenated blood) --> Left Atrium --> Mitral/Bicuspid Valve --> Left Ventricle --> Aortic Semilunar Valve --> Ascending/Abdominal Aorta--> Body

➤ **Vena Cava:**

Note that the Vena Cava is split into the Superior Vena Cava, bringing deoxygenated blood from the upper extremities, and the Inferior Vena Cava bringing deoxygenated blood from the lower extremities.

➤ **Aorta:**

The Ascending aorta has three branches:

    a. The Left Subclavian
    b. The Left Common Carotid
    c. The Brachiocephalic
        1) The Brachiocephalic then splits into the Right Subclavian and Right Common Carotid Arteries.

The abdominal aorta brings blood to the lower extremities.

Systemic circulation: *Includes all the arteries and arterioles that carry oxygenated blood from the left ventricle to systemic capillaries, plus the veins and venules that carry deoxygenated blood returning to the right atrium after flowing through the body organs.*

Pulmonary circulation: *When blood returns to the heart from the systemic route, it is pumped out of the right ventricle to the lungs. In pulmonary capillaries of the alveoli of the lungs, it loses some of its CO2 and takes on O2. Bright red again, it returns to the left atrium of the heart and reenters the systemic circulation as it is ejected by the left ventricle.*

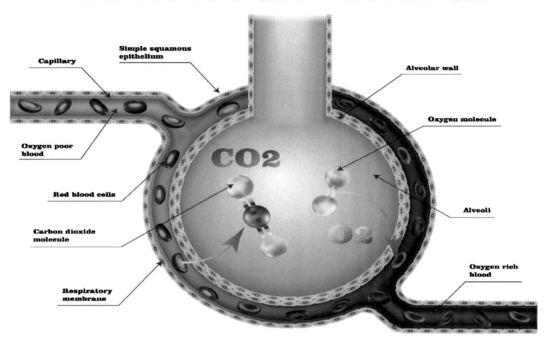

These are the circulatory structures that are specific to fetuses.

FETAL STRUCTURE	ADULT STRUCTURE
Foramen ovale	fossa ovalis
Ductus arteriosus	ligamentum arteriosum
Ductus venosus	ligamentum venosum
Umbilical arteries	lateral umbilical ligaments
Umbilical vein	ligamentum teres of the liver

THE CIRCULATORY SYSTEM - BLOOD VASCULAR SYSTEM

(Heart, blood vessels, and blood)

- ➤ **Heart:** Muscular organ that pumps blood throughout the system
- ➤ **Chambers:** 4 chambers of the heart.

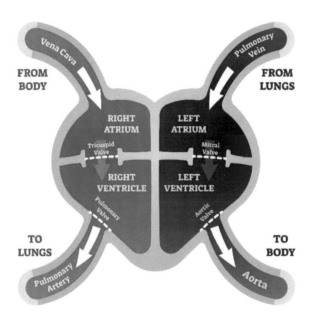

(a) *Right atrium*: Receives deoxygenated systemic blood from the superior and inferior vena cava and the coronary sinus.

(b) *Right ventricle*: Pumps blood from the heart to the lungs. Pulmonary circulation.

(c) *Left atrium*: Receives blood from the lungs.

(d) *Left ventricle*: Pumps blood from the heart throughout the body. Origin of systemic circulation.

- o **Location**: Rests on the diaphragm near the middle of the thoracic cavity in the mediastinum between the lungs. About two-thirds of the mass of the heart lies to the left of the body's midline.
- o **Structure**: 12 cm (5") long, 9 cm (3 ½") wide, and 6 cm (2 ½") thick.
    - ▪ Layers (tunics): Heart wall.
        - (a) Endocardium: Innermost layer, a thin layer of endothelium overlying a thin layer of connective tissue. Provides a smooth lining for the inside of the heart and covers the valves of the heart. It is continuous with the endothelial lining of the large blood vessels associated with the heart.
        - (b) Myocardium: Middle layer, cardiac muscle tissue. Make up the bulk of the heart and is responsible for the pumping action.
        - (c) Epicardium (visceral pericardium): Outermost layer is composed of mesothelium and delicate connective tissue that imparts a smooth, slippery texture to the outermost surface of the heart.

312

- Pericardium: A triple-layered sac that surrounds and protects the heart. Between the parietal and visceral layers of the serous pericardium is a thin film of serous fluid known as the pericardial fluid that reduces friction between the membranes as the heart moves.
  - (a) Visceral: Inner layer of the serous pericardium, also called the epicardium. Adheres tightly to the surface of the heart.
  - (b) Parietal: Outer layer of the serous pericardium that is fused to the fibrous pericardium.

- **Other structural features:**
  - Anastomoses: Most tissues of the body receive blood from more than one artery. The union of the branches of two or more arteries supplying the same body region is called anastomosis. The Circle of Willis is the most famous example.
  - Collateral circulation: The alternate route of blood flow to a body part through an anastomosis.

THE CIRCULATORY SYSTEM - VESSELS

Arteries: These are vessels that carry blood from the heart to the tissues	a. Tunica intima (internal): Composed of a lining of endothelium that is in contact with the blood. b. Tunica media: thickest layer, consists of elastic fibers and smooth muscle fibers. c. Tunica adventitia (external): Composed of elastic and collagen fibers.
Arterioles: Medium-sized arteries divide into small arteries, which in turn divide into still smaller arteries called arterioles.	a. Tunica intima (internal): Composed of a lining of endothelium that is in contact with the blood. b. Tunica media: thickest layer, consists of elastic fibers and smooth muscle fibers. c. Tunica adventitia (external): Composed of elastic and collagen fibers.
Capillaries: As the arterioles enter a tissue, they branch into countless microscopic vessels called capillaries. Substances are exchanged between the blood and body tissues through the thin walls of capillaries. Capillaries connect arterioles and venules.	a. Endothelium: Single layer of epithelial cells. b. Connective tissue: Capillaries are endothelium cells made of connective tissue.

Veins: Convey blood from the tissues back to the heart. Venules are the smallest veins. Vein walls are not as thick as arterial walls.	a. Tunica intima (internal): Composed of a lining of endothelium that is in contact with the blood. b. Tunica media: thickest layer. Consist of elastic fibers but relatively few smooth muscle fibers. c. Tunica adventitia (external): Composed of elastic and collagen fibers.
Vasa vasorum: Because blood vessels require oxygen and nutrients just like other tissues of the body, larger blood vessels especially have their own blood vessels called vasa vasorum	

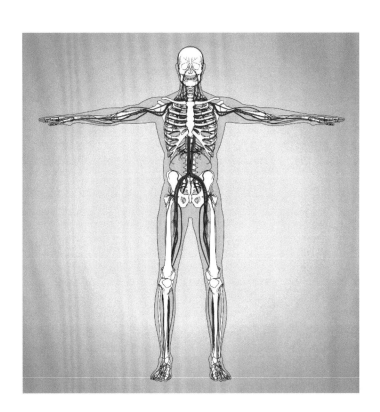

THE CIRCULATORY SYSTEM- ARTERIAL SYSTEM

Aorta: The main systemic trunk of the arterial system of the body that emerges from the left ventricle. It is about 3 cm (1") in diameter at is origin in the upper surface of the left ventricle.	a. Location: Begins at the left ventricle. It passes upward as the ascending aorta, turns backward and to the left (arch) at the level of the fourth thoracic vertebra, and then passes downward as the descending aorta, which is divided into the thoracic and abdominal aorta. The latter terminates at its division into the two common iliac arteries.
Ascending aorta: Two branches. Two coronary arteries provide blood to the myocardium.	a. Aortic valve: Prevents back flow. b. Origin of coronary arteries.
Arch of the aorta: Three branches	a. Brachiocephalic artery b. Left Common Cortaid c. Left Subclavian

Brachiocephalic artery (innominate artery)	The first branch of the arch of the aorta is found only on the right side.
	
	It bifurcates to form:
	    a. the right subclavian artery
	    b. right common carotid artery.

Right subclavian artery	Extends from the brachiocephalic to the first rib and then passes into the armpit, where it becomes the axillary artery.
Right vertebral artery	Branch of the subclavian. Passes through the foramina of the transverse process of the cervical vertebrae and enters the skull through the foramen magnum to reach the inferior surface of the brain. Here it unites with the left vertebral artery to form the basilar artery.
Right internal thoracic artery	Provides blood to the chest wall.
Right axillary artery	Continuation of the subclavian extends from the lateral border of the first rib to the lower border of the tendon of the teres major muscle, where it becomes the brachial artery.
Right brachial artery	Continuation of the axillary bifurcates just below the elbow to form radial (lateral) and ulnar (medial) arteries.
Right deep brachial artery	Bifurcates at the bend of the elbow. a. Right radial artery – Right deep palmar arch – Right digital arteries b. Right ulnar artery – Right superficial palmar arch – Right digital arteries
Right common carotid artery	Begins at the bifurcation of the brachiocephalic artery behind the sternoclavicular articulation and is confined to the neck. At the superior border of the larynx, it divides into the right external and right internal carotid arteries.

Right external carotid artery	Becomes the:
	  a. Right facial artery
	  b. Right superficial temporal artery
	  c. Maxillary
	  d. Posterior auricular

Right internal carotid artery	Supplies the brain, right eye, and right sides of the forehead and nose.

Cerebral arterial circle (Circle of Willis)	a. Location: At the base of the brain stem around the sella turcica.
	
	b. Components: Nine vessels form the Circle of Willis.
	  1) Internal carotid arteries (2)
	  2) Anterior cerebral arteries (2)
	  3) Posterior communicating arteries (2)
	  4) Posterior cerebral arteries (2)
	  5) Anterior communicating artery (1): Only unpaired artery in the circle.

Left common carotid artery	Arises from the highest part of the arch of the aorta at the second costal cartilage. Branches in the same manner as the right common carotid.
Left subclavian artery	3rd branch off the arch of the aorta. Branches in the same manner as the right subclavian artery.
Descending aorta	From the arch of the aorta to bifurcation into common iliac arteries.
Thoracic aorta: From the arch of the aorta to the diaphragm.	a. Bronchial arteries: 2 or more. Provide blood for bronchi. b. Pericardial arteries: Provide blood to the pericardium. c. Esophageal arteries: 4 or 5. Provide blood to the esophagus. d. Intercostal arteries: 9 pairs. Supply blood for intercostal areas (ribs). e. Subcostal arteries: Supply blood to subcostal areas beneath the ribs. f. Superior phrenic arteries: Supply the diaphragm.

Abdominal aorta: From diaphragm to bifurcation into common iliac arteries	a. Celiac artery (trunk or axis): Supplies the stomach, liver, and spleen.
	  1) Left gastric artery: Stomach
	  2) Splenic artery: Spleen
	b. Common hepatic artery: Liver
	c. Superior mesenteric artery: Supplies all of the small intestine except the superior portion of the duodenum.
	d. Inferior mesenteric artery: Supplies all of the colon and rectum except the right half of the transverse colon.
	e. Middle suprarenal arteries: Supply the adrenal glands.

	f. Renal arteries: Supply the kidneys, ureters, and adrenals. g. Gonadal arteries (testicular): Supply testicles and ureter. Ovarian arteries (correspond to the internal spermatic arteries of the male) supply the ovaries, part of the ureters, and uterine tubes. h. Inferior phrenic arteries: Supply the diaphragm and esophagus. i. Lumbar arteries: Supply lumbar and psoas muscles and part of the abdominal wall musculature. j. Middle sacral arteries: Supplies the sacrum and coccyx.
Terminal branches: **Common iliac arteries:** Supply lower pelvic and abdominal areas and the lower extremities.	a. Internal iliac arteries: Uterus, prostate gland, and muscles of buttocks and urinary bladder. b. External iliac arteries: Lower limbs. Once past the inguinal ligament, it becomes the femoral artery.
Femoral	Continuation of the external iliac artery. It extends from the inguinal ligament down through the femoral (Scarpa's) triangle and the adductor (Hunter's) canal, where it becomes the popliteal artery.
Popliteal	The continuation of the femoral artery is located at the back of the knee. It descends from the opening of the adductor magnus muscle to the lower border of the popliteus muscle, passing behind the knee joint. Just below the knee joint, it divides into the posterior and anterior tibial arteries.
Anterior tibial	Originates at the bifurcation of the popliteal artery at the lower border of the popliteal space. At its point of termination, it becomes the dorsalis pedis artery.
Posterior tibial	Begins at the lower border of the popliteal space opposite the interval between the tibia and fibula. Arises as a bifurcation of the popliteal artery.
Dorsalis pedis	Continuation of the anterior tibial artery lies between the tendon of the extensor hallucis longus muscle and the tendon of the extensor digitorum longus muscle on the dorsal surface of the foot.

THE CIRCULATORY SYSTEM - VENOUS SYSTEM

Dural sinuses	Inside the skull, blood bathes the brain, then collects into the dural sinuses, then pours into the internal jugular veins.
Internal jugular veins	Parallel the internal carotid arteries.
External jugular veins	Run inferiorly in the neck along the outside of the internal jugulars. They drain blood from the parotid glands, facial muscles, scalp, and other superficial structures into the subclavian veins.
Cephalic veins	Superficial veins, Begins in the lateral part of the dorsal venous arch and winds superiorly around the radial border of the forearm. Anterior to the elbow, it is connected to the basilic vein by the median cubital vein. Ultimately empties into the axillary vein.
Basilic veins	Superficial veins, Originate in the medial part of the dorsal venous arch. Extends along the posterior surface of the ulna to a point near the elbow where it receives the median cubital vein. The basilic continues ascending on the medial side until it reaches the middle of the arm. There it penetrates the tissues deeply and runs alongside the brachial artery until it joins the brachial vein. As the basilic and brachial veins merge, they form the axillary vein.
Deep veins	Run parallel with and have the same names as arteries.
Brachiocephalic veins	Formed by the union of subclavian and internal jugular veins. Unite to form the superior vena cava.
Superior vena cava	About 7-½ cm (3") long and empties its blood into the superior part of the right atrium. Begins posterior to the right first costal cartilage by the union of the right and left brachiocephalic veins and ends at the level of the right third costal cartilage, where it enters the right atrium.
Right brachiocephalic vein	Formed by a union of the right subclavian and internal jugulars.
Left brachiocephalic vein	Formed by a union of the left subclavian and internal jugulars.
Azygos system	Collects blood from the thorax and may serve as a bypass for the inferior vena cava that drains blood from the lower body. Several small veins directly link the azygos system with the inferior vena cava.
Greater saphenous veins	Superficial veins are the longest vein in the body. Begins at the medial end of the dorsal venous arch of the foot. Passes anterior to the medial malleolus and then superiorly along the medial aspect of the leg and thigh just deep to the skin. It receives tributaries from superficial tissues and connects with the deep veins as well. It empties into the femoral vein near the groin.
Lesser saphenous veins	Superficial veins, Begins at the lateral end of the dorsal venous arch of the foot. Passes posterior to the lateral malleolus and ascends deep to the skin along the posterior aspect of the leg. Empties into the popliteal vein posterior to the knee.

Common iliac veins	Formed by the union of the external and internal iliac veins.
Inferior vena cava	Formed by the union of the right and left common iliac veins.
Portal system	Delivers blood to the liver for detoxification.
Lumbar veins	Drain lumbar and psoas muscles and part of the abdominal wall musculature.
Gonadal veins	Drain the testes or ovaries.
Renal veins	Drain kidneys.
Suprarenal veins	Drain the adrenal glands.
Inferior phrenic veins	Drain the diaphragm.
Hepatic veins	Drain the portal system and empties into the inferior vena cava.

Blood is classified as a viscous liquid type of connective tissue composed of plasma and corpuscles (formed elements). The functions of blood include the transportation of gases (Oxygen, Carbon Dioxide), food, waste, and hormones; regulation of temperature, pH, and water balance; and protection against infection. Blood comprises roughly 8% of body weight (approximately 5-6 liters in the adult female and 4-5 liters in the adult male). Blood has a relatively neutral pH of approximately 7.35-7.45. Blood also has a higher temperature than normal body temperature, hovering around 37 degrees Celsius (98.6 F).

Plasma is a watery liquid that contains dissolved substances (91.5% water, 8.5 % dissolved substances). The dissolved substances can be either blood proteins or non-protein components. Blood proteins include:

- **Serum albumin**: 54% plasma proteins. Smallest plasma proteins. Produced by the liver and exert considerable osmotic pressure, which helps maintain the water balance between blood and tissues and regulate blood volume. Also function as transport proteins for fatty acids, some lipid-soluble hormones, and certain drugs.
- **Serum globulin**: 38% plasma proteins. Most are produced by hepatocytes. Alpha globulins include high-density lipoprotein (HDL), which transports lipids, thyroxine-binding globulin (transports thyroid hormones), and other proteins. Antibodies (also known as gamma globulins or immunoglobulins) are produced by plasma cells, which develop from B-lymphocytes. They help defend against viral and bacterial invaders, such as those that cause measles, hepatitis, polio, and tetanus.
- **Fibrinogen**: 7% of plasma proteins. Produced by hepatocytes. Plays an essential role in blood clotting.

Non-protein components include electrolytes, nutrients, enzymes, hormones, gases, urea, uric acid creatinine, ammonia, and bilirubin.

Corpuscles contain cells and cell fragments. Corpuscles include Erythrocytes, Leukocytes, and Thrombocytes.

- ➢ **Erythrocytes** (red blood cells): More than 99% of the formed elements in blood are RBCs. Erythrocytes contain the oxygen-carrying protein hemoglobin, which is a pigment that gives whole blood its red color. A healthy adult male has about 5.4 million RBCs per cubic millimeter (mm^3) of blood, and a healthy female has about 4.8 million per mm^3.
  - o **Structure**: Biconcave discs (much greater surface area). Lack a nucleus and other organelles and can neither reproduce nor carry on extensive metabolic activities. Only live 120 days. New RBCs are produced by bone marrow.
  - o **Function**: Transport oxygen to cells.
- ➢ **Leukocytes** (white blood cells): They have a nucleus and do not contain hemoglobin. Live only a few days, or during a period of infection, phagocytic WBCs may live only a few hours. Far less numerous than red blood cells, about 5000-10,000 cells per cubic millimeter (mm^3). RBCs outnumber WBCs by about 700:1.
  - o **Structures**:
    - ▪ Agranulocytes (agranular leukocytes): Do not have cytoplasmic granules that can be seen under a light microscope, owing to their small size and poor staining qualities.
      1. Lymphocytes: Develop from monoblasts. The nuclei of lymphocytes are darkly stained and round or slightly indented. The cytoplasm stains sky blue and forms a rim around the nucleus.
      2. Monocytes: Usually kidney-shaped or horseshoe-shaped, the cytoplasm is blue-gray and has a foamy appearance. The blood is merely a conduit for monocytes, which migrate out into the tissues, enlarge, and differentiate into macrophages.
    - ▪ Granulocytes (granular leukocytes): Develop from myeloblasts. Have conspicuous granules in the cytoplasm that can be seen under a light microscope.
      1. Neutrophils: Have granules that are "neutral," staining a pale lilac with a combination of acidic and basic dyes.
      2. Eosinophils: Have granules that stain red or orange with acidic dyes.
      3. Basophils: Have granules that stain blue-purple with basic dyes.
  - o **Functions**: Once pathogens enter the body, the general function of WBCs is to combat them by phagocytosis or immune responses.

- ➢ **Thrombocytes** (platelets): Platelets have a short life span, normally just 5-9 days.
  - o **Structure**: Besides the immature cell types that develop into erythrocytes and leukocytes, hemopoietic stem cells also differentiate into megakaryoblasts. Under the influence of a hormone known as thrombopoietin, megakaryoblasts transform into meta megakaryocytes, huge cells that splinter into 2000-3000 fragments. Each fragment, enclosed by a piece of the cell membrane, is a platelet.
  - o **Function**: Help stop blood loss from damaged blood vessels by forming a platelet plug. Their granules also contain chemicals that, upon release, promote blood clotting.

Blood can clot. This is due to substances found in the blood. These include Thromboplastin (an intracellular substance that accelerates blood clotting), Prothrombin (Interacts with calcium to produce thrombin), Calcium, and Fibrinogen. There are also substances that inhibit blood's ability to clot, including Antithrombin and Antiprothombin (Heparin).

The Lymphatic System

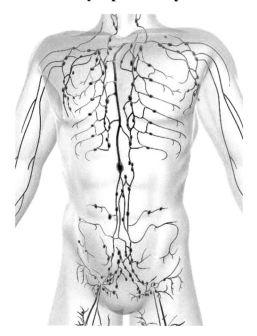

The lymphatic system contains vessels, cells, organs, and tissues that work to filter fluids and pathogens from the bloodstream. It works closely with the immune system, which works to destroy or neutralize pathogens. During normal blood flow and due to blood pressure, about 20 liters of plasma and fluid a day can build up in the interstitial space between cells (17 liters are reabsorbed, and the other 3 are taken care of by the lymphatic system). This system works to protect the body from pathogens and bacteria and assists the immune system in the formation of white blood cells.

- ➢ **Lymphatic Vessels:** Begin as closed-ended vessels in spaces between cells. These unite to form lymphatic vessels. Resemble veins but have thinner walls and more valves.
- ➢ **Cisterna chyli:** Part of the thoracic duct as dilation. Anterior to the second lumbar vertebrae. Largest lymph node in the body, reservoir before draining into the thoracic duct.
- ➢ **Thoracic duct:** About 38-45 cm (15-18") long. The main collecting duct of the lymphatic system. Receives lymph from the left side of the head, neck, and chest, the left upper limb, and the entire body inferior to the ribs.
- ➢ **Right lymphatic duct:** About 1.25 cm (½") long and drains lymph from the upper right side of the body.
- ➢ **Lymph nodes:** Oval or bean-shaped structures located along the length of lymphatic vessels. Filter lymph by having it enter at one end and exit at another.
- ➢ **Tonsils:** Located in depressions of the mucous membrane of the fauces and pharynx.
- ➢ **Spleen:** Largest single mass of lymphatic tissue in the body, about 12 cm (5") in length, and is situated in the left hypochondriac region between the stomach and the diaphragm lateral to the liver.
- ➢ **Thymus:** Usually a bilobed lymphatic organ, it is in the mediastinum, posterior to the sternum, and between the lungs.

The Endocrine System

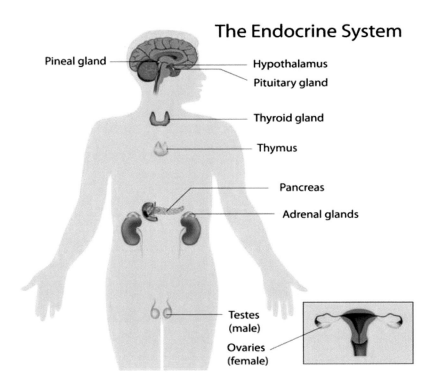

The Endocrine System

Pineal gland
Hypothalamus
Pituitary gland
Thyroid gland
Thymus
Pancreas
Adrenal glands
Testes (male)
Ovaries (female)

Adenology *is the study of glands.* **Endocrinology** is the study of the endocrine glands.

The Endocrine system deals with hormone regulation. The endocrine system, along with the nervous system, works to keep the body in homeostasis. They both work via signals with the endocrine system working with chemical (hormone) signals. Hormones are substances that originate in endocrine glands and, once secreted, are transported through the blood. The four classes of hormones are Steroids, Biogenic Amines, Peptides/Proteins, and Eicosanoids.

There are three types of glands in this system: Exocrine, Endocrine and Heterocrine Glands.

Exocrine glands secrete their products into ducts, and the ducts carry the secretions into body cavities, into the lumen of an organ, or to the outer surface of the body. Include sudoriferous (sweat), sebaceous (oil), mucous, and digestive glands.

Endocrine glands secrete their products (hormones) into the extracellular space around the secretory cells rather than into ducts.

Heterocrine glands can secrete their product as either exocrine or endocrine. The Pancreas is the only gland of this type.

> **Pituitary:** Secretes HGH (human growth hormone). The pituitary gland is a pea-shaped structure lying in the sella turcica of the sphenoid bone and attached to the hypothalamus via a stalk called the infundibulum. The pituitary is also called the hypophysis. For years

it was called the "master" endocrine gland because it secretes several hormones that control other endocrine glands. The pituitary gland itself has a master – the hypothalamus.

➢ **Thyroid:** Has right and left lateral lobes on either side of the trachea connected by an isthmus located anterior to the trachea just inferior to the cricoid cartilage of the larynx; secretes thyroxine (T4) and triiodothyronine (T3).

➢ **Parathyroids:** One of four (usually) small glands embedded in the posterior surfaces of the lateral lobes of the thyroid gland. Secretes PTH, a hormone that increases blood calcium level and decreases blood phosphate level.

➢ **Suprarenals** (adrenals): Two glands located superior to each kidney. Produce a group of hormones called mineralocorticoids, glucocorticoids, and androgens.

➢ **Gonads:** A gland that produces gametes and hormones; the ovary in the female and the testis in the male. Ovaries produce estrogens, inhibin (this is also found in semem), and progesterone. Testes produce testosterone.

➢ **Pancreatic islets** (islets of Langerhans): A cluster of endocrine gland cells in the pancreas that secretes insulin, glucagon, somatostatin, and pancreatic polypeptide.

THE NERVOUS SYSTEM

The functions of the nervous system include sensory, integrative, and motor control. The nervous system is comprised of the Central nervous system (CNS - contains the brain and spinal cord) and the Peripheral nervous system (PNS - contains sensory receptors, muscles, and glands).

Cerebrospinal fluid continuously circulates through the subarachnoid space to help nourish and protect the brain and spinal cord from injuries (both chemical and physical).

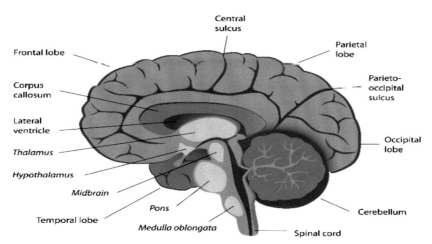

Median section of the brain

THE CENTRAL NERVOUS SYSTEM

➢ **Brain** (encephalon): Consists of gray and white matter. White matter refers to aggregations of myelinated processes from many neurons. The whitish color of myelin gives white matter its name. Gray matter contains either neuron cell bodies, dendrites, and axon terminals or bundles of unmyelinated axons and neuroglia. It looks grayish rather than white because there is no myelin in these areas. *Three parts: cerebrum, cerebellum, and brain stem.*

1. **Cerebrum** (Latin for the brain): Supported on the diencephalon like the cap of a mushroom and forming the bulk of the brain. The superficial layer of the cerebrum is gray matter and is called the cerebral cortex. The cortex, which is only 2-4 mm (0.08 – 0.16 in. thick), contains billions of neurons. Deep in the cortex lies the cerebral white matter. The cerebrum is the seat of intelligence and provides us with the ability to read, write, speak, make calculations and compose music, remember the past, plan for the future, and create works that have never existed before. The cerebrum occupies most of the cranium and has right and left halves called cerebral hemispheres. Each hemisphere can be further subdivided into four lobes, named after the bones that cover them: Frontal, parietal, temporal, and occipital lobes.

2. **Cerebellum** (Latin for little brain): Second largest portion of the brain and occupies the inferior and posterior aspect of the cranial cavity. Posterior to the medulla and pons and inferior to the posterior portion of the cerebrum. It is separated from the cerebrum by a deep groove known as the transverse fissure and by an extension of the cranial dura mater called the tentorium cerebelli. Shaped somewhat like a butterfly.

3. **Brain stem:** Connects the spinal cord to the diencephalon and consists of the medulla oblongata, pons, and midbrain. The diencephalon is the second portion of the brain, or that lying between the telencephalon and mesencephalon. It includes the epithalamus, thalamus, metathalamus, and hypothalamus.

➢ **Ventricles** (little belly or cavity): Four cavities filled with cerebrospinal fluid. Each of the two lateral ventricles are located in the hemisphere of the cerebrum. The third ventricle is a narrow cavity at the midline superior to the hypothalamus and between the right and left halves of the thalamus. The fourth ventricle lies between the brain stem and the cerebellum.

➢ **Meninges:** Surrounds the brain and spinal cord. Have three layers.
   o Pia mater (pia = delicate): The deep, thin transparent connective tissue layer that adheres to the surface of the spinal cord and brain.
   o Arachnoid (Arachne = spider): The middle meninx of the three coverings of the brain and spinal cord, called arachnoid because of its spider's web arrangement of delicate collagen fibers and some elastic fibers. Acts as a baffle system to break up waves in the cerebrospinal fluid.
   o Dura mater (dura = tough, mater = mother): Composed of dense, irregular connective tissue. Outer, most superficial of the three spinal meninges.

➢ **Spinal cord:** Ovoid column of nervous tissue averaging about 44 cm in length, flattened anteroposteriorly, extending from the medulla to the 2nd lumbar vertebra in the spinal canal. All nerves to the trunk and limbs are issued from the spinal cord.
   o **Structure**: In cross-section, it does not fill the vertebral space, being surrounded by the pia mater, the cerebrospinal fluid, the arachnoid, and the dura mater, which fuses with the periosteum of the inner surfaces of the vertebrae. The gray substance approximates the shape of an "H," there being a posterior and anterior horn in either half. The anterior horn is composed of motor cells from which the fibers making up the motor portions

of the peripheral nerves arise. Sensory neurons enter posteriorly. The "H" also divides the surrounding white matter into posterior, lateral, and anterior bundles. These serve to connect the brain and cord in both directions (i.e., with efferent and afferent nerves) as well as various portions of the cord itself.

THE PERIPHERAL NERVOUS SYSTEM

➢ **Cranial nerves:** Twelve pairs of nerves that have their origin in the brain. Ten originate from the brain stem, but all pass through the foramina of the skull. In addition to the 12 pairs of cranial nerves, there is a small combined efferent and afferent nerve that goes from the olfactory area of the brain to the nasal septum. The cranial nerves are designated with Roman numerals and with names. The Roman numerals indicate the order in which the nerves arise from the brain from anterior to posterior. The names indicate the distribution or function.

I.	Olfactory
II.	Optic
III.	Oculomotor
IV.	Trochlear
V.	Trigeminal
VI.	Abducens
VII.	Facial
VIII.	Vestibulocochlear
IX.	Glossopharyngeal
X.	Vagus: Found in the anterior cervical triangle.
XI.	Accessory
XII.	Hypoglossal

➢ **Spinal nerves:** Nerves arising from the spinal cord, each spinal nerve is attached to the spinal cord by two roots; a dorsal or posterior sensory root and a ventral or anterior root. The former consists of afferent fibers conveying impulses to the cord; the latter consists of efferent fibers conveying impulses from the cord. A typical spinal nerve, on passing through the intervertebral foramen, divides into four branches, a recurrent branch, a dorsal ramus or posterior primary division, a ventral ramus or anterior primary division, and two rami communicantes (white and gray) that pass to ganglia of the sympathetic trunk.

a. 31 pairs corresponding with the spinal vertebrae:

8 cervical
12 thoracic
5 lumbar
5 sacral
1 coccygeal

THE MUSCULAR SYSTEM

The muscular system works for the protection, structure, and movement of the body.
There are three types of muscle tissue: Cardiac, Skeletal, and Smooth.

Skeletal muscle works by attaching to bones and moving parts of the skeleton. Skeletal muscle is striated because of the appearance of alternating light and dark bands. This type of muscle can consciously be made to contract and relax, making it a type of voluntary muscle. Skeletal muscles are named after their: shape, location, divisions, attachments, fiber direction, superficial/deep location, size, and action.

MUSCLE ACTION

Flexion	The act of bending or condition of being bent.
Extension	A movement that brings the members of a limb into or toward a straight condition.
Adduction	Movement of a limb toward the median plane of the body, or in the case of digits, toward the axial line of a limb.
Abduction	The lateral movement of the limbs away from the median plane of the body.
Supination	Turning the palm or the hand anteriorly or upward or the foot inward and upward.
Pronation	The act of turning the hand so that the palm faces downward or backward
Eversion	Turning outward.
Inversion	Reversal of normal relationship. Turn inward.
Constriction	A binding or squeezing of a part.
Dilation	Expansion of an organ, orifice, or vessel.
Elevation	A raised area that protrudes above the surrounding area.
Depression	A hollow or lowered region.
Rotation	Process of turning on an axis.
Circumduction	The action or swing of a limb, such as an arm, in such a manner that it describes a cone-shaped figure, the apex of the cone being formed by the joint at the proximal end, while the complete circle is formed by the free distal end of the limb.

Tendons *are fibrous connective tissue that is used for attachment of muscles to bones, and other parts.* **Aponeuroses** *are flat, fibrous sheets of connective tissue that attach muscle to bone or other tissue. They also serve as fascia.* The **origin** is where the muscle tendon attaches to the stationary bone. The **insertion** is where the muscle tendon attaches to the movable portion of a bone. The **belly of a muscle** is the fleshy portion between the tendons of origin and insertion.

THE MUSCULAR SYSTEM- HEAD/NECK

(See Restorative Art Section pp. 125 & 126)

THE MUSCULAR SYSTEM-TRUNK

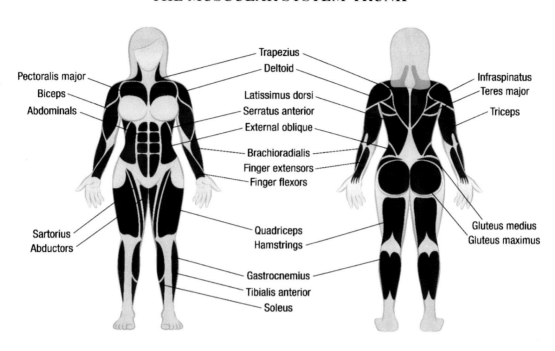

- ➢ **Back**
  - • **Trapezius:** Elevates clavicle, adducts scapula, rotates scapula superiorly, elevates or depresses scapula, and extends head.
  - • **Latissimus dorsi:** Extends, adducts, and rotates arm medially; draws arm inferiorly and posteriorly.
- ➢ **Chest**
  - • **Pectoralis major:** Flexes, adducts, and rotate arm medially.
  - • **External intercostals:** Elevate ribs during inspiration and thus increase lateral and anteroposterior dimensions of the thorax.
  - • **Internal intercostals:** Draw adjacent ribs together during forced expiration and thus decrease lateral and anteroposterior dimensions of the thorax.
- ➢ **Abdomen**
  - • **External oblique:** Contraction of both compresses' abdomen; contraction of one side alone bends vertebral column laterally; laterally rotates vertebral column. Anterolateral
  - • **Internal oblique:** Compresses abdomen; contraction of one side alone bends vertebral column laterally; laterally rotates vertebral column. Anterolateral
  - • **Transverses abdominis:** Compresses abdomen. Anterolateral
  - • **Rectus abdominis:** Flexes vertebral column and compresses abdomen to aid in defecation, urination, forced expiration, and childbirth. Anteromedial.
  - • **Iliopsoas:** The compound iliacus and psoas magnus muscles. Posterior.
- ➢ **Diaphragm:** Forms floor of thoracic cavity; pulls central tendon inferiorly during inspiration and as the dome of diaphragm flattens increases the vertical length of thorax.

327

THE MUSCULAR SYSTEM- UPPER EXTREMITIES

> **Deltoid:** Abducts, flexes, extends, and may alternately medially or laterally rotate the arm.
> **Teres major:** Extends arm; assists in adduction and medial rotation.
> **Biceps brachii:** Flexes and supinates forearm; flexes arm.
> **Triceps brachii:** Extends forearm; extends arm.
> **Coracobrachialis:** Flexes and adducts arm.
> **Brachialis:** Flexes forearm.
> **Flexor carpi radialis:** Flexes and abducts wrist.
> **Flexor carpi ulnaris:** Flexes and abducts wrist.
> **Flexor digitorum superficialis:** Flexes the middle phalanges of each finger.
> **Brachioradialis:** Flexes forearm.
> **Supinator:** Supinates forearm and hand.

THE MUSCULAR SYSTEM- LOWER EXTREMITIES

> **Gluteus maximus:** Extends and rotates thigh laterally.
> **Sartorius:** Flexes leg; flexes thigh and rotates it laterally, thus crossing leg. "Tailor's muscle." The longest muscle in the body.
> **Quadriceps femoris:** Comprised of 4 muscles, the rectus femoris, vastus lateralis, vastus medialis, and vastus intermedius. All four heads extend their leg. The rectus portion alone also flexes the thigh. Laterally rotates and adducts the thigh.
> **Adductor longus:** Adducts, medially rotates, and flexes thigh. The medial border is the medial border of the femoral triangle (Scarpa's triangle).
> **Adductor magnus:** Adducts and medially rotates thigh, anterior part flexes, and posterior part extends thigh. Hunter's canal is in the adductor magnus.
> **Biceps femoris:** Flexes leg and extends thigh.
> **Semitendinosus:** Flexes leg and extends thigh.
> **Semimembranosus:** Flexes leg and extends thigh.
> **Tibialis anterior:** Dorsiflexes and inverts foot.
> **Calcaneal or Achilles tendon:** connects the three muscles to the calcaneal bone of the foot. The largest and strongest tendon in the body.
> **Gastrocnemius:** Plantar flexes the foot and flexes the leg.
> **Soleus:** Plantar flexes foot.
> **Plantaris:** Plantar flexes foot.

ANATOMICAL LIMITS AND GUIDES

Anatomical limits and guides are utilized by embalmers to know how and where to make incisions to find crucial vessels for embalming (See Embalming Section pp. 39-44).

Glossary for Human Anatomy

Accessory (auxiliary) - This term is applied to a lesser structure that resembles a similar organ in structure and function, such as the accessory pancreatic duct.

Albumin – A protein found in blood plasma.

Alimentary canal - The digestive system tube from the mouth to the anus, including the mouth or buccal cavity, pharynx, esophagus, stomach, and small and large intestines.

Anatomy - The branch of science dealing with the study of the structure of the body.

Anastomoses - The connection between vessels; the union of two vessels going to the same body part.

Anterior (ventral) - Before or in front of; refers to the front side of the body or structure.

Appendicular skeleton - The 126 bones that make up the pectoral girdle, upper extremities, pelvic girdle, and lower extremities.

Articulation - The connection between two or more bones; a joint.

Axial skeleton - The 80 bones composing the skull, vertebrae, thorax, and hyoid bone; the central structure to which the appendicular skeleton is attached.

Bilateral symmetry - Refers to the symmetry of paired organs or to an organism whose right and left halves are similar images of each other.

Biliary - Pertaining to bile.

Biliary tract - The organs (liver and gall bladder) and ducts that participate in the secretion, storage, and delivery of bile to the duodenum.

Bladder - A membranous sac or receptacle for secretion or excretion.

Buccal - Relating to the cheek or mouth.

Cardiology - The study of the heart.

Carotid canal - The canal or passageway in the temporal bone through which the internal carotid artery passes.

Central - Situated at or pertaining to a center or central point.

Colon - The part of the large intestine beginning with the ascending colon and ending with the sigmoid colon

Conchae - Means shell; ridges in the walls of the nasal cavity.

Condyle - A curved protuberance at the end of a bone forming part of an articulation.

Curvature - A normal or abnormal bending away; an arc.

Cystic - Of or pertaining to a sac-like structure.

Deep - Below the surface or toward the central part of a structure.

Detoxification - Reduction of the harmful properties of a poisonous substance.

Distal - Farther away from the point of attachment or from the trunk; opposite of proximal.

Dorsal - Posterior; toward the back; opposite of anterior.

Eminence - A prominence or projection.

Endocrine - Pertaining to a ductless gland that secretes directly into the bloodstream.

Exocrine - Pertaining to a gland that delivers its secretion through a duct.

External - Pertaining to the exterior; the opposite of internal.

External auditory meatus - The lateral, outer opening of the ear or auditory canal.

Fontanel - A temporarily unossified area on the surface of the cranium of an infant.

Fossa - A shallow depression.

Gland - A secretory organ or structure that can manufacture a secretion.

Heterocrine - A gland that has both endocrine and exocrine functions.

Histology - The study of tissues.

Inferior - Beneath; lower; the undersurface of an organ or a structure below another structure. The opposite of superior.

Integumentary - Relating to the outer surface of a structure.

Internal - Within the body; within or on the inside; the opposite of external.

Islets of Langerhans (pancreatic islets) - clusters of cells in the pancreas that produce insulin.

Joint - The connection between two bones; an articulation.

Lateral - Pertaining to the side of the body, away from the median plane.

Lobes - Well-defined parts of an organ separated by boundaries.

Mandibular fossa - The depression in the temporal bone into which the condyle of the mandible fits.

Meatus - A passage or opening through a bone.

Medial - Pertaining to the middle, toward the median plane of the body.

Myology - The study of muscles.

Nares - Openings of the nose; nostrils.

Nasal septum - The partition that divides the nasal cavities.

Neurology - The study of the nervous system.

Oral - Pertaining to the mouth.

Orifice - The entrance or outlet of any anatomical structure; an opening.

Ossicles - Any small bone.

Parietal - Pertaining to, or forming, the wall of a cavity.

Pectoral - Pertaining to the front of the chest.

Peripheral - Located at, or pertaining to, the outer surface of the body or body part; located away from the center.

Perpendicular - At right angles to another surface.

pH (potential of hydrogen) - A number signifying the acidity or alkalinity of a solution.

Portal - An entrance to an organ.

Posterior (dorsal) - Behind or in back of; refers to the back side of the body or structure; opposite of anterior.

Protuberance - An anatomic landmark that appears as a blunt projection.

Proximal - Nearest to the point of attachment of a limb to the trunk of the body, the opposite of distal.

Pubic symphysis - The slightly movable junction of the anterior portion of the os coxae.

Pyloric sphincter - The smooth muscle around the exit of the stomach into the duodenum.

Respiratory - Referring to the organ system that carries out the gas exchange.

Salivary - Pertaining to or the formation of saliva.

Salivary gland - One of the three pair of glands that secretes saliva into the mouth.

Septum - A wall dividing two cavities.

Serum - Blood plasma, excluding the clotting factors; the watery, amber-colored portion of the blood after coagulation occurs.

Sesamoid bone - Bone shaped like a sesame seed, a bone embedded in a tendon.

Sinus - A paranasal cavity within a bone; a dilated channel for venous blood.

Sphincter - A circular muscle constricting an orifice.

Superficial - Pertaining to or situated near the surface of the body or body part.

Superior - Toward the top of the head; a structure situated above another structure; the opposite of inferior.

Suprarenal (adrenal) - Located on the superior portion of the kidney.

Sutural - Relating to the line of the union in an immovable articulation, such as between the cranial bones.

Symphysis - A joint in which the bones are connected by fibrocartilage.

System - A group of organs arranged for the performance of a specific function.

Tunic - A covering or layer.

Urinary - Pertaining to the secretion or storage of urine.

Urinary system - Composed of the kidneys, ureters, bladder, and urethra, the function of which is to filter wastes from the bloodstream.

Valve - Any one of various membranous structures in a hollow organ or passage that temporarily closes to permit the flow of fluid in one direction only.

Vascular - Pertaining to or composed of vessels.

Vascular system - The blood vessels, including arteries, capillaries, veins, and lymphatics.

Ventral - Located toward the front of the body; anterior.

Vermiform appendix - A narrow, worm-shaped tube connected to the cecum.

Visceral - Pertaining to the internal organs contained within a cavity.

Viscosity - Resistance to the flow of a liquid.

Zygomatic - Pertaining to the cheekbone.

References

Anatomy

American Board of Funeral Service Education. (n.d.). *Curriculum.* ABFSE.

https://www.abfse.org/html/curriculum.html

Betts, J. G. (2013). *Anatomy & physiology.* OpenStax College, Rice University.

Taggart, T. R. (2016). *National board examination review book for students of funeral service education/mortuary science: Science.* Mesa, Arizona.

Embalming

American Board of Funeral Service Education. (n.d.). *Curriculum.* ABFSE.

https://www.abfse.org/html/curriculum.html

Gee-Mascarello, S. L. (2022). *Embalming: History, theory, and practice* (6th ed.). McGraw Hill Medical.

Mayer, R. (2011). *Embalming history, theory, practice.* McGraw-Hill.

Taggart, T. R. (2016). *National board examination review book for students of funeral service education/mortuary science: Science.* Mesa, Arizona.

Microbiology and Pathology

Alcamo, I. E. (1983). *Fundamentals of microbiology* (5th ed.). Benjamin/Cummings.

American Board of Funeral Service Education. (n.d.). *Curriculum.*

https://www.abfse.org/html/curriculum.html

Engelkirk, P. G., & Duben-Engelkirk, J. L. (2008). *Laboratory diagnosis of infectious diseases: Essentials of diagnostic microbiology.* Wolters Kluwer, Lippincott Williams & Wilkins.

332

Madigan, M. T., & Martinko, J. M. (2006). *Brock biology of microorganisms* (11th ed.). Pearson Prentice Hall.

Mullins, D. F. (2006). *Pathology and microbiology for mortuary science.* Delmar, Cengage Learning.

Taggart, T. R. (2016). *National board examination review book for students of funeral service education/mortuary science: Science.* Mesa, Arizona.

Zelman, M., Raymond, J., Tompary, E., Holdaway, P., & Mulvihill, M. L. (2010). *Human Diseases: A Systemic Approach* (7th ed.). Pearson Education.

Occupational Health and Safety (OSHA)

American Board of Funeral Service Education. (n.d.). *Curriculum.* ABFSE. https://www.abfse.org/html/curriculum.html

Taggart, T. R. (2016). *National board examination review book for students of funeral service education/mortuary science: Science.* Mesa, Arizona.

United States Department of Labor. (n.d.). *Formaldehyde – Overview.* Occupational Safety and Health Administration. https://www.osha.gov/formaldehyde

United States Department of Labor. (n.d.). *Occupational Safety and Health Administration.* OSHA. https://www.osha.gov/laws-regs/regulations/standardnumber/1910/1910.1030

United States Department of Labor. (n.d.). *Occupational Safety and Health Administration.* OSHA. https://www.osha.gov/laws-regs/regulations/standardnumber/1910/1910.1200

Preparation for Final Disposition Section

American Board of Funeral Service Education. (n.d.). *Curriculum.* ABFSE.
https://www.abfse.org/html/curriculum.html

Cleveland, L. J. (2022a). *Funeral service rites and customs: A guide for funeral service students.* Hudson Valley Professional Services.

Klicker, R. L. (2020). *21st century funeral directing and funeral service management & study guide.* Thanos Institute.

Taggart, T. R. (2016). *National board examination review book for students of funeral service education/mortuary science: Arts.* Mesa, Arizona.

Restorative Art

American Board of Funeral Service Education. (n.d.). *Curriculum.* ABFSE.

https://www.abfse.org/html/curriculum.html

Fritch, J. B. (2020). *Restorative art: Foundation & practice.* Funeral Service Education Resource Center.

Kie, G. (2022). Photographs.

Klicker, R. L. (2003). *Restorative art and science.* Thanos Institute.

Mayer, J.S. (1961). *Restorative art.* Graphic Art Press.

Taggart, T. R. (2016). *National board examination review book for students of funeral service education/mortuary science: Arts.* Mesa, Arizona.

Tips on How to Pass the National Board Exam

The International Conference of Funeral Service Examining Boards. (2022). *National Board exam science study guide* (Vol. 13). The International Conference of Funeral Service Examining Boards.

Thanatochemistry

American Board of Funeral Service Education. (n.d.). *Curriculum.*

https://www.abfse.org/html/curriculum.html

Bettelheim, F. A., Brown, W. H., Campbell, M. K., Farrell, S. O., Torres, O. J., & Madsen, S. (2020). *Introduction to general, organic, and biochemistry* (12th ed.). Cengage.

Boyd, R. & Morrison, R. (1992). *Organic chemistry* (6th ed.) Prentice Hall.

de la Cruz, D., & Holmes, R. (2018). *Turning art into science: Applying chemistry to funeral service*. Tuesday Evening Publications.

Dorn, J., & Hopkins, B. (2010). *Thanatochemistry, A survey of general, organic, and biochemistry for funeral service professionals* (3rd ed.) Pearson.

Taggart, T. R. (2016). *National board examination review book for students of funeral service education/mortuary science: Science.* Mesa, Arizona.

Index